T0354265

SECRETS OF
PREDICTIVE
ASTROLOGY

About the Author

Anthony Louis (CT) is a physician and psychiatrist. Astrology has been his avocation for more than fifty years, and he has authored five books on the topic. He has taught courses and lectured internationally on horary and predictive astrology, and has published numerous articles in magazines such as *American Astrology*, *The Mountain Astrologer*, and *The Horary Practitioner*.

SECRETS OF
PREDICTIVE
ASTROLOGY

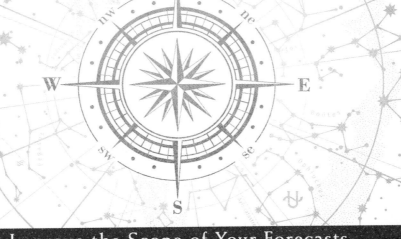

Improve the Scope of Your Forecasts
Using William Frankland's Techniques

ANTHONY LOUIS

Llewellyn Publications
Woodbury, Minnesota

Secrets of Predictive Astrology: Improve the Scope of Your Forecasts Using William Frankland's Techniques Copyright © 2023 by Anthony Louis. All rights reserved. No part of this book may be used or reproduced in any manner whatsoever, including internet usage, without written permission from Llewellyn Worldwide Ltd., except in the case of brief quotations embodied in critical articles and reviews.

FIRST EDITION
First Printing, 2023

Cover design by Shannon McKuhen
Charts created using Solar Fire software, published by Astrolabe, Inc., www.alabe.com
Interior art by the Llewellyn Art Department

Llewellyn is a registered trademark of Llewellyn Worldwide Ltd.

Library of Congress Cataloging-in-Publication Data

Names: Louis, Anthony, author.
Title: Secrets of predictive astrology : improve the scope of your
   forecasts using William Frankland's techniques / by Anthony Louis.
Description: First edition. | Woodbury, Minnesota : Llewellyn Worldwide,
   2023. | Includes bibliographical references and index. | Summary: "This
   book is an overview of the predictive techniques of William Frankland, a
   well-known London astrologer who published two books in the late 1920s
   about symbolic directions. The book is focused on how to use Frankland's
   techniques in order to create a chart that will show what years/times of
   someone's life will be favorable or not favorable. It allows the reader
   to prepare for good and not-so-good times in their life"— Provided by
   publisher.
Identifiers: LCCN 2023030446 (print) | LCCN 2023030447 (ebook) | ISBN
   9780738774640 (paperback) | ISBN 9780738774749 (ebook)
Subjects: LCSH: Predictive astrology. | Zodiac. | Astrology.
Classification: LCC BF1720.5 .M68 2023 (print) | LCC BF1720.5 (ebook) |
   DDC 133.5—dc23/eng/20231002
LC record available at https://lccn.loc.gov/2023030446
LC ebook record available at https://lccn.loc.gov/2023030447

Llewellyn Worldwide Ltd. does not participate in, endorse, or have any authority or responsibility concerning private business transactions between our authors and the public.

All mail addressed to the author is forwarded, but the publisher cannot, unless specifically instructed by the author, give out an address or phone number.

Any internet references contained in this work are current at publication time, but the publisher cannot guarantee that a specific location will continue to be maintained. Please refer to the publisher's website for links to authors' websites and other sources.

Llewellyn Publications
A Division of Llewellyn Worldwide Ltd.
2143 Wooddale Drive
Woodbury, MN 55125-2989
www.llewellyn.com

Printed in the United States of America

Other Books by Anthony Louis

Horary Astrology:
The Theory and Practice of Finding Lost Objects
(Llewellyn, 2021)

Llewellyn's Complete Book of Tarot
(Llewellyn, 2016)

Tarot Beyond the Basics
(Llewellyn, 2014)

The Art of Forecasting Using Solar Returns
(The Wessex Astrologer, 2008)

Horary Astrology Plain & Simple
(Llewellyn, 2002)

Tarot Plain & Simple
(Llewellyn, 1996)

"There is a tide in the affairs of men
Which, taken at the flood, leads on to fortune;
Omitted, all the voyage of their life
Is bound in shallows and in miseries.
On such a full sea are we now afloat,
And we must take the current when it serves,
Or lose our ventures."

—Brutus speaking to Cassius in Shakespeare's *Julius Caesar*, act 4, scene 3

"I had made my way to Mr. Frankland's office intent on complaining bitterly to him of the inadequacy of our science, when a crisis of outstanding consequence could strike one unawares.

"But I had neither time nor opportunity to state my grievance and the nature of my mission. Mr. Frankland took the offending chart in his hand, looked at it for a few moments, and proceeded to describe the very events in question, their nature, and the time of their occurrence.

"In view of the hours I had spent vainly trying to account for them myself, my feelings of astonishment can be imagined."

—L. Protheroe Smith, client and student of William Frankland, in his foreword to Frankland's *New Measures in Astrology*, 1928

Contents

List of Charts..xi

Foreword...xv

Introduction 1

Chapter 1: An Overview of Frankland's *Astrological Investigations*......13

Chapter 2: The Vocabulary of Directions and Progressions 21

Chapter 3: Alan Leo's Zodiac Signs as Periods of Life........................39

Chapter 4: Planetary Periods and Ptolemy's *Seven Ages of Man* 51

Chapter 5: Frankland's *Point of Life Measure* 75

Chapter 6: Birth Numbers Identify Potentially Significant Years 79

Chapter 7: Frankland on Methods of Prediction and Their Scope......115

Chapter 8: Judging the Overall Tenor of the Chart 131

Chapter 9: *Age Along the Zodiac (Age Point)* 147

Chapter 10: Midpoints and Areas of Life...167

Chapter 11: The 12 Houses 193

Chapter 12: Combining Cusps of Houses to
Produce Sensitive Points...219

Chapter 13: Average Positions and Midpoints 249

Chapter 14: Aspects and Orbs: The Knatchbull Twins 267

Chapter 15: The *4/7° Age Point* 275

Chapter 16: Frankland's Measures with Unknown Birth Times 303

Chapter 17: Frankland's Student L. Protheroe Smith 317

Chapter 18: Forecasting Methods of Wynn and Adams 333

Chapter 19: Atacirs (Symbolic Directions) 349

Chapter 20: Found by the Aid of the Stars 357

Epilogue 363

Appendix A: The *Point of Life* 371

Appendix B: The *4/7° Per Year Measure (4/7° Age Point)* 379

Appendix C: Ptolemy's *Seven Ages of Man* 385

Appendix D: Alan Leo's Zodiac Signs Combined with
    Ptolemy's *Seven Ages of Man* 387

Appendix E: Keywords for the Planets, Ascendant, and Midheaven 389

Bibliography 399

Index 407

Charts

Introduction
1: Jennifer Aniston   8

Chapter 2
2: Miguel de Unamuno   26
3: Woman Who Divorced   28
4: Evangeline Adams   30

Chapter 3
5: Shinzo Abe   47

Chapter 4
6: Alan Leo   53
7: Male Chart with Uranus Square Saturn   58
8: King George V   68

Chapter 5
9: Charles Carter   77

Chapter 6
10: Alan Leo, Birth Chart, with Secondary Progressions
    for 7 August 1890 in Outer Wheel   87
11: Charles Lindbergh   89
12: Sophia Frances Hickman   93
13: Ruth Ellis   97
14: Lad Who Died in a Windstorm   104
15: Martha Stewart   106
16: Man Whose Arm Was Torn Off   110

Chapter 7
17: Robert Louis Stevenson   120
18: Wilson Barrett   124
19: Jim Henson   128

Chapter 8
20: Fateful Chart   135
21: Dorit Schmiel   144

Chapter 9
22: Death by Hanging   150
23: Pope Francis   152
24: Diana Spencer, Princess of Wales   155
25: Elizabeth II, Queen of England   158
26: Elizabeth II, Queen of England, Solar Return 2022   161
27: George Eliot   163

Chapter 10
28: George Bernard Shaw   169
29: A Modern Example (Anonymous)   175
30: Rudolph Valentino   179
31: Christa McAuliffe   182
32: Christopher Reeve   186

Chapter 11
33: $35 Million Lottery Winner   215

Chapter 12
34: Ramsay MacDonald   223
35: Benito Mussolini   225
36: Yusuf Islam (Cat Stevens)   229
37: William Ewart Gladstone   235
38: Justin Bieber   239
39: Stanley Conder   241
40: Valerie Percy   246

Chapter 13
41: William Frankland   251
42: Astrologer Who Died at Age 46   255

43: Deborah Houlding   258

44: Woman from Madrid   261

45: Garry Hoy   264

Chapter 14

46: Nicholas Knatchbull   268

Chapter 15

47: Private Client of Frankland   277

48: Frida Kahlo   279

49: Pat Harris   284

50: George Michael   287

51: Man Whose Mother Died   291

52: Man Whose Mother Died, Solar Return 1936   295

53: Boy Whose Father Died by Suicide   297

Chapter 16

54: Emperor Hadrian   306

55: Emmett Till   312

Chapter 17

56: L. Protheroe Smith   319

57: Boris Cristoff   327

Chapter 18

58: Sidney K. Bennett (Wynn), Birth Chart, with Secondary Progressions
    for 18 May 1926 in Outer Wheel   336

59: Sidney K. Bennett (Wynn), Wynn Key Cycle Return for 18 May 1926,
    with Birth Chart in Outer Wheel   338

60: Man Who Drowned on Vacation, Wynn Key Cycle Return
    for 31 October 1908   340

61: Woman with Liver Function Tests, Wynn Key Cycle Return
    for 18 August 2022   343

Chapter 20
62: Edward Whitehead Vanishes, Horary Chart   359

Epilogue
63: Anthony Louis   367

Appendix A
64: Yevgeny Prigozhin   376

FOREWORD

I first met Anthony Louis in 2018 while attending a course on horary astrology at the School of Traditional Astrology (STA). Although he was already quite knowledgeable about horary—he had even written a book on the subject—he was taking part in the fundamentals of horary course, and I was lucky to have him in my study group. To me, his enrolling in this course was evidence of a man with an immense openness to knowledge and a deep love of learning. I saw in Anthony someone with a true passion for studies, willing to revisit and review topics about which he already had expertise in order to learn new things and continue to grow. At the time, he was one of my favorite authors, and having him in my study group was more than I could ever wish for. I felt that life was giving me a gift that I should cherish.

I admired his open attitude towards learning, his capacity for analysis and the investigative spirit that led him to test every technique before accepting it as useful and reliable. In addition, his love for transmitting knowledge stood out; Anthony is curious, detail-oriented, and rigorous. In no time he became my tutor and a great ally on my path as an astrologer. With him by my side, I started to improve my techniques and grow professionally.

In this text, Anthony revisits the work of William Frankland, a prestigious English astrologer who was active during the inter-war period of the 1920s and 1930s and who developed his own predictive techniques. Unfortunately, Frankland's work has fallen into oblivion, and his techniques are not widely known among contemporary astrologers. Anthony thus seeks to bring his methods back into the spotlight and give Frankland the recognition he deserves. In this book, Anthony explains the predictive techniques that Frankland developed and that are still quite useful for their accuracy and simplicity. To do so, he has carried out exhaustive research in which he himself acted as a guide to Frankland's symbolic predictive measures.

Frankland's techniques are simple but also surprisingly original and effective. He used symbolic language in a creative way and thus opened new possibilities for interpretation. As Anthony explains, Frankland believed that every major event in a person's life is accompanied by a symbolic aspect that highlights a sector of the individual's life and that may be "activated" by operative astrological influences during a particular period. Frankland proposed symbolic measures that can be easily calculated in a few minutes without using any software and that help the astrologer to decide where to put the focus when analyzing a natal chart.

As an astrologer, I know firsthand that we often feel discouraged by complicated calculations, and I believe that Frankland's measures are excellent additions to the astrologer's toolbox. I truly hope that the reader of this volume finds these techniques and measurements as useful as I do.

Maria Blaquier
Director, Academia de Astrología Avanzada MB
Buenos Aires, Argentina
May 15, 2022

INTRODUCTION

In the midst of the COVID-19 pandemic in the year 2021, I began reviewing the works of William Frankland, a London-based astrologer who published two volumes in the late 1920s. He developed a remarkable approach to astrological forecasting that has been lost to many modern astrologers. Carefully testing his system on a large number of charts, I found Frankland's techniques to be both simple and impressive in their results. Quite frankly, I was rather astounded.

My first acquaintance with Frankland's work came in the 1980s, when I read Charles E. O. Carter's 1929 book *Symbolic Directions in Modern Astrology*. Carter makes several references to Frankland's "new measures" and mentions other symbolic directions that British astrologers were testing at the time. Unfortunately, Carter only focused on some key details of Frankland's texts and did not explain that he had developed a well-integrated system of natal chart interpretation, grounded in years of astrological practice, that could quickly and reliably generate an outline of the major periods and events of the native's life.

I didn't pay much attention to these experiments with new ways of astrological forecasting because my focus was more on learning traditional techniques. I was heavily into William Lilly at the time. The Regulus edition of *Christian Astrology* (1647) had recently become available, and I was determined to read it cover to cover.

The final section of Lilly's *Christian Astrology* has to do with the unfolding of the birth chart as revealed by primary directions, annual profections, solar returns, and transits. I was already familiar with transits, which were the backbone of prediction in the work of Evangeline Adams, whose books had initially introduced me to astrology during my teenage years. I was also somewhat familiar with primary directions, having used Llewellyn George's primary direction method in his *A to Z Horoscope Maker and Delineator* (first published in 1910) to rectify my own chart.

Lilly's use of continuous annual profections was new to me, and I found it hard to believe that such a simple technique could be reliable. Although Lilly did not mention secondary progressions in his seventeenth-century text, I had been using them routinely and effectively in predictive work. With so many traditional tools at my disposal, I looked askance at the modern experiments of the British school being described by Charles Carter.

William Frankland again caught my attention in the 1990s in Geoffrey Cornelius's *The Moment of Astrology* (1994), which focuses mainly on horary, a great interest of mine at the time. Cornelius describes a case from Lancashire, UK, in which astrologer William Frankland cast a horary chart to locate the body of a 63-year-old depressed man who had gone missing and likely died by suicide. The son-in-law of the missing man used Frankland's delineation to trace a route that led directly to the body. The story made headlines in England in 1926.

Cornelius remarked that Frankland's methods deserved to be better known, stating in *The Moment of Astrology* that Frankland "was known to an earlier generation of English astrologers for his pioneering development of 'symbolic directions' which much influenced Carter in the late 1920s. He was a full-time consultant astrologer with an office in the West-End of London and a thriving practice in the period between the wars. He was also one of the very few gifted horary astrologers of his period" (Cornelius 1994, 132).

Frankland's skill as a horary astrologer made me wonder whether his experiments with new "symbolic" techniques was worthy of reconsideration. I resolved to investigate Frankland's methods as time permitted, but never quite got around to it. Finally, after a long hiatus, during the pandemic in the year 2021 I returned to Frankland's writings. The result is this book that you have before you. My hope is that, as a reader of this text, you will be as impressed by Frankland's astrological skill and creative genius as I have been in researching his approach to forecasting.

In many ways, Frankland's discontent with traditional predictive techniques resembles the dissatisfaction mentioned by Michael Harding and Charles Harvey in their 1990 text on midpoints and harmonics, *Working with Astrology*, in which they address the problem of charts that do not reveal the known qualities of the moment in an obvious or well-established manner. Harding and Harvey begin their book by noting that the commonly used zodiacal birth chart "is a distorted attempt to fit a highly-complex set of geometric relationships into a single diagram … which omits the majority of planetary relationships in favour of simplifying a few of them" (Harding and Harvey 1990, 3).

Frankland gives an overview of his system for forecasting in *New Measures in Astrology* (1928):

> The various methods are simple of calculation—just an addition of the cusps of houses (if known) and the age [of the native] in degrees, the measure round the signs at seven years per sign for areas [of life], and the moving of the planets along at four-sevenths of a degree per year of life. Yet these simple calculations will give us *the power to estimate the important periods and years of life, without confusing the mind by a multitude of systems.* (Frankland 1928, 90; italics mine)

Frankland's research led to the development of a handful of *symbolic* measures, which he found to be reasonably reliable. Let me list them here as bullet points:

- Adding together the zodiacal positions of the cusps of two houses to create a sensitive point, similar to a lot or Arabic part, which is symbolically related to the combined significations of the two houses.

- Converting the current age of the native to an equivalent number of degrees of arc along the ecliptic, and then directing that arc, commencing at 0° Aries. This measure is similar to a solar arc direction but is symbolic rather than based on the real-time movement of the Sun.

- Converting the current age to an arc of ecliptic degrees at the rate of one zodiac sign (30° degrees) per 7 years of life, which is 4.286° per year (the orbital speed of Uranus around the zodiac, an idea expounded by Alan Leo in the late 1800s), and directing that ecliptic arc from 0° Aries.

- Advancing the planets through the zodiac at a rate of 4/7 of a degree per year of life, an idea of Frankland's based on the long-standing occult significance of the numbers 4 and 7.

In the remainder of this book, I will explain these symbolic measures in detail with case examples. At this point, it is important to point out that Frankland viewed the function of his new **symbolic** measures as **intensifiers** of certain regions and configurations of the birth chart, which represent particular areas of life and natal promises, but he did not view these symbolic measures as **operative astrological influences**, such as progressions, which functioned to precipitate the natal promise into **manifestation**.

In his second book, however, Frankland appeared to treat his new *4/7 of a degree per year of life* symbolic measure in two ways: both as an intensifier of configurations in the natal chart and as a method to symbolically direct points in the chart that serves as an operative influence, resulting in the manifestation of the "natal promise." In Frankland's system, the *4/7° per year measure* is a symbolic direction that advances at the slowest rate in his system of forecasting, and, as we shall see, its contact with midpoints in the midpoint modal sort (90° midpoint sort) is quite useful in prediction.

Although Frankland routinely utilized midpoints in his work, he did not have available the type of midpoint modal sort that astrologers use today. The advantage of the modern 90° midpoint sort is that it compresses the 360° horoscope into the space of 90°, thereby grouping together zodiac signs according to mode (cardinal, fixed, mutable), as if layering all the signs of a single mode on top of one another. Such a layering of all four signs of a single modality into one-third of the 90° dial allows the astrologer to see at a glance which planets will be affected by the transits (or progressions or directions) of a planet through the sign of a particular modality. For example, if Saturn were to enter a cardinal sign, where it will spend the next 2½ years, the astrologer can easily see which natal planets in the Grand Cross of cardinal signs Saturn will aspect during those 2½ years, and in what order those aspects will perfect.

Frankland often uses metaphors to explain his new measures. For example, he compares the native's natal promise to fruit growing in an orchard. At certain times of life, various fruits will *ripen* and become ready for picking. His new symbolic measures indicate when the fruit will be ripe, but the actual harvesting will be done by operative astrological influences, such as directions or progressions, that are in effect around the same time. From this perspective, Frankland's methods resemble the timelord systems of Hellenistic astrology and the dasha systems of Indian astrology.

Alternatively, one might compare Frankland's symbolic measures to the act of priming a pump. The symbolic directions do not cause the water to flow; rather, they indicate when the pump will be ready to produce water. Then, if an appropriate astrological operative influence activates the pump's lever, water will issue forth.

Frankland explains why he developed these new measures, highlighting the fact that when he was forecasting with traditional methods, such as secondary progressions, it sometimes happened that strong progressed-to-natal aspects formed without an appropriate corresponding event, and, conversely, significant events sometimes occurred for which there was no corresponding secondary progression. As a result, he spent years searching for a simpler and more reliable way to assess a chart as quickly and accurately as possible.

Using his "new measures," Frankland maintains that aspects may still form without corresponding events of importance, but no significant event will occur without aspects of an appropriate nature. In other words, he claims that **every major life event will be accompanied by a meaningfully related aspect in his system of symbolic directing.** He argues that when traditional methods of directing (primary directions, secondary progressions, major transits) coincide with his "new measures," a significant event always occurs.

In judging the influence of his new measures, Frankland studied "hits" to natal planets and sensitive points in the chart as well as hits to significant *midpoints*. Although he does not mention Alfred Witte by name, Frankland frequently uses midpoints in a manner reminiscent of Witte, which leaves the impression that he was familiar with the work of the Hamburg School of Astrology during the period between World War I and the late 1920s.

The material in this text draws primarily upon Frankland's first two books, published almost a hundred years ago: *Astrological Investigations* (1926) and *Key Measures in Astrology* (1928). Oddly, my copy of the first edition of *Astrological Investigations* does not indicate its date of publication. However, in that book, Frankland discusses the death of actor Rudolph Valentino; hence, the book must have been published after August of 1926, when the actor died. In addition, his first volume discusses George Bernard Shaw but does not mention his Nobel Prize in Literature, which was awarded in November of 1926. These facts suggest that *Astrological Investigations* went to press between late August and early November of 1926.

Frankland's books inspired Charles E. O. Carter to publish his own text about symbolic directions, *Symbolic Directions in Modern Astrology* (1929). In it, Carter describes the methods of Frankland, stating:

> The *Age along the Zodiac* is a method by which an imaginary point may be assumed to pass along the ecliptic from 0° Aries, at a rate of 1° to the year, forming aspects. (Carter 1929, 25–26)

Strictly speaking, this is not a "new measure" in astrology. In his book on annual revolutions from the ninth century, *On the Revolutions of the Years of Nativities*, Abu Ma'shar recommended directing the birth chart at a rate of 1° per year. Haly Abenragel in his eleventh-century *Complete Book on the Judgment of the Stars* devoted an entire chapter to various symbolic directions, including the *1° per year measure*. The source of Ma'shar's and Abenragel's *1° per year measure* appears to have been Claudius Ptolemy in the second century, who maintained that one *equatorial* degree could be equated to one year of life.

Unlike Ptolemy, Frankland's method of symbolic directing involves one *ecliptic* degree per year, which is similar to, but not the same as, the real-time-based solar arc method of directing, which takes into consideration the difference in arc between the position of the secondary progressed Sun and natal Sun at a particular moment in time. Carter further states in *Symbolic Directions in Modern Astrology* (1929):

> The *Point of Life* is an imaginary point which, starting from 0° Aries in every case, passes through the Zodiac at the rate of one sign for every seven years, or $4\frac{2}{7}°$ per annum, forming aspects with radical positions.
>
> My experience of this method is that it is of some value and merits the attention of all students, although its influence may be of a diffused character indicating the general diathesis of a period rather than special events.
>
> In his second book, *New Measures in Astrology*, Mr. Frankland sets forth, among other things, a uniform measure of $\frac{4}{7}°$ to the year.
>
> [...]
>
> I can only give it as my opinion that this ratio is of value and a brilliant contribution to astrological science. (Carter 1929, 25)

Carter also cites an article in the April 1929 *British Journal of Astrology* in which Sepharial (aka Walter Gorn Old) compares Frankland's 4/7 ratio to the mystical 600-year Naronic cycle (a "true secret of god" according to Theosophist H. P. Blavatsky), because the 360° of a circle divided by the 600 years of Naros equals 3/5, or 21/35, which is quite close to Frankland's ratio of 4/7, equivalent to 20/35. This type of woo-woo thinking, based on the tenets of Theosophy, apparently pervaded British astrology in the early decades of the 1900s.

Frankland explains in *New Measures in Astrology* that the aim of his research into symbolic measurements was "to establish a system whereby estimation of all important years and affairs of life can be calculated from the birth map alone" (Frankland 1928, 51). One of his clients, L. Protheroe Smith, who first consulted Frankland at the end of 1926, writes in the foreword to *New Measures in Astrology* that his consultation with the astrologer was startling: "It was evident that Mr. Frankland had something at his disposal that was not only 'simple, logical and orderly,' but also **uncommonly effective**" (Frankland 1928, 8; bold highlighting mine).

Example Chart: Jennifer Aniston

Let's take a quick look at a chart to see how "simple, logical and orderly" Frankland's method can be. As I was writing this introduction, I happened to hear an astrologer discussing the chart of actress Jennifer Aniston and the life-altering experience of her father abandoning the family when she was only 9 years old. As an adult, Aniston recalled in an interview that when she returned home from a birthday party at age 9, her mother told her that her father was not going to be around for a little while, but "a little while" turned out to be a year before she again saw him. How would Frankland have interpreted Aniston's natal chart?

After eyeballing her chart to get the big picture and assess its overall pattern, Frankland might have begun by stating that what immediately caught the eye is the cluster of planets and points in Aries in the 6th house opposing the planets and points in Libra in the 12th house (chart 1). The 6th and 12th houses can indicate difficult periods of life, which is especially the case here because the contrary-to-sect malefic Saturn occupies the Aries group, with disruptive Uranus across the wheel in Libra, the sign of intimate relationships. Frankland consistently found that hard aspects involving Saturn and Uranus, even by whole sign, mark stressful times in clients' lives.

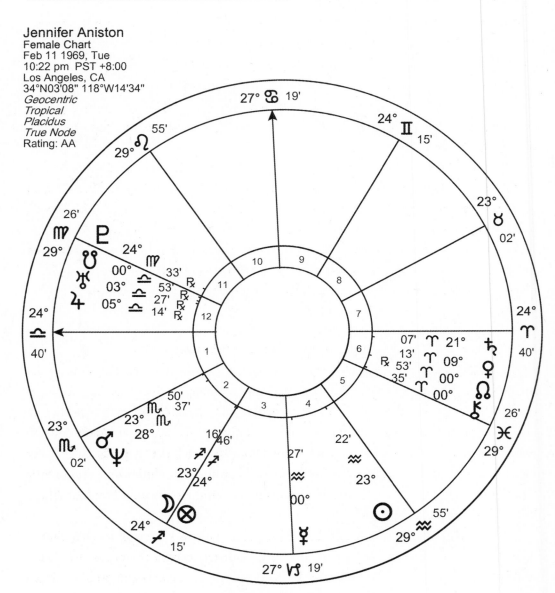

Jennifer Aniston
Female Chart
Feb 11 1969, Tue
10:22 pm PST +8:00
Los Angeles, CA
34°N03'08" 118°W14'34"
Geocentric
Tropical
Placidus
True Node
Rating: AA

Chart 1: Jennifer Aniston
11 February 1969, 10:22 p.m. PST, Los Angeles, California, 34N03 118W15

For timing, Frankland considered his symbolic measures, which he'd been testing for a number of years. For example, starting with 0° Aries as a universal symbol of the birth moment and measuring from there at a rate of 1° for every year of life, this so-called *Age along the Zodiac Point* crosses over Chiron and the North Lunar Node during Aniston's first year of life. The *Age Point*'s next encounter is with Venus in 9° of Aries when she is 9 years old. The planetary goddess of love symbolizes ties of affection, but Venus is not comfortable in Aries, which is ruled by Mars, whose motto is "make war, not love."

In addition, Venus at Aniston's birth is opposed by Uranus, as well as by the South Lunar Node and Jupiter. Jennifer needs to be aware that Uranus, the planet of sudden and disruptive change, when paired with Venus can signify breakups, separations, or divorce. Around age 9, her *Age along the Zodiac* conjoins natal Venus, and she may experience events related to the disruptive nature of Uranus opposing Venus at that time. Conjunctions of symbolic measures to natal planets often indicate significant events related to the nature of the planet, its house position, and its rulerships and aspects.

Glancing at a list of eclipses around the time Jennifer was 9 years old, we find that a Total Lunar Eclipse at 3° 40' Libra "hit" her natal Uranus in March of 1978, and a Partial Solar Eclipse at 8° 43' Libra almost exactly opposed her natal Venus in October of that same year. Eclipses are powerful transits, which Frankland called "excitants," and as such they can trigger the natal potentials of the birth chart, in this case, the natal opposition of Uranus to Venus. Frankland regards this natal Saturn-Uranus square as the most challenging feature of the birth chart

What form might these Venus-Uranus events take? A possible manifestation is a separation from a parent or a dissolution of family happiness when Jennifer is about 9 years old. Frankland would make this statement on the basis of his "new measure," which advances from 0° Aries by *4/7° for each year of life* and arrives at 5° 09' Aries when Aniston turns 9 years old. This *4/7° measure* triggers Jupiter at 5° 14' Libra Rx and intensifies Jupiter's opposition to Venus from the 12th house. Jupiter rules the natal 6th house, a traditionally unfortunate house, and also rules the natal 3rd house, which is the derived 12th house of the natal 4th house of parents and early family life. The 12th house from any house represents the dissolution or negation of the matters signified by that house. Thus, for Aniston at age 9, by the *4/7° measure*, the dissolution of early family happiness becomes a distinct possibility.

Frankland would caution Jennifer that she needs to deal with this early disruption in the family, which occurred around age 9, because it could have long-term consequences. For example, the slow-moving planet Saturn, by secondary progression (at a rate of one day after birth equals one year of life), will strongly affect the natal 7th house cusp of marriage during her adult life. In Jennifer's chart, Saturn lies in the sign of its "fall" in Aries and is also linked to Pluto by a stressful quincunx, a configuration that will remain in the background by secondary progression during much of her life. She might wish to enter psychotherapy to deal with this early childhood disruption so that it will not affect her potential to become happily married.

Frankland, no doubt, would have continued with his other measures and assessment of the natal potentials of the chart, but let me stop here because my intent was merely to give a taste of how simple and powerful his methods can be.

In reality, Jennifer's father unexpectedly abandoned her when she was 9 years old. She came home one day from a birthday party to discover that her dad had abruptly left without even saying goodbye, and she had no further contact with him for about a year. Not long after her father left, her mother moved with Jennifer and her half-brother from California to New York City. Her parents finalized their divorce on 20 August 1980, when Jennifer was 11 years old.

In the remainder of this book, we will flesh out Frankland's system in detail and test how well it works in a variety of case examples. His writing style is somewhat terse, and he doesn't always explain fully what he is thinking. As a result, I have had to piece together some of his methodology from his sample charts, and I hope I have done so accurately.

As you work through the examples in this book and apply his techniques to your own chart, I suspect that your ability to interpret a birth chart will grow in ways that surprise you, as they did for his client and future student Protheroe Smith, who first consulted William Frankland in 1926. Working though Frankland's books, I too have been repeatedly impressed by the power, simplicity, and brilliance of the approach of this master astrologer.

Perhaps the most valuable lesson I have learned from Frankland is to start with the big picture and overall pattern or plan of the birth chart and avoid getting lost in the details. In some ways, Frankland's approach is contrary to the teachings of other astrologers, who start with the details and work diligently to synthesize them into an overall and coherent scheme.

Let me conclude this introduction by expressing my gratitude to Maria Blaquier, an astrologer from Argentina, who read early drafts, made recommendations, and agreed to write a foreword. Her comments and suggestions have been invaluable. I am also grateful to a host of other astrologers whose names are too numerous to mention. Among them are Geoffrey Cornelius, who first drew my attention to William Frankland in his book *The Moment of Astrology* back in 1994, and to Deborah Houlding, whose research identified a possible birth date for Edward Whitehead, the elderly man who went missing in 1926 and whom Frankland helped to find with the aid of a horary chart. This case study is the subject of the final chapter of this book.

Chapter I
AN OVERVIEW OF FRANKLAND'S
ASTROLOGICAL INVESTIGATIONS

"It has struck me that it is possible for the astrological student to sacrifice too much on the altar of exact science, and it may not be out of place if here we attempt to reclaim some of that ground which has been ceded by Cosmic Symbolism to exact methods."

—Sepharial (Walter Gorn Old), *Transits and Planetary Periods*, 1920, p. 43

William Frankland was born in or near Burnley, England, on 26 September 1878, with his 10th house ruler, Mercury, and 9th house ruler, Venus, conjoined to the Virgo Ascendant. Given that the 10th house signifies career and the 9th is closely allied to astrology and divination, it is not surprising that he became a professional astrologer.

Around 1916, Frankland moved from Burnley to London and set up a practice as a consulting astrologer. In 1915, Alan Leo (aka William Frederick Allen) established the Astrological Lodge of London, which may have been one of the reasons that Frankland decided to relocate there. Leo had previously been active in the Astrological Society (founded in 1895) and in the Society for Astrological Research (founded in 1903). After Leo's death in 1917 at the age of 57, the Astrological Lodge languished until it was revived by Charles E. O. Carter, who served as its president from 1920 until 1952.

In the foreword to his *Astrological Investigations* (1926), Frankland states that he spent more than twelve years (beginning around 1913) studying natal charts, during which time his frustration with established predictive techniques motivated him to seek easier and more reliable methods of forecasting. He summed up his approach as follows:

> Test all things. Hold fast to that which proves itself of value, irrespective of any bias or prejudice. (Frankland 1926, 30)

Frankland tested the standard methods of astrological prediction that were in vogue early in the twentieth century (primary directions, secondary progressions, transits). Such techniques were grounded in a view that astrology was a form of exact science whose methods could predict events precisely. Frankland found that such "operative aspects" were powerful and effective tools, but only some of the time. Major events sometimes occurred in the lives of his clients with no corresponding directions, progressions, or transits. Conversely, significant directions, progressions, or transits took place with no corresponding event in his clients' lives. With a cluster of planets in Virgo in his own birth chart, Frankland sought a more thoroughgoing, logical, efficient, and orderly predictive technique.

From 1922 to 1925, Frankland researched other techniques, that is, symbolic measures that might identify when the standard predictive techniques ("operative aspects") were likely to trigger the manifestation of the astrological symbolism in the chart. He realized that the majority of standard predictive measures were based on real-time or actual movement of the planets. Primary directions, for example, project the apparent rotation of the sky around the Earth in the 6 or so hours after birth onto the human life span (at a rate of one degree on the equator being equivalent to one year of life). Secondary progressions project the image of the sky as seen from Earth as it travels on its orbit around the Sun during roughly 3 months after birth onto the human life span (at a rate of one day after birth being equivalent to one year of life). Transits are the actual celestial positions of the planets at a given moment (at a rate of each day after birth being equivalent to a day of life).

Frankland wondered whether there existed symbolic measures, based on number mysticism or symbolic measurements of time not linked to the actual movement of the planets, that might indicate when real-time-based "operative influences" would likely become effective. His twelve years of practice and recent astrological investigations had yielded several symbolic measures that fairly reliably identified which of the active directions, progressions, or transits would manifest as important events. Frankland's books published in the late 1920s describe these novel measures and give numerous examples of their use. A fundamental principle for using these symbolic measures is that *the more of them that are active in a given year, the more significant the year will be.* In the words of a popular adage, "One swallow does not a summer make." Frankland's "new measures" include:

- The **Birth Numbers** are calculated by adding together the digits of one's date of birth. The sums thereby generated are believed to highlight potentially significant years of life, depending on which astrological factors, if any, are active at the given age.

- The *Point of Life* is calculated by assigning 7 years to each sign of the zodiac, commencing from 0° Aries to the current age of the client at a rate of 4 2/7° per year. For example, 21 years old would symbolically equate to 0° Cancer. The *Point of Life* highlights areas of life that may be significant at a given age, depending on which astrological factors, if any, are active at the time. Because the *Point of Life* is a sign-based, rather than a house-based, technique, the 7-year periods that the *Point of Life* is traversing will be characterized in a general way by the zodiac sign's element (fire, water, air, earth) and modality (cardinal, fixed, mutable). In appendix A, you will find a table to determine the *Point of Life* at each year of life at a glance, along with examples of how to calculate the *Point of Life* at a specific age.

- The *Age along the Zodiac* (which I sometimes refer to as the *Age Point*) is calculated by converting the client's age to an arc of ecliptic longitude and advancing by this arc from 0° Aries. For example, 17 years old would symbolically equate to 17° of Aries, and 32 years old would match with 2° of Taurus. This symbolic measure is similar to one described by Abu Ma'shar in the ninth century and by Haly Abenragel in the eleventh, based on Ptolemy's rate of 1° of equatorial arc representing one year of life. It also resembles real-time-based solar arc directions, measured from 0° Aries. Solar arc, however, refers to the actual (not symbolic) difference in ecliptic longitude between the positions of the secondary progressed Sun and the natal Sun on any given day.

- **Symbolic "house-based" sensitive points** are calculated by adding together the zodiacal longitudes of house cusps; the point so generated is then directed by adding the age of the client to this sensitive point whose meaning combines the significations of the two houses. The method is similar to the generation of lots or Arabic parts.

- The *4/7 of a degree per year of life Age along the Zodiac measure (4/7° Age Point)* is calculated by taking 4/7 of the current age and adding that value to 0° Aries. Frankland also used the *4/7° measure* to symbolically direct any point or stellar body in the chart, a procedure that he explains in his second book, *New Measures in Astrology* (1928). In appendix B, you will find a table to determine the *4/7° per year of life Age along the Zodiac measure (4/7° Age Point)* at each year of life at a glance, along with an example of how to calculate the *4/7° Age Point* at a specific age.

- Frankland also considers the ***Period of Life*** through which the native is passing, which is essentially a timelord (chronocrator) technique that assigns each of the seven traditional visible planets to particular spans or "planetary periods" of human life. Specifically, Frankland employs as timelords the rulers of **Ptolemy's** *seven ages of man* and the signs of **Alan Leo's** *seven years per zodiac sign* to highlight which transits, progressions, and directions will produce the most noticeable effects at certain ages.

Charles E. O. Carter, in his 1929 text *Symbolic Directions in Modern Astrology*, commented that in addition to directing the *4/7° Age Point*, starting at 0° Aries, Frankland also applies the *4/7° per year of life measure* to symbolically direct any planet or point in the chart. According to Carter, Frankland uses only two of his measures—the *1° per year of life Age along the Zodiac* and the *4 2/7° per year Point of Life*—to symbolically direct the age of the client, commencing at 0° Aries. Carter calls Frankland's *4 2/7° per year Point of Life* (or, in decimal form, 4.285714° per year) the *septenary* measure, because it divides each zodiac sign into 7 equal parts. Expanding on Frankland's findings, Carter applies this symbolic measure (*4 2/7° per year Point of Life*) to symbolically direct all the factors of the chart, and finds it to be an effective method of direction.

Carter apparently failed to notice that Frankland gave examples in which he calculated a symbolic point by adding together the cusps of two houses and then used the

1° per year measure to symbolically direct the house-related sensitive point. Carter also missed the fact that Frankland also directed the natal planets at a rate of 7 years per zodiac sign and used Ptolemy's planetary periods from the *seven ages of man* as symbolic directions.

Frankland, convinced of the utility of his "new" measures, which were based on symbolic rather than real time, wrote in the foreword to his *Astrological Investigations* (1926):

> The various points put forth in this book are the result of those [twelve] years of practical experience. They are not merely theories. They are theories that by dint of actual test have proved themselves, sufficiently, to become convictions to me. They are points or factors, that in my actual judgments, I never lose sight of. (Frankland 1926, 7)

In his 1928 *New Measures in Astrology*, Frankland added, "Given a combined influence of either house influence, or sign influence, or *Point of Life*, together with operative influence, you always have important events" (Frankland 1928, 93).

In other words, Frankland found that *when real-time-based operative configurations occurred simultaneously with one or more of his symbolic measures, a symbolically related event almost always took place in the life of the native.*

By "real-time-based," we mean transits, primary directions, secondary progressions, eclipses, planetary stations, solar returns, etc., all of which have, at their root, the real movement of the heavens. For example, primary directions are based on the real motion of the sky in the six or so hours after birth. To quote Charles Carter from his 1929 book *Symbolic Directions in Modern Astrology*: "In the primary and secondary systems [of directing] the movements of the planets are not symbolic but actual, whether denominated real or apparent. In the symbolic methods the movement is a mere arbitrary assumption, used for the sake of practical convenience" (Carter 1929, 9).

Although Frankland does not mention annual profections (an ancient symbolic measure) and may not have had access to the works of Abu Ma'shar, I was struck in reading his 1920s texts by the similarity of Frankland's ideas to those of the ninth-century astrologer. In the introduction to his translation of Ma'shar's work on annual revolutions from the ninth century, *On the Revolutions of the Years of Nativities*, Benjamin

Dykes makes the point that reliable interpretation of solar returns (a *real-time* technique) requires the simultaneous use of at least one *symbolic* measure, such as annual profections. Frankland appears to be making the same point, on the basis of his own extensive work with clients' charts.

Dykes explains that symbolic measures, such as the timelords of the annual profections, serve to put the indications of the birth chart into an orderly sequence. Like Frankland in the 1920s, Dykes concludes, after studying Abu Ma'shar's methods, that to adequately interpret real-time operative influences, such as solar returns, the most reliable results are obtained when you combine a real-time measure with at least one technique based on a symbolic measure of time. In his twelve years of research on the charts of his clients, Frankland apparently rediscovered what Abu Ma'shar had found to be true in the ninth century.

The century-old booklet *Transits of the Planets*, attributed to Dr. J. Heber Smith, makes a similar point: "Never lose sight of the fact that most of the events of life are produced by combinations of transits, affecting radical and progressed places, and that no one transit over a single place is ever productive of important events; it is always the combinations that are of consequence" (Smith 1968, 16).

A more modern text, Robert Blaschke's 1998 *Progressions*, further clarifies the interrelationships between the natal chart and its progressions and transits during the life cycle: "In most cases, I have found that when a pair of planets that aspect one another natally then move into a subsequent progressed aspect, while simultaneously undergoing a transit-to-natal or transit-to-progressed episode, [it] will coincide with the most lasting major changes and transformations in life" (Blaschke 1998, 72).

Frankland also suggests that real-time measures (operative influences such as directions and transits) serve to trigger events, whereas symbolic measures (Birth Numbers, *Point of Life*, *Age along the Zodiac*, etc.) function mainly to highlight certain areas of the birth chart and intensify the natal configurations found in those regions, which the operative influences may then more easily trigger into manifestation.

Frankland gives the example of a man born with several personal planets in Cancer opposed by both Uranus and Neptune in Capricorn. These oppositions, from the outer planets to several personal planets, contained a natal promise of difficulties at some point in life. The symbolic *Point of Life* (measured at a rate of 7 years of life per zodiac sign, starting from 0° Aries) would traverse Libra between ages 42 and 49, squaring the natal planets in both Cancer and Capricorn and thus sensitizing and intensifying these natal oppositions during this period. When this man was 46 years old, transiting Uranus entered Cancer, conjoining his natal Cancer planets and opposing natal Neptune. At the same time, transiting Neptune entered Aries, squaring these natal oppositions. The native died in that year. In this example, we see Frankland's *modus operandi* of *searching for major themes and patterns in the birth chart as the point of entry into forecasting*—a fundamental principle that should always be kept in mind.

In *Astrological Investigations* (1926), Frankland identifies what he considers the essential features of astrology to be used in delineating a birth chart. These include:

- The planets
- The twelve signs of the zodiac
- Astrological houses (Placidus cusps)
- Astrological aspects
- Additional chart factors such as the lunar nodes, Part of Fortune, fixed stars, sensitive points, and critical degrees
- Correct birth data, including an accurate date, time, and location of birth
- Birth Numbers—a numerological method of adding together the digits of the birth date to generate numbers that symbolize potentially significant ages

Frankland then judges the natal chart in two broad categories:

1. **The nature of the native and character of their life.** Frankland always begins with the big picture, *focusing on the overall pattern and plan of the birth chart.* He pays special attention to *dominating features* and core themes of the birth chart, including the strength or weakness of the planets, angular planets, exact or nearly exact aspects, planetary stations, the presence of stelliums, and configurations such as T-squares and Grand Crosses. In discussing dominating features, he cites the example of Alan Leo, who is a "solar type" because his birth chart has Leo rising, the Sun and three non-luminary planets in Leo, and the Sun aspecting several planets. As a solar type, Alan Leo

would be expected to have a commanding presence and exhibit good organizational and management skills.

2. **An estimation of the timing of favorable and adverse periods of life,** based on the natal promise being highlighted or "ripened" (like fruit in an orchard) by symbolic directions during specific periods of life. Frankland also studied "operative influences," especially "progressed directions" but really any of the various ways in which the planets and significant points in the birth chart "are apparently carried into relationship with others" on the basis of the actual movement of planets and the apparent rotation of the sky around the Earth.

The Symbolic Nature of Frankland's "New Measures"

Frankland stresses that his new measures are symbolic in nature and not intended to provide precise timing of events. Instead, he emphasizes that these measures identify significant years, or periods of years, in the life of the native. Symbolic Birth Numbers, for example, become important if and only if they coincide with years during which there are also significant astrological influences.

In *New Measures in Astrology* (1928), Frankland discusses his *4/7° per year measure* and states that "these influences **affect the year as a whole rather than any point of the year,** and the time of operation may be ascertained by transits, lunar aspects, etc." (Frankland 1928, 78; bold highlighting mine). The implication is that, much like secondary progressions, the symbolic measures, especially the *Point of Life*, are valid within an orb of influence of about a year both before and after the symbolic direction becomes exact. For example, the *Point of Life* at age 50½ would relate to the period from about 49½ to about 51½ years of age.

This type of orb makes sense in the context of human life. Major events usually have a prior period of buildup and a subsequent period of reaction and aftermath. For example, a death in the family is often preceded by a period of illness and followed by a period of grieving, yet the specific event occurs on a single day in the life of the native. Or, as an example from the judicial system, the sentencing for a crime on a specific date entails a prior period in which the crime was committed and the offender was apprehended and a subsequent period of imprisonment. We will review orbs in more detail when we discuss the charts of the Knatchbull twins in chapter 14.

Chapter 2
THE VOCABULARY OF DIRECTIONS AND PROGRESSIONS

Various technical terms appear repeatedly in the astrological literature regarding directions and progressions. This chapter is intended to clarify some key words and phrases of this terminology.

The birth chart is called the "root" or "radix" of the nativity. As such, it contains the "natal promise," which may manifest at various stages of life. All prediction begins with a study of the birth chart, because it shows what is possible in the life of the native. William Lilly, in book 3 of *Christian Astrology* (1647), writes:

> The Art of Direction being only to find out in what part of time the Significator shall meet with his Promittor; or in more plain terms, When, and at what time, or in what year such or such an accident [event] shall come to pass, viz. In what year Preferment; When Marriage; When Travel; When increase of Estate, &c. The general judgment upon any Nativity informs us, by the consideration of the twelve houses, what the general fortune of the Native may be in the whole course of his life, but the Art of Direction measures out the time unto Years, Months, Weeks and Days, informing us beforehand when we may expect in particular, what is generally promised us in the Root of the Nativity; and although many times it pleases God that we do not hit the mark aright, as to point of time. (Lilly 1647, 651–52)

Lilly explains that the natal chart informs us "what the general fortune of the Native *may be in the whole course of his life*," whereas a predictive method, such as a primary direction, "*measures out the time unto Years, Months, Weeks and Days*, informing us beforehand when we may expect in particular, what is generally promised us in the Root of the Nativity."

Note also that Lilly uses the words "Significator" and "Promittor" (sometimes referred to as "Promissor"). Let's explore these terms in more detail.

"Significator" and "Promissor" refer to two different functions that a planet, star, or point in a chart can perform. The geocentric model of astrology imagines that at the moment of birth, all celestial bodies and points in the heavens are "imprinted" on the radix or radical celestial sphere—the map of which is the native's birth chart. Each planet or point in the natal chart signifies some feature of the native for the duration of the entire life.

Robert DeLuce, in his 1978 book *Complete Method of Prediction*, defines a significator as "any point, place or heavenly body, taken to represent or symbolize an individual, an organ, a function or vital center" (DeLuce 1978, 26). For example, the cusp of the 11th house will signify the native's friends throughout life. The Sun will permanently signify the native's vitality, dignity, and honor, and so on for the other points and planets of the birth chart. The function of being a significator refers to the enduring imprint of the heavens at the moment of birth onto the radical sphere. Such imprints are permanent and fixed; they do not move from their natal positions as the native grows older. These imprints are like a snapshot of the heavens at the moment of birth and are viewed as being located on the stationary radical or "root" celestial sphere.

However, the heavenly bodies and their projections onto the ecliptic of the birth chart can move over time by transit, progression, or direction. As they move, they carry with them their natal promise and can act as promissors that make contact with the various stationary significators of the birth chart. In other words, the promissors are regarded as being located on the moving celestial sphere, which rotates around the stationary radical celestial sphere, represented by the "root" or birth chart. When a point or stellar body (a promissor) on the moving celestial sphere aligns with a stationary point (significator) on the radical celestial sphere, we say that the transit, direction, or progression has "perfected," signaling that a symbolically related event is ripe to take place.

To illustrate, consider a birth chart with natal Mars in the 1st house about ten degrees below the Ascendant. As the Earth continues to rotate after birth, Mars will rise and at some moment cross the Ascendant. Here, the Ascendant degree is a permanent significator, symbolizing the native's body and vitality. The promissor Mars (a natural symbol of strife, conflict, and injuries) is rising due to the primary motion of the heavens. When the "promise" of Mars arrives at the stationary significator, the Ascendant (body, health), the native may get into a fight or suffer some type of bodily injury.

William Lilly makes another useful observation. He views the stationary significator, which is a point or planet in the birth chart, as an indicator of the type of event related to the direction, the subject matter and the people involved, and the area of life that will be affected when the direction perfects. Judgment is made on the basis of the universal symbolism of the significator, the natal house that the significator occupies, and the natal houses that it rules in the chart.

The promissor, or moving planet, on the other hand, indicates the *cause* of the event, which is judged on the basis of the universal symbolism of the promissor, the houses that it occupies and rules in the birth chart, and especially the house in which the perfected direction takes place. In this last statement, Lilly is referring to directing the aspect rays of planets. For example, Mars might be at 10° Aries in the 1st house and the square of Mars at 10° Cancer in the 4th. If the Moon were at 15° Cancer and we symbolically directed Mars at a rate of 1° per year along the zodiac, then the directed square of Mars would conjoin the Moon at age 5, bringing the natal promise of Mars to the Moon, significator of the native's emotional life. Perhaps in this case, at age 5 the native's temper tantrums (Mars) might be the cause of a disturbance to his mother's ability to nurture (Moon).

Traditionally, only five points or planets were used as significators: the Ascendant (eastern horizon), Midheaven (meridian), Sun, Moon, and Part of Fortune. Transits, progressions, and directions to these five main significators were considered highly indicative of significant changes and dynamic events in the native's life. Sepharial (1920) used only four of these as primary significators, omitting the Part of Fortune, but he acknowledged that in some sense every planet can act as a significator. William Lilly (1647) extended the list of five significators to include all of the visible planets. Jean-Baptiste Morin (1661) further amplified the list by adding the cusps of the houses, arguing that significators include any significant points or planets present in the birth chart that indicate a radical disposition of the native toward particular types of experiences during their lifetime.

Frankland's measures are essentially symbolic directions in which he directs the ecliptic degree of the vernal equinox, 0° Aries, at a rate of 1°, 4/7°, or 4 2/7° per year of life. In each of these cases, the point 0° Aries (which I will refer to in this text as the *Aries Point*) acts as the promissor as it advances along the ecliptic. The significator in this case is any planet, planetary aspect, star, or sensitive point that the moving *Aries Point* contacts as it advances around the zodiac circle, commencing at 0° Aries. In addition, Frankland sometimes advanced (symbolically directed) all the points and planets in the birth chart at these rates (1°, 4/7°, or 4 2/7° per year)—an approach advocated by Charles Carter.

Furthermore, Frankland was likely familiar with the work of Alfred Witte in Germany and used Witte's understanding of the *Aries Point* as reflecting the native's interface with the outside world. As a *promissor*, 0° Aries indicates how the native's sense of self, or will to be, can manifest in external reality. As a *significator*, 0° Aries symbolizes the native's involvement with the world at large, and the directions of natal planets to the *Aries Point* tend to correlate with observable external events of the nature of the planet in the native's life. Thus, symbolic directions involving 0° Aries, as either the promissor or the significator, and the points and planets of the birth chart can indicate *when the natal promise of those natal points and planets is likely to manifest*. Because we are dealing with symbolic directions, the timing is not precise but is usually accurate to within a year.

Another important point regarding forecasting from the birth chart is that future aspects formed by transits, progressions, or directions will indicate when the promise of two *aspectually linked natal planets* is likely to manifest, *regardless of the type of future aspect involving the same two planets*. As Celeste Teal explains in her book *Identifying Planetary Triggers* (2000):

> When planets that were in aspect in the natal chart are once again linked together through progressed [or directed] aspects, it indicates current conditions and circumstances that are especially inviting for the natal potential to surface and operate. *The type of aspect does not matter, only that the two are once more linked together.*... It is most often the natal aspect that furnishes the clearest picture of a later link between two planets. The birth aspect shows the probable or most likely way in which the new aspect will operate. Transits work much the same way. (Teal 2000, 15–16; italics mine)

Alan Leo made a similar comment more than a century earlier in his 1906 book *The Progressed Horoscope*:

> All directions are conditioned by the state of the horoscope at birth. If a planet is fortunately aspected and free from affliction in the horoscope, even serious directions to it, such as squares and oppositions, will have only a limited power to harm, while good directions to it will mark periods of decided good fortune. And *vice-versa* with those which are heavily afflicted at birth; evil directions to them will be serious and dangerous, and good ones will be restricted in their scope. ...
>
> Two planets in strong good aspect at birth mark fortunate points in the horoscope all through life; and two that seriously and closely afflict each other will always be a source of trouble or danger under adverse directions and transits. (Leo 1906, 59)

Unamuno's Spiritual Crisis at Age 14

In 1929, Charles E. O. Carter suggested directing, by Frankland's various symbolic rates, any point or stellar body in the chart and not just the 0° *Aries Point*. Carter apparently had not read Frankland's books carefully, because, in fact, Frankland was already using the 1° per year symbolic direction in this way.

Let's consider an example of the 1° per year symbolic direction in the chart of Spanish philosopher Miguel de Unamuno, who describes his spiritual crisis at age 14 in his 1908 memoir, *Recuerdos de niñez y de mocedad*:

> **A mis catorce años**, *cumplióse en mí, en lecturas de vela y por la obra de la Congregación de San Luis Gonzaga, la labor **de la crisis primera de espíritu**, de la entrada del alma en su pubertad.* [At the age of fourteen, I underwent the labor of my first crisis of spirit, of the entrance of the soul into puberty, through candlelight readings and the works of the Congregation of St. Aloysius Gonzaga.] (Unamuno 1968, 103)

During his spiritual crisis, Unamuno sometimes burst into tears without explanation. Astrologically, this crisis of faith ought to be reflected in a symbolic direction involving 14° of separation between planets meaningfully linked to his spiritual life, a 9th house issue.

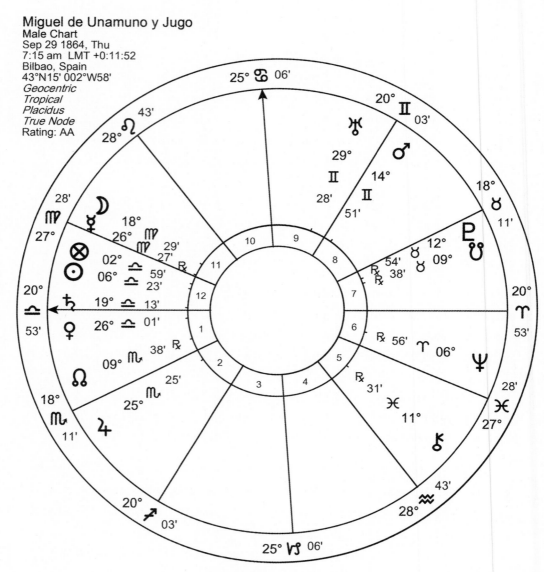

Chart 2: Miguel de Unamuno
29 September 1864, 7:15 a.m. LMT, Bilbao, Spain, 43N15 2W58

Looking at Unamuno's birth chart (chart 2), we find Uranus in the 9th house in Gemini, acting as a significator of his attitude toward religion, ethics, faith, and spirituality. In this position, Uranus represents an original, individualistic, unorthodox, or rebellious approach to religion. In volume 4 of Unamuno's *Obras completas* [Complete works], we learn that Unamuno was brought up in a strictly Roman Catholic environment and found himself at age 14 profoundly questioning his orthodox religious beliefs in search of a "pure faith totally free from dogmas" ["*fe pura y libre todavía de dogmas*"] (Unamuno 1958, vol. 4, p. 1020).

Like Uranus, the planet Mars in Unamuno's birth chart also occupies the intellectual sign Gemini but lies in the natal 8th house at a distance of 14° 37' from Uranus, which would correspond to an age of about 14.6 years by the *1° per year measure*. Symbolically, the warrior planet Mars in Gemini likes to challenge ideas, and Mars in the 8th house of occult knowledge is inclined to probe deeply into the meaning of life. In this case, Mars acts as the promissor that approaches Uranus, the significator, and the two meet when Unamuno is 14 years old, indicating a spiritual crisis.

In addition, his *Point of Life* at age 14 had just entered the sign Gemini, *highlighting natal issues related to Gemini, its ruler, and any planets therein, for the next seven years.*

Modern astrologers regard Neptune as a spiritual planet. In Unamuno's chart, Neptune directed by 14° arrives at the 7th house cusp, opposite the natal Ascendant, at age 14. Because the Sun opposes Neptune in his birth chart, the directed Sun at age 14 conjoins the natal Ascendant and directed Neptune conjoins the natal Descendant, placing the natal Sun-Neptune opposition directly on the horizon—a further indication of a spiritual crisis.

Directing natal Chiron (a symbol of physical or emotional hurts and painful crises) by 14° advances it to trine natal Jupiter (ruler of the 3rd house of the Moon goddess) and oppose natal Mercury (ruler of the 9th house of the Sun god). Directed Chiron is also quincunx Ascendant-ruler Venus in Libra in the 1st house at age 14 (an age ruled by Venus in Ptolemy's *seven ages of man*). Unamuno linked his spiritual crisis to the entrance of his soul into puberty (5th house). During this period, he sometimes found himself crying for no apparent reason (Chiron in Pisces).

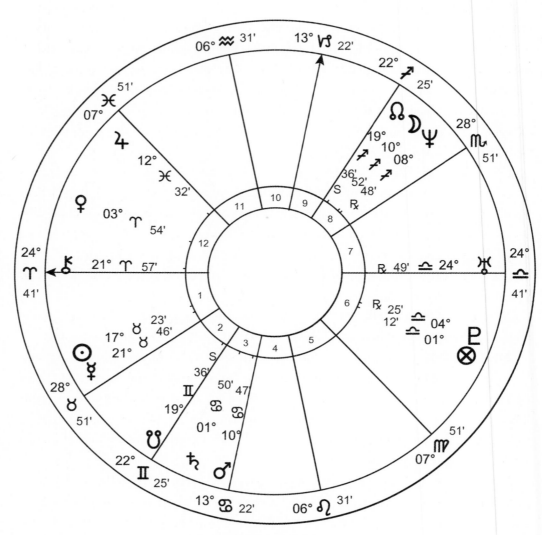

Chart 3: Woman Who Divorced
(No data)

A Woman Who Divorced Shortly before She Turned 37 Years Old

This next example is of a woman who married at age 23 and whose husband left her ten years later, about three months before her 33rd birthday. The period of marital separation lasted another four years, and the divorce was finalized a couple of months before she turned 37 years old. She was kind enough to give me permission to use her natal chart; her birth data has been withheld (chart 3).

Frankland would have begun by looking for major themes in the chart. Almost immediately we are struck by natal Uranus conjunct the 7th house cusp (marriage, partnerships) opposing Chiron (wounding) on the Ascendant. Furthermore, natal Venus rules the 7th house and also opposes Pluto and squares Saturn, forming a T-square, which indicates the natal promise of challenges in close relationships. Mars rules the natal Ascendant, conjoins Saturn, and squares both Venus and Pluto. A theme of potential hurts or breakups in relationships pervades this birth chart.

In this woman's symbolic directions, the *Point of Life* enters the sign of Cancer at age 21, where it conjoins Saturn, triggering the natal T-square in the cardinal signs. Two years later, at age 23, the *Point of Life* conjoins natal Mars in Cancer and the cusp of the 4th house (domestic life). During this period, she gets married.

Ten years after the wedding, around age 33, by the *1° per year measure* natal Saturn is directed to about 4° 50' Leo, which is sextile to natal Pluto in Libra in the 6th house, activating the natal Pluto-Venus opposition. In her birth chart, Venus rules the 7th house cusp (her spouse). Her husband left at this time. A few months after her birthday (age 33), they legally separated.

Four years later, at age 37, directed Uranus (a promissor of breakups and disruptions) has advanced 37° by the *1° per year measure* and lies in the 8th house at about 1° 49' Sagittarius, almost exactly quincunx natal Saturn in the 3rd house, and the divorce is finalized. Saturn is a significator of her 10th (public status) and 11th (friendships) houses.

At age 34 (a year after the separation), her *Point of Life* was traversing the final degrees of Leo, where it conjoined her natal Sun/Moon midpoint in her natal 5th house of romance at 29° 07' Leo. The *Sun/Moon midpoint* is a particularly sensitive point in any chart, and it characteristically becomes active at important moments in close relationships. According to Alfred Witte, keywords for the Sun/Moon midpoint include friendship, marriage, parents, and husband and wife. At age 34, with her *Point of Life* highlighting her natal Sun/Moon midpoint, she met someone new and began a significant long-term relationship.

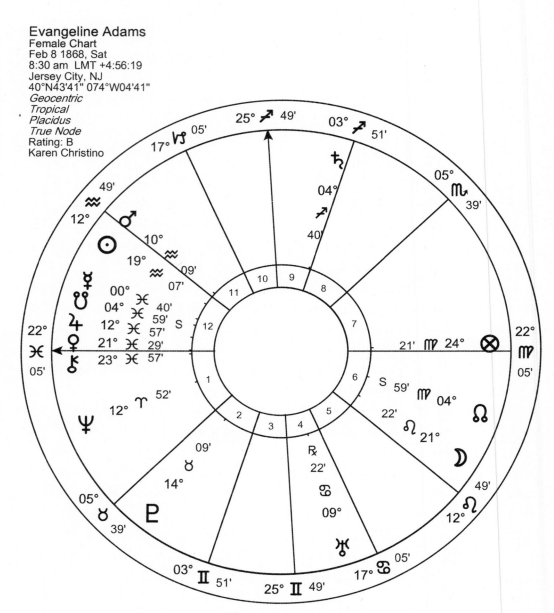

Evangeline Adams
Female Chart
Feb 8 1868, Sat
8:30 am LMT +4:56:19
Jersey City, NJ
40°N43'41" 074°W04'41"
Geocentric
Tropical
Placidus
True Node
Rating: B
Karen Christino

Chart 4: Evangeline Adams
8 February 1868, 8:30 a.m. LMT, Jersey City, New Jersey, 40N44 74W05

Evangeline Adams Breaks a Leg

In her autobiography, *The Bowl of Heaven* (1926), the noted astrologer Evangeline Adams describes her first meeting with her mentor Dr. J. Heber Smith:

> The first time I went to see the great diagnostician, he asked me the date and hour and place of my birth. . . . Then he amazed me by saying: "Didn't you break your leg when you were nine years old?"
>
> "I broke my leg, all right," I replied, "but I can't be sure now how old I was."
>
> When I reached home, I asked my mother about the accident, and she told me that it happened in January and I was nine the following month! (Adams 1926, 28–29)

Adams doesn't tell us how Dr. Smith saw her broken leg from her birth chart (chart 4). Let's look at Frankland's symbolic measures to see if they reveal such an accident.

At age 9, Adams's *Age along the Zodiac* (a rate of 1° per year, commencing at 0° Aries) would be at 9° Aries in the 1st house in square to Uranus at 9° 22' Cancer in the 4th house. A "hard" (4th harmonic) aspect to Uranus could certainly signify an accident, a sudden change, or an unexpected disruption. Like Dr. Smith, William Frankland would have glanced at Evangeline's chart and asked whether she'd had a significant accident or health crisis, perhaps a broken leg, around age 9.

The Sun, which rules the Leo 6th house cusp (illness and injuries) in Adams's chart, occupies the 12th house of hospitalization and confinement. Mars, which naturally signifies injuries, rules the 8th house cusp and is separated from the natal Sun by 9 degrees. If we symbolically direct Mars at a rate of 1° per year, the red planet will arrive at the natal Sun just before age 9. The planet Mars, as *promissor*, carries by symbolic direction the "promise" of the 8th house to the Sun, which is a *significator* of 6th house matters in her chart. When the Sun and Mars meet in the 12th house, Evangeline breaks a leg and undergoes a period of confinement.

Frankland's *4/7° per year measure* at age 9 lies at 5° 9' Aries (9° × 4/7) in quincunx to the cusp of the 8th house. This *4/7 Age Point* also trines her natal Saturn (bones), which lies "*at the bendings*," that is, forms a T-square with the Moon's nodes, which are activated by the *4/7° per year measure* via a semisextile and quincunx of *the 4/7° Age Point* to the lunar nodal axis, spanning the 6th and 12th houses. Natal Saturn in Sagittarius in the 9th house indicates the leg or thigh as the part of the body that may be affected.

At age 9, Adams's *Point of Life* (7 years of life per zodiac sign, commencing at 0° Aries) would be at 8° 34' Taurus, in square to the *midpoint* Saturn/Neptune at 8° 46' Aquarius, which falls near natal Mars at 10° 09' Aquarius. The planet Saturn signifies bones and structure, and the action of Neptune is to weaken, undermine, rarefy, and diffuse.

Note that in this example the *Point of Life* at age 9 does not make a direct hit (within orb) to any natal point or stellar body, but it does activate the natal Saturn/Neptune midpoint, which is descriptive of the situation. Frankland was keenly aware of the value of directions, progressions, transits, and aspects involving midpoints, but, lacking a modern computer, he was limited in his ability to use midpoints as extensively as we can today. Studying the "hits" that Frankland's symbolic directions make to natal midpoints substantially enhances the astrologer's predictive ability.

Different Rates, or "Keys," for Directions and Progressions

In the second century CE, Claudius Ptolemy discussed *primary directions* (based on the rotation of the heavens in the hours after birth), proposing the timing of events by allowing each degree of the celestial equator that passes over the Midheaven to signify one year of life. Degrees on the equator are measured in "right ascension." The primary directed Ascendant is calculated from the latitude of the chart and the value of the directed MC. The rate at which the astrologer advances the MC will obviously affect the timing of events based on directions involving the angles.

In the sixteenth century CE, the German astrologer Valentine Naibod (1523–93) argued that a more accurate method to estimate the timing of events would be to modify Ptolemy's rate and equate 00° 59' 8.33" of right ascension to one year of life. This arc is based on dividing the 360° of a circle by 365.24219 days in a tropical year, which calculates the *mean daily motion* of the Sun in right ascension:

360°/365.24219 days = 0.985647359° per tropical day, that is, 00° 59' 8.33" per day, which is called the *Naibod key* or *Naibod rate*

Several other "keys," or rates, for advancing the Midheaven are available to astrologers using primary directions, but the keys of Ptolemy and Naibod are most commonly used. As with primary directions, secondary progressions also allow different strokes for different folks when it comes to progressing the MC.

Secondary progressions equate each day after birth with one year of life. The Midheaven of the secondary progressed chart advances at a rate chosen by the astrologer, and the Ascendant and other angles of the secondary progressed chart are derived from the progressed MC and the latitude for which the chart is cast. The positions of the "progressed" planets are those of the transits of the day after birth that corresponds to the native's age. The "Chart Angle Progression Type" section of the *Solar Fire 9 User Guide* explains:

> When charts are progressed, it is normal to progress all the planets according to the prescribed progression rate, but to apply a separate calculation to determine the position of the Midheaven (MC), and then to derive the other chart angles (Ascendant, Vertex, Equatorial Ascendant) from that newly calculated MC. (Esoteric Technologies 2019)

The Solar Fire astrology software program offers several choices of rates for progressing the MC:

- *True Solar Arc in Ecliptic Longitude*, in which the MC is advanced at a constant *annual rate* of the natal daily solar arc, in ecliptic degrees, for each year of life.

- *True Solar Arc in Right Ascension* (equatorial degrees), in which the MC is advanced at a constant *annual rate* of the true solar arc, in equatorial degrees, for each year of life.

- *Naibod (or mean solar arc) in Ecliptic Longitude*, in which the MC is advanced at a constant *annual rate* of 00° 59' 08.33" ecliptic degrees for each year of life.

- *Naibod (or mean solar arc) in Right Ascension*, in which the MC is advanced at a constant *annual rate* of 3 minutes 56.5 seconds of equatorial arc (right ascension) for each year of life. This is the preferred rate of many astrologers.

- *Mean Quotidian* (*quotidian* means "daily"), in which the MC is progressed in right ascension at a constant *daily rate* of 24h 03m 58s of equatorial arc, which is based on the *mean solar day* (360° divided by 365.24219879 days in a tropical per year). The MC advances each day by one complete rotation of the Earth plus the Earth's daily movement on its orbit around the Sun. This method is sometimes called *Daily Houses*.

Secondary progressions are based on equating each day after birth with a corresponding year of life. Western astrologers generally work with tropical years and ephemeris days of 24 hours each to determine the rate of progression of the MC (the so-called Q2, or standard day, progression rate). Sidereal astrologers may choose to progress the MC at a rate based on sidereal years, which are about 20 minutes longer than tropical years, and sidereal days, which have a duration of 23 hours, 56 minutes, and 4.09 seconds (the basis for the Bija "correction," or Q1 day progression rate, proposed by Cyril Fagan).

Although the topic of progression rates is rather technical, astrologers need to have an understanding of the different methods of progressing of the MC, because the choice of progression rate will affect the timing of events indicated by aspects involving the progressed angles. As Michael Munkasey explains in his 1998 paper "Comments on Progression, Direction and Return Techniques," available on the website for the San Diego chapter of the NCGR:

> There are *two parts to calculating a progressed chart*: (1) *calculating the progressed chart's angles*, and (2) *calculating the progressed chart's planetary positions*. Within all progression methods the planetary movements are set by the planets themselves, but *the chart angles move distances according to the rules of the particular method of progression chosen*. There are three described ways for moving the planets (see the "Variations" section of this paper, paragraph four), but *twenty-four different techniques for progressing or directing the chart angles*. With such a large choice of methods people can and do get different chart planetary positions and angles when using different techniques. (Munkasey 1998; numbers and italics mine)

Unlike primary directions and secondary progressions, *symbolic directions* advance every planet or point in a chart at a uniform rate. For example:

- Annual profections advance the entire chart at a rate of 30° along the ecliptic per tropical year of life, which is equivalent to 00° 04' 55.69" ecliptic degrees per tropical day.

- Frankland's *Age along the Zodiac* symbolic direction advances the entire chart at a rate of 1° along the ecliptic per tropical year.

- Frankland's *4/7° Age along the Zodiac* symbolic direction advances the entire chart in ecliptic degrees at a rate of 4/7° (or 0° 34' 17") per tropical year. The arc 0° 34' 17" is almost exactly identical to the maximum angular diameter of the Moon at perigee. Thus, it is as if Frankland is progressing the chart at the rate of the maximum size of the Moon as observed from Earth per each year of life.

- Frankland's *Point of Life* symbolic direction advances the entire chart in ecliptic degrees at a rate of 30° per 7 tropical years, which is equivalent to 4.285714286° (or 4 2/7°, or 4° 17' 9") per tropical year.

Charles Carter's Law of Excitation

Like Frankland, Charles Carter viewed transits as "excitants" that stimulate natal and progressed configurations into manifestation. Carter explains his approach in his 1939 text *The Principles of Astrology*, in which he distinguishes three distinct classes of planetary positions: *current* (transiting), *radical* (natal), and *progressed* or *directed* (by primary direction, secondary progression, or symbolic direction). Aspects can form between planets in different classes, giving rise to the following possible combinations:

- Natal to natal aspects (Radical aspects reflect the "natal promise.")
- Progressed to natal aspects
- Progressed to progressed aspects
- Transit to natal aspects
- Transit to transit aspects
- Transit to progressed aspects

Carter explains that all forecasting begins with, and is inexorably limited by, the birth chart: "*No direction can bring to pass what is not shown in the nativity*" (Carter 1939, 174).

Any attempt to predict the future must begin with a thorough understanding of the nativity: "The radix shows what will happen; the directions, when" (Carter 1939, 174).

In other words, progressions reveal the development of the radical promise over time and indicate *when* the natal promise will be ripe for manifestation. Transits act as stimuli or "excitants" that trigger the natal and progressed configurations into action at a particular time. Carter calls this principle the "Law of Excitation" and defines it as follows:

> If at the time that a progressed body is in aspect to another by direction, either of these bodies forms an aspect by transit with either of the two directional bodies, then this transit will excite the direction into immediate operation. (Carter 1939, 175)

To rephrase Carter's Law of Excitation: If two planets, A and B, are involved in a progressed-to-progressed or progressed-to-natal aspect and, at the same time, transiting planet A or transiting planet B makes an aspect to either planet in the directional aspect, then planet A or B by transit will trigger the direction into manifestation.

Carter uses the terms *progression* and *direction* interchangeably. He also states that the Law of Excitation explains why some transits seem quite powerful while others go by almost unnoticed. When the same planet takes part in a direction and in a transit to one of the planetary positions in that direction, it acts to release the pent-up energy of the direction.

Robert Blaschke, in his 1998 book on progressions, states that Carter's Law of Excitation is valid for various types of directions, including secondary, tertiary, and minor progressions. Secondary progressions (a day for a year) were described by Vettius Valens in the second century in book 4, chapter 3, of his *Anthologies*. Tertiary progressions (a day for a month) equate one day with one lunar month (29.531 days) of life, and minor progressions (a month for a year) advance the planets by one lunar month for each year of life. Blaschke does not deal with primary directions (one degree of right ascension passing over the MC for each year of life) or with symbolic directions, which are the main focus of Frankland's approach.

Carter's Law of Excitation implies that directions and progressions remain active for an extended period of time (sometimes several years) and are exquisitely sensitive to "hits" by the transits of one of their component parts. Celeste Teal, in her 2000 book *Identifying Planetary Triggers*, points out that transits of faster-moving planets, especially the Sun or Mars, to a point or body involved in a direction can trigger that direction into action. Alan Leo, in his 1906 book *The Progressed Horoscope*, notes that progressed aspects also manifest when accompanied by *analogous* transits or progressions and not just by direct hits by transits, that is, when similar lunar progressions, eclipses, or transit-to-transit aspects coincide in signification with the direction under consideration.

This latter concept can also be found in the seventeenth-century writings of Morin in France and Placidus in Italy. For example, Placidus de Titus, in Canon XXXIX: Of Secondary Direction in his *Primum Mobile* (1814, Cooper translation), describes day-for-a-year secondary directions in much the same way that Vettius Valens did in the second century; that is, the transiting aspects that form on the first day after birth refer as "secondary directions" to the first year of life, those that form on the second day after birth refer to the second year of life, and so on. Placidus adds that the effect of these *secondary directions* is all the more remarkable "if at that time there are *primary directions* of the same kind and nature" (Placidus de Titus 1814, 110; italics mine).

Different authors use different orbs of influence for directions. Frankland considers the period of one year before and after the date when a symbolic direction perfects. In her book on secondary progressions, Nancy Hastings takes a similar approach. Astrologer Sophia Mason, on the other hand, uses a wider orb of 18 months before and after the perfection of a secondary progression.

In delineating the aspects formed by directed or progressed planets, Alan Leo cautions in *The Progressed Horoscope* (1983) that "preference should always be given to the rulers of the *natal* houses, and too much stress should never be laid upon the houses governing the progressed horoscope" (Leo 1983, 10). In other words, throughout the native's life, a planet always signifies the affairs of the house that it occupies and the house cusps that it rules in the birth chart.

Chapter 3
ALAN LEO'S ZODIAC SIGNS AS PERIODS OF LIFE

After the discovery of Uranus in 1781, astronomers noticed that this new planet, which spends about seven years in each sign of the zodiac, is weirdly oriented in space; its axis of rotation is quite tilted and points almost directly at the Sun. How unique and bizarre! Frankland was so impressed by the astrological significance of Uranus that he adopted Alan Leo's idea of a symbolic equivalence of the average human life span with the 84-year cycle of Uranus, at a rate of one sign every seven years.

Early in his assessment of a birth chart, Frankland studied the zodiac signs and the corresponding ages that each sign represented in the native's life. In this sense, he took a "whole sign" approach, similar to that found in ancient Hellenistic texts or in the practice of Jyotish in India. He paid particular attention to tenanted whole signs that formed T-squares or Grand Crosses in the natal chart.

Although Frankland used Placidus houses and regarded Placidian cusps as power points in the chart, he appeared to view his symbolic measures as activating entire signs, together with the rulers of those signs and the planets and house cusps contained within them. In this sense, he was using a timelord system in which the zodiac signs and their rulers acted as chronocrators for 7-year periods, and the planets within the activated signs functioned as timelords for subperiods of the 7-year stretch.

In chapter 13 of his 1904 book *Everybody's Astrology*, Alan Leo wrote:

To the deep thinker, much food for thought is furnished by the twelve divisions of the zodiacal circle, taken in connection with the various periods of vital activity that determine the physical (and also to some extent the emotional and mental) course of life.

The planet Uranus makes the circle of the heavens in eighty-four years, which is its "year"; and as this planet is stated by occultists to be one that has a special influence over man in a spiritual sense, its "month," or passage through a twelfth part of the circle, might well be expected to exercise an influence on the life of man comparable to that exhibited in the physical world by the Sun during the various monthly stages of its annual course. The fact that during each period of seven years a complete change is known to take place in the physical body, as testified to by physiologists, tends to support this **theory of a sign ruling over each seven years of life;** and certainly, **the period of eighty-four years may be reasonably taken as a** *life cycle,* without necessarily regarding it as marking the limit of normal human life. In this sense, **these eighty-four years of life will correspond to one earth year,** or, in other words, to the circle of the zodiac.

Let us consider the division of the zodiacal circle into four grand quarters resembling: *Spring,* ♈ ♉ ♊; *Summer,* ♋ ♌ ♍; *Autumn,* ♎ ♏ ♐; and *Winter,* ♑ ♒ ♓. (Leo 1910, 73–74; bold highlighting mine)

Alan Leo's Zodiac Signs and Their Associated Ages

Thus, Alan Leo associates each season and each zodiac sign with specific ages and periods of the human life span:

SPRING (ages 0–21, and ages 84–105)
    Aries (ages 0–7, and ages 84–91)
    Taurus (ages 7–14, and ages 91–98)
    Gemini (ages 14–21, and ages 98–105)

SUMMER (ages 21–42, and ages 105–126)
    Cancer (ages 21–28)
    Leo (ages 28–35)
    Virgo (ages 35–42)

AUTUMN (ages 42–63)
    Libra (ages 42–49)
    Scorpio (ages 49–56)
    Sagittarius (ages 56–63)

WINTER (ages 63–84)

    Capricorn (ages 63–70)

    Aquarius (ages 70–77)

    Pisces (ages 77–84)

Using the association of zodiac signs with specific ages, Alan Leo describes twelve stages of life (see illustration) and further outlines a method for identifying fortunate and unfortunate times of life. In Chapter XIII: The Fortunate and Unfortunate Periods of Life in *Everybody's Astrology*, Alan Leo describes the stages of human development attributed to each of the twelve signs:

> They may be briefly illustrated by reference to the four quarters. In the spring-quarter of life (1 to 21), the first seven years under *Aries* are the impulsive, uncontrolled and irresponsible years of life, the centralising stage being from 7 to 14 under *Taurus*, when obedience and respect for superiors must be learned, while youth is established under *Gemini* from 14 to 21, the period of mind-growth and the mingling of subjective with objective thought, the mental processes being actively at work.
>
> From 21 to 28 is the domestic stage, in which home life begins, with all its cares and responsibilities (*Cancer*); from 28 to 35 the social life is established and the magnetic forces are in full activity (*Leo*); from 35 to 42 the business and external life is fully established and manhoods ripe (*Virgo*).
>
> From 42 to 49 the life-forces settle and equilibrium is attained (*Libra*); from 49 to 56 is the critical stage, when the generative system undergoes its change, and the emotional life is fully established (*Scorpio*); from 56 to 63 the subjective, religious or philosophic conception of life is more seriously entertained, and preparation for old age is made (*Sagittarius*).
>
> From 63 to 70 old age is setting in, and the physical body is making its final stand before the quickening of the higher mind (*Capricorn*); from 70 to 77 fruition is established, in the wisdom of a well-lived life (*Aquarius*); and finally the sinking into the subjective or death stage is attained from 77 to 84 (*Pisces*). The grand cycle of Uranus (84 years) marks the limit of ordinary human life; beyond

that stage is usually the chaos of abnormal old age, when the circle is re-entered under the fruitful or wasteful side of Neptune's rule. (Leo 1910, 77)

[...]

In seeking for the best period in life, in quite a general sense the place of Jupiter will mark that period when the Jupiterian influences will be prominent, and, if supported by good "directions" to Jupiter, it then becomes *the* time in life when all things will tend to go well according to the general quality of the nativity. In the author's case, for instance, the period of Jupiter was reached at the 30th year of life (♃ *in* ♌, 8° 25'); *Modern Astrology* was started under that influence and his affairs in general took a decided turn for the better; the current "directions" being moreover very favourable (Jupiter having progressed to the conjunction of the Sun), the Jupiterian period had therefore a doubly beneficial influence. (Leo 1910, 77B)

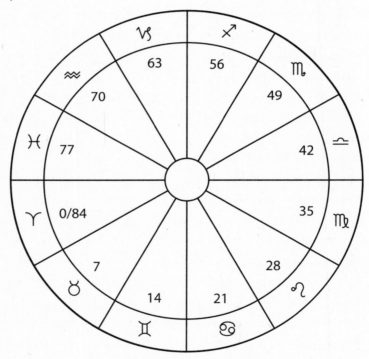

Alan Leo's 12 Stages of Life

Echoing Alan Leo, Frankland writes in *New Measures in Astrology* (1928):

The period of **Uranus,** i.e., its passing through the Zodiac, is about **84 years,** roughly **7 years per sign,** and by reason of its galvanising influence, acting upon a humanity brought to a high degree of sensitiveness, marks off these **7-year periods** as very important.

As there are analogies between the symbols employed in astrology and human nature, so I believe there is **an analogy between the vernal equinox, or 0 degrees of Aries** as we term it, **and the commencing of a human life.**

There is, as it were, the commencing of life's pathway. The electrical nature of this planet and its corresponding nature in our life and being can be seen by noting its average motion and comparing it to some powerful current along life's pathway, **at the rate of about 7 years per sign,** which stirs up or ripens anything along that pathway for effective expression. (Frankland 1928, 40)

Frankland calls the point that commences at birth at 0° Aries and advances through the zodiac at a rate of seven years per zodiac sign the *Point of Life.* He chose to begin directing from 0° Aries at birth because the vernal equinox, as the intersection of the celestial equator with the ecliptic (path of the Sun), is the point where, by convention, we say that the tropical zodiac begins. As in Uranian astrology, 0° Aries plays a crucial role in Frankland's system. The *Point of Life*, directed at a rate of seven years per zodiac sign, signals observable changes in the outer world as it interacts with natal planets, house cusps, midpoints, and other sensitive points, which by symbolic direction it "stirs up or ripens … for effective expression."

Frankland illustrates his ideas with his own birth chart, stating that he has a stellium in Virgo, including Ascendant, Moon, Mercury, Venus, and Uranus—making Virgo a *dominant sign* in his nativity. Because Virgo rules his Ascendant, this sign has a major impact on his health and vitality.

In this manner of forecasting with the *Point of Life*, Frankland is employing whole signs and whole-sign aspects to highlight 7-year periods of the native's life. In Alan Leo's scheme, for example, Virgo rules ages 42 to 49, and the signs in square aspect to Virgo (Gemini and Sagittarius) rule periods of life that are likely to be challenging to Frankland's health and well-being. Gemini rules ages 14 to 21, and Sagittarius governs ages 56 to 63. Late in life, his Virgo stellium might undergo a stressful opposition from Pisces, from ages 77 to 84.

Thus, Frankland was not surprised that he suffered a serious illness at age 18.5, during his Gemini *Point of Life* period (ages 14 to 21). Given that Gemini forms a whole-sign square aspect to Virgo, adverse directions occurring during the Gemini period could take a significant toll on his health. He does not describe the exact nature of his illnesses.

His approach, in Frankland's own words from *New Measures in Astrology*, goes as follows:

> Seek to ascertain which sign has the strongest influence in your nativity. This may be a sign containing a galaxy of planets, such as, for instance, in the author's case Virgo rises with Uranus, Mercury, Venus, and Moon in that sign—therefore this sign has dominant claim. In some cases it is by reason of the Sun, Moon, and Mercury being in one sign, or, in others like Mr. Gladstone's, where Mercury and the Sun are in the ascendant. [The British politician and Prime Minister William Ewart Gladstone was born 29 December 1809 around 8:00 a.m., about a half hour before sunrise, in Liverpool, England. He has Capricorn rising with Mercury conjunct the Sun early in that sign.]
>
> If one sign be thus dominant, especially by reason of a galaxy of planets, note carefully its nature and the house it occupies.
>
> Measure its period of 7 years. This in the author's case was the period from 35 to 42 years, the period of Virgo. (Frankland 1928, 37–38)
>
> [...]
>
> Mark the exact period of the signs thus occupied as most eventful. (Frankland 1928, 39)
>
> [...]
>
> Then measure 21 years [corresponding to 90°, or a square aspect] on either side of this, in my own case 21 years either side would be from 14 to 21 years, and from 56 to 63 years.
>
> Watch these years carefully. If there be any adverse directions they are detrimental, and certainly cause bodily changes that require care. (Frankland 1928, 38)

Fortunately, there also exist favorable periods of the nature of the 60° sextile and 120° trine aspects:

Then measure 14 [corresponding to the 60° sextile] and 28 years [corresponding to the 120° trine] either side, for benefit. Thus 14 years either side in the above case would be 21 to 28 years and 49 to 56. If benefics operate these are exceptionally good periods, if adverse influences these periods lessen the adversity. They are better for bodily changes. (Frankland 1928, 38)

When there is no "dominant" sign, Frankland states that **important degrees of planets** should be noted:

In nativities where the planets are evenly distributed then important degrees should be noted and measured in the same manner, 7 years per sign, particular attention being given to **degrees where ponderous planets are situated,** *if strongly placed and aspected.* Thus **an exact square of Saturn and Uranus would give sensitive degrees,** which, measured in this way, would prove very illuminating. (Frankland 1928, 39)

Frankland published his books in the 1920s before the discovery of Pluto. Thus, his list of "ponderous," or slow-moving, planets included only Jupiter, Saturn, Uranus, and Neptune. If he were writing today, he most likely would have included Pluto, the centaur-object Chiron, and perhaps the various dwarf planets.

Uranus as the "Developer"

We have seen how Frankland viewed the passage of Uranus through a sign as a "developer" that "stirs up or ripens anything along that pathway for effective expression." This idea is also found in the booklet *Transits of the Planets* attributed to Dr. J. Heber Smith, which delineates Uranus as follows:

Uranus is the developer, the bringer to the surface of the latent possibilities, and he augments the powers of the planets he aspects to the nth power. If any point in the horoscope awaits development, there is nothing that will bring it out more than the transits of Uranus, and there is nothing that will afford experiences of the unusual type more readily than the conjunction or adverse aspects of this planet. (Smith 1968, 26)

Astrologer Karen Ober Savalan also utilizes this notion of Uranus as "developer," which she combines with Alan Leo's emphasis on the 7-year passage of Uranus through each zodiac sign. For example, in her discussion of Uranus transiting the fixed segment of the 90° dial in her book *Midpoint Interpretation Simplified* (1978), she writes:

> From the time Uranus enters a Fixed sign until the time it leaves the same Fixed sign it plays a Uranus "developing" role in your life. If your chart shows stellar bodies in the Fixed section, you know immediately that there will be Uranus activity during the coming seven years of your life. Using keywords for the stellar bodies in the fixed section that Uranus transits will give you an approximate idea of the ways of Uranus development in your life during its seven-year transit. (Savalan 1978, 92)

In a similar way, Uranus transiting the cardinal or mutable signs will stimulate the development of the stellar bodies contained within the signs of those modalities during its 7-year transit. We will see an example of these principles in action in the chart of Princess Diana in chapter 9.

The Assassination of Shinzo Abe

As I was writing this chapter, the former prime minister of Japan, Shinzo Abe, was shot to death while giving a speech at a campaign event in Nara, Japan. His murder occurred on 8 July 2022.

Shinzo Abe was born on 21 September 1954 in Shinjuku City, Tokyo, Japan (time unknown), so he would have been 67.8 years old at the time of his demise. The Japanese website www.horoscope-tarot.net gives an unverified birth time of 2:35 a.m. JST, as no source is cited. I calculated Abe's chart with noon positions in Tokyo and used the Aries rising wheel since we are not certain of the actual Ascendant (chart 5).

How would Frankland have approached this chart?

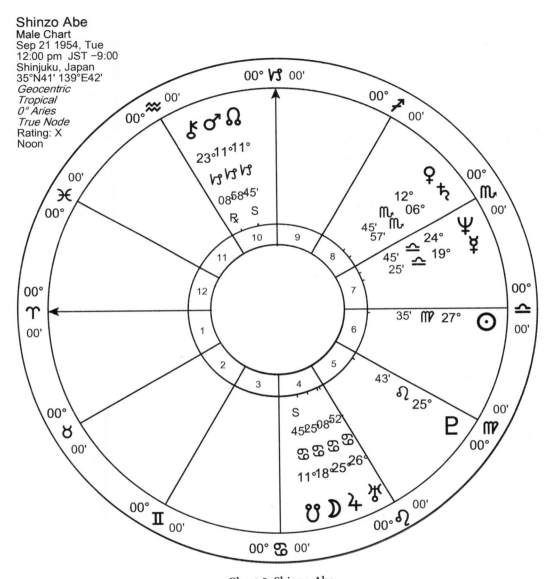

Shinzo Abe
Male Chart
Sep 21 1954, Tue
12:00 pm JST −9:00
Shinjuku, Japan
35°N41' 139°E42'
Geocentric
Tropical
0° Aries
True Node
Rating: X
Noon

Chart 5: Shinzo Abe
21 September 1954, 12:00 p.m. JST (time unknown), Shinjuku, Japan, 35N41 139E42

First, he would have noticed the clusters of planets in the signs Cancer, Libra, and Capricorn forming a cardinal T-square as a dominant feature of this nativity. Using Alan Leo's *seven years per zodiac sign*, commencing at 0° Aries, Frankland would have identified stressful and potentially dangerous periods (Mars opposing Uranus and square Neptune) as:

Cancer, ages 21–28

Libra, ages 42–49

Capricorn, ages 63–70 (He died at 67.8 years of age.)

Using Ptolemy's *seven ages of man*, Frankland would have noted the timelords of the following ages:

Ages 22–41, ruled by the Sun in Virgo

Ages 41–56, ruled by Mars in Capricorn

Ages 56–68, ruled by Jupiter in Cancer

Frankland also would have noticed that, around age 42, Uranus would oppose its natal position at the same time that Libra and Mars were active by symbolic measures.

In addition, if he were practicing today, Frankland would have known that Pluto was passing through Capricorn between 2009 and 2023, during which time Pluto would conjoin the natal planets in Capricorn, square those in Libra, oppose the ones in Cancer, and also quincunx its own birth position. The quincunx is a stressful configuration because it links planets that are 6 or 8 houses apart and thus has a 6th and 8th house significance (bodily ailments and mortality).

Particularly concerning would have been the fact that transiting Pluto would oppose natal Jupiter and quincunx natal Pluto in 2021 and would then oppose natal Uranus in 2022, marking the years 2021 and 2022 as particularly stressful. Abe turned 66 years old in September of 2020 and 68 years old in September of 2022. His *Point of Life* at age 66 would have been at 12° 51' Capricorn and at age 68 at 26° 26' Capricorn, activating his natal T-square in cardinal signs. When he was shot at age 67.8, his *Point of Life* was at 20° 34' Capricorn.

How to Calculate Frankland's *Point of Life* at a Given Age

Shinzo Abe was 67.8 years old when he was fatally wounded. To calculate his *Point of Life* at that age, divide 67.8 years by Alan Leo's rate of 7 years per zodiac sign:

67.8/7 = 9.685714

This result means that at that age, the *Point of Life* has passed through 9 entire zodiac signs and through 0.685714 of the next one. The *Point of Life* commences in Aries and has passed through the first 9 zodiac signs (Aries through Sagittarius) and is partway through Capricorn. Each sign contains 30°, so to find the number of degrees of the *Point of Life* in Capricorn, multiply 30° by the decimal part of 9.685714:

0.685714 × 30° = 20.57142° = Capricorn

Each sign contains 60', so to find the number of minutes of the *Point of Life* in Capricorn, multiply 60' by the decimal part of 20.57142:

0.57142 × 60' = 34.2852' = 34' Capricorn
20° + 34' = 20° 34' Capricorn

Having used his symbolic measure in combination with real-time influences, Frankland would have further studied the years 2021–22 for other indications. Glancing at his list of eclipses for the period, he would have noticed these eclipses in the fixed signs in 2022:

Partial Solar Eclipse: 20 April 2022 at 10° 21' Taurus
Total Lunar Eclipse: 16 May 2022 at 25° 16' Scorpio
Partial Solar Eclipse: 25 October 2022 at 2° 01' Scorpio
Total Lunar Eclipse: 8 November 2022 at 15° 59' Taurus

The Lunar Eclipse of 16 May 2022 squares Shinzo Abe's natal Pluto and trines his natal Jupiter-Uranus conjunction in Cancer, activating his natal cardinal T-square.

Furthermore, if we symbolically direct the birth chart at the *Point of Life* rate of 4 2/7° per year to the time of Abe's demise, we see that directed Jupiter arrives at 15° 41' Taurus, and directed Neptune at 15° 19' Leo. These positions are closely hit by the November 2022 Lunar Eclipse at 15° 59' Taurus.

If we calculate the secondary progressions of the noon chart (birth time unknown) for 2022, we find that secondary progressed Mars opposes natal Pluto during this year. Thus, the symbolic and real-time measures highlight the natal cardinal T-square and its most stressful planets (Mars, Pluto, Uranus, Neptune) during the year of Shinzo Abe's assassination.

Chapter 4
PLANETARY PERIODS AND PTOLEMY'S *SEVEN AGES OF MAN*

The Hellenistic astrologer Claudius Ptolemy (83–161 CE) divided the human life span into seven stages and taught that each of the seven visible planets acted as a *timelord* (*chronocrator*) managing a particular *planetary period* of human development:

Moon: Infancy, the 4-year period from birth until age 4.

Mercury: Childhood, the 10-year period beginning at age 4 until age 14.

Venus: Adolescence, the 8-year period beginning at age 14 until age 22.

Sun: Early Adulthood (End of Youth), the 19-year period beginning at age 22 until age 41. Nineteen years is the duration of the Metonic cycle of the Sun.

Mars: Middle Adulthood, the 15-year period beginning at age 41 until age 56.

Jupiter: Full Adulthood (Transition to Old Age), the 12-year period beginning at age 56 until age 68.

Saturn: Old Age, the 30-year period from age 68 onward. Presumably, most people will die during their Saturn period.

The ninth-century astrologer Abu Ma'shar, in his book about annual revolutions translated by Benjamin Dykes, *On the Revolutions of the Years of Nativities*, stressed the importance of Ptolemy's *seven ages of man* in predictive work. In fact, Ma'shar began his delineation of the annual return with this technique:

> In the revolutions of the years of nativities you ought to *begin by knowing the age level which the native is at* (of childhood, youth, maturity, old age, and senility) *because each one of the seven planets has an indication whose nature is rooted in*

one of the periods of his lifespan, and his condition in the revolutions of years does not proceed by any other [means]. (Ma'shar, 2019 Dykes translation, 165; italics mine)

Like Abu Ma'shar, Frankland took seriously Ptolemy's *seven ages of man* and carefully studied the planetary timelord of the Ptolemaic stage of life that the native was traversing. For example, he notes that Alan Leo launched *Modern Astrology* at age 30 while in the midst of his *solar* Ptolemaic planetary period (ages 22–41). In his birth chart, Alan Leo's Sun makes a favorable sextile to Uranus (associated with astrology) and a beneficial trine to the Moon (chart 6).

Thus, one would expect Alan Leo's solar period from ages 22 to 41 to be beneficial and productive, and to reflect especially the symbolism of the Sun, Uranus, and the Moon, and the houses that they rule and occupy in his chart. In Alan Leo's birth chart, using Placidus houses, the natal influences at age 30, during this favorable solar Ptolemaic period, include:

- Leo rising, ruled by the Sun
- Sun in the 12th house in Leo
- Sun conjunct Jupiter in Leo in the 12th house
- Sun conjunct Mercury in Leo in the 12th house, with Mercury acting as dispositor of Uranus in Gemini
- Sun sextile Uranus, which lies in Gemini in the 10th house of career
- Sun trine the Moon, which lies in Aries in the 9th house and conjunct the 9th house cusp (associated with astrology, publishing, and higher learning)

Using Symbolic Stages of Life as Timelords in Predictive Work

For predictive purposes we can combine Ptolemy's *seven ages of man* with Alan Leo's *zodiac signs as stages of life* into a kind of dasha system. In appendix D, I have organized the combination of Alan Leo's zodiac sign system and Ptolemy's *seven ages of man* into a table for easy reference.

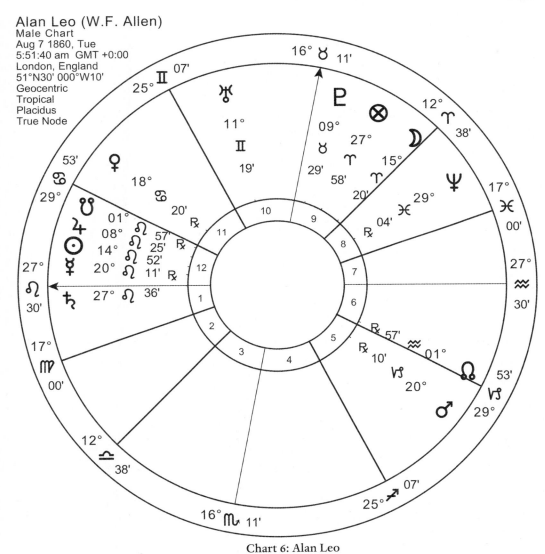

Chart 6: Alan Leo
7 August 1860, 5:51:40 a.m. GMT, London, England, 51N30 0W10

SPRING (ages 0–21)

Aries (ages 0–7); Moon period until age 4, when the Mercury period begins

Taurus (ages 7–14); Mercury period, age 4 until age 14

Gemini (ages 14–21); Venus period, age 14 until age 22

SUMMER (ages 21–42)

Cancer (ages 21–28); Sun period, age 22 until age 41

Leo (ages 28–35); during the Sun period

Virgo (ages 35–42); Sun period until age 41, at which time the Mars period begins

AUTUMN (ages 42–63)

Libra (ages 42–49); Mars period, age 41 until age 56

Scorpio (ages 49–56); Mars period

Sagittarius (ages 56–63); Jupiter period, age 56 until age 68

WINTER (ages 63–84)

Capricorn (ages 63–70): Jupiter period until age 68, at which time the Saturn period begins

Aquarius (ages 70–77); Saturn period, age 68 until age 98

Pisces (ages 77–84); Saturn period until age 98, at which time the "second infancy" begins with a Moon period, age 98 until age 102

Stages of Life in Frankland's Birth Chart

In *New Measures in Astrology*, Frankland tells us how Alan Leo's scheme of life stages played out in his own birth chart (chart 41, which will be examined in chapter 13):

> To use my own nativity again, Virgo rising and four planets therein, the qualities of Virgo and those planets would be most active and provocative of events during the [Virgo] period from 35 to 42, which was exactly the case. The period which challenged the health most was the one of Gemini [a sign in square to Virgo], from 14 to 21 years. The period in which the qualities of Virgo may bring most expression is from 49 to 56 [the Scorpio period, which forms a favorable sextile to Virgo], which period I have commenced as I write these sentences. (Frankland 1928, 42)

The sign Scorpio (ages 49 to 56) is on the cusp of Frankland's natal 3rd house (writing, communication) and is also in whole-sign sextile to Capricorn, which is on the cusp of his 5th house (creative activities), where his natal Jupiter resides. Thus, by merely looking at his birth chart with the schemes of Ptolemy and Alan Leo in mind, he is able to foresee major themes that will occupy him during various periods of his life.

Utilizing Stages of Life in Prediction

In summary, Frankland's use of the ideas of Alan Leo and Claudius Ptolemy regarding stages of life consists of the following steps:

1. Study the birth chart to identify important themes and configurations, which represent the natal promise of the nativity. Among such patterns, modern astrologers would include the stellium (Frankland calls this aspect a "galaxy of planets"), Grand Cross, T-Square, Yod, Hammer of Thor, Hard Rectangle, Magic Rectangle, Grand Trine, Kite, and so on. Symbolic directions that "hit" any planet or midpoint that forms part of the aspect pattern tend to activate the entire configuration, which can then manifest if it is also "hit" by a real-time predictive factor.

2. Note which zodiac signs are associated with these natal configurations, and identify the corresponding 7-year periods assigned to those signs. These 7-year spans are the ages at which the qualities of the sign, its ruler, and any planets therein will be most active and provocative of events.

3. Identify the zodiac signs in sextile or trine (by whole sign) to the natal configuration to predict which 7-year periods will blend most harmoniously with it.

4. Make note of the zodiac signs that form a whole-sign square to the natal configuration. These will be the most difficult and challenging years with regard to it.

5. The sign opposite the natal configuration will also indicate active years, but the way in which the opposition manifests will depend on the condition of the natal planets being highlighted.

6. Look up in the ephemeris the number of days after birth when any natal planet makes a station, either direct or retrograde. Convert the number of

days to years to identify important ages with regard to the significations of
the planet.

7. Note also the retrograde periods of any planets after birth. These correspond
to times of life when that planet's significations are hampered or weakened.

8. In a given year, pay attention to Solar or Lunar Eclipses that closely conjoin or
aspect a natal (or progressed or directed) planet involving one of Alan Leo's
zodiac signs that corresponds to the age of the native. According to Charles
Carter in *The Principles of Astrology*, "Eclipses, if falling on a radical or progressed planet, may exert great power and rank equally with almost any
direction" (Carter 1939, 179).

The Resonant or Ripple Effect of Ptolemy's *Seven Ages of Man*

In *New Measures in Astrology*, Frankland gives an example of the way in which he uses
Ptolemy's *seven ages of man* together with Alan Leo's system of *seven years per sign* to
symbolically direct planets in the birth chart.

In his example, Frankland has us imagine a nativity in which slower, "heavy" planets
are involved in a Grand Cross formation, for example, Uranus in Libra squaring Saturn
in Cancer as part of a cardinal Grand Cross. According to Frankland, the Saturn-Uranus
square will be associated with the most challenging features of the native's life. The most
sensitive points in this regard are the natal degrees of Saturn and Uranus, and the first of
these to be stimulated will trigger the entire complex.

Frankland then directs the natal positions of Saturn and Uranus at a rate of seven
years per zodiac sign (Alan Leo's scheme). Because Capricorn and Aries are the other
signs involved in this cardinal Grand Cross, the same degrees of Saturn and Uranus, but
in the signs Capricorn and Aries, will also be sensitive points that can stimulate the natal
Saturn square Uranus into action.

Furthermore, Frankland considers the planetary rulers of Cancer and Libra, which
are the Moon and Venus, respectively.

If I understand Frankland correctly, he symbolically directs natal Venus at Alan Leo's
rate of seven years per sign to determine its first contact by symbolic direction with Saturn or Uranus. Then, because the Ptolemaic period of Venus is 8 years of life, he regards
each 8-year period thereafter as a "ripple" of Venus, which again stimulates the natal
Saturn-Uranus square into action. Frankland uses the word "ripple" to evoke the image

of a stone cast into a pond, producing Venusian overtones, which in the case of Venus are spaced eight years apart. In other words, Frankland views the actions of each planet as producing particular *resonances, ripples,* or *overtones* at intervals associated with the Ptolemaic period of the planet. Frankland also uses the metaphor of the seasonal *ripening* of crops, in which each planet resembles a fruit that becomes *ready for harvesting at its own particular intervals.*

For the Moon, however, Frankland uses the approximately 28-year secondary progressed cycle rather than the 4 years attributed by Ptolemy's *ages of man.* He then determines when the Moon will first contact Saturn or Uranus by secondary progression, and considers every 14 and 28 years thereafter to be resonant lunar triggers to the natal Saturn-Uranus square.

In the case of Mars, he begins by calculating the first contact that Mars makes with the heavy planets at a rate of 7 years per sign, and then uses Ptolemy's Mars period of 15 years of life for future "ripples" of directed Mars, which trigger the sensitive points at 15-year intervals.

Frankland's does not mention Mercury in his example. My assumption is that he would allot, as "ripple intervals," Ptolemy's 10 years to Mercury, 19 years to the Sun, and 12 years to Jupiter. For Saturn, he appears to prefer to use the transits of Saturn (whose tropical orbit is about 29.4 years) rather than its Ptolemaic period of 30 years, but the two periods are very close in duration.

Frankland's Example of the Ripple Effect of Ptolemy's *Seven Ages*

In *New Measures in Astrology,* Frankland discusses the chart of a person born with Saturn in Cancer closely square to Uranus in Libra (Frankland 1928, 44–45). He does not give the birth data of this client, so I have generated a chart that meets Frankland's conditions (chart 7).

We can see from the birth chart that this individual has the following:

Saturn at 4° 18' Cancer in the 8th house
Uranus at 4° 18' Libra Rx in the 10th house

Frankland regards this natal Saturn-Uranus square as the most challenging feature of this birth chart. He notes that Saturn "will draw its adversity from matters under Cancer, while Uranus will draw its adversity or disturbing power from the sign Libra" (Frankland 1928, 44)

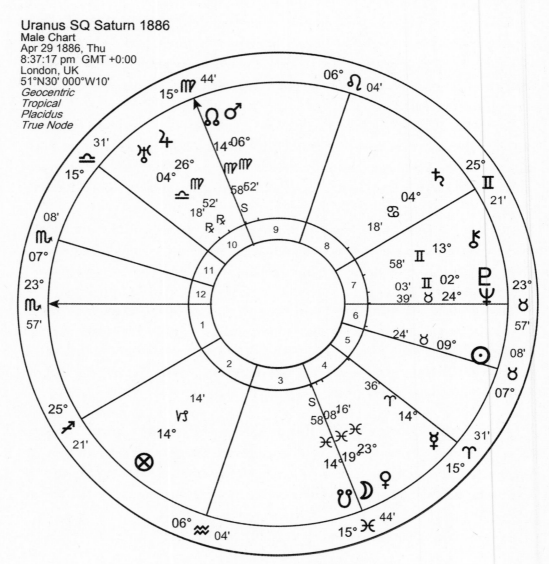

Chart 7: Male Chart with Uranus Square Saturn
29 April 1886, 8:37:17 p.m. GMT, London, England, 51N30 0W10

To determine when these adverse effects of Saturn square Uranus are likely to manifest, Frankland considers the positions of the planets measured at Alan Leo's rate of seven years per sign, which is equivalent to 4.286° per year.

Uranus lies at the beginning of the 2nd year of the sign Cancer (ages 21–28), indicating that the effects of Uranus will be felt around age 22 when the *Point of Life* conjoins Uranus. Saturn lies at the beginning of the 2nd year of the sign Libra (ages 42–49), and thus the effects of Saturn will be felt around age 43 when the *Point of Life* conjoins Saturn. Hence, ages 22 and 43 are significant times when the natal Saturn-Uranus square is ripe to manifest in this native's life.

Frankland continues:

> The most receptive periods of life for such [for the adverse effects of Saturn square Uranus to manifest] are the position[s] of the two planets measured at 7 years per sign, and the same degree of Capricorn or Aries [the two cardinal signs that complete the Grand Cross formation]. (Frankland 1928, 44)

In other words, the four sensitive points that, when activated by direction or transit, can trigger the adverse effects of Saturn square Uranus are the positions of Saturn and Uranus in Cancer and Libra, respectively, and the positions exactly opposite to Saturn and Uranus in Capricorn and Aries. These positions form a cardinal Grand Cross. Elsewhere, Frankland notes that the midpoints of this cardinal Grand Cross also act as sensitive points that can trigger it into manifestation.

Next, Frankland considers the dispositors of Saturn and Uranus, and the "ripples" of those dispositors in the life of the native. Venus disposes Uranus in Libra, and the Ptolemaic period of Venus is 8 years. Frankland advises us to note when Venus (presumably by direction or progression) passes over the sensitive points of the cardinal Grand Cross, and "then measure every 8 years as another ripple" (Frankland 1928, 45). In other words, the effect of progressed or directed Venus "hitting" natal Saturn or Uranus will reverberate throughout the native's life at 8-year intervals. Modern astrologers, like Arielle Guttman and David Cochrane, have further elaborated the symbolism of the 8-year synodic cycle of Venus, which produces a five-pointed "Venus Star" pattern.

As for the Moon, which disposes Saturn in this chart, Frankland prefers to use the progressed lunar cycle rather than Ptolemy's 4-year period:

The [progressed] Moon cycles round in about 28 years. Mark the first passage [of the Moon] by [*secondary*] *progression* over either of these points [the positions of natal Saturn and Uranus] and each 14 years [the opposition aspect] after. (Frankland 1928, 44)

We will see another example of the "ripple effect" later in chapter 13 when we discuss the case of a male astrologer who died at age 46.

A Numerological Rationale for Ptolemy's *Seven Ages of Man*

In book 4, chapter 10, of the *Tetrabiblos* (Loeb edition), Claudius Ptolemy discusses the "division of times." He assigns a specific number of years of the human life cycle to each of the seven visible planets, based on the planet's symbolism, analogy with a particular phase of life (for example, the Moon with mothering and early childhood, Saturn with advanced age, etc.), and the planet's observed astronomical properties as it orbits the Earth in his geocentric model. Thus, each planet is considered a timelord, or chronocrator, of a certain period of the human life cycle.

Our astrological forebears developed many systems of timelords, as can be seen in the *Anthologies* of Vettius Valens of the second century CE. In India, astrologers created numerous dasha systems. The Persian astrologers invented the *Firdaria*. These timelord systems are based on a view of time as cyclic rather than simply linear, and they assign the governance of a recurring period of years to each of the planets. Among the most influential systems of chronocrators are the so-called "lesser" and "greater" planetary periods, as shown in the following table.

LESSER AND GREATER PERIODS OF THE PLANETS		
Planet	**Lesser Period (Minor Years)**	**Greater Period (Greater Years)**
Moon	25	108 (Sun's maximum semi-arc minus the orb of the Moon)
Mercury	20	76 (sum of degrees of terms)
Venus	8	82 (sum of degrees of terms)
Sun	19 (Metonic period)	120 (idealized maximum semi-arc of the Sun)
Mars	15	66 (sum of degrees of terms)
Jupiter	12	79 (sum of degrees of terms)
Saturn	30	57 (sum of degrees of terms)

The *greater periods of the non-luminary planets* are the sums of the degrees allotted to each planet in the Egyptian and Ptolemaic systems of terms (bounds), which is a minor essential dignity. Note that the sum total of the degrees allocated to the non-luminary planets in these systems of bounds is Saturn (57°) + Jupiter (79°) + Mars (66°) + Venus (82°) + Mercury (76°) = the 360° in a complete circle.

The *greater periods of the luminaries*, the Sun and Moon, derive from the maximum semi-arc of the Sun in the Northern Hemisphere of the ancient civilized world, which has an idealized value of 120°, or one-third of a circle. For example, the northernmost boundary of the Roman Empire extended to Hadrian's Wall, which passed through Wallsend (latitude 55° North) in the UK around 122 CE in the second century during the lifetime of Claudius Ptolemy (born 100 CE in Alexandria, Egypt). On the day of the summer solstice in 2022, the longest day of the year, the Sun rose in Wallsend at 4:36 a.m. and culminated at the Midheaven at 1:07 p.m.—a difference (or semi-arc of the Sun) of 8 hours and 31 minutes. Converting this time interval to degrees, we divide the 8.5 hours of the semi-arc by 24 hours in a day and multiply the result by the 360° in a circle. The result is almost 128° at the northernmost frontier of the ancient Roman Empire. On the same day in Paris, France (latitude 48° 58' North), the Sun rose at 5:54 a.m. and culminated at 1:52 p.m.—a difference (or semi-arc of the Sun) of almost exactly 8 hours, or one-third of a day, which corresponds to the idealized figure of 120° of a circle.

Converting this idealized 120° maximum semi-arc of the Sun to years (perhaps chosen because it constitutes a perfect trine aspect), ancient astrologers assigned 120 years as the *greater period of the Sun*. In the astrology of India, this ideal numerical value was adopted as the maximum life span of a human being and incorporated into the Vimshottari dasha system. According to the Theosophist/astrologer Sepharial, 120 years is the period allotted to the process of incarnation.

The *Moon's greater period* derives from the greater period of the Sun. The traditional orb of the Moon is 12°, which is the minimal distance the Moon must be from the Sun to be visible to the human eye. Thus, the Sun's maximal semi-arc of 120° minus the 12° orb of the Moon gives 108° as the greater period of the Moon. The astrologers of India used 108 years as the length of the full life of a human being in the Ashtottari dasha system. The number 108 is highly significant in Jyotish and in the Hindu religion.

The *Sun's lesser or minor period* is based on the Metonic cycle, described by the Athenian astronomer Meton in the fifth century BCE. It is a period of 19 years consisting of 235 lunations (synodic months), after which the lunar phases recur on the same days of the solar year. In other words, every 19 years the New Moon and Full Moon repeat their ecliptic longitude at, or extremely close to, the same degree of the zodiac. The arithmetic underlying the Metonic cycle is straightforward:

(19 years) × (365.24219 days per tropical year) / (29.53059 days per synodic month) = 234.99705, or almost exactly 235 synodic months per Metonic cycle

The *Moon's lesser or minor period* is based on the belief of Pythagoras (sixth century BCE) in the mystical properties of whole numbers and the relationship between the ancient Egyptian civil year of exactly 365 days and the synodic month (lunation) of 29.53059 days. Sepharial (1920) implies that the Pythagorean teachings about the mystical properties of whole numbers are an essential part of the fundamental "Cosmic Symbolism" of Western astrology. The whole number periods represent the idealized form of an empirical astronomical observation, which can only approximate the ideal, however closely. The arithmetic underlying the lesser or minor period of the Moon goes as follows:

25 years × 365 days per civil year = 9,125 days (a whole number)
9,125 days divided by 29.53059 days per lunation = 309.002, or almost exactly 309 lunations (a whole number) per 25 civil years (a whole number)
In other words, 309 lunations (a whole number) = 24.9999, or almost exactly 25 civil years (a whole number)

The *lesser or minor years of the non-luminary planets* are also based on the Pythagorean belief in the mystical properties of whole numbers and the relationship of the synodic periods of the planets with respect to the Sun and the ancient Egyptian civil year of exactly 365 days. The synodic period of a planet is the amount of time it takes for the planet to return to the same position in the heavens relative to the Sun, as viewed from Earth. To determine the lesser years of a given planet, we seek to equate an idealized whole number of civil years with an idealized whole number of synodic periods. In other words, we want to find the *smallest whole number of 365-day civil years* it takes for the Sun and a particular non-luminary planet to meet at, or extremely close to, the very same position in the sky:

Mercury: 20.0005, or almost exactly **20** civil years = 63 Mercury-Sun synodic periods

Venus: 7.99889, or almost exactly **8** civil years = 5 Venus-Sun synodic periods, which occur at 19.2-month intervals tracing the shape of a five-pointed star

Mars: 14.9577, or almost exactly **15** civil years = 8 Mars-Sun synodic periods

Jupiter: 12.0212, or almost exactly **12** civil years = 11 Jupiter-Sun synodic periods

Saturn: 30.0402, or almost exactly **30** civil years = 29 Saturn-Sun synodic periods

The *lesser or minor years of Venus, Mars, Jupiter, and Saturn* pair nicely with the phases of human life to which they are assigned. For example, Venus symbolically governs the activity of human semen and correlates with the onset of puberty and the eight years of adolescence and early adulthood (ages 14 through 21). Every eight years, Venus conjoins the Sun at the same place in the sky. Frankland calls this 8-year cycle of the influence of Venus, rooted in its period of lesser years, the "ripple" effect of Venus through the life span of the native.

The two stellar bodies in Ptolemy's scheme of the *seven ages of man* that do not fit well with their lesser years are the Moon and Mercury. The Moon's lesser years are 25, but the Moon governs only the first 4 years of life, that is, the period of infancy. Mercury's lesser years are 20, but Mercury governs only the 10 years of latency and early education, which follow the 4 lunar years of infancy.

In his translation of Ptolemy's *Tetrabiblos,* F. E. Robbins explains the discrepancy between the lesser or minor years of the Moon and Mercury and their corresponding periods in Ptolemy's *ages of man* by quoting the anonymous commentator in a footnote on page 443 of his translation of the *Tetrabiblos*:

Four years is assigned to the moon [instead of 25] because after a period of that length [of 4 years] its phases again occur in the same degrees. Only half the period [10 years instead of 20] is assigned to Mercury because of the latter's double nature [Mercury rules the dual signs Gemini and Virgo]. (Ptolemy 1980, 443)

Sepharial, in his *Transits and Planetary Periods* (1920), suggests an alternate explanation based on "Cosmic Symbolism" and Pythagorean numerology. The following table illustrates the remarkable interrelationships that exist among the planetary periods in Ptolemy's *seven ages of man.*

RELATIONSHIPS AMONG PLANETARY PERIODS		
Inner Planets Ruling Signs Opposite Those of the Outer Planets	**Idealized Maximum Semi-arc of the Sun = 120°**	**Outer Planets in Chaldean Order**
MOON Ptolemaic Ages Period: **4** years (Minor Years: 25)	4 × 30 = **120** years	**SATURN** Minor Years: **30** Ptolemaic Ages Period: 30 years
MERCURY Ptolemaic Ages Period: **10** years (Minor Years: 20)	10 × 12 = **120** years **EARTH/SUN** Moon (**4**) + Mars (**15**) = **19** years, the **Metonic cycle** of the SUN	**JUPITER** Minor Years: **12** Ptolemaic Ages Period: 12 years
VENUS Ptolemaic Ages Period: **8** years (Minor Years: 8)	8 × 15 = **120** years	**MARS** Minor Years: **15** Ptolemaic Ages Period: 15 years

This table represents a kind of hybrid of the geocentric and heliocentric models of our solar system. The Earth and Sun are placed at the center, surrounded by the three "outer" visible planets (Saturn, Jupiter, and Mars) in the right-hand column and the three "inner" visible planets (the Moon, Mercury, and Venus) in the left-hand column. In Ptolemy's scheme for the *seven ages of man*, the following relationships apply:

- *Saturn*, which is farthest from the Earth and governs the last 30 years of life, is paired with the *Moon*, which is closest to the Earth and governs the first 4 years of life: 4 × 30 = 120, the ideal maximal number of degrees of semi-arc of the Sun and years of the human life span. Saturn rules Capricorn, which lies opposite Cancer, ruled by the Moon.

- *Jupiter*, the next planet in from Saturn toward the Earth, governs 12 years and is paired with *Mercury*, which is the next planet in from the Moon and governs 10 years of life: 12 × 10 = 120 years, the ideal length of the human life span. Jupiter rules Sagittarius and Pisces, which lie opposite Gemini and Virgo, respectively, which are both ruled by Mercury.

- *Mars*, the next planet in from Jupiter toward the Earth, governs 15 years and is paired with *Venus*, the next planet in from Mercury toward the Earth. Venus governs 8 years: $15 \times 8 = 120$, the ideal human life span. Mars rules Aries and Scorpio, which lie opposite Libra and Taurus, respectively, which are both ruled by Venus.

- Another feature is that the sum of the periods of the inner planet and outer planet closest to the Earth, the Moon (4 years) and Mars (15 years), is 19 years, the idealized duration of the Metonic cycle of almost exactly 19 years, after which the phases of the Moon, including eclipses, repeat on the same days of the solar year. It is also interesting that $19 \times 19 = 361$, which is one more than the number of degrees in a perfect circle.

If Sepharial is correct, Ptolemy used numerological reasoning to assign 4 years to the Moon so that the product of the Moon's period and that of the planet ruling the sign *opposite* to Cancer would be 120 years, the idealized human life span. Similarly, he assigned 10 years to Mercury so that the product of Mercury's period and that of the planet ruling the signs *opposite* to Gemini and Virgo would be 120 years, the idealized human life span.

Like Frankland (1926), Sepharial (1920) believed that the Ptolemaic *ages of man* periods represented intervals at which the influence of the planet would recurrently manifest in the life of the native—like *ripples* on a pond, or musical *resonances*, or the *seasonal ripening* of a crop at harvest time. This concept of resonant influence is not new and can be found in the writings of Vettius Valens (second century CE) and Firmicus Maternus (fourth century CE).

Valens, for example, assumes that the influence of a planet is likely to be experienced at intervals (Frankland's "ripples" or "ripenings") corresponding to the minor or lesser years of the planet. Thus, the influence of Jupiter, which has a period of 12 minor years, may manifest, "ripple" or "ripen," around ages 12, 24, 36, 48, and so on.

Valens also adds together the intervals associated with planets to predict years when the combined influence of the two planets may manifest. For example, a natal configuration of Jupiter sextile Saturn highlights the period around age 42, because Jupiter's 12 minor years plus Saturn's 30 minor years sum to 42 years. In summary, Valens's techniques for working with planetary years include the following:

- Summing the minor years of planets that are in aspect in the birth chart
- Summing the minor years of a planet and the number of years associated with the rising time of the sign it occupies
- Summing the minor years of a planet and the minor years of its dispositor
- Considering multiples or fractional parts of planetary years and combinations of planetary periods

Like Valens (second century CE), Sepharial (1920) and Frankland (1926) considered fractional parts of planetary periods, especially those associated with astrological aspects. For example, Sepharial, noting that the minor period of Saturn is 30 years, so that its square to its natal position *by symbolic direction* occurs 7.5 years later, wrote in *Transits and Planetary Periods*:

> If Saturn is in evil aspect to any of the Significators at birth, then it will repeat that aspect every 7½ years, by coming to the successive squares of its radical place, and every 15 years it will be in opposition to its radical place. (Sepharial 1920, 37–38)

The following table shows the yearly intervals at which the symbolic directions (of 1° per year) occur for each planet, based on Ptolemy's *ages of man* period.

YEARLY INTERVALS OF SYMBOLIC DIRECTIONS (1° PER YEAR) BASED ON PTOLEMY'S *AGES OF MAN*					
Planet	Ptolemaic Age Period (Years)	Opposition (Years)	Trine (Years)	Square (Years)	Sextile (Years)	Average Degrees Per Year
Saturn	30	15	10	7.5	5	12
Jupiter	12	6	4	3	2	30
Mars	15	7.5	5	3.75	2.5	24
Sun	19	9.5	6.333	4.75	3.167	18.95
Venus	8	4	2.667	2	1.333	45
Mercury	10	5	3.333	2.5	1.667	36
Moon	4	2	1.333	1	0.667	90

Planetary Periods, Emily Davison, and King George V of the UK

King George V of the UK was born in London on 3 June 1865 at 1:18 a.m. GMT, Rodden Rating AA (chart 8). He became king on 6 May 1910 upon the death of his father. George V died on 20 January 1936 at the age of 70. Let's explore some of the ideas about planetary periods in King George V's nativity.

A prominent feature of this chart is the elevated Jupiter Rx in its own domicile Sagittarius in the 9th house, conjunct the Capricorn MC. Jupiter rules the 9th house and also rules Pisces, which is intercepted in the 12th house. Jupiter's aspects include a sesquisquare to Venus in Taurus, a sextile to Saturn and the North Lunar Node in Libra, a square to the Moon in Libra, and an opposition to Uranus in Gemini.

Jupiter's lesser or minor years are 12; hence its "ripples" occur every 12 years, that is, at ages 12, 24, 36, 48, 60, 72, and so on.

Jupiter in Sagittarius is its own dispositor. Thus, summing the planetary periods of Jupiter and its dispositor produces a result of 24 years, and multiples of 24, such as 48 and 72, are ages when the influence of Jupiter is "ripe" to manifest. At age 24 (in 1889), George V was honored for chivalry in the Kingdom of Prussia (a 9th house foreign land), receiving awards from the Prussian Orders of the Black Eagle and the Red Eagle (a bird ruled by Jupiter, according to William Lilly).

Jupiter (minor years, 12) sextiles 10th house ruler Saturn (minor years, 30). The sum of the minor years of these two planets is 12 + 30 = 42, which suggests that age 42 (the year 1907) would be a time when this sextile was "ripe" to manifest. In March of 1907, just three months before he turned 42 years old, George V, who had joined the cadet training ship HMS Britannia at age 12 (a Jupiter "ripple") in 1877, rose to the rank of full admiral (a 10th house theme).

When King George V was 48 years old, his horse Anmer struck suffragette Emily Davison on 4 June 1913 at the Epson Downs Derby. She fell into a coma and died four days later. As a result, Emily Wilding Davison (born in London on 11 October 1872 around 00:30 a.m.) became an internationally recognized martyr for the cause of women's right to vote. Jupiter in the 9th house is associated with justice and human rights. As the ruler of Pisces intercepted in the 12th house, Jupiter is linked to large animals such as horses. The close opposition from an angular Uranus to George V's natal Jupiter suggests accidents and unexpected disruptive happenings regarding Jupiterian themes.

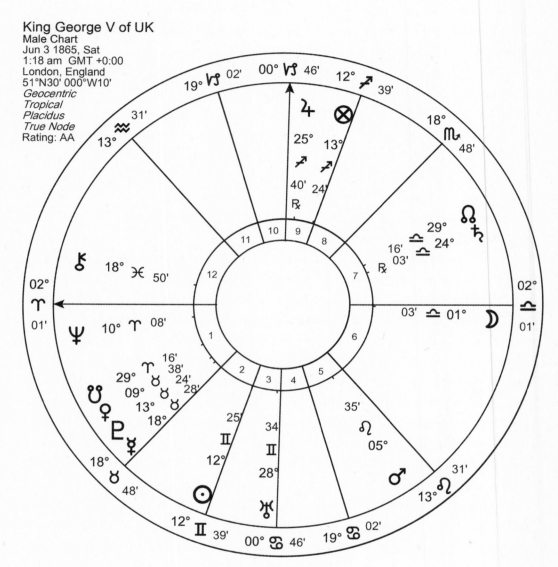

King George V of UK
Male Chart
Jun 3 1865, Sat
1:18 am GMT +0:00
London, England
51°N30' 000°W10'
Geocentric
Tropical
Placidus
True Node
Rating: AA

Chart 8: King George V
3 June 1865, 1:18 a.m. GMT, London, England, 51N30 0W10

At age 48, George V's *Age along the Zodiac* (at a rate of 1° per year, commencing at 0° Aries) was at 18° Taurus, closely conjunct his natal Mercury and 2nd house cusp and opposite his 8th house cusp of death. Natal Mercury rules his 3rd house of news and local travel and is closely sextile to Chiron, the wounded healer, in the radical 12th house of horses and undoing. The news of the killing of Emily Davison by the king's horse Anmer, as she was attempting to petition the king for women's right to vote, dominated the news in the UK in June of 1913. In addition, at age 48 the king's *Point of Life* was at 25° 43' Libra in the radical 7th house of women's issues and almost exactly sextile to George V's natal Jupiter in Sagittarius in the 9th house.

At Davison's funeral in London on 14 June 1913, five thousand woman from all parts of Britain marched in the procession. The women wore white dresses with black armbands and carried Madonna lilies to commemorate their suffragette heroine and to protest being denied the vote because they were regarded as inferior to men in British society. King George V expressed his sympathy for the jockey, who recovered, and for his horse, which emerged unhurt, but he regarded the behavior of trampled Emily Davison as regrettable and scandalous. The queen's immediate reaction to the suffragette's encounter with the king's horse was to comment that Emily Davison was "a horrid woman."

As one might expect from George V's chart, the king was prone to Uranian-type accidents with Jupiter-ruled horses. His natal Moon closely opposes his Ascendant (the body and vital forces of the native) and forms a T-square with his natal Jupiter-Uranus opposition. The lesser or minor years of the Moon are 25, with resonances at ages 50 and 75. On 28 October 1915, at age 50, King George V was thrown by his horse at a troop review on the Western Front in France (a 9th house matter). He suffered serious chronic health problems as a result of the accident.

As with other symbolic directions, those involving planetary periods, such as minor years of planets or Ptolemy's *ages of man,* serve to highlight areas of the chart and ages when the natal promise becomes "ripe" and more likely to manifest. Events related to these areas tend to occur only when and if there is also a concurrent real-time-based astrological influence in effect. For example, astrological influences within orb at the time of the king turning 48 years old included transiting Pluto conjunct natal Uranus and opposite natal Jupiter, transiting Neptune in the radical 5th house (sporting events) square natal Saturn in the radical 7th house, a Lunar Eclipse almost exactly conjunct his natal Moon (a female symbol) and the 7th house cusp of women's issues, secondary progressed Venus (a symbol of women) conjunct his natal Sun, transiting Saturn sesquisquare natal Saturn on 8 June 1913, just two days after the death of Emily Davison, and transiting Saturn conjunct his natal Sun on 7 July 1913.

Sepharial's Influence on William Frankland

Walter Gorn Old (born on 20 March 1864 in Handsworth, UK) was a Theosophist and astrologer who wrote under the pen name Sepharial. He was editor of *Old Moore's Almanac* and wrote several books and articles on astrology beginning in 1887 until his death in 1929. Sepharial's writings influenced several prominent British astrologers of the period, including Alan Leo, Charles Carter, and William Frankland. Sepharial's interest in Theosophy and mysticism was fundamental to his approach to astrology. In fact, he felt that contemporary astrologers were abandoning the mystical "Cosmic Symbolism" that lies at the root of astrology and thereby sacrificing too much on the altar of exact science. Freud might have diagnosed such astrologers as suffering from "science envy."

In his 1920 book *Transits and Planetary Periods*, Sepharial emphasized the predictive value of the planetary cycles associated with Ptolemy's *seven ages of man*. He also made extensive use of the symbolic directions of the "Significators" of the natal chart (Asc, MC, Sun, and Moon) at the rate of 1° per year. Frankland incorporated both of these ideas into his own work on symbolic directions.

Like Frankland, Sepharial was seeking forecasting techniques that were quicker and easier to calculate than the more complex primary directions and secondary progressions. Other areas upon which the two authors agreed included the importance of Solar and Lunar Eclipses that impact the natal chart and of transiting planets that station direct or retrograde within orb of a radical point or planet. Sepharial noted that stationary planets in transit were equivalent in force to primary directions, and he commented that "by observing eclipses and transits we may be reliably notified of any great event which may be portentous in the life" (Sepharial 1920, 56).

Eclipses are special types of New and Full Moons ("lunations"). Sepharial found that lunations in general indicate the course of events during the ensuing month-long period. Lunar returns to the birth chart can also be used to forecast for a month ahead.

Eclipses, however, "have a more enduring influence and may influence the import of successive transits over the same point" (that is, transits that closely aspect the place where the eclipse occurred) (Sepharial 1920, 59–60). He also noted that "the visibility of an eclipse plays no part in horoscopy" (Sepharial 1920, 57), so that an eclipse impacting a significant point or planet in the birth chart will have an effect regardless of whether or not the eclipse is visible at the location of the native. According to Sepharial, ancient astrologers with a knowledge of the Metonic lunisolar cycle of 19 years and the lunar nodal cycle of 18.612958 years (18 years, 7 months, 9 days) have a practical means of predicting eclipses regardless of their region of visibility, which enabled them to use "eclipses as primary pointers, and the transits as secondary pointers, thus timing events with considerable accuracy" (Sepharial 1920, 57).

In addition, eclipses were traditionally considered malefic influences portending misfortune, and sometimes fatality, with regard to the symbolism of the significators that they impacted. For example, on the day of death of King Edward VII of the UK (6 May 1910), transiting Uranus was at 25° 12' Capricorn Rx conjunct his secondary progressed Sun at 26° 28' Capricorn and conjunct his symbolically directed Sun (at 1° per year) at 25° 23' Capricorn. King Edwards's natal Sun at 16° 54' Scorpio was "hit" by a Total Solar Eclipse at 17° 43' Scorpio on 9 May 1910, just three days after his passing. King Edward VII was born on 9 November 1841 at 10:48 a.m. LMT in London, and his natal Sun was the *hyleg*, or life-giving planet, in his birth chart.

Yet another example that Sepharial gives of the importance of eclipses is the chart of Kaiser Wilhelm II, who governed Germany during World War I. Kaiser Wilhelm was born on 27 January 1859 at 3:00 p.m. LMT in Potsdam, Germany. His was a difficult and prolonged breach birth, the baby's bottom appearing at 2:45 p.m. and the birth finally concluding at 3:00 p.m. The kaiser was 55½ years old when World War I began on 28 July 1914. At that time his *Point of Life* was at 28° Scorpio applying to square his secondary progressed Ascendant at 29° 27' Leo, which conjoined the fixed star Regulus and was about to be "hit" by a Total Solar Eclipse at 27° 35' Leo less than a month later on 21 August 1914. Sepharial commented about the impact of this eclipse on the kaiser's progressed chart:

A solar eclipse happening on the place of the [secondary] progressed Ascendant is sinister in the highest degree and its influence lasts for three years. (Sepharial 1920, 48)

To assess the combined influence of active transits, symbolic directions, and secondary progressions at a given age, Sepharial developed a comprehensive method of forecasting, which he called "gradial" transits and applied to the four principal significators: the MC, Asc, Sun, and Moon. The MC as a significator represents the professional life and the native's actions in the world. The Ascendant signifies the native and their body, life, and health. The Moon, according to Sepharial, is a signifier of the mother, mutability, change, the functional properties of the physical system, and the opening up of new avenues in life. Finally, the Sun represents the father, the fixed or constitutional element of affairs, and the organic properties of the organism.

By *gradial transits* to a significator, Sepharial meant the continuing influence of a transiting planet through an *arc* formed by the radical position of the significator, as a starting point, and the symbolically directed position of the same significator at a given age at a rate of 1° per year of life, as a terminal point. Sepharial made an exception for symbolically directing the Ascendant as significator. He advanced the Sun, Moon, and MC at a rate of 1° per year, but he calculated the directed Ascendant on the basis of the symbolically directed MC and the latitude of the birthplace. To quote directly from *Transits and Planetary Periods* (1920) regarding "continuous," or *gradial,* transits:

Transits are continuous from the moment that they impinge upon the radical position of a Significator up to the time when they finally pass the progressed position of the same ... at the rate of one day after birth for every year of life. ...

[...]

... During the progress of the Significator from its radical position in the horoscope of birth to that which it has attained at any subsequent time, the [directed] Significator forms aspects to the planets, both radical and [secondary] progressed, which constitute periods of good and ill fortune. The planet in transit picks up these aspects in its gradial transit from the radical to the progressed [directed at a rate of 1° per year] position and undergoes a modification of its action. (Sepharial 1920, 22–24)

To illustrate, consider King George V's *gradial transits* to his Midheaven *arc* (a signifier of his professional and political life) at 48 years of age when the trampling of suffragette Emily Davison by the king's horse dominated the news. The king's natal MC at 0° 46' Capricorn becomes the initial point of the *arc*, to which we must add 48°, corresponding to his age, to arrive at the terminal point of 18° 46' Aquarius. Rounding to the nearest degree, the limits (terminals) of his *gradial transit arc* at age 48 in 1913 are 1° Capricorn and 19° Aquarius. Sepharial likens the terminal points of the gradial arc to human nerve endings. In this analogy, the peripheral nerve ending would be at 1° Capricorn and the its ending in the brain at 19° Aquarius.

Uranus transited this region (1° Capricorn to 19° Aquarius) between 1905 and 1916, suggesting an extended period of political disruptions and social unrest in the empire over which the king reigned, due to the continuous influence of transiting Uranus. In 1913, Uranus was transiting opposite natal Mars (an aspect indicating accidents), which occupies the king's 5th house of sporting events such as the Epsom Derby. Jupiter began to transit the *gradial arc* of the Midheaven around January of 1913. During the summer of 1913, Jupiter was transiting in quincunx to the king's natal Sun. Also, in the summer of 1913 the king's secondary progressed MC perfected a semisquare to his natal MC. Finally, at age 48 the king's symbolically directed Saturn (at a rate of 1° per year), the ruler of his radical and directed MC, arrived at 12° 03' Sagittarius, at the cusp of the 9th house and directly opposite his natal Sun.

Also affecting this Midheaven's *gradial arc* at age 48 (1° Capricorn to 19° Aquarius) were oppositions from transiting Neptune and Pluto. Neptune entered Cancer in 1901 and made its final exit from Cancer in May of 1916. In the summer of 1913, Neptune was transiting the king's natal 5th house in square to radical Saturn in the 7th house and in quincunx to radical Jupiter in the 9th house. Pluto entered Cancer in July of 1913, not long after the funeral of Emily Davison. Transiting Pluto in Cancer in the radical 4th house opposed the king's natal MC on 28 June 1914, a month before the onset of World War I.

Sepharial's Guidelines for Interpreting Transits

Sepharial summarizes his approach to interpreting transits in six guidelines:

1. Observe the nature of the transiting planet and the type of aspect it forms to the radical, secondary progressed, and symbolically directed positions in the birth chart.

2. If the point of transit forms an exact aspect to a radical position, judge its influence by whether the radical planet is afflicting or benefiting the planet in transit. By "exact," I think he means partile, or in the same numerical degree.

3. A transit to a radical significator will have its effect in terms of the radical house position of the planet in transit. However, a transit to a progressed significator will have its effect in terms of the progressed house position of the planet in transit. For example, suppose transiting Saturn conjoins the natal Sun in the 8th house of the birth chart, and natal Saturn lies in the radical 4th house. Then the effect of the natal 4th house Saturn has come to the natal 8th house Sun by transit. At age 33, however, the progressed Sun may be in the 8th house, but progressed Saturn may occupy the 3rd house of the progressed chart. In this case, transiting Saturn conjunct the 8th house progressed Sun will have an effect related to progressed Saturn in the 3rd house.

4. Transits are continuous in their action from the point at which they first impact the radical significator to the point at which they impact the same significator symbolically directed at a rate of 1° per year. Breaks may occur in the general period of a particular *gradial* transit, depending on the aspects that the symbolically directed significator makes to radical and progressed planets and points in the birth chart.

5. The stationary position of a transiting planet is similar in force to a primary direction and has a marked and lasting effect.

6. Transits that fall on the position of an eclipse that affects a significator will have a major and enduring impact on the native's life.

Chapter 5
FRANKLAND'S *POINT OF LIFE MEASURE*

In chapter 5 of *Astrological Investigations* (1926), Frankland defines his **Point of Life** as follows:

> The planet Uranus moves through the Zodiac at the **rate of one sign in seven years,** or about **4 degree two-sevenths per year (4²⁄₇°)** [or 4.286° per year].
>
> Imagine *Life* to be moving along the Zodiac at this Ratio. The 49th year would equal the end of the 7th sign, or 30 degrees Libra. [In other words, the **Point of Life** commences at 0° Aries at birth and advances along the zodiac at the rate of 4.286° per year of life.] The age of 17½ would equal the 15th degree of Gemini, and so on with all the signs.
>
> Mark off the positions of the Planets at Birth as comparable with certain years [of life]. Thus Saturn in Virgo 8½ degrees would equal about 37 years. Jupiter in Leo 8½ [degrees] would equal 30 years, etc.
>
> Call these "Important areas," *allow 4 degrees* (which covers one year), and judge them weak or strong, good or adverse, as the nature of the Planet may be.
>
> You will find that at the year comparable with the Planet's position, its nature and aspects, there is generally some corresponding event or experience. [Note that Frankland is using an orb of 4° for *Point of Life symbolic directions*, which covers a period of one year before or after the exact aspect.]
>
> In any case should there be aspects formed at the time by [secondary] progression, such aspects will be strengthened or mitigated.
>
> If a Planet be well aspected and situated, mark off its sextiles and trines, and judge beneficial periods.

Conversely, if the Planet is adversely placed or aspected, then mark off its squares and oppositions and judge adverse periods.

It should be understood that the **Point of Life** opposed to a Planet, even a Malefic, would lose its adversity if that Planet were *well* aspected at Birth. [In other words, the effect of the *Point of Life* opposing a natal planet will depend on the favorable or adverse condition of that planet in the birth chart.] (Frankland 1926, 72–73; bold highlighting mine)

Charles. E. O. Carter and Frankland's *Point of Life*

Frankland illustrates these principles with the chart of the renowned British astrologer Charles E. O. Carter, born on 31 January 1887 at about 11:00 p.m. GMT in Parkstone, England. Let's look at the birth chart that Carter rectified for himself (chart 9).

Frankland explains that at 35 years of age, Carter's *Point of Life* would be in 0° of Virgo, opposite to his natal Mars, which lies at 0° 26' Pisces. Without any mitigating factors, an opposition from Mars would indicate an adverse event. In this chart, however, Mars is trine benefic Jupiter, sextile natal Moon, and in an out-of-sign conjunction with benefic Venus. The only adverse aspect involving Mars is an out-of-sign square to Neptune, from which Mars is separating. Overall, this period should be favorable because the directed *Point of Life* is applying harmoniously to sextile Jupiter and trine the Moon.

The corresponding event is that in 1922, at age 35, Carter became president of the Astrological Lodge of London. At that time, his directed *Point of Life* was opposing natal Mars, and his directed *Age Point* (one year of life per degree, measured from 0° Aries) was at 5° Taurus, opposing natal Jupiter. In his birth chart, Mars and Jupiter are in trine aspect and in mutual reception. Mars occupies Pisces, ruled by Jupiter, which occupies Scorpio, ruled by Mars. Thus, even though two of Frankland's "new measures" were in opposition to natal planets, the planets being opposed were favorably configured with each other by trine and mutual reception, the manifestation of which was his assuming leadership of the Astrological Lodge.

In addition, Frankland paid attention to Ptolemy's *seven ages of man* and would have noticed that at age 35 Carter was in the midst of his 19-year Sun period. In Carter's chart, the Sun is powerfully placed in Aquarius in the angular 4th house, from which it makes a favorable trine to both Uranus and the natal Ascendant, both in Libra. The trine to Uranus, a modern planet associated with astrology, is extremely close and quite favorable for the practice of astrology.

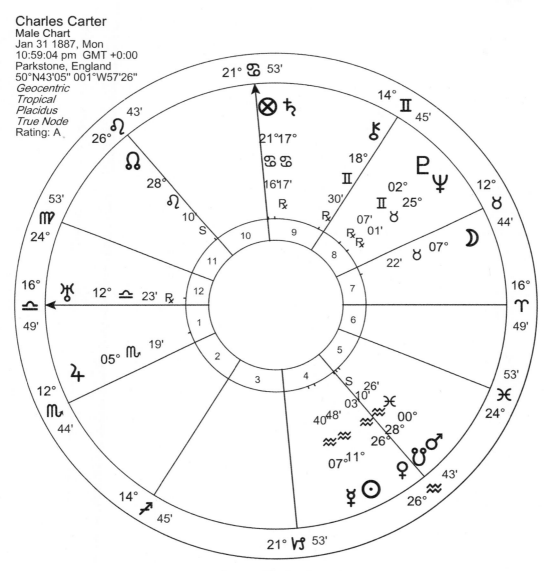

Charles Carter
Male Chart
Jan 31 1887, Mon
10:59:04 pm GMT +0:00
Parkstone, England
50°N43'05" 001°W57'26"
Geocentric
Tropical
Placidus
True Node
Rating: A

Chart 9: Charles Carter
31 January 1887, 10:59:04 p.m. GMT, Parkstone, England, 50N43 1W57

Charles Carter married at the age of 26¾, also during his solar Ptolemaic period. His natal Sun lies sextile the 7th house cusp of his birth chart. Frankland notes that measuring an arc of 26¾ degrees from 0° Aries places Carter's *Age along the Zodiac Point* at 26° 45' Aries at the time of his marriage, within orb of a sextile to his natal Venus. With Carter's natal Venus at 26° of Aquarius, Frankland's method would identify points in the chart in sextile or trine to Venus (namely, 26° of Aries, Libra, Gemini, Sagittarius) as indicating suitable periods for Venusian matters, such as love and marriage.

Carter's directed *Point of Life* at age 26¾ fell at 24.5° of Cancer (at a rate of one sign per 7 years of life, beginning at 0° Aries at birth). At that time the directed *Point of Life* was closely applying to sextile natal Neptune and trine secondary progressed Mercury, ruler of the 9th house of religious ceremonies. During this same period, his secondary progressed Uranus had retrograded back to an almost perfect trine to his natal Sun.

Chapter 6
BIRTH NUMBERS IDENTIFY POTENTIALLY SIGNIFICANT YEARS

One of the stranger features of Frankland's method was his use of Birth Numbers to identify potentially significant years of life. Birth Numbers are found by adding together the digits in one's date of birth in particular ways. Numerologists and many tarot readers use Birth Numbers in their readings. I was skeptical at first, but Frankland's many examples convinced me that there may be something to this technique.

In Frankland's case examples, he appears to use Birth Numbers to identify important birthdays in the life of the native and uses an orb of about a year before and after the age indicated by the Birth Number. The periods surrounding these birthdays appear to have heightened significance when they correlate with significant operative astrological influences.

Unlike the numerologists, however, Frankland emphasizes that he does not regard Birth Numbers as important in and of themselves. Rather, only if Birth Numbers coincide with a period during which the native also experiences a significant direction, progression, or transit does that period stand out prominently in the native's life—all the more so if one of Frankland's new symbolic measures or another astrological influence also falls within the year identified by the Birth Number. The chart of Queen Elizabeth II, discussed elsewhere in this text, is a good example of this principle. Specifically, in chapter 4 in *Astrological Investigations*, Frankland describes his research into Birth Numbers as follows:

I have studied hundreds of these Dates and have come to the conclusion that *should important directions*, etc., *fall* in a *year* comparable with the important totals, etc., of the birth Date, the *added* weight may be given to *those Directions*. (Frankland 1926, 68)

The following table summaries key definitions from Frankland's approach to Birth Numbers, which is explained in detail in this chapter. To "reduce" a number means to add together all the single digits in that number to generate a sum.

CALCULATING PRIMARY AND ADDITIONAL BIRTH NUMBERS	
Birth Date Format (Day-Month-Year)	DD-MM-YYYY
Single Digits Birth Number	The sum of all the single digits in the birth date: D + D + M + M + Y + Y + Y + Y
Double Digits Birth Number	The sum of the day and month as double-digit numbers plus the single digits of the year of birth: DD + MM + Y + Y + Y + Y
Additional Birth Number(s)	Add the *Single Digits Birth Number* (or *Double Digits Birth Number*) to the 4-digit year of birth (YYYY), and reduce this 4-digit sum to its reduced double-digits and single-digits forms. Then add the original Birth Number to the reduced forms to generate the *Additional Birth Number* (and its reduced forms).
Day Number	DD of the date of birth. Frankland sometimes adds the *Day Number* to the Birth Numbers or their reduced forms to identify important years.

How to Calculate Birth Numbers, According to Frankland

Frankland had a particular way of calculating the Birth Numbers, and it took me a while to figure it out. As I understand it, he followed the following sequence.

First, add together the individual digits of the year of birth to arrive at the sum that corresponds to the native's year of birth. The individual digits of the year are always summed together in this way. For example, the year 2019 produces the sum $2 + 0 + 1 + 9$, which totals 12. The day and month digits can be added as either single-digit or double-digit numbers, as will be explained below.

For example, the astrologer Charles E. O. Carter was born on 31 January 1887. His year of birth is 1887, so we add the individual digits 1 + 8 + 8 + 7 to arrive at a sum of **24**, which is the number corresponding to the year of his birth. We can call this his "birth year number."

Second, add together the *individual* digits of his day and month of birth, and then add this total to the birth year sum to obtain his *Single Digits Birth Number.*

Carter was born on 31 January, which contains the digits 31 and 01. Thus, we add the *individual* digits 3 + 1 + 0 + 1 and arrive at the sum of **5**, which we must add to his birth year number (24), for a total of 5 + 24, which equals **29**. Frankland calls **29** his *Single Digits Birth Number* because it is found by adding together all the single digits in his date of birth.

Third, if either the day or the month is a double-digit number, then add the two numbers together as double-digit numbers, and continue by adding that sum to the birth year number to obtain the *Double Digits Birth Number.*

In Carter's case, he was born on 31 January (31/01). The *Day Number* (31) is a double-digit number. Therefore, we must add 31 + 01 as double digits, which gives a total of 32, which we then add to the birth year number (24) to arrive at a grand total of 32 + 24, which equals **56**, his *Double Digits Birth Number.* In this method, the period within a year of his birthday when he turns 56 years old is potentially significant.

Thus far we have established that Carter has two significant (primary or basic) Birth Numbers: his *Single Digits Birth Number,* **29**, and his *Double Digits Birth Number,* **56**. Thus, an important direction, progression, or transit occurring around the time when he turns 29 or 56 years old could potentially leave an indelible mark on Carter's life.

Fourth, Frankland calculates *Additional Birth Numbers* by adding the *Single Digits Birth Number* or *Double Digits Birth Number* to the 4-digit year of birth.

In Carter's case, his *Single Digits Birth Number* is **29** and his *Double Digits Birth Number* is **56**. To obtain his *Additional Birth Numbers,* we add each of his Birth Numbers separately to his actual birth year (**1887**) and reduce each result to its single-digit sum:

29 (*Single Digits Birth Number*) + **1887** (birth year) equals **1916**, which reduces to 1 + 9 + 1 + 6, or **17**, which further reduces to 1 + 7, or **8**.

We then add the *Single Digits Birth Number* (**29**) to the reduced values of the sum of the Birth Number plus the birth year (29 + 1887 = 1916, which reduces to **17** and **8**) to arrive at **29 + 17 + 8**, which equals **54** and identifies turning 54 years old as a potentially significant period of life for him.

In a similar way, **56** (*Double Digits Birth Number*) + **1887** (birth year) equals **1943**, which reduces to 1 + 9 + 4 + 3, or **17**, which further reduces to 1 + 7, or **8**.

We then add the *Double Digits Birth Number* (**56**) to the reduced values of the sum of the Birth Number plus the birth year (56 + 1887 = 1943, which reduces to **17** and **8**) to arrive at **56 + 17 + 8**, which equals **81** and identifies the period around his birthday when he turns 81 as a potentially significant time of life. Charles Carter (born 31 January 1887) died on 4 October 1968 at the age of 81.

Thus far we have identified the following ages as potentially significant in Carter's life: 29, 54, 56, and 81. According to Frankland, these Birth Numbers give added weight to major transits, primary directions, and secondary progressions that occur around the same age. Age 81 was obviously significant because Carter died during that year. Let's consider Carter's life at age 29 in the year 1916, in the midst of World War I, which lasted from 28 July 1914 until 11 November 1918.

According to the biographical sketch of Carter by Mari Garcia and Joy Usher on the Skyscript website:

> Carter studied law at the University of London and worked as a barrister until WWI when he enlisted in the army. He returned safely from the Western Front, but his war experiences brought on claustrophobia, so that he was no longer able to work within the confines of a courtroom. Instead, he worked with his father, helping post-war families to resettle through the Homeland's Trust initiative. (Garcia and Usher 2013)

Is there evidence in Carter's birth chart and directions, progressions, transits and in Frankland's "new measures" of the risk of severe claustrophobia around age 29, in the year 1916, during Carter's tour of duty in World War I? A logical place to start would be to look at the 6th, 8th, and 12th houses of his horoscope.

Charles Carter has Virgo on the 12th house Placidus cusp and Pisces on the 6th house cusp. Thus, Mercury rules his 12th house and Jupiter rules his 6th house. In his birth chart, Jupiter at 5° 19' Scorpio squares Mercury at 7° 40' Aquarius, and his natal Moon (symbolic of his emotions) lies at 7° 22' Taurus opposite Jupiter and square to Mercury. This natal T-square involving Jupiter-Mercury-Moon would form a Grand Cross if there were a significant point or stellar body around 6° or 7° of Leo.

Frankland instructs his readers of *Astrological Investigations* (1926) to note carefully those nativities in which a Grand Cross occurs, because *"when some strong direction is formed between or on the points of the square, a most drastic or eventful time is indicated"* (Frankland 1926, 45; italics mine). By "between" the points of the square, Frankland means the *midpoints* of the planets involved in the Grand Cross. The importance of symmetry and midpoints in astrology has a long and distinguished history, as can be seen in the use of half-sums by Ptolemy in the second century CE, the calculation of lots in Hellenistic texts, the symmetrical placement of sign rulers in the Thema Mundi, and the discussions of antiscia and contra-antiscia in literature dating back to at least the first millennium CE.

Although Frankland does not mention Alfred Witte by name, he appears to have been aware of the German astrologer's use of midpoints in predictive work. In 1913, Witte gave a presentation to the Hamburg Kepler Circle in which he discussed his research into planetary symmetries and midpoint configurations. Like Frankland, Witte became frustrated with traditional techniques because they did not always reveal the quality of the moment. Upon further research, Witte discovered that the midpoints of planets in well-timed birth charts provided an effective method to delineate natal charts and to make predictions. It is not surprising, then, that Frankland also incorporated midpoints into his "new measures" in astrology. A useful feature of Witte's research is that midpoint combinations can be activated by hard aspects that are multiples of 45°, that is, the so-called 8th harmonic aspects, which include the semisquare, square, sesquisquare, and opposition.

Like Frankland, Charles Carter was also interested in Witte's work. In a footnote to the entry about "Abscesses" in his book *An Encyclopedia of Psychological Astrology* (1924), Carter comments that the "special degrees" that he is delineating "may be brought into action by being 'bracketed' between two [planetary] bodies; that is to say, two bodies will fall exactly on each side of the degree in question . . . . Such *mid-points* are recognized in modern astrology as being important" (Carter 1924, 26; italics mine).

If we calculate Carter's *Point of Life* at age 29 (allowing 7 years per zodiac sign, commencing from 0° Aries), we find that his directed *Point of Life* at that age ranged from 4° 17' Leo to 8° 34' Leo in his 10th house of career, opposite to natal Mercury and square to both Jupiter and the Moon. As for major transits in 1916, on July 30th a Solar Eclipse occurred at 6° 33' Leo, aspecting the natal Mercury/Jupiter and Moon/Jupiter midpoints within a few seconds of arc.

In 1916, Carter's secondary progressed Ascendant opposed his natal Moon, triggering the natal T-square with Mercury and Jupiter. In addition, in 1916 by primary direction (Placidus semi-arc method, 0° latitude, with Ptolemy's key), the directed Sun was semisquare natal Mars, directed Mercury was semisquare the natal 8th house ruler Venus and also square the natal Ascendant, and directed Mars was square his natal Moon.

Thus, 1916 (age 29) appears to have been of major significance in Carter's life, leaving him with lifelong claustrophobia that altered his career path.

Birth Numbers and the Chart of Alan Leo

In each of his books, Frankland cites the birth chart of Alan Leo to illustrate his techniques. He calculated the Birth Numbers of Alan Leo as follows:

Alan Leo was born on 07 August 1860, expressed in numbers as 7/8/1860.

His *Single Digits Birth Number* is calculated like this:

7 + 8 + 1 + 8 + 6 + 0 equals **30**, which can be further reduced to 3 + 0, or 3. Thus, if other astrological factors concur, age 30 may be highly significant in Leo's life.

Because Alan Leo's month and day of birth are single-digit numbers, there is no need to calculate a *Double Digits Birth Number*.

An *Additional Birth Number* is found by adding his original *Single Digits Birth Number* to his year of birth, which is then further reduced:

30 + 1860 (his year of birth) equals **1890**, which reduces to 1 + 8 + 9 + 0, or **18**, and then to 1 + 8, or **9**.

An *Additional Birth Number* is generated by adding **30** + **18** + **9**, which equals **57**.

Frankland points out that Alan Leo died on 30 August 1917 (1917 = 1860 + 57) at the age of 57. As with the chart of Charles Carter, the *Additional Birth Number* identified the age of Leos death.

Frankland also notes that when Alan Leo was about to turn 30 years old, he launched the journal *Modern Astrology,* with a publication date of 20 July 1890 (1890 = 1860 + 30)—again a highly significant period in Leo's life.

To illustrate Frankland's methods using Alan Leo's chart, let's review his recommended steps from pages 57–58 of *Astrological Investigations* (1926):

1. Calculate the Birth Numbers based on the date of birth to see whether there is any correlation between the age under consideration and the Birth Numbers.

2. Count the age in years along the zodiac at the rate of 1° of ecliptic longitude per year, commencing from 0° Aries. Note whether such degrees highlight favorable or adverse points or stellar bodies in the birth chart. (In his next book, *New Measures in Astrology* (1928), Frankland included the "new measure" of 4/7° of longitude as equivalent to one year of life.)

3. Direct the *Point of Life*, commencing from 0° Aries, at the rate of 7 years per zodiac sign, and note whether the directed *Point of Life* corresponds to favorable or adverse positions in the nativity.

4. Calculate "the areas over which the more ponderous Planets spread the influence of their aspects, as Saturn square Jupiter, Saturn square Uranus, Neptune slowly moving to square of radical Sun, etc., or other movements of similar nature." What Frankland has in mind is that the secondary progressions of the slow-moving natal planets influence extended periods of time during the life of the native.

5. Note "the *periods of Planets* and whether they tend to benefit such periods or otherwise." Frankland is referring to the *seven ages of man* proposed by Claudius Ptolemy in the second century CE. For example, Ruth Ellis, who was hanged at age 28, had the Sun in tight square to Pluto in her birth chart and would have experienced this natal Sun-Pluto square as quite challenging during her Ptolemaic Sun period (ages 22 to 41).

"By such methods as these one can make a survey as it were of the strength or weakness of the Native's position at the time when the operative Influences are being directed" (Frankland 1926, 58). By "operative influences," Frankland means primary directions, secondary progressions, and major transits—all of which are based fundamentally on the actual movement of the sky and the planets projected onto the life span, as opposed to some arbitrary rate chosen for symbolic reasons.

Applying These Five Steps to the Chart of Alan Leo

At age 30, Alan Leo launched the journal *Modern Astrology*. Frankland used a chart for Alan Leo that has 27° 30' Leo on the Ascendant (chart 10, inner wheel). The secondary progressions at age 30 included progressed Jupiter tightly conjunct natal Sun, progressed Moon conjunct natal MC within a 2° orb, progressed Ascendant closely trine the progressed Moon in the 10th house, and progressed Venus trine natal Neptune (chart 10, outer wheel). Age 30 corresponds to Alan Leo's Birth Number 30.

At age 30, Alan Leo's *Age along the Zodiac*, at 1° per year starting at 0° Aries, falls at 0° Taurus and lies in square to progressed Venus on the cusp of the natal 12th house.

Leo's directed *Point of Life* at age 30 ranged from 8° 34' to 12° 51' Leo, so that it conjoined natal Jupiter in the 12th house, made a square to natal Pluto in the 9th house, and formed a sextile to natal Uranus in the 10th house.

With regard to "calculation of area of Ponderous Aspects," at age 30 Alan Leo's secondary progressed Jupiter moved to an exact conjunction of the natal Sun. Frankland, in his first book, *Astrological Investigations* (1926), devotes an entire chapter to the secondary progressed aspects of "ponderous" planets, namely, Jupiter, Saturn, Uranus, and Neptune. (Pluto was unknown in 1926.) Because these planets move so slowly, their aspects at birth will influence a large area of life by secondary progression. Frankland advises his students "to examine the Chart of Birth in the light of time from 0 degrees of Aries to 30 degrees of Pisces. Call any afflicted point *a weak or adverse area* and count it in years at the rate of seven years to a sign" (Frankland 1926, 60; italics mine).

Additionally, at age 30 Alan Leo was passing through his 19-year Ptolemaic solar planetary period (ages 22 to 41). The Sun in his birth chart rules the Leo Ascendant, sextiles natal Uranus in the 10th house, and trines the natal Moon on the cusp of the 9th house, which is related to astrology.

Frankland's *4/7° Per Year of Life Measure* in Alan Leo's Chart

New Measures in Astrology (1928) introduces Frankland's symbolic direction in which he equates each *4/7 of a degree of ecliptic longitude to one year of life*. He illustrates this symbolic measure in the chart of Alan Leo, who died on 30 August 1917 at 10:00 a.m. in Bude, England. Leo was 57.065 years old at the time. Four-sevenths of Alan Leo's age at the time of his demise was 4 × 57.065 divided by 7, which is equivalent to 32.6° of longitude in Frankland's *4/7° measure*.

Next, Frankland uses the *4/7° measure*, which is 32.6° at age 57, to direct points that are symbolically related to death in the birth chart:

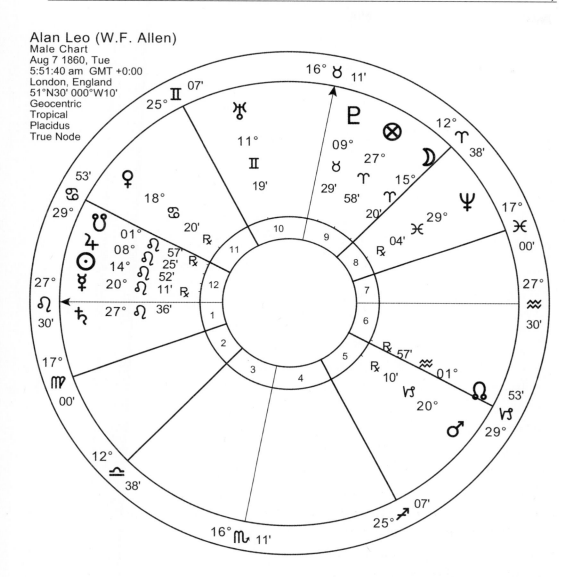

Chart 10: Alan Leo, Birth Chart, with Secondary Progressions for 7 August 1890 in Outer Wheel
Inner Wheel: 7 August 1860, 5:51:40 a.m. GMT, London, England, 51N30 0W10
Outer Wheel: 7 August 1890, 5:51:40 a.m. GMT, London, England, 51N30 0W10

- The Placidus cusp of the natal 8th house of death at 17° 00' Pisces plus 32.6° equals 19° 36' Aries, which is applying within orb to square Leo's natal Mars at 20° 10' Capricorn. Thus, the symbolically directed cusp of the natal 8th house squares Leo's out-of-sect malefic Mars at the time of his passing.
- Alan Leo's Ascendant-ruler Sun (symbolizing his body and life force) lies at 14° 52' Leo in the birth chart. Adding 32.6° to the position of the natal Sun gives a symbolically directed position of 17° 28' Virgo, which opposes the natal 8th house cusp of death.
- The ruler of the natal 8th house cusp, Jupiter, lies at 8° 25' Leo in his birth chart. Adding 32.6° to the position of Jupiter symbolically directs the lord of the 8th to 11° 01' Virgo, which closely squares natal Uranus at 11° 19' Gemini.

Charles Carter, in his 1929 book *Symbolic Directions in Modern Astrology*, commented that Frankland's *Age along the Zodiac*, at a rate of 1° for each year of life, could be used effectively to symbolically direct any point or planet of the natal chart, with good results.

Birth Numbers and the Lindbergh Kidnapping

Charles Lindbergh, famous for his transatlantic flight in May of 1927, was born in Detroit, Michigan, on 4 February 1902 at 1:30 a.m. LMT, Rodden Rating AA (chart 11). The birth time was verified by biographer A. Scott Berg, who had access to family records stored at Princeton University, in which his mother indicates 1:30 a.m. as the time of birth.

Perhaps the most significant event in Lindbergh's life was the kidnapping and murder of his infant son in 1932. Lindbergh was 30 years old at the time.

Lindbergh's son, Charles Jr., was born on 22 June 1930. About a year and a half later, on 29 February 1932, Charles Jr. was kidnapped from the Lindbergh home near Hopewell, New Jersey. The child's body was found on 12 May 1932 in a shallow grave in the woods. In response, the US Congress passed the Lindbergh Law (1932), which made interstate kidnapping a federal offense. The kidnapper was eventually caught and executed in 1936.

Let's begin with Lindbergh's Birth Numbers. He was born on 4 February 1902.

By adding the individual digits of his birth date, $4 + 2 + 1 + 9 + 0 + 2 = \textbf{18}$, we calculate his *Single Digits Birth Number*.

The *Single Digits Birth Number* (18) reduces to $1 + 8$, or **9**, which is also a significant number.

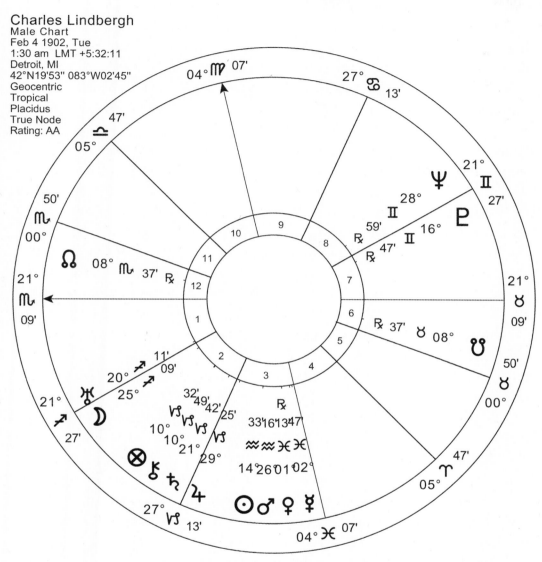

Chart 11: Charles Lindbergh
February 4, 1902, 1:30 a.m. LMT, Detroit, Michigan, 42N20 83W03

Lindbergh's *Additional Birth Number* is found by adding 18 to his year of birth: **18** + 1902 (his year of birth) = 1920, which reduces to 1 + 9 + 2 + 0, or **12**, which further reduces to 1 + 2, or **3**. We then we add **18** + **12** + **3** and arrive at **33** as his *Additional Birth Number*, which further reduces to 3 + 3, or **6**.

Hence, Lindbergh's potentially significant ages, based on these Birth Numbers, are **18** and **33** and combinations of these Birth Numbers with each other or with their reduced forms, that is, **3, 6, 9,** or **12.**

As an example of a combination of basic Birth Numbers, in 1953 at age 51 (**18** + **33** = 51) Lindbergh won the Pulitzer Prize for his autobiography, *The Spirit of St. Louis.*

Age 30, when Lindbergh's son was kidnapped, shows up as potentially significant in the combination **12** + **18**, which equals 30. According to Frankland, if a symbolically relevant astrological influence were to occur at this age, it would be powerfully reinforced.

Calculating Lindbergh's secondary progressions at age 30, we find that on 31 May 1932, secondary progressed Mars in the natal 4th house squared natal Uranus in the 1st house. Mars rules the 5th house of children and also the 12th house, which is the derived 8th house of death of his children. Uranus symbolizes sudden and unexpected disruptions. The natal 4th house, where progressed Mars was located at the time, is the derived 12th house of dissolution of the 5th house of children. Progressed Mars square Uranus, from the 4th house to the 1st house, is certainly a symbolically relevant astrological influence at age 30.

Other important astrological influences are Solar and Lunar Eclipses, which act as especially powerful transits, or "excitants," to use Frankland's terminology. A significant Annular Solar Eclipse took place on 7 March 1932 (just a week after the kidnapping) at 16° 33' Pisces, almost exactly square Lindbergh's natal Pluto. This Solar Eclipse activated the natal configuration of Pluto Rx in Gemini near the cusp of the natal 8th house of death together with Neptune in Gemini in the 8th house, opposing both Uranus and the Moon in Sagittarius, thereby creating a T-square with the eclipse at the apex. Pluto is lord of the underworld, Neptune can signify dissolution and deception, and Uranus symbolizes sudden disruptive events. The 4th house, where the eclipse occurred, represents home, family, and domestic security.

Lindbergh's *Point of Life* at age 30 falls in his 6th house at about 8° 34' Taurus and advances to 12° 51' Taurus over the course of the year. Thus, at age 30, the *Point of Life* is exactly conjunct the true lunar South Node (Ketu), a point signifying depletion and material loss.

Lindbergh's *Age along the Zodiac* at age 30 has progressed a total of 30° from 0° Aries, arriving at 0° Taurus, where it conjoins the cusp of the 6th house and opposes the cusp of the 12th house, which is the derived 8th house of death of the child.

If we symbolically direct the points and planets of the natal chart by the number of degrees indicated by the *Age Point* (30° at age 30), we find that the directed 8th house cusp opposes natal Saturn and, in turn, directed Saturn squares the horizon axis, giving the Greater Malefic much prominence. Since Lindbergh was born at night, Saturn is his contrary-to-sect malefic and can indicate particularly adverse conditions.

Lindbergh's *4/7° per year measure* at age 30 gives an arc of about 17° 09'. If we direct the 4th house cusp of home, family, and final endings by this amount, we arrive at 21° 16' Pisces, which is almost exactly square the natal 8th house cusp. The square of the directed 4th house cusp of domestic life to the natal 8th house cusp of death becomes exact around the time the baby's body was discovered in the woods.

The Case of the Missing Lady Doctor: Sophia Frances Hickman

In August of 1903, posters appeared in London offering a substantial reward for information about the "Missing Lady Doctor, Miss Sophia Frances Hickman." On Saturday, 15 August 1903, the 29-year-old doctor left the Royal Free Hospital during her lunch break and disappeared. On 20 August 1903, *The Times* published her father's plea for help. His daughter, Dr. Sophia Hickman, had begun a tour of duty at the hospital on Friday, the 14th of August, to cover for another physician who was away for a brief period. Her father wrote that, although his daughter was devoted to helping the poor, she may have felt overwhelmed by the severity of the cases at the Royal Free Hospital, or alternatively she may have been kidnapped during one of her visits to the home of a sick person whom she cared for.

Weeks went by without a trace of the missing doctor. On October 8th, her father again wrote to *The Times*, as recounted in the article "A Poster Speaks" by Elizabeth Crawford (2013):

> It is quite possible that my daughter, overwhelmed with the responsibilities of a
> resident surgeon, which serious work she commenced on August 15 for the first

time in her life, and feeling all alone and without the usual support of the very capable visiting surgeon and his *locum tenens* being also away for a holiday on Saturday, August 15 last, coupled with her horror of the work she was told she would have to do on the evening of that date at the gate of the hospital in attending to the awful cases resulting from quarrels between drunkards on pay day— may well have upset her balance of mind, caused loss of memory, and made her wander. (Crawford 2013)

The father also hinted that his daughter might have been kidnapped by "Roman Catholic Italians," who were held in especially low regard in London at the time.

Finally, on 19 October 1903, a boy playing in Richmond Park stumbled upon the body of the missing doctor in the undergrowth of Sidmouth Wood. A syringe with traces of morphine sulphate was found near the body, and an autopsy revealed that Dr. Hickman had died of morphia poisoning, most likely due to suicide.

According to Alan Leo's *1001 Notable Nativities* (1917), Sophia Frances Hickman was born in London on 22 June 1874 at 7:00 a.m. GMT (chart 12). Frankland mentions Dr. Hickman's birth chart as one of the many he studied in developing his new measures.

What would Frankland have noticed when he first glanced at Dr. Hickman's chart? Given his interest in Ptolemy's *seven ages of man*, he would have considered the condition and aspects of the Sun, which rules the period of adult life (ages 22 to 41) during which she died by suicide.

The Sun disposes her Leo Ascendant and is conjunct Mars, ruler of her 10th house of profession. As a young doctor, Hickman was focused on advancing in her medical career. Natal Mars in Cancer, the sign of its "fall," conjoins the 12th house cusp, which might symbolize the stress of working in a hospital with severely ill patients. Making her professional life even more difficult is the square from the Moon, ruler of the 12th house of hospitals and a symbol of her emotional state, to the Sun-Mars conjunction near the cusp of the 12th house.

Having been sensitized in his research to the importance of T-squares and Grand Crosses as indicating "a most drastic and eventful time," Frankland would have observed that the planets and points in the fixed signs (Leo, Aquarius, Taurus, and Scorpio) were in a broad Grand Cross formation. The fact that the ponderous planets (Uranus, Saturn, Neptune, and Pluto) were all in fixed signs added more gravity to this Grand Cross configuration.

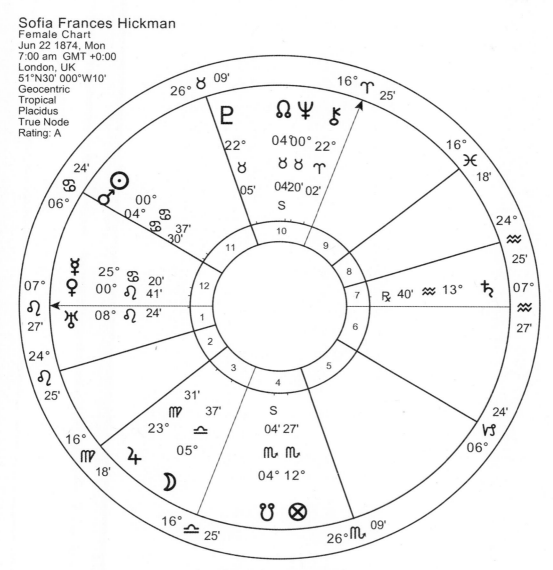

Chart 12: Sophia Frances Hickman
22 June 1874, 7:00 a.m. GMT, London, England, 51N30 0W10

Knowing that Dr. Hickman was 29 years old when she disappeared, Frankland would have realized immediately that she was in the midst of her first Saturn return to its natal sign Aquarius, a fixed sign. Thus, transiting Saturn was acting as an "excitant" to the entire fixed Grand Cross configuration. In other words, when Dr. Hickman left the hospital at lunchtime on 15 August 1903, a powerful astrological influence was operating, namely, transiting Saturn opposing natal Uranus, Venus, and Ascendant and squaring natal Neptune and the lunar nodes. In addition, transiting Saturn squares natal Pluto during its return to the sign Aquarius.

Saturn, in Dr. Hickman's birth chart, rules the 6th, 7th, and 8th houses. The 6th house rules illness and bodily injury, the 8th house governs death and life-threatening conditions, and the 7th house cusp directly opposes the Ascendant, which represents the native's body and vitality. Symbolically, the 7th house cusp at the western horizon can signify the "sunset" of our lives.

Furthermore, by secondary progression, Uranus was moving forward in the zodiac and Saturn was traveling retrograde, so that in the months after birth these two planets were approaching an opposition across the cusps of the 1st and 7th houses—a progressed aspect that would hover in the background during much of Dr. Hickman's adult life. Not needing to look at an ephemeris or compute any complex mathematics, Frankland could simply look at her birth chart and forecast serious danger to the life of Sophia Hickman around age 29.

If we apply Frankland's *Point of Life* technique to Dr. Hickman's chart, we find that at age 29 it ranges from about 4° 17' Leo to 8° 34' Leo, making close aspects to her natal Ascendant, Uranus, and lunar nodes and thereby intensifying the influence of the natal Grand Cross, which is being excited by the "operative influence" of transiting Saturn returning to its birth sign Aquarius.

Dr. Hickman's Birth Numbers

Dr. Hickman was born on 22 June 1874: 22/6/1874.

Adding the day and month as single digits to the birth year, $2 + 2 + 6 + 1 + 8 + 7 + 4 = 30$, we calculate her *Single Digits Birth Number*, which further reduces to 3.

Her *Additional Single Digits Birth Numbers* are found by adding **30** to her year of birth (1874): **30** + 1874 equals 1904, which reduces to $1 + 9 + 0 + 4$, or **14**, and further reduces to **5**. Then, **30** + **14** + **5** = **49** as her *Additional Single Digits Birth Number*, which further reduces to $4 + 9 = 13$ and then to $1 + 3 = 4$ as other significant numbers.

Adding the day and month as double digits to the birth year, 22 + 6 + 1 + 8 + 7 + 4 = **48**, we calculate her *Double Digits Birth Number*, which further reduces to **12**, which in turn reduces to 1 + 2, or **3**.

Her *Additional Double Digits Birth Numbers* are found by adding **48** to her year of birth (1874): **48** + 1874 = 1922, which reduces to 1 + 9 + 2 + 2, or **14**, and further reduces to **5**. Then **48** + **14** + **5** equals **67** as her *Additional Double Digits Birth Number*, which reduces to 6 + 7 = **13** and in turn to 1 + 3, or **4**.

In summary, potentially significant ages based on these *Single Digit* and *Double Digit Birth Numbers* are **30, 48, 49,** and **67** and combinations of these Birth Numbers with each other or with their reduced forms, that is, 3, 5, 9, 12, and 13. Astrological influences occurring around these ages are likely to be especially noticeable in the life of the native. In this case, Dr. Hickman died at age 29, but her core Birth Numbers point to age 30 as a potentially significant year. However, Frankland also combined the Birth Numbers and their reduced forms to indicate significant ages. In this case, the Birth Number 49 minus the sum of three of the reduced forms (3 + 5 + 12 = 20) produces age 29 (49 − 20 = 29) as potentially significant.

Whether we regard 30 or 29 as a significant age based on Birth Numbers and their combinations, around the time of Dr. Hickman's death the operative astrological influence, transiting Saturn, perfected its conjunction to natal Saturn on 18 February 1904, just 4 months prior to the doctor turning 30 years old on 22 June 1904.

Another feature that this example illustrates is Frankland's focus on the broad picture, the overall patterns in the birth chart, rather than the fine details. He insisted first on being able to see the forest before studying any of the individual trees. His ability to consider the major patterns in the birth chart, to find the central thread, is the key to successful use of his method. Frankland eloquently expressed this idea in part 2 of *New Measures in Astrology*:

> During the course of my studies in astrology, many students have asked the best way of delineating a horoscope.
>
> It would be impossible to give any definite plan, as the reading of a horoscope must be individual, free, allowing the reasoning powers and the intuition full play.
>
> There are, however, a few points of advice that might be given, or a few suggestions made.

The first thing to be emphasised, in my opinion, is the grasping of the main plan.

Just as, in a play, drama, or narrative, one looks for the thread, the central point around which the whole narrative revolves, so should the horoscope be studied in regard to the principal features, etc.

Unless this can be done, then must the reading be disjointed and scattered, and lacking that individual note thereby being less arresting and convincing. (Frankland 1928, 94–95)

Dance with a Stranger: The Hanging of Ruth Ellis

Dance with a Stranger is a 1985 film about Ruth Ellis, the last woman to be hanged in Great Britain. Ruth led a tragic life. At age 23, while working as a nightclub hostess, she became pregnant by one of her customers and decided to terminate the pregnancy. In November 1950, she married George Ellis, a violent alcoholic who fathered a daughter with her but refused to acknowledge his paternity. She and George ended up separating.

In 1953, Ruth became manager of a nightclub where she met David Blakely, a heavy-drinking, philandering race car driver who got her pregnant. She decided to have an abortion. David became increasingly violent and unfaithful. In January of 1955, she was again pregnant, and David punched her in the stomach, causing her to miscarry. The previous year Ruth had also had a miscarriage after David beat her, but she remained in the relationship. On Easter Sunday, 10 April 1955, Ruth shot David Blakely several times at close range, killing him, and turned herself in to the police. She was tried and sentenced to death by hanging.

Born on 9 October 1926, Ruth Ellis was 28.76 years old when she was hanged on 13 July 1955. Her birth chart here is based on data from Astro.com, Rodden Rating C (chart 13).

The Birth Numbers of Ruth Ellis

Ruth Ellis's date of birth was 9 October 1926, or 1926-10-09 in international standard notation.

Adding the single digits gives a sum of **28** as her *Single Digits Birth Number*, which reduces to **10** and then to **1**. Ruth died when she was 28 years old.

Her *Additional Single Digits Birth Number* is calculated as **28** + 1926 (her birth year) = 1954, which reduces to 1 + 9 + 5 + 4 = **19**, and further to **10** and then to **1**. Then 28 + 19 + 10 + 1 = **58**, which reduces to 5 + 8 = **13** and then to 1 + 3 = **4**.

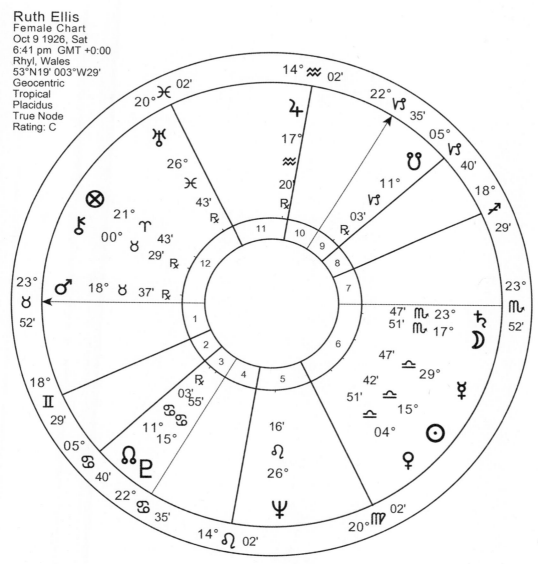

Chart 13: Ruth Ellis
9 October 1926, 6:41 p.m. GMT, Rhyl, Wales, 53N19 3W29

Adding the double-digit month produces the sum of 9 + 10 + 1 + 9 + 2 + 6 = **37,** which is her *Double Digits Birth Number,* which reduces to **10** and **1.**

Ruth's *Additional Double Digits Birth Number* is calculated as **37** + 1926 (her birth year) = 1963, which reduces to 1 + 9 + 6 + 3 = **19,** and further to **10** and then to **1.** Then 37 + 19 + 10 + 1 = **67** is her *Additional Double Digits Birth Number.*

Thus, potentially significant ages based on Ruth's single- and double-digit Birth Numbers are **28, 37, 58,** and **67** and combinations of these Birth Numbers with each other or with their reduced forms, that is, 1, 4, 10, and 13.

Ruth Ellis's *Point of Life* at Age 28 and Her Grand Cross

At age 28, Ruth Ellis's *Point of Life* ranges from 0° to 4° Leo 17', occupying her 4th house of endings and squaring her natal Chiron in the 12th house. Activation of Chiron often correlates with some type of physical or emotional wound.

Because Frankland began by looking at the big picture and the overall patterns in the chart, he would have viewed the *Point of Life* entering Leo as highlighting all of the fixed signs (Leo, Scorpio, Aquarius, and Taurus), which contain a Grand Cross configuration involving Jupiter, ruler of her 8th house, in opposition to Neptune and in square to both traditional malefics, Mars and Saturn, as well as the Moon. The passage of the *Point of Life* through Leo begins at age 28 and lasts until age 35, and Frankland would have viewed this period as especially dangerous and problematic. In addition, during this 7-year Leo period, she is in the Ptolemaic age of the Sun, with the Sun occupying her natal 6th house of bodily infirmities and squaring her natal Pluto and lunar nodes.

Ruth Ellis's *Age along the Zodiac*

At age 28, Ruth Ellis's *Age along the Zodiac (Age Point)* lies at 28° Aries. On the day of her execution, the *Point of Life* would have been at 28.76° Aries (28° 46' Aries), within orb of opposition to her natal Mercury, which rules her 6th house of bodily injury.

If we symbolically direct her natal Sun (at 15° Libra 42') by the *Age along the Zodiac* arc of 28.76° at the time of her execution, we arrive at 14° 28' Scorpio, which is the position at which transiting Saturn stationed direct at 14° 30' Scorpio on 19 July 1955, less than a week after her demise. Because Pluto closely squares her Sun at birth, the symbolically directed Pluto will square the transiting Saturn station around the time of her execution.

Ruth Ellis's *4/7° Measure*

At age 28, the *4/7° measure* lies at 16° Aries in Ruth's 12th house, in close opposition to her natal Sun and close square to her natal Pluto, highlighting the natal Sun-square-Pluto aspect. Frankland would have given extra weight to this aspect because, at age 28, she is traversing her Ptolemaic 19-year solar phase of life (ages 22–41) and her *Single Digits Birth Number* is 28.

On the day of Ruth's hanging at age 28.76, the *4/7° Age Point* lies at 16° 26' Aries. If we symbolically direct the cusp of her Placidus 8th house of death (at 18° 29' Sagittarius) by the *4/7° measure* (16.43°), we arrive at 4° 55' Capricorn, which closely squares her Ascendant-ruler Venus in the 6th house of bodily ailments.

If we direct natal Chiron by the *4/7° measure* of 16.43° at age 28.76, we arrive at 16° 55' Taurus, which squares 8th house ruler Jupiter and opposes the natal Moon. The Moon, in turn, conjoins natal Saturn, squares both natal Neptune and Jupiter, and opposes natal Mars.

Operative Primary Directions of Ruth Ellis

Significant operative influences in Ruth Ellis's chart in 1955 include the following primary directions (Placidus semi-arc, 0° latitude, Naibod key):

- Primary directed Uranus sesquisquare natal Pluto in March
- Primary directed Mars arrives at the 12th house cusp in March
- Primary directed Sun quincunx natal Uranus in July
- Primary directed Saturn conjunct natal Venus (natal Ascendant ruler) in August
- Primary directed Descendant conjunct Venus (natal Ascendant ruler) in September

Operative Transits (Excitants) in Ruth Ellis's Chart

A Lunar Eclipse in January 1955 took place at 17° 21' Cancer, exactly quincunx Ruth's natal 8th house ruler Jupiter, closely quincunx the 8th house cusp, closely conjunct natal Pluto, and closely square to her natal Sun. This eclipse appears to have set the tone for the year.

On 6 May 1955, transiting Pluto stationed direct at 24° 18' Leo, conjunct natal Neptune and closely square to natal Saturn. In August, not long after Ruth's execution, transiting Pluto semisquared the natal true North Lunar Node and conjoined natal Neptune.

On 20 June 1955, a Solar Eclipse occurred at 28° 04' Gemini, in square to natal Uranus in the 12th house and sextile to natal Neptune in the 4th house.

On 7 July 1955, transiting Neptune stationed direct at 25° 27' Libra in Ruth's 6th house, in quincunx to natal Uranus in the 12th house.

On 19 July 1955, six days after Ruth was hanged, transiting Saturn stationed direct at 14° 30' Scorpio in her 6th house, conjunct natal Moon-Saturn, opposite natal Mars in the 12th house, and square natal Jupiter (ruler of the 8th house of death), thus activating the natal Grand Cross involving Mars, Jupiter, Neptune, Saturn, and the Moon. As mentioned previously, transiting Saturn was highlighted by the symbolically directed natal Sun at a rate of 1° equals one year of life.

The station of transiting Saturn in the 6th house in July of 1955 closely squared Ruth's natal Placidus 5th house cusp, which may symbolically relate to her difficulties with love affairs, pregnancies, miscarriages, and abortions. In her birth chart, Saturn conjoins the 7th house cusp of intimate partnerships and is opposed by Mars in its fall in Taurus, an indicator of potential violence in relationships.

Are Birth Numbers Just Surprising Coincidences?

In a discussion about Birth Numbers with Maria Blaquier, she raised the question "What happens when the Birth Number is just a single digit, for example, a birth that took place in the first few days of January of 2000? Then the Birth Number would be 1 (January) plus 2 (year 2000) plus an early day, like 1, 2, 3, and so on?"

In Frankland's texts and the cases I'd studied, I hadn't come across any charts with such a small Birth Number. Curious, I did an online search for births in early January of 2000, and the first one that appeared was the American actress Rhiannon Leigh Wryn, who was born on 4 January 2000. Wryn had lead roles in the films *The Last Mimzy* (2007) and *Monster Mutt* (2010), and was nominated for a Saturn Award for Best Performance by a Younger Actor for her performance in *The Last Mimzy*.

Rhiannon Leigh Wryn's Birth Numbers

Adding the digits of 4 January 2000, we have 4 + 1 + 2 + 0, which equals **7** as her *primary or basic Birth Number*.

At age 7, Wryn played the lead role in a film as a child actor, for which she was nominated for an award.

Wryn's *Additional Birth Number* is calculated as follows: **7** (Birth Number) + 2000 (year of birth) = 2007, which reduces to 2 + 7, or **9**. Then we add the main Birth Number **7** to **9,** which results in **16** as her *Additional Birth Number*, which further reduces to **7**.

Thus, potentially significant ages for Wryn, based on these Birth Numbers, are **7** and **16** and combinations of these Birth Numbers with each other or with their reduced forms, that is, **7**.

An Example from Frankland: Lord Kitchener's Birth Numbers

To further illustrate how Frankland calculated Birth Numbers, let's review an example from *Astrological Investigations* (1926).

Horatio Herbert Kitchener (24 June 1850–5 June 1916) was a senior British Army officer noted for his role in the Boer Wars and the early part of World War I. Frankland calculates Kitchener's Birth Numbers as follows:

Kitchener was born on 24 June 1850: 24/6/1850.

Single Digits

Adding by single digits, 2 + 4 + 6 + 1 + 8 + 5 + 0 = **26**, we determine his *Single Digits Birth Number*, which reduces to 2 + 6 = **8**.

Then we add Kitchener's *Single Digits Birth Number* **(26)** to the year of birth (1850): **26** + 1850 equals 1876, which reduces to 1 + 8 + 7 + 6, or **22**, and further reduces to 2 + 2, or **4**. Then his *Additional Single Digits Birth Number* is 26 + 22 + 4 = **52**, which reduces to **7**.

Double Digits

Adding the double-digit day of birth (24) to the month and year, 24 + 6 + 1850, produces 24 + 6 + 1 + 8 + 5 + 0, which equals **44**, his *Double Digits Birth Number*.

Adding the *Double Digits Birth Number* **(44)** to his year of birth (1850), we get 44 + 1850 = 1894, which reduces to 1 + 8 + 9 + 4, or **22**, which further reduces to **4**. Thus,

Kitchener's *Additional Double Digits Birth Number* is 44 + 22 + 4, or **70**, which reduces to 7 + 0 = **7**.

Thus, potentially significant ages for Kitchener based on these single- and double-digit Birth Numbers are **26, 44, 52,** and **70** and combinations of these Birth Numbers with each other or with their reduced forms, that is, 7 and 8.

Combining Birth Numbers

24 (Kitchener's day of birth, the 24th of the month) + 22 = **46** was his age during the Egyptian campaign.

26 + 22 = **48** was the age when he was honored for a military campaign.

44 + 22 = **66** was the age when Kitchener died.

In this example, Frankland uses the *number of the day of the month* (the 24th of June) as an important number, which he combines with a principal Birth Number.

Birth Numbers of William Ewart Gladstone

For another example of Frankland's calculation of Birth Numbers, let's consider the chart of the British statesman W. E. Gladstone (29 December 1809–19 May 1898).

Gladstone was born on 29 December 1809: 29/12/1809.

Single Digits Birth Number

2 + 9 + 1 + 2 + 1 + 8 + 0 + 9 equals **32** as Gladstone's *Single Digits Birth Number*, which reduces to 3 + 2, or **5**.

Additional Single Digits Birth Number

32 + 1809 equals 1841, which sums to 1 + 8 + 4 + 1 = **14** and reduces to 1 + 4, or **5**. Then we add **32** + **14** + **5**, which gives **51** as his *Additional Single Digits Birth Number* and reduces to 5 + 1, or **6**.

Double Digits Birth Number

29 + 12 + 1 + 8 + 0 + 9 = **59** as Gladstone's *Double Digits Birth Number*, which reduces to 5 + 9, or **14**, which further reduces to 1 + 4, or **5**.

Additional Double Digits Birth Number

59 + 1809 equals 1868, which sums to $1 + 8 + 6 + 8 = $ **23**, which reduces to 2 + 3, or **5**. Then, we add **59** + **23** + **5**, which equals **87** as his *Additional Double Digits Birth Number*, which reduces to 8 + 7, or **15**, and further reduces to 1 + 5, or **6**.

Thus, potentially significant ages for Gladstone based on these single- and double-digit Birth Numbers are **32, 51, 59** and **87** and combinations of these Birth Numbers with each other or with their reduced forms, that is, 5, 6, and 15.

In this case, Frankland adds Gladstone's day of birth (the 29th of December) to the *Double Digits Birth Number* (59) and arrives at 29 + 59 = 88, the age at which Gladstone died.

Frankland also could have arrived at 88 by combining the *Single Digits Birth Number* (32) with the *Additional Single Digits Birth Number* (51) and the reduced form of 32 (3 +2 = 5), the total of which is 32 + 51 + 5 = 88, Gladstone's age at the time of his demise.

The Lad Who Died in a Windstorm:
A Case from Charles Carter

To further test Frankland's method, I selected a chart that Frankland hadn't seen, from Carter's book *Symbolic Directions in Modern Astrology*. In the section "Case No. Three" (pp. 41–43), Carter discusses the chart of a young man who was killed in a severe windstorm just as he was turning 17 years old. Judging from the chart, the youth was born on the 11 May 1903 at 8:00:17 p.m. MST in Victor, Colorado (chart 14). Carter is a bit unclear about whether the lad died just before or after his 17th birthday. My sense from Carter's text is that the youth was 16 years old, going on 17, when he perished, probably in early May of 1920. Here are his Birth Numbers:

Single Digits Birth Number: $1 + 1 + 5 + 1 + 9 + 0 + 3 = $ **20**, which reduces to **2**.

Additional Single Digits Birth Number: **20** + 1903 = 1923, which reduces to **15** and **6**. Then 20 + 15 + 6 = **41** as the *Additional Single Digits Birth Number*, which reduces to **5**.

Double Digits Birth Number: $11 + 5 + 1 + 9 + 0 + 3 = $ **29**, which reduces to **11** and then to **2**.

Additional Double Digits Birth Number: **29** + 1903 = 1932, which reduces to **15** and **6**. Then 29 + 15 + 6 = **50** as the *Additional Double Digits Birth Number*, which reduces to **5**.

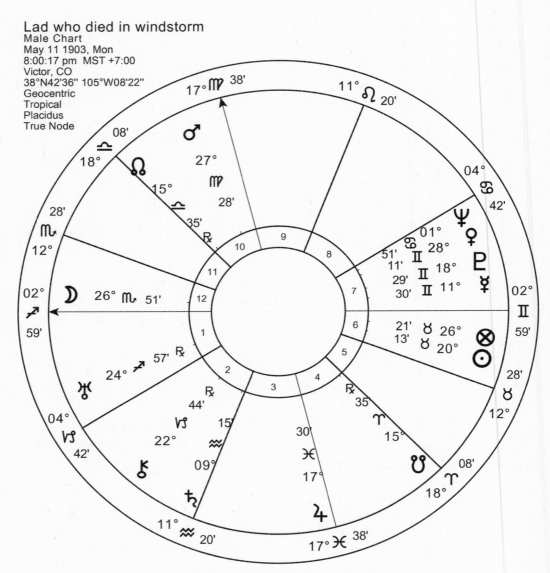

Lad who died in windstorm
Male Chart
May 11 1903, Mon
8:00:17 pm MST +7:00
Victor, CO
38°N42'36" 105°W08'22"
Geocentric
Tropical
Placidus
True Node

Chart 14: Lad Who Died in a Windstorm
11 May 1903, 8:00:17 p.m. MST, Victor, Colorado, 28N43 105W08

The young man was born on the 11th of May. Thus, **11** (his day of birth) + **5** (his reduced *Additional Single Digits Birth Number*) = **16**, his age when he died.

Does a combination of Birth Numbers also indicate age **17**? The *Single Digits Birth Number* (**20**) plus the reduced *Double Digits Birth Number* (**2**) minus the reduced *Additional Single Digits Number* (**5**) produces the sum of **17**. Hence, both ages 16 and 17 are potentially significant for this lad.

Looking at the boy's chart, Frankland would have immediately been struck by the stressful mutable Grand Cross involving Ascendant-ruler Jupiter, with all the planets in angular houses. With a stellium of planets in Gemini, this configuration would "ripen" between ages 14 and 21, when the *Point of Life* passed through Gemini. The aspect Mars square Uranus is a classic indicator of serious accidents. Mercury, the dispositor of the stellium and the earliest planet in this Grand Cross at 11° 30' Gemini, would be "hit" by the *Point of Life* at age 16.7 (mid-January of 1920), marking the beginning of a high-risk period that would last until the youth turned 21 years old.

At age 16.7, the *Age along the Zodiac* would be at 16° 42' Aries, applying to semisextile Ascendant-ruler Jupiter, a stressful aspect that would perfect when the lad was 17.5 years old. Natally, Jupiter is afflicted by a close square from Pluto in Gemini, which would be activated by the *Age along the Zodiac measure* around age 17.5 (mid-November of 1920). No doubt Frankland would have identified 1920 as a highly significant and potentially dangerous year.

Looking in his ephemeris, Frankland would have noticed the following troublesome celestial events:

- Transiting Jupiter and Neptune turning stationary direct at 8° of Leo in the natal 8th house in April of 1920, closely opposite natal Saturn.

- A Lunar Eclipse on 2 May 1920 at 12° 19' Scorpio, almost exactly conjunct the cusp of the natal 12th house of undoing and within orb of a square to natal Saturn.

- A Solar Eclipse on 17 May 1920 at 26° 59' Taurus, conjunct the lad's Part of Fortune in the 6th house of bodily injury and exactly opposite his natal Moon in the 12th house, with the Moon ruling the cusp of the 8th house of death.

- If Frankland had been aware of the existence of Pluto, he would have noticed Pluto turning stationary direct on 19 March 1920 at 5° 40' Cancer, conjunct the cusp of the natal 8th house.

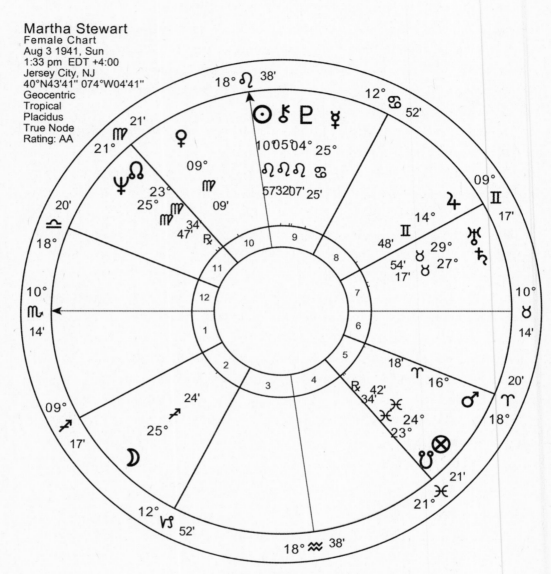

Chart 15: Martha Stewart
3 August 1941, 1:33 p.m. EDT, Jersey City, New Jersey, 40N44 74W05

Martha Stewart Goes to Prison

On 4 June 2003, at age 62, entrepreneur and TV personality Martha Stewart (born 3 August 1941) was indicted for securities fraud (chart 15). She was found guilty on 5 March 2004 and entered prison to serve a five-month term on 8 September 2004 at 63.1 years of age.

Let's start with Stewart's Birth Numbers.

First, 03 August 1941 produces the sum 3 + 8 + 1 + 9 + 4 + 1 = **26** as her *Single Digits Birth Number*, which further reduces to 2 + 6, or **8**.

To calculate Stewart's *Additional Birth Number*, we begin by adding her basic Birth Number to her year of birth: **26** plus 1941 (year of birth) equals 1967, which reduces to 1 + 9 + 6 + 7, or **23**, and further to 2 + 3, or **5**. Then we must combine **26, 23,** and **5,** that is, 26 (her basic Birth Number) + 23 + 5 = **54** as her *Additional Birth Number*, which further reduces to **9**.

Thus, potentially significant ages for Martha Stewart based on her *Single Digits Birth Number* are **26** and **54** and combinations of these Birth Numbers with each other or with their reduced forms, that is, **8** and **9**.

In this example, 8 + 54 = 62, Stewart's age when she was indicted, and 9 + 54 = 63, her age when she was convicted and sent to prison. Frankland reminds us that these ages will be significant only if concurrent astrological factors are in operation.

Let's calculate Martha's primary directions (Placidus semi-arc, 0° latitude, Naibod key) for the year 2004, when she was found guilty and sent to prison. We find several difficult primary directions involving the rulers of the 12th house (imprisonment), 7th house (lawsuits), 9th house (legal guidance), and 6th house (stressful conditions). These include:

- Primary directed Venus square natal Mars
- Primary directed Sun square natal Venus
- Primary directed Mars semisquare natal Moon
- Primary directed Venus semisquare natal Saturn

Martha Stewart's Natal Yod

Martha Stewart's *Point of Life* at ages 62 and 63, when her legal proceedings were transpiring, ranged from the last 5 degrees of Sagittarius through the first 5 degrees of Capricorn, which highlighted her natal Moon's square to Neptune and its quincunx to both Mercury and her Saturn-Uranus conjunction, forming a triangular pattern in the shape of a slingshot.

In other words, there is a 60° aspect between Stewart's natal Mercury and her natal Saturn-Uranus conjunction, both of which are in a quincunx to the Moon. This pattern is called a *Yod, Finger of God*, or *Finger of Fate*. The most sensitive point of the Yod formation is the "tip of the Finger," sometimes called its "action point," which lies 150° from the two planets in sextile (60°) to each other. In Stewart's Yod, the action point is the Moon. The point opposite the action point—that is, the midpoint of the planets in sextile—is also a sensitive point of the Yod.

When activated, Yods indicate memorable, life-changing events that have a fated quality. The fact that Mercury rules her 8th house (loss, crisis, financial obligations, the money of others) and both Saturn and Uranus are at a vertex of the slingshot triangle suggests an event that is unexpected, difficult, limiting, and disruptive. When she was 62 years old, Stewart's directed *Point of Life* highlighted her natal Moon, which is the action point of this Yod.

If we direct the natal Moon (at 25° 24' Sagittarius) by the *Age along the Zodiac* when Stewart was sent to prison (age 63.1, corresponding to 63.1°), we arrive in the 4th house at 28° 30' Aquarius, which squares her Saturn-Uranus conjunction in Taurus in the 7th house. One signification of the 4th house is the "end of the matter" in a lawsuit. The midpoint of the Saturn-Uranus conjunction lies at 28° 35' Taurus, almost exactly square the directed Moon. Her natal Saturn and Uranus occupy the 7th house of lawsuits, and the Moon rules the 9th house of lawyers and legal advice. As a general signifier, the Moon also represents the jury in a trial.

A note about the 9th house: Deborah Houlding, in her book *The Houses* (2006), clarifies that the 9th house rules the study of law, scholars and practitioners of the law, and also lawyers and solicitors who offer legal advice and counsel, but the 9th does not represent those who enforce the law. People in authority, such as judges and magistrates who enforce the law, are signified by the 10th house.

A Case in Which Frankland's System Failed?

While testing Frankland's symbolic measures against charts with established birth times, I came across a case in Charles E. O. Carter's book on symbolic directions. At first glance, I thought that Frankland's system was not going to work with Carter's example. Looking more carefully, however, I realized that Frankland's methods were again effective. I do not mean to imply that Frankland's measures are infallible, and there are certainly charts in which they do not appear to provide significant information. More often than not, however, Frankland's symbolic techniques do highlight important years in the native's life.

In chapter 1 in *Symbolic Directions in Modern Astrology* (1929), Carter discusses the chart is of an engineer who nearly died when his arm was torn off in an industrial accident. The man was born on 25 June 1891 at about 8:10 a.m. GMT in Wiltshire County in South West England (chart 16). Carter does not give the exact location of birth, so I used Trowbridge, the capital of Wiltshire, and adjusted the time to match the cusps on the birth chart in Carter's book (Carter 1929, 17).

The accident occurred on 30 October 1923, when the man was 32.35 years old. Frankland would quickly have calculated his Birth Numbers to identify potentially significant years in which astrological influences would be greatly intensified. The engineer's Birth Numbers for 25 June 1891 are as follows:

Single Digits Birth Number: Adding together the **single digits,** we get 2 + 5 + 6 + 1 + 8 + 9 + 1, which equals **32** as the engineer's *Single Digits Birth Number*, which reduces to 3 + 2, or **5**. His arm was torn off while he was inspecting the driving belt of a machine in a factory at age 32, a near-fatal accident.

Double Digits Birth Number: Adding together the **double digits** of the day or month of birth, we get 25 + 6 + 1 + 8 + 9 +1, which equals **50** as his *Double Digits Birth Number*, which reduces to 5 + 0, or **5**. Frankland would have paid special attention to astrological influences at ages **32** and **50** and to any combinations of these two Birth Numbers with each other or with their reduced form, **5**.

Frankland's symbolic measures for the engineer at age 32, when he had the accident, include the following:

The *Point of Life* ranges from 17° 09' to 21° 26' Leo, conjoins the Ascendant (the body and vitality of the native), and quincunxes Jupiter, ruler of the 8th house of life-threatening experiences. The quincunx is a stressful configuration with 6th house (injury, illness) and 8th house (death, life-threatening crises) connotations.

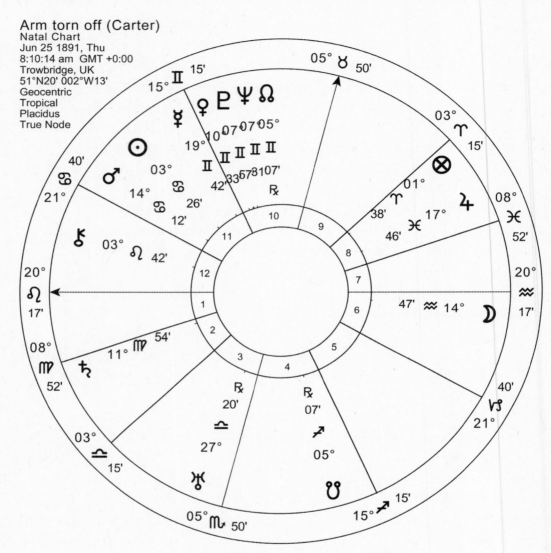

Chart 16: Man Whose Arm Was Torn Off
25 June 1891, 8:10:14 a.m. GMT, Trowbridge, England, 51N20 2W13

The *Age along the Zodiac* at the time of the injury has advanced 32.35°, starting from 0° Aries, that is, it lies at 2° 21' Taurus and does not closely aspect any planet in the chart. However, as we shall see, 2° 21' Taurus squares the engineer's directed *house-related Point of Life-Threatening Injury or Illness* at age 32.

The *4/7° measure* at the time of the near-fatal accident is 4/7° × 32.35, which equals 18.48°, or 18° 29' of arc. Measured from 0° Aries, the *4/7° Age Point* lies at 18° 29' Aries and is separating from a semisextile to Jupiter in the 8th house. As mentioned previously, the semisextile is a stressful aspect belonging, with the quincunx, to the family of inconjuncts, which link houses that are in aversion to each other.

If we wish to symbolically direct the points and planets in the birth chart by the *4/7° measure* at age 32.35, we must add 18° 29' to each of their positions, which produces the following symbolic directions:

- The directed 8th house cusp of near-death experiences arrives at 27° 21' Pisces in the 8th house, exactly quincunx natal Uranus at 27° 20' Libra in the 3rd house of local travel. This symbolic direction is quite impressive.

- The directed Ascendant (the native's body and vitality) arrives at 8° 46' Virgo, almost exactly opposite the 8th house cusp of life-threatening conditions. This symbolic direction is also impressive.

- Directed Mars arrives at 2° 41' Leo, applying to conjoin Chiron in the 12th house within a 1° orb.

We can calculate the house-related sensitive *Point of Life-Threatening Illness* by adding the 6th and 8th house cusps, as follows:

6th house cusp: 21° 40' Capricorn

8th house cusp: 08° 52' Pisces

The sum is 0° 32' Capricorn as the *Point of Life-Threatening Injury or Illness* at birth.

If we direct this combined 6th plus 8th house sensitive point (0° 32' Capricorn at birth) by 32.35° (the arc of his age at the time of the accident), we arrive at 2° 53' Aquarius in the 6th house, opposing Chiron in the 12th house and forming a quincunx to the natal Sun in the 11th house.

Desiring a quick and easy way to see what is happening in a chart, Frankland would have calculated the *Point of Life-Threatening Illness* more simply by rounding the house cusps to the nearest integer. In other words, he would have rounded the 6th house cusp to 22° Capricorn and added this value to the 8th house cusp, rounded to 9° Pisces, arriving at the sum of 1° Capricorn as the *6th plus 8th house-related sensitive point* at birth.

Knowing that the accident occurred four months after the man turned 32 years old, Frankland would have quickly estimated his age to be about 32⅓ years old at the time he lost his arm, and would have added 32⅓° to 1° Capricorn, arriving at 3⅓° of Aquarius, that is, 3° 20' Aquarius, as the *house-related sensitive point* directed to the date of the accident. Glancing at the chart, he would have seen that this directed sensitive point occupies the 6th house of bodily ailments, opposes Chiron (which can signify wounds to the body) in the 12th house of undoing and hospitalization, and forms a quincunx to the natal Sun, a symbol of the life force and vitality of the native.

Excitants: Transits, Including Eclipses, to the Engineer's Chart

Frankland regarded important transits as "excitants" that could precipitate the potentials of the natal chart, and its directions and progressions, into manifestation. Among the most powerful transiting influences are the eclipses of the Sun and Moon. If the engineer had consulted the astrologer prior to 1923 (the year of his accident), Frankland no doubt would have mentioned the following easily observable facts.

The *Single Digits Birth Number* is **32**, which implies that age 32 (from 25 June 1923 to 25 June 1924) is potentially a highly significant and memorable year for the engineer.

The eclipses at age 32 include a Total Solar Eclipse on 10 September 1923 at 17° 06' Virgo, close to the engineer's natal Saturn, ruler of his 6th house of bodily infirmities, and almost exactly opposite natal Jupiter, ruler and occupant of the 8th house of life-threatening situations. This eclipse is disposed by natal Mercury, which squares both the eclipse and natal Jupiter in the 8th house, creating a T-square formation and indicating a potentially dangerous period in which the native will need to be especially cautious to avoid serious illness or bodily injury.

Eclipses have an orb of influence that can affect the entire year. Just a few months prior to this man turning 32 years old, there was a Partial Lunar Eclipse on 3 March 1923 at 11° 38' Virgo, almost exactly conjunct his natal Saturn, ruler of the 6th house of bodily injury.

Being a good astrologer, Frankland would have noticed in his ephemeris that transiting Saturn was passing through mid- to late Libra in 1923 and turning stationary direct on 16 June 1926 at 13° 21' Libra, closely square to natal Mars. Saturn would then continue transiting Libra and arrive at natal Uranus at 27° 20' Libra on 22 November 1923. These highly stressful transits of Saturn to the natal chart reinforce the warnings given by the eclipses of 1923.

With ephemeris in hand, Frankland might also have considered the native's secondary (day for a year) progressions at age 32 by consulting the planetary positions on 27 July 1891, 32 days after the engineer's birth, which correspond to age 32. He would have quickly seen that on the day the engineer turned 32 years old, the secondary progressed Moon (at 22° 52' Aries) applied within orb to oppose natal Uranus (at 27° 20' Libra), and the secondary progressed Sun (at 3° 57' Leo) closely conjoined natal Chiron (3° 42' Leo, if Frankland had known about Chiron). Also, secondary progressed Saturn (at 14° 44' Virgo) closely quincunxed the natal Moon (at 14° 47' Aquarius), ruler of the 12th house in the 6th house. Because 32 is a Birth Number for this man, these secondary progressions are strongly intensified.

Chapter 7
FRANKLAND ON METHODS
OF PREDICTION AND THEIR SCOPE

William Frankland explains that astrologers can predict, with accuracy, only likely trends rather than specific events. Knowledge of impending difficulties or favorable opportunities can help the client prepare for what is to come.

According to Frankland, the main methods of prediction prior to his "new measures in astrology" were primary directions, secondary progressions, and transits. He refers to such factors as "operative influences."

Primary directions are based on the rotation of the Earth during the hours immediately after birth, and equate one degree on the equator passing over the meridian with one year of life. Secondary progressions are based on the supposition that each day of life after birth is symbolically related to the corresponding year of life after birth: the first day to the first year, the second day to the second year, and so on.

In *New Measures in Astrology* (1928), Frankland writes:

It is generally thought that the astrologer can predict *events*. The real fact is that, with his knowledge of operative or directional influences at any given year of life upon the native, and his general knowledge of human nature in its *average*, he is in the position of being able to say fairly correctly **what conditions will beset the native, and the probable effects such are likely to have upon his subject.**

He cannot, however, with surety name the effects. His surmise will often prove correct, because he has particular knowledge of one factor—i.e. operative influence, and general knowledge of human nature.

Therefore, he can describe conditions to be met with, and surmise probable results, but **cannot give with certainty the effects such will stimulate.**

Even with this limit, the advice thus given, or obtained by study, must be of value to the balanced, intelligent person, for to have estimation in advance of opportunities or difficulties likely to be encountered **allows one to prepare *oneself*,** to harvest with greater vigour or skill, or in case of difficulties to entrench oneself or gird one's loins for the obstacle.

There are various systems of directing, as this branch of astrology is termed, in use at present. The two chief systems are **Primary** and **Secondary** There are other methods of more or less note, such as Lunar Figures, Solar Revolutions, etc.

Transits, or the passing of heavenly bodies over important points of the nativity, are also used, and with important effect.

These latter, in my opinion, are very important as **excitants** in any otherwise important year.

The **first system, Primary,** has been used by the most learned, mathematical minds. This system is too difficult for the average student. As to its accuracy in results, those using it are most entitled to say.

The **second system, Secondary Directions,** as they are termed, are most commonly used. They are easier to calculate, and, therefore, understood by the average student.

Their value is best known to those who use them. **I have known wonderful results from both Primary and Secondary Directions.**

Primary Directions are based upon the theory that the rotation of the earth on its axis carries all the heavenly bodies from the mundane position they occupied in the horoscope. The measure of time employed is the time that elapses while one complete degree of Right Ascension is passing across the Meridian, or about four minutes of Sidereal Time. Each period of four minutes after birth measures one year of life (see text-books on directing by Sepharial, Bailey, Leo, Robson, Simmonite, and other well-known authors).

The **Secondary Directions** are based upon the theory that the changes in the heavenly bodies during the first day of life are analogous to events in the first year of life, and so on at the rate of a day for a year of life.

This is also fully explained in text-books. (Frankland 1928, 17–19; bold high-lighting mine)

Having outlined traditional predictive methods, Frankland goes on to explain his newly discovered symbolic measures. His aim in developing these techniques is to identify, quickly and easily, all the important years and events of life from the birth map alone, without having to resort to other methods, such as primary and secondary directions.

To avoid the need for primary directions and secondary progressions, Frankland defines a measure that depends solely on the significance of house cusps. In *New Measures in Astrology* (1928), he explains the theoretical basis for this technique:

> I maintain that if the houses have the influence attributed to them, then it should be that, at the time of an event such as financial gain or loss the 2nd house should be directly affected.
>
> The Sun opposition to Saturn can be termed an adverse aspect, and is likely to vent its nature upon the native, *but*, while it gives sad or retarding events, etc., of its nature, yet the 8th house should be directly affected or very sensitive at that time if an important death occurs, and so on with the other houses. If this is not the case, then any adverse aspect could be made to fit any adverse event.
>
> **The aim of this book is to demonstrate that the house concerned with any particular affair *is* affected at the time of events,** and that if we have sickness we shall find that by these simple calculations the signs or houses of such nature are in accordance with activities of that nature. (Frankland 1928, 52–53; bold highlighting mine)

The Importance of Operative Influences on the Birth Chart

Frankland stresses repeatedly that all prediction begins with the birth chart, which encodes the natal promise. A careful study of the nativity will reveal the natal planets' strengths and weaknesses, areas where stressful and beneficial aspects may fall, and the likely timing of favorable and adverse periods of life. In other words, the natal chart will give an overview of the native's character, the most active departments of life (the astrological houses), and the general timing of events.

In Frankland's system, predictive measures based on the real-time motion of the sky and planets are referred to as "operative influences." These include primary directions, secondary progression, major transits, solar returns, eclipses, stations of transiting planets, and so on. From Frankland's point of view, a thoroughgoing study of the natal chart is essential to effective predictive work because "the *Effect* of operative influence depends largely upon the material upon which it is operative [the birth chart]" (Frankland 1926, 56). He offers the analogy that a "flaming brand" cast upon wet ground will cause little harm, but the same brand, cast upon a flammable substance, could trigger a conflagration.

Of all the real-time-based measures, the transits tend to be the fastest and act as "excitants," indicating a specific range of dates when the effects of operative influences are likely to become evident. The transits of the slower, more ponderous planets (Saturn, Uranus, Neptune, Pluto) spread their influence over a longer period of time. During these periods, the faster-moving planets, like Mars, may trigger the manifestation of the transits of the slower planets. In addition, transits will be more effective during periods when deeper influences, such as directions or progressions of a similar nature, are also in effect.

Symbolic versus Real-Time-Based Operative Influences

If I understand Frankland correctly, in his 1926 text *Astrological Investigations* he regards predictive techniques grounded in the real-time motion of the planets as operative influences. These include primary directions based on the rotation of the Earth in the first six hours or so after birth; secondary progressions, at a rate of each day after birth being equivalent to one year of life; and transits, which are the actual positions of the planets at a given moment.

In contrast, Frankland discusses "symbolic measures," which include numerological Birth Numbers, Alan Leo's *assignment of ages to zodiac signs*, Ptolemy's *seven ages of man*, and Frankland's own *Point of Life* and *Age along the Zodiac* measures. These symbolic measures do not act as operative influences; instead, they highlight "areas of life" symbolized by the natal houses and configurations that are "ripe" and ready to manifest at a certain age. When a symbolic measure highlights such a "ripe" area of the natal chart, an operative influence is more likely to trigger the significations of the natal promise of that part of the chart into manifestation.

In Frankland's *New Measures in Astrology* (1928), however, he introduces a novel symbolic direction, *4/7 of a degree for each year of life*, which he appears to treat as an operative influence when it is used to direct the planets and points of a birth chart. Directing at a rate of *4/7° per year* means that *each 30° of the zodiac is equivalent to 52.5 years of life* (30 × 7/4 equals 52.5)—a fact worth remembering as you practice with this technique.

Frankland cites as examples the charts of the actor Wilson Barrett and the writer Robert Louis Stevenson (author of *Dr. Jekyll and Mr. Hyde* and other classics). Unfortunately, Frankland calculates Barrett's chart with an incorrect year of birth. (Barrett was born in 1846, but Frankland uses the birth data given in Alan Leo's *1001 Notable Nativities*, which erroneously uses 1845.) Thus, his discussion of Barrett's chart is based on inaccurate data.

Author Robert Louis Stevenson

Frankland also takes the birth data for Robert Louis Stevenson from Alan Leo's unreliable *1001 Notable Nativities*, which uses the 1:30 p.m. birth time found in Stevenson's family records but calculates the chart for LMT rather than GMT. In contrast, Astro.com calculates the birth chart for 1:30 p.m. GMT, which produces angles and house cusps that are several degrees different. Unsure of which chart was correct, I researched time zones in Edinburgh and found that Scotland adopted GMT on 30 January 1848, so that when Stevenson was born in 1850, all the clocks in Scotland were set to GMT.

Unfortunately, Alan Leo used LMT to calculate Stevenson's chart, and Frankland was unaware of the error. In any case, here is Stevenson's more accurate birth chart (chart 17), to which we will apply Frankland's measures, even though this chart differs somewhat from the one Frankland used in his book.

Frankland begins his discussion of Stevenson's chart with his marriage to Fanny Osbourne in San Francisco, California, in May of 1880 at the age of 29.5. Frankland calculates a *sensitive Point of Marriage* by adding the longitudes of the cusps of the 11th (friendship) and 7th (marriage) houses:

11th house cusp: 28° 25' Sagittarius equals 268.42°

7th house cusp: 11° 42' Leo equals 131.7°

Thus, 268.42° + 131.7° equals 399.9°, from which we must subtract 360° (a complete circle) to arrive at 39.9°, which is equivalent to 9° 54' Taurus as Stevenson's *Point of Marriage*.

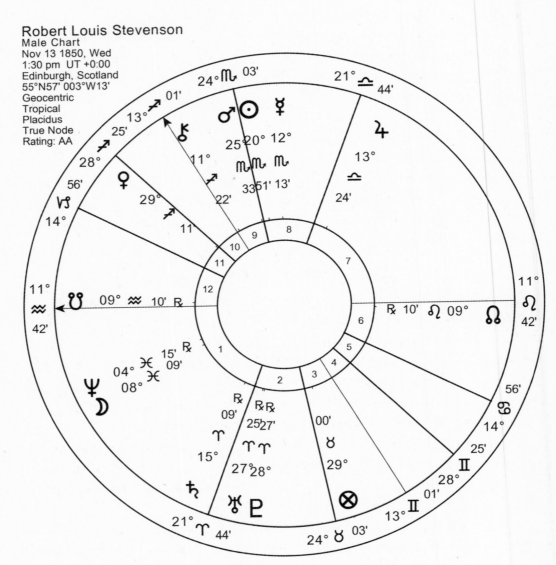

Chart 17: Robert Louis Stevenson
13 November 1850, 1:30 p.m. UT, Edinburgh, Scotland, 55N57 3W13

In his quick and easy method, Frankland would have rounded the 11th house cusp to 28° Sagittarius and the cusp of the 7th house to 12° Leo. He then would have added mentally, 28° + 12° = 40°, or one sign and 10°. He would have summed Sagittarius (8) with Leo (4) and gotten 12, which is equivalent to Aries, to which he would add one sign and 10° and arrive at 10° Taurus as the *Point of Friendship Leading to Marriage* in this chart.

We next add Stevenson's *Age along the Zodiac* (29.5 years) to his *Point of Marriage*, which locates it at 9° 24' Gemini at the time of his wedding, almost exactly sextile the North Lunar Node (fateful connections with others) at the cusp of the 7th house.

If we calculate the *4/7° measure* of Stevenson's age at the time of his marriage, we arrive at 4/7 × 29.5 equals 16.857°, or 16° 51' of arc. Adding this value to the cusp of the 7th house (marriage) directs the 7th house cusp to 28° Leo 33', which forms a Grand Trine with natal Venus in Sagittarius on the cusp of the 11th house of friendship and the natal Uranus-Pluto conjunction in Aries in the 2nd house. The directed 7th house cusp is also sextile the 5th house cusp of love affairs. In his 1928 text, Frankland considers the symbolic directions performed with the *4/7° measure* (4/7 of a degree represents one year of life) to be "operative influences."

Stevenson met his future wife, the American short story writer Fanny Osbourne, in September of 1876 while traveling in France. He was 25 years old at the time; she was 36 and had recently separated from her philandering husband, with whom she had two children. Robert Louis and Fanny felt an immediate mutual attraction, but he had to return to England and was unable to pursue the relationship in person. They managed to meet again early in 1877, at which time they began a love affair. Robert spent much of the following year with Fanny and her two children in France. In August of 1878, however, she had to return to the United States.

In August of 1879, Robert, who chronically suffered from ill health, decided to travel to San Francisco to reunite with his lover Fanny. The trip was arduous, and by the time he arrived in Monterey, California, he was almost fatally ill. Fearing that Stevenson might die, some local ranchers managed to nurse him back to reasonable health, and in December of 1879 he made his way to San Francisco, where Fanny was waiting for him. Robert's health again severely declined in the winter months of 1880, but Fanny, now divorced, nursed him back to health. In May of 1880 they tied the knot.

Can we see the risk of death in late 1879 and early 1880 by applying Frankland's symbolic measures to Stevenson's birth chart? The 8th house of death has 21° Libra 44' on its cusp, making Venus the ruler. Frankland was about 29 years old when he first arrived in California, gravely ill and near death. If we add 29° to the position of 8th-ruler Venus, at 29° 11' Sagittarius, we arrive at 28° 11' Capricorn, which is square to his natal Uranus-Pluto conjunction at the end of Aries.

If we use the *4/7° measure*, then 4/7 of 29 years is 16.57 years, which when added as 16.57° to the position of Venus symbolically directs Venus to 15° 45' Capricorn, closely square to his natal Saturn at 15° 09' Aries Rx in the 1st house and the sign of its fall. Frankland would consider this symbolic direction of natal Venus to the square of natal Saturn by the *4/7° measure* to be an operative influence, indicating the risk of death during this period in his life. Saturn, of course, rules Stevenson's natal Ascendant (his body and vitality), and Venus is the ruler of his natal 8th house of death and near-death experiences.

Being sickly all his life, Stevenson died young on 3 December 1894, having turned 44 years of age on November 13th of that year. He succumbed during the Ptolemaic stage of life ruled by Mars (ages 41 to 56). Could Frankland's measures have foreseen his early demise?

Frankland calculated two sensitive points related to death by combining house cusps: (a) the *Point of Life-Threatening Illness* (6th plus 8th house cusps) and (b) the *Point of Illness in One's Final Days* (6th plus 4th house cusps). He viewed the 4th house as indicating conditions at the end of life.

Point of Life-Threatening Illness (6th plus 8th house cusps):

6th house cusp: 14° 56' Cancer = 104.93° longitude

8th house cusp: 21° 44' Libra = 201.73° longitude

The sum of the two cusps is 306.66°, which is equivalent to 6° 40' Aquarius, Stevenson's *Point of Serious Illness*.

If we add 44 years (his age at death) to 6° 40' Aquarius (*Point of Serious Illness*), we arrive at 20° 40' Pisces, which is quincunx the natal Placidus 8th house cusp of death and trine his natal Sun at 20° 51' Scorpio.

Point of Illness in One's Final Days (6th plus 4th house cusps):

6th house cusp: 14° 56' Cancer = 104.93° longitude

4th house cusp: 13° 01' Gemini = 73.03° longitude

The sum of the two cusps is 177.96°, which is equivalent to 27° 58' Virgo as his *Point of Illness at the End of Life*.

If we add 44 years (his age at death) to 27° Virgo 58', we arrive at 11° Scorpio 58', which conjoins his natal Mercury in the 8th house and squares his natal Ascendant.

In Stevenson's chart, Mercury rules the 4th house, which is a house of endings. In addition, this directed *Point of Illness at the End of Life* is closely quincunx natal Uranus at 27° 25' Aries Rx, symbolizing sudden unexpected events. On 3 December 1894 at about 8:00 p.m., Stevenson was opening a bottle of wine at his home in the Samoan Islands when he began to feel strange and suddenly collapsed. He died a few hours later, most likely of a cerebral hemorrhage. On the day of his demise, his secondary progressed Moon (ruler of his natal 6th house of illness) was passing through Libra in his 8th house of death, exactly opposite natal Uranus at 27° 25' Aries Rx (an operative influence).

Actor Wilson Barrett

Wilson Barrett, a noted British actor in the late 1800s, was born on 18 February 1846 (not in 1845, as in Frankland's text) to a farming family in Essex, England. Of small stature but possessing a powerful voice and handsome, masculine appearance, he was perfect for melodrama. On 21 July 1866 at the age of 20.42, he married Caroline Heath. The couple had two sons and three daughters.

Barrett toured the United States in 1894 and 1895. His most popular and successful role was in the play *The Sign of the Cross* in 1895. He died in a London nursing home on 22 July 1904 at the age of 58. Frankland tested his symbolic measures against Barrett's marriage at age 20 and his demise at age 58.

As best as I can reconstruct the chart from Frankland's text and Alan Leo's erroneous *1001 Notable Nativities*, Wilson Barrett's birth chart has a birth time of about 1:03:30 a.m. LMT (chart 18). In *Notable Nativities*, Alan Leo gives the following positions (rounded to whole numbers) for the cusps of Barrett's chart, presumably based on the correct birth time but the wrong year of birth. (The 20° Scorpio Ascendant does not make sense if he was born in Essex and suggests that Alan Leo either printed a typo or believed incorrectly that Barrett was born in the north of England.)

I: 20° Scorpio
II: 21° Sagittarius

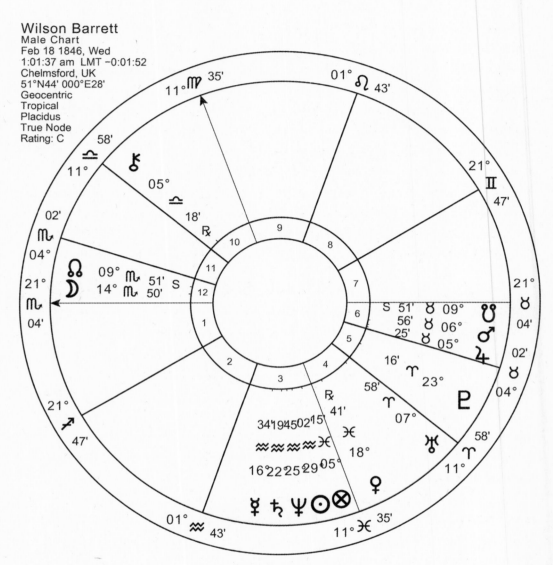

Wilson Barrett
Male Chart
Feb 18 1846, Wed
1:01:37 am LMT −0:01:52
Chelmsford, UK
51°N44' 000°E28'
Geocentric
Tropical
Placidus
True Node
Rating: C

Chart 18: Wilson Barrett
18 February 1846, 1:01:37 a.m. LMT, Chelmsford, England, 51N44 0E28

III: 01° Aquarius
X: 12° Virgo
XI: 12° Libra
XII: 04° Scorpio

Barrett's Marriage at Age 20

To estimate Barrett's birth time, I calculated the Placidian primary directions (0° latitude, Ptolemy's key) that were in effect at age 20.42 and identified the time at which the primary directed 7th house cusp of marriage conjoined natal Jupiter (expansion, good fortune, lord of the 4th house of domestic life) in October of 1866. The symbolism of this primary direction is appropriate for a marriage in July of 1866. Unfortunately, I do not have a verifiable source for Barrett's birth time, and this chart remains somewhat speculative, even though the cusps are quite close to those used by both Frankland and Alan Leo.

House Measures for Wilson Barrett

11th house cusp (friendship): 11° 58' Libra = 191.966° longitude

7th house cusp (marriage): 21° 04' Taurus = 51.066° longitude

Adding these two house cusps together produces a *Point of Friendship Leading to Marriage*, the result being 242.726° of ecliptic longitude, which is equivalent to 2° 44' Sagittarius.

Adding age 20.42° to the above result takes us to 23° 09' Sagittarius, which is just separating from a sextile to natal Saturn (serious matters) and closely approaching a trine to natal Pluto at 23° 16' Aries in the 5th house of romance.

By the *Point of Life* symbolic measure, age 20 corresponds to the span from 25° 44' Gemini to 30° Gemini in Barrett's chart, and trines both natal Neptune and the Sun in late Aquarius, suggesting a favorable year. The Sun rules his natal 9th house, which signifies religious ceremonies, including weddings.

Another of Frankland's techniques was to add the cusp of a house to the Ascendant degree (or to the 4th house cusp) to generate a *symbolic point related to the matter signified by the house in question*. For marriage, he would add the longitude of the 7th house cusp to that of the 1st (or 4th) house:

1st house cusp: 21° 04' Scorpio = 231.066° longitude

7th house cusp: 21° 04' Taurus = 51.066° longitude

Adding the longitudes of these two house cusps together gives the result 282.132° longitude, which is equivalent to 12° 08' Capricorn as a *Point of Marriage*.

Adding Barrett's age at the time of marriage (20.42 years), converted to 20.42°, to the above result takes us to 2° 22' Aquarius as a *house-related sensitive Point of Marriage*, which in this case conjoins the 3rd house cusp and opposes the 9th house cusp (religious ceremonies) but does not aspect any planet in the chart.

Operative Influence of the *4/7° Measure* at Age 20 in Barrett's Chart

Using 20.42 (Barrett's age when he wedded), we calculate the *4/7° symbolic measure* to be 4/7 × 20 equals 11.668°, which we can add to the planets and points in the chart to symbolically direct them to that age. Do any of these symbolic directions suggest marriage?

11.668° + 7th house cusp = 2° 44' Gemini, which is sextile the 9th house cusp of religious ceremonies within an orb of 1 degree.

11.668° + Venus (ruler of the 7th house of marriage) = 0° 21' Aries, which is approaching a trine to the 9th house cusp within an orb of about a degree.

11.668° + Mars (signifying the native as ruler of the Ascendant) = 18° 36' Taurus, which is almost exactly sextile Venus (the 7th house ruler) at 18° 41' Pisces, strongly signifying marriage.

Wilson Barrett's Demise at Age 58.42

Wilson Barrett died in London on 22 July 1904 when he was 58.42 years old. To calculate a symbolic point for his passing, Frankland would add the cusp of the 1st house (the Ascendant, signifying the beginning of the native's life) to the cusp of the 4th house (the end of matters).

1st house cusp: 21° 04' Scorpio = 231.066° zodiac longitude

4th house cusp: 11° 35' Pisces = 341.5833° zodiac longitude

Adding the longitudes of the two cusps together gives the result of 212.65° of longitude, which is equivalent to 23° 39' Scorpio as a *sensitive point related to the end of life*.

Adding Barrett's age of 58.42 years to this "end of life" point takes us to longitude 271.07°, equivalent to 1° 04' Capricorn, which does not aspect any planet or significant point in his birth chart, except perhaps a quincunx to the 9th house cusp of long journeys.

However, in Barrett's secondary progressed chart for the day of his demise, progressed Chiron lies at 1° 03' Libra Rx in the progressed 8th house, square to the directed end of life point at 1° 04' Capricorn. Frankland, of course, would have been unaware of the existence of Chiron.

If we use the *4/7° measure*, 4/7 of Barrett's age of 58.42 is 33.38 years. Adding 33.38° to the cusp of the 8th house of death takes us to 25° 10' Cancer in the 8th house, which is closely quincunx natal Neptune at 25° 45' Aquarius in the 3rd house. Natal Neptune is combust the Sun and afflicted by a conjunction with Saturn. In modern astrology, Neptune is considered a ruler of the Pisces 4th house of final endings. The stressful quincunx between natal Neptune, ruling the 4th house of endings, and the symbolically directed 8th house cusp of death is consistent with a life-threatening period.

If we add 33.38° of longitude to the position of Venus at 18° 41' Pisces in the 4th house of endings, we arrive at 22° 04' Aries, which is closely sextile to natal Saturn at 22° 19' Aquarius, again a potential symbol of a peaceful demise. Natal Venus symbolically directed to 22° 04' Aries is also sextile to the natal 8th house cusp of death.

Frankland was not aware of the existence of Pluto (a modern signifier of death and the afterlife), which lies at 23° 16' Aries in Barrett's natal chart. If we add his age at death in degrees (58.42°) to the longitude of natal Pluto, we arrive at 21° 41' Gemini, closely conjunct the natal Placidus 8th house cusp of death.

Jim Henson: Looking at the Big Picture

An essential feature of Frankland's method of forecasting is to begin with the major themes and patterns in the chart. The astrologer can then focus in on the details. Consider the chart of *Muppets* creator Jim Henson, who died unexpectedly of septic shock on 16 May 1990. The birth time of this chart (chart 19) is taken from the 2013 biography of Henson by Brian Jay Jones, *Jim Henson: The Biography*.

How would Frankland have approached this chart? Looking at the big picture, he most likely would have noticed the following themes and patterns.

There is a mutable Grand Cross (Grand Square) pattern, and the planets Neptune, Jupiter, and Saturn form a close T-square at 17° to 18° of the mutable signs. The 18th degree is extremely sensitive and can trigger the Grand Cross into action. In *Astrological Investigations*, Frankland wrote: "When some strong direction is formed *between* or *on* the points of the square, a most drastic or eventful time is indicated" (Frankland 1926, 45; italics mine). By "between," he means the midpoints of the Grand Cross.

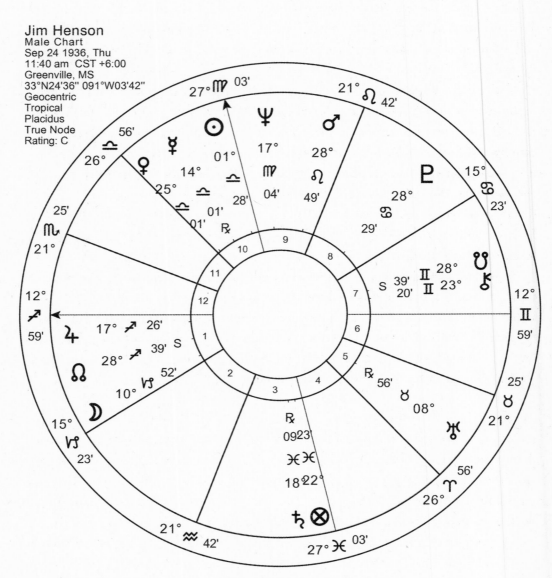

Chart 19: Jim Henson
24 September 1936, 11:40 a.m. CST, Greenville, Mississippi, 33N25 91W04

The midpoints of the 18th degree (17°–18°) of mutable signs lie at the 2nd degree (2°–3°) of the fixed signs (Taurus, Leo, Scorpio, Aquarius). Hence, a direction to these degrees in the fixed signs can also portend a drastic or eventful period in the life of the native.

The 29th degree (28°–29°) is also prominent in Henson's birth chart. The true South Lunar Node has stationed at 28° Gemini in the 7th house. Pluto in 28° Cancer occupies the 8th house. The 12th house ruler Mars, which is the planetary ruler of this Ptolemaic age (41–56 years old) and the contrary-to-sect malefic, occupies 28° Leo in the 9th house. Claudius Ptolemy, in book 3, chapter 12, of the *Tetrabiblos*, associates planets in the last degrees of the signs with injuries and illnesses.

The 30° interval separating the South Node from Pluto and Pluto from Mars means that when the South Node is directed to Pluto in the 8th house, Pluto will simultaneously be directed to Mars in the 9th house. These are difficult directions because they involve Mars, Pluto, and the South Node as well as the 8th and 12th houses. By the *4/7° per year measure*, these directions will perfect at about 52.5 years of age, which will mark a highly stressful time in Henson's life (30° × 7/4 equals 52.5°). Because of the involvement of the 8th and 12th houses, the year or so surrounding this *Age Point* could be dangerous to his health.

Glancing at Henson's chart, we see that Pluto in the 8th house looks quite close to the midpoint of Venus and Uranus. With Venus ruling the 6th house, this midpoint could indicate an unexpected injury or illness. If we calculate the Venus/Uranus midpoint exactly, we find it to be at 1° 59' Leo, almost exactly at a midpoint of the 18th degree of the mutable Grand Cross. Thus, triggering the Grand Cross could also involve some type of sudden health crisis.

Keeping in mind the 30° spacings among the South Node, Pluto, and Mars, we look to see whether directing any other natal point or planet by 30° will produce a "hit." Directing Mars by 30° will take it to 28°–29° Virgo, in partile square to the natal lunar nodes, placing directed Mars "*at the bendings*" (in this case, the point on the ecliptic at which the Moon reaches its southernmost latitude), which often heralds a crisis related to the nature of the planet. With directed Mars at the MC, the symbolism fits with the stressful negotiations Henson was having with Disney Productions at the time. It also correlates with his developing pneumonia, which led to his death in May of 1990. Ptolemy, in book 3, chapter 12, of the *Tetrabiblos*, connects the Moon being "at the nodes or her bendings" with disease, injury, burns, attacks, lameness, paralysis, and deformations of the body.

Directing the natal Sun (a symbol of the life force and the traditional hyleg in this chart) by 30° takes the Sun to 1° 28' Scorpio, opposite the Venus/Uranus midpoint (at 1° 59' Leo) and conjunct 2° Scorpio, one of the midpoints of the natal Grand Cross. The Sun perfects this direction to 1° 59' fixed at 53.4 years of age.

If we do the math for the midpoint of the Grand Cross, the Jupiter/Neptune midpoint lies at 2° 16' Scorpio, which is 30° 48' distant from the Sun. By the *4/7° per year measure*, 30° 48' times 7 divided by 4 equals 53.9°, which is equivalent to 53.9 years of age.

Jim Henson was 53.64 years old when he died.

In this example, we see how Frankland's method allows us to begin with the big picture to identify the year or so surrounding age 52.5 as a particularly stressful and potentially dangerous time in Henson's life, and then to focus in on the details to narrow the period of highest risk to the period between 53.4 and 53.9 years of age (roughly February to August of 1990).

Chapter 8
JUDGING THE OVERALL TENOR OF THE CHART

In chapter 5 of *Astrological Investigations* (1926), Frankland recommends judging the overall tenor of the chart prior to making specific predictions. His judgment is based on the zodiacal and mundane condition of the planets and their combined interactions with each other and with significant points or house cusps in the nativity. Frankland identifies three broad categories of birth charts: favorable, adverse, and fateful.

Favorable charts have planets that are in signs of their essential dignity and fast in motion; benefic planets occupy the angular houses, especially the 1ˢᵗ and 10ᵗʰ; and the majority of aspects are soft (sextiles, trines, and harmonious conjunctions).

In contrast, **adverse charts** tend to have many planets that are retrograde and in signs of their fall or detriment; malefic planets tend to occupy the angular houses, especially the 1ˢᵗ and 10ᵗʰ; and the majority of aspects are hard (squares, oppositions, and stressful conjunctions).

Astrologers of the early 1900s considered certain charts as more **fateful** than others. The term "fateful" has various meanings, including (1) momentous, or of great import; (2) controlled by fate rather than by the individual's will; (3) disastrous or fatal; and (4) ominously prophetic. For example, the booklet *Transits of the Planets* published by the AFA, probably written around 1913 and erroneously attributed to Dr. J. Heber Smith, the mentor of Evangeline Adams, states:

> There are what I call *unimportant nativities, or such wherein the planets are mostly cadent, and in common [mutable] signs.* In such cases the directions [primary direction or secondary progressions] must be very potent to produce any great

result, and many small directions will pass without being observed. (Smith 1968, 39; italics mine)

A similar comment appears in Alan Leo's 1906 text *The Progressed Horoscope:*

The most *fateful* horoscopes are those in which the *majority of planets are in the Common or Mutable signs*, and those where *Saturn afflicts the luminaries. Jupiter afflicted by Mars*, or the *Sun by Uranus* are fateful nativities, as in the case of [the poet] P. B. Shelley. (Leo 1906, 7; italics mine)

In other words, birth charts with a predominance of planets in *cadent houses* and *mutable signs* belong to individuals who are less able than average to determine their own destiny and are therefore subject to whatever fate has in store for them. If the chart also happens to contain significant adverse aspects, the life is likely to be unfortunate.

In his 1906 book on progressions, Alan Leo argues that one of the most difficult adverse configurations in the natal chart is "Saturn hunting the Moon," which occurs when transiting Saturn forms a hard aspect to the position of the secondary progressed Moon. Because the cycle of the progressed Moon (roughly 28 years) is close to that of transiting Saturn (roughly 30 years), transiting Saturn and the progressed natal Moon will travel at almost the same speed round the chart. As a result, a natal aspect between Saturn and the Moon will remain in effect *as a transiting Saturn-to-progressed Moon aspect* for many years, coloring a considerable period of the native's life. Leo explains:

The *most unfortunate aspect in a nativity* is the affliction of the Moon by Saturn, either by square or opposition, and when the aspect is very close and the progressive Moon is moving slowly, or at the same rate as Saturn, the transit of Saturn goes on for the best part of the life. For *the Moon by progressive motion moves through one sign of the zodiac in two years and a half, and Saturn's motion by transit is at the same rate*, therefore, unless the Moon is moving fast and moving out of the sphere of influence of Saturn, *a double affliction is kept up for the best part of the life*. This, of course, can only be the case where the Moon is in conjunction, square or opposition with Saturn at birth. (Leo 1906, 202; italics mine)

Of the adverse charts, the most *fateful* ones, according to Frankland, are as follows:

1. Charts in which most planets occupy *mutable* signs (Gemini, Virgo, Sagittarius, Pisces).

2. Charts in which Saturn or Uranus afflicts both of the luminaries (Sun and Moon) or afflicts one luminary and the ruler of the Ascendant.

3. Charts in which the majority of planets occupy the critical degrees that mark the cusps of the 28 Arabic lunar mansions (360° divided by 28 gives a size of 12° 51' to each mansion). In Frankland's usage of the term, the critical degrees are points spaced 12° 51' apart around the zodiac, beginning at 0° Aries. The boundaries of the Arabic lunar mansions are 0°, 12° 51', and 25° 43' of the *cardinal* signs; 8° 34' and 21° 26' of the *fixed* signs; and 4° 17' and 17° 09' of the *mutable* signs.

4. Frankland may have encountered this idea of critical degrees in the writings of his contemporary Vivian Robson, who remarked that the passage of the Moon from one lunar mansion to the next marks a change in the general current of events. Both Robson and Frankland were likely influenced by Sepharial's *Manual of Occultism* (1914), which popularized the idea that the boundaries between the lunar mansions, whether they be the 28 Arabic or 27 Hindu lunar mansions (*nakshatras*), were "critical degrees," that is, "points of change" at which "the Moon changes its signification as it goes from one to another Mansion" (Sepharial 1914, 19).

5. Sepharial also associates the boundaries of the Hindu lunar mansions with eminence:

> It has been observed that when planets are on the cusps of the Lunar Mansions, the person then born rises to eminence (Section I, chap. iii).
>
> The majority of planets in or near any such degrees, viz. the 1st, 13th and 25th of the cardinal signs, the 9th and 22nd of the fixed signs, or the 4th and 17th of the common signs, denotes one born to distinction. King George V has 5 planets, as well as the Midheaven and Ascendant, close to such degrees. (Sepharial 1914, 53).

If Frankland had been aware of the existence of Pluto, he surely would have included it as one of the slow malefic planets whose afflictions to the luminaries or the Ascendant ruler could indicate a fateful chart.

As an example of a fateful chart, Frankland mentions a person born on 27 April 1893 at 11:30 p.m. with Mars exactly opposing the Ascendant (*Astrological Investigations*, 43). Assuming that this person was born in the UK, a tables of houses would indicate the he was born near Carlisle (54N54 02W55), which would place Mars on his 7th house cusp (chart 20).

In this "fateful" chart, Frankland notes the following features:

- Sagittarius rises, so that Jupiter rules the Ascendant.
- The slow-moving malefic planet Uranus opposes natal Venus.
- Mars exactly opposes the Ascendant degree.
- Ketu, the South Lunar Node symbolizing loss, occupies the angular 10th house of career.
- Uranus at birth lies at 08° 44' Scorpio Rx in the 10th house, so that by secondary progression it applies to oppose both natal Jupiter at 7° 54' Taurus and natal Sun at 7° 53' Taurus during this man's 20s.
- Saturn at birth lies at 7° 21' Libra Rx and is stressfully quincunx (150°) to both his natal Sun and Jupiter.

The outcome of this adverse fateful chart was that the native was "practically ruined" at age 27.

If we calculate this man's directed *Point of Life* at age 27, we find that it advances from 25.7° to 30° of Cancer. Thus, at age 27 his *Point of Life* will square the natal MC (career) and also the natal lunar nodes. The *Point of Life* in Cancer is disposed by the Moon, which at birth is closely conjoined to Saturn. At the same time, both his natal Sun and his natal Ascendant-ruler Jupiter are opposed by Uranus from the 10th house. Finally, at age 27 his secondary progressed Mars will be at about 7° of Cancer, squaring his natal Saturn.

If we measure his *Age along the Zodiac* (which I also refer to as his *Age Point*), allowing one degree for each year of life, commencing from 0° Aries, then at age 27 his *Age Point* lies at 27° Aries, square to his meridian axis and applying to square his lunar nodes within the year. The overall symbolism is adverse and fateful. Not surprisingly, he faced nearly total ruin during this period.

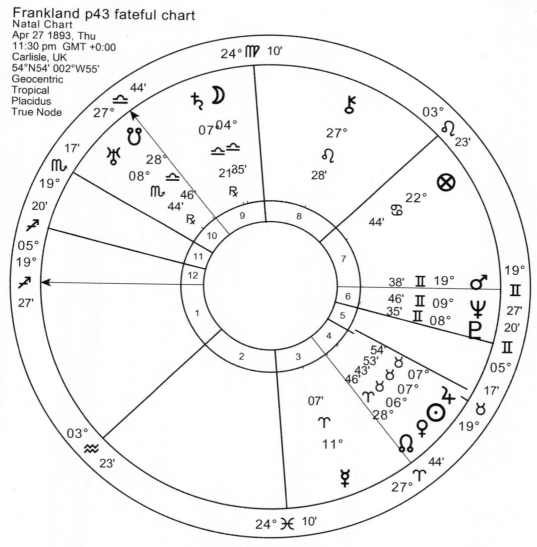

Frankland p43 fateful chart
Natal Chart
Apr 27 1893, Thu
11:30 pm GMT +0:00
Carlisle, UK
54°N54' 002°W55'
Geocentric
Tropical
Placidus
True Node

Chart 20: Fateful Chart
27 April 1893, 11:30 p.m. GMT, Carlisle, England, 54N54 2W55

In his 1928 *New Measures in Astrology*, Frankland also summarizes, in terse form, many principles of natal chart interpretation gleaned from his years of research. In many ways his comments read like lists of aphorisms in the traditional astrological literature. I will highlight his basic principles in the following paragraphs:

> The setting of the whole horoscope is of far greater importance than the playing of influences upon it. … (Frankland 1928, 43)
>
> […]
>
> … Therefore, *before* one seeks to estimate critical years of life, the setting and symbolism of the horoscope should be well studied.
>
> In this system of directing, one consideration is that the setting of the nativity is [always] before us even in directing, whereas in secondary directions, with the different maps, unless one is careful the mind is apt to lose sight of the original plan. (Frankland 1928, 48)

In other words, forecasting is done first, foremost, and always in the context of the natal chart and never solely from derivative charts read independently of the birth chart.

Keep in mind that there are three main types of influences in a natal chart: planetary, zodiacal, and mundane (houses influence).

The planets represent basic principles of the self. For example, Venus can symbolize our capacity to form loving relationships.

The signs of the zodiac are characterizing influences that describe *how* the planets will behave. For example, Venus in Taurus may act to love self-indulgently. The signs function to "mold" the behavior of the planets. Zodiacal strength has to do with how well, or badly, a planet behaves.

The mundane houses are based on the native's geographical latitude and the rotation of the Earth. They represent the practical, material, and physical side of existence. Mundane strength derives from a planet's relationship to the angles (Asc, MC, Dsc, IC) and has to do with the extent to which, or how powerfully, a planet can manifest its significations in the real world. For example, the Sun exalted in Aries in the 10th house might signify an honorable and powerful leader in a practical, material sense. The same Sun in Aries but in the 12th house might represent a highly dignified leader in exile, with little worldly power at their disposal.

Pay attention to *midpoints* and the planets involved in them. Especially important are the Sun/Moon midpoint and the midpoint that the Ascendant ruler forms with either luminary or with other vital chart points. Midpoints involving the Ascendant or MC gain importance when the time of birth is well established. If a symbolic measure, such as the *Point of Life* or the *Age Point*, conjoins such midpoints, it signals a potentially highly significant year in the life.

Note whether the Ascendant ruler or the benefics are besieged by the malefics. One of Frankland's clients with much trouble in his life had his Ascendant-ruler Mercury conjunct the Moon, and both of these planets were besieged between Mars and Saturn.

Note any "curious positions" of the Ascendant ruler. For example, the chart of a notable person "of strange fame and short career" had Sagittarius rising with Jupiter simultaneously conjunct both the Part of Fortune and Ketu, the South Node of the Moon.

Acutely difficult conditions prevail when malefics "hold the Ascendant and Midheaven" and the benefics are weakly placed, especially when the malefics are in adverse aspect. However, when benefics "hold the Ascendant and Midheaven," even if there be adverse aspects, much success is indicated.

Planets in the angular 1st, 4th, 7th, and 10th houses will strongly impact the native.

Planets conjunct the angles (the horizon or meridian axis) will be especially prominent during the life of the native, and their condition and configurations in the birth chart should be carefully assessed. Interestingly, Harding and Harvey closely echo Frankland's comments when they write in their 1990 book *Working with Astrology*:

> Experience demonstrates that when a planet is configured with the Ascendant or MC, it is almost certainly going to be expressed in that person's life.... The Angles make a planet's energy *personal* and thus liable to be expressed strongly in the world. (Harding and Harvey 1990, 29)

When several planets are grouped together in a single sign in the birth chart, extremely eventful periods are likely when the stellium is stimulated. For example, one of Frankland's clients with a stellium of five planets in the *fixed* sign Taurus complained that he felt as if his life were stuck "in a deadly groove." Fortunately, this person (probably born 23 June 1881) had Uranus in mid-Virgo, and Frankland was able to forecast correctly that when the trine of Uranus (the "Developer") to the Virgo stellium became activated by the *Point of Life* (around age 37), "beneficial changes would be made of a progressive nature" (Frankland 1926, 46).

When several planets lie close together in a birth chart, the progressed aspects of these planets will have a significantly stronger effect and be spread over a longer period of time. Pay special attention to periods when the slowest planets arrive at these groupings. In his practice prior to the discovery of Pluto in 1930, Frankland found that the directions from Saturn and Uranus by hard aspect to natal points and planets caused the most difficulties.

Always note when a close grouping of planets receives a major aspect from a ponderous planet (Saturn, Uranus, Neptune, Pluto) in the birth chart. The transits of these ponderous planets, especially the hard aspects to their own natal positions, will be especially significant during the life cycle.

Note carefully nativities that contain a Grand Cross. Major events are likely to occur when a strong direction arrives at the points or midpoints of this cross. A similar situation can occur when a major transit, direction, or progression aspects a natal T-square, converting it into a Grand Cross by opposing the focal planet, or apex, of the natal configuration.

Even when benefics rule or occupy the Midheaven, success may be delayed if the benefic receives a stressful aspect from Saturn. For example, a client born 4 April 1891 at 10:25 a.m. in England had Jupiter ruling his Pisces MC and approaching the MC from the 9th house. Venus was with Jupiter in Pisces in the 9th house. Saturn was across the wheel, opposing natal Jupiter and Venus from Virgo. Saturn was in the 3rd house and conjunct the IC. This client experienced career setbacks arising from conditions in his domestic life.

Pay special attention to the Ascendant ruler "in all its movements and aspects" (Frankland 1926, 47). Retrograde periods of the Ascendant ruler will be significant.

In nativities, note whether the strength or weakness of a planet is zodiacal (based on sign position) or mundane (based on house position). Zodiacal position relates to the character of the native, while mundane position has more to do with material benefit or adversity.

"The position of a planet counts more than the aspect" (Frankland 1926, 49). A well-placed planet can withstand ill aspects. A badly placed planet will receive little help from beneficial aspects.

Aspects to planets that rule or occupy natal house cusps will affect the affairs symbolized by those houses in the birth chart. In judging houses, however, consider *first* any planets that occupy the house, as they will find expression in such matters. *Second,* consider the ruler of the house cusp, which "lies at the root" of the house's affairs and disposes any planets in the house. *Third* and last, consider any progressed planets that influence the house.

Thus, Frankland gives more weight to the placement of a planet in a house than to house rulership. Wynn (aka Sidney K. Bennett), a contemporary of Frankland, makes a similar point about a planet's house position in *Your Future: A Guide to Modern Astrology* (1935):

> The most important of all considerations is that of position. Make this your unforgettable rule. (Wynn 1935, 84)

Both Frankland and Wynn appear to be echoing the teachings of the seventeenth-century French astrologer Jean-Baptiste Morin de Villefranche, who argued that the physical placement of a planet within a house is its most immediate determining factor.

Only after considering any planets within a house does Frankland proceed to the *second* step of studying the ruler of the house cusp, which "lies at the root of the affairs [of the house], and disposes of all other influences (if strong enough)" (Frankland 1926, 47). Morin would next assess the aspects formed by any planets that occupy or rule the house cusp. Frankland would next proceed to study the secondary progressions of the planets in question.

Note whether the ruler of a house is placed in another house, because such a placement establishes a link between the two houses.

Check whether a particular planet becomes the *"Dominant Note"* of the birth chart. For example, Alan Leo's chart is strongly *solar* because he has Leo rising (ruled by the Sun), with several planets in Leo. His natal Sun is also abundantly aspected by other planets. On pages 50–51 of *Astrological Investigations*, Frankland uses the following keywords to characterize the dominant planet:

Sun: A large type of Nature, organization, management.

Moon: Change, impressions, moods.

Mercury: Mental, nervous, intellectual, like quicksilver.

Venus: Harmony, beauty, sociability, artistic ability, tendency toward indolence.

Mars: Executive ability, motive, initiative, constructive or destructive energy, fiery, energetic, impulsive, combative, difficult to restrain.

Jupiter: Expansive, jovial, sociable, enthusiastic, large, sportive, majestic, fortunate, prone to excess or overindulgence.

Saturn: Earnest, serious, cautious, practical, concrete, sterling, responsible, conscientious, systematic, disciplined, concerned about reputation and status, focused on long-term results, liable to gloom and trial.

Uranus: Electric, explosive, original, unexpected, unconventional, self-willed, independent, difficult to deal with. In hard aspect, Uranus often indicates tension, sudden change, or a stressful bolt from the blue.

Neptune: Mysterious, uncommon, psychic, magnetic, imaginative, sensitive, too much swayed by emotions, idealistic, languid, dreaming, illusory, deceptive, escapist, lacking a sound or tangible basis. In hard aspect, Neptune can signify the dissolution, weakening, or unreliability of previously established structures. There is sometimes a tendency to escape into drugs or alcohol.

Pluto: This planet had not yet been discovered in 1926. Modern astrologers associate Pluto with transformation, regeneration, radical change, intense emotion, transcendence, points of inflection, death, rebirth, elimination of waste, obsession, and the afterlife.

If the Moon's nodes are strongly positioned or aspected at birth, then the transits of the lunar nodes, and the aspects cast to them at various points in life, will have noticeable effects. Frankland's research led him to view the Moon's nodes in a manner similar to that of the astrologers of India, who regard Rahu (North Node) and Ketu (South Node) as *shadow planets*, capable of marked effects that are indistinguishable from those of the traditional visible planets.

Regarding the Moon's nodes, Frankland gives the example of a man born in England before sunrise in mid-April of 1887. His North Lunar Node was in Leo, close to the 6th Placidus house cusp. His South Lunar Node was in Aquarius, near the 12th house cusp. His natal Neptune was in Taurus in square to the lunar nodes. This man suffered from a spinal deformity (Dragon's Head in Leo near the 6th house cusp). When suitable operative influences activated the natal T-square involving Neptune (which was at 26° Taurus) and his lunar nodal axis (at 26° Leo/Aquarius), he almost died of food poisoning. At the same time, a symbolic measure coinciding with his age was in effect.

In predictive work, care must be taken to assess not only the seed that is falling but also the ground on which it falls.

When interpreting transits, always keep in mind the house position that the planet holds in the birth chart, for planets act most immediately and directly in the place where they are located and more indirectly as rulers that "lie at the root" of the house's affairs and act as dispositors of other influences, if they are strong enough. In a similar way, the conjunctions, or body-to-body contacts of two planets, take precedence over aspects that join the body of only one planet with the rays of another. (See Chapter V: Type of Horoscope in *Astrological Investigations*.)

When the native is passing through a period in which a planet is strongly activated by a direction or progression, then the transits of that same planet will be particularly effective.

The effects of a transit must be interpreted with respect to, and in proportion to, the operative influences that lie at the root of the year.

Keep in mind the birth positions and aspects among the more ponderous planets (Saturn, Uranus, Neptune, Pluto), because *by secondary progression they will move only a few degrees during the lifetime of the native* and will thus have a background influence for many years. For example, the following table shows the movement of the slower planets by transit during the first 100 days of life (which corresponds to the first 100 years in secondary progressions) for someone born on 1 January 2022:

100-YEAR MOTION OF PONDEROUS PLANETS BY SECONDARY PROGRESSION				
Transits	**Saturn**	**Uranus**	**Neptune**	**Pluto**
1 Jan 2022	11° Aqu 54'	10° Tau 57' Rx	20° Pis 40'	25° Cap 56'
11 Apr 2022 (100 Days Later)	22° Aqu 54'	13° Tau 25' D	23° Pis 55'	28° Cap 30'
Movement by Secondary Progression in 100 Years	11°	2° 28'	3° 15'	2° 34'

In addition to natal aspects between ponderous planets, aspects at birth formed by the Sun with the meridian axis will be effective by secondary progression for the entire life of the native because the progressed Sun and the progressed MC each advance at a rate of roughly 1° per year. For example, Pope Benedict XVI was born on 16 April 1927 in Marktl, Germany, at 4:15 a.m. CET. His natal Sun was at 25° 08' 43" Aries in an almost exact trine to the MC at 25° 17' 58" Sagittarius. When he was elected pope in 2005 at the age of 78, this secondary progressed Sun was at 10° 13' 14" Cancer in almost exact trine to his secondary progressed MC at 10° 13' 57" Pisces.

The Purpose of Prediction in Astrology

Frankland had a busy practice as a consulting astrologer in London between the two world wars. His understanding of astrology was strongly influenced by his years of direct contact with clients, advising them on the basis of their birth charts. His experience with clients led him to develop an interpretive approach with certain underlying principles.

His first step was to seek the main idea embedded in the chart, the thread or central point around which the narrative being told in the nativity revolves. The pattern of the astrological symbols in the horoscope tells a story, and the astrologer must enter into its main theme and get a sense of how the symbolism of the chart reflects the course of the native's life.

Frankland was not deterministic in his understanding of how astrology functions. His approach, like that of modern evolutionary astrologers, takes into account karma. While he notes that, having been born with a particular birth chart, we cannot select the pattern of life depicted therein, nonetheless "we may previously have brought it about" (Frankland 1928, 101). In other words, we may have chosen our current nativity because it will allow us to encounter issues we need to address in this lifetime.

From this perspective, the purpose of astrological prediction is to increase the client's understanding and awareness of the life pattern that the native has chosen to experience in the current reincarnation. As Frankland states in *New Measures in Astrology* (1928):

> We can, however, increase our power of understanding. The same type of ground plot can be utilised to various advantages. The interpretation of the nativity exerts an influence that cannot easily be estimated. (Frankland 1928, 101)

Frankland also addresses the issue of fate versus free will. He believes that no planet can be regarded as truly malefic or benefic. Each planet represents a certain type of expression of energy, which the native may experience either as an external condition being imposed or alternatively as a resource at their disposal. He notes that we rarely thank fiery Mars for our cup of hot coffee in the morning, but we readily complain about Mars when we get cut, burned, or injured. "We all have this fiery principle of Mars in our nature, without which we should indeed be insipid" (Frankland 1928, 104).

Frankland also notes that astrologers commonly comment that the stars incline, but they rarely add that we also incline. Thus, when interpreting a birth chart,

> the aim should be that of *awakening the native to a knowledge, not only of the conditions to which he is subjected, but also to the wonderful resources which may reward his efforts to extract them.* (Frankland 1928, 100; italics mine)

Dorit Schmiel: A Stellium Aspected by Ponderous Planets

Dorit Schmiel, a young woman from East Germany, was shot to death on 19 February 1962 while trying to escape to West Berlin. Dorit was born in East Berlin on 25 April 1941, time unknown. Here is her generic Aries rising chart cast for noon to give the mean positions of the planets on her day of birth (chart 21).

According to the website *Prabook*, Dorit Schmiel was born in Berlin during the Second World War, during which her father was killed. As a child, she traveled regularly to visit relatives in West Berlin. When the East German authorities completely restricted travel to the West, she acutely felt the loss of freedom. When she and some friends tried to escape on 19 February 1962, the border guards began to shoot at them, hitting Dorit in the abdomen. She died later the same day of her bullet wounds.

Without a time of birth for Dorit, we cannot know her Ascendant, MC, or house cusps. However, we can apply Frankland's technique of studying the transits of slow-moving planets to a stellium in the birth chart. Frankland writes in *Astrological Investigations* (1926):

> In Nativities where there is a group of Planets [a stellium], Progressed aspects are also bound to have much stronger effect and to spread over a much longer period. In cases of this kind note carefully the Periods when Uranus and Neptune arrive on these points. (Frankland 1926, 44–45)

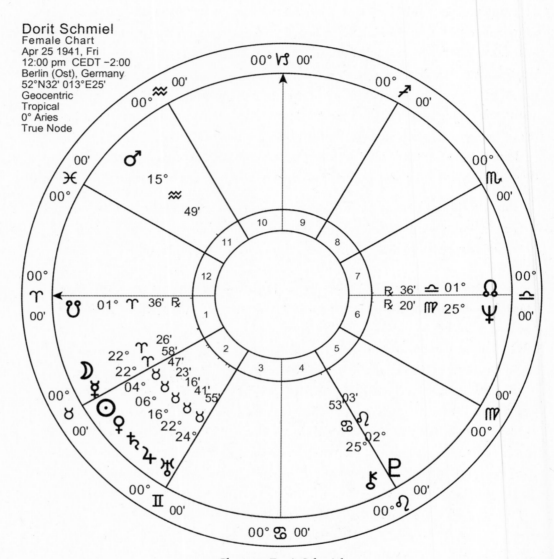

Dorit Schmiel
Female Chart
Apr 25 1941, Fri
12:00 pm CEDT −2:00
Berlin (Ost), Germany
52°N32' 013°E25'
Geocentric
Tropical
0° Aries
True Node

Chart 21: Dorit Schmiel
25 April 1941, 12:00 p.m. CEDT (time unknown), Berlin, Germany 52N32 13E25

Frankland regarded the transits of ponderous planets, like Uranus and Neptune, as being similar in effect to the secondary progressions of the faster planets. In addition, Frankland quickly estimated the future aspects of Uranus and Neptune to their natal positions. Uranus spends about 7 years in each sign, and Neptune about 14 years in each sign; that is, Neptune travels at about half the rate of Uranus.

Frankland would have glanced at this birth chart and immediately estimated that Dorit might face great danger in her late teens or early 20s, especially around age 21. How would he have come to this conclusion? By doing the following calculations in his head.

Natal Uranus at about 25° Taurus will square its birth position by transit when Dorit is around 21 years old. Because Uranus travels about 4° per year, it will square natal Jupiter around age 20 and will square natal Saturn and oppose natal Mars around age 19.

About the same time that Uranus squares its birth position, natal Neptune will be roughly 45° from its birth position and will be in Scorpio, opposing the stellium in Taurus.

Natal Saturn, which takes 29 years to circle the entire zodiac, will oppose its birth position in about 14.5 years and will make a superior square to its natal position and also conjoin natal Mars around age 21 or 22.

Dorit's *Point of Life* at age 20 will be at 25° 43' Gemini, in square to natal Neptune in Virgo and in semisextile to both Uranus in Taurus and Chiron in Cancer. The natal Sun/Mars and Sun/Saturn midpoints are also involved in this planetary picture.

Frankland used the *4/7° per year Age Point* to symbolically direct the chart. At age 21, the *4/7° measure* is 12° (4 × 21 / 7 equals 12), which would direct the natal Sun to conjoin Saturn shortly before she turned 21 years of age. This symbolic direction of natal Sun to Saturn would simultaneously activate both natal Sun square Pluto and natal Saturn square Mars during the first few months of 1962.

Although Frankland does not mention which reference books he kept handy during his consultations, he almost certainly had access to an ephemeris and a list of eclipses, such as the one found in Sepharial's *Astrology: How to Make and Read Your Own Horoscope*, first published in 1904 and reissued in 1920 in a revised and expanded edition.

Frankland would have noticed the Total Solar Eclipse of 5 February 1962 at 15° 43' Aquarius, almost exactly conjunct Dorit's natal Mars at 15° 49' Aquarius and square to natal Saturn in the noon birth chart. She was shot to death two weeks later on 19 February 1962 at 20.82 years of age, a couple of months before her next birthday.

In estimating the approximate age at which the slow planets form hard aspects to their birth positions, Frankland kept the cycles of the planets in mind, as in the following table based on NASA's data about tropical planetary orbits (Williams 2023).

TROPICAL PLANETARY ORBITS, SQUARES, AND OPPOSITIONS				
	Tropical Orbit (Years)	First Square	Opposition	Superior Square
Neptune *Rounded:*	163.73 *164*	40.93 *41*	81.86 *82*	122.79 *123*
Uranus *Rounded:*	83.75 *84*	20.94 *21*	41.88 *42*	62.82 *63*
Saturn *Rounded:*	29.42 *29*	7.36 *7*	14.72 *15*	22.08 *22*
Jupiter *Rounded:*	11.86 *12*	2.97 *3*	5.94 *6*	8.91 *9*

Chapter 9
AGE ALONG THE ZODIAC (AGE POINT)

One of Frankland's simplest and most basic symbolic measures is the *Age along the Zodiac*, which I sometimes refer to as the *Age Point*. The *Age along the Zodiac* simply converts the native's age into degrees, *at a rate of 1° for each year of life*, and adds that number to 0° Aries. For example:

Age 5 corresponds to 5° Aries.

Age 27 corresponds to 27° Aries.

Age 30 corresponds to 0° Taurus.

Age 45 corresponds to 15° Taurus.

Age 61 corresponds to 1° Gemini.

Age 77 ¾ corresponds to 17° 45' Gemini.

Age 90 corresponds to 0° Cancer.

And so on.

I don't know whether this measure was Frankland's own idea or he borrowed it from the astrological literature. For example, Abu Ma'shar in the ninth century directed natal charts by 1° per year, and in the eleventh century astrologer Haly Abenragel (Abū l-Ḥasan 'Alī ibn Abī l-Rijāl al-Shaybani) included a chapter on *atacirs* in his *Complete Book on the Judgment of the Stars*, in which he describes a predictive method using primary directions to advance the five hylegiacal points at the rate of 1° per year, measured in right or oblique ascension, depending on whether they are being directed to the meridian or the horizon. In the same chapter, Abenragel also describes *profections*, which advance the entire chart at the uniform rate of one 30° zodiacal sign per each year of life, to be used in combination with forecasting from solar returns.

A Case from Haly Abenragel: Death by Hanging at Age 52

Haly Abenragel mentions several case examples of symbolic directions (*atacirs*) at a rate of 1° per year. For example, in chapter 7, book 4, of his *Complete Book on the Judgment of the Stars*, he describes the chart of a man who died by hanging: "the hyleg was the Sun in the 9th house and, when the atacir of the MC arrived at the opposition of Mars, he was hanged and died" (Abenragel 1485; my translation of the Castilian text).

Based on Haly's comments, I did some astrological sleuthing to reconstruct the birth chart of this hanged man based on the following assumptions.

The hanged man was most likely a contemporary of Haly in Tunisia in the late tenth and early eleventh centuries. Haly served as court astrologer to a Tunisian prince during the first half of the eleventh century. Historians date Haly's death to a time after 1037 or 1040 CE.

For the Sun to act as hyleg, it must have been dignified in either Aries or Leo.

For the opposition of Mars to symbolize death by hanging, Mars must have been debilitated and in an unfortunate place in the chart.

For the directed MC to oppose Mars, it had to be directed through the 10th, 11th, and 12th houses toward the Ascendant, which would correspond to the periods of youth, young adulthood, and middle adulthood, respectively. Haly most likely used Alcabitius houses.

It is unlikely that the man was hanged as a youth, while the MC was progressing through the 10th house, with Mars in the 4th house. It is also unlikely that Mars was in the 5th house of good fortune when he died violently.

More likely is that he was hanged when the directed MC was passing through the 12th house of misfortune, confinement, and undoing, with Mars in the 6th house of bad fortune and bodily harm.

If the Sun were in Aries, then Taurus would be on the MC and Capricorn on the 6th house cusp, a sign in which Mars is exalted. Hence, Mars was probably not in Capricorn.

If the Sun were in Leo, Virgo would be on the MC and Taurus on the 6th house cusp, a sign in which Mars is debilitated.

Thus, the chart described by Haly Abenragel most likely has Virgo on the MC, the Sun in Leo in the 9th house as hyleg, and Mars debilitated in Taurus in the 6th house and in square aspect to the Sun. Under these conditions, the directed MC arriving at the opposition of Mars could symbolize a violent death.

With Virgo on the MC and Scorpio on the 12th house cusp, the man must have been middle-aged at the time of his demise, and therefore must have been born in the latter part of the tenth century.

Using Solar Fire's "electional search," I looked for birth dates between 960 CE and 1010 CE when the Sun was in Leo, the MC in Virgo, and Mars in Taurus.

The search produced a small number of charts, from which I selected the one that has Mars on the cusp of the 6th house and the Sun closely square Mars. My reasoning is that the directed MC arriving at the 12th house cusp would simultaneously activate both the 12th and 6th houses and also the opposition from debilitated Mars, the out-of-sect malefic, in Taurus (the neck)—a combination that could readily symbolize death by hanging.

The chart shown here meets all these criteria and is probably close to the actual date of the nativity that Haly was describing (chart 22).

In this chart, the Sun is dignified in Leo, occupies the 9th house, and trines the Ascendant, meeting criteria for being hyleg. Mars conjoins the cusp of the 6th Alcabitius house. Directed Mars will oppose the MC degree of 12° 56' Virgo in an arc of 54° 52' along the *ecliptic*. However, Haly was demonstrating the *atacir* that *1° along the equator equals 1 year of life*, so we must find the difference in right ascension between the position of Mars (36° 07' R.A.) and that of the IC (344° 17' R.A.), which turns out to be 51° 50' of *equatorial* arc. Thus, this man must have been hanged around age 52 in the year 1032 CE.

Using his symbolic directions measured along the ecliptic, Frankland would immediately have noticed that in his 50s, this man was in the Mars period (ages 41–56) of Ptolemy's *seven ages of man*. Beginning with the overall pattern or plan of the chart, he would have focused on the Grand Cross among the fixed signs, with Mars (the timelord of this period) debilitated in Taurus, intensified by the North Node of the Moon, and conjunct the cusp of the 6th house of bodily harm, from which it makes a square aspect to the Sun (the life force). Thus, this native's middle age years carried the risk of serious illness or bodily harm.

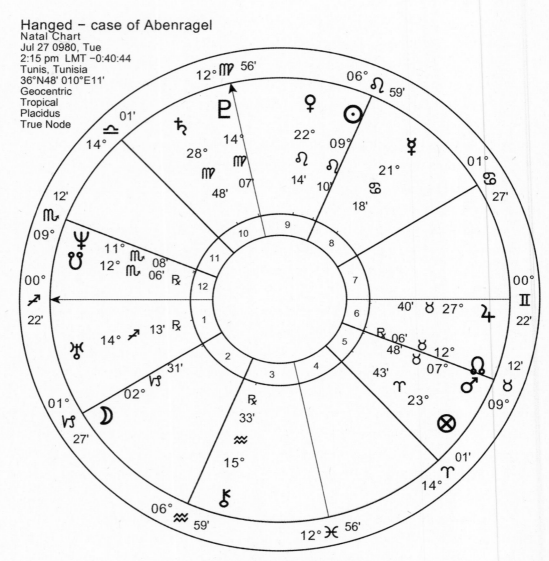

Hanged – case of Abenragel
Natal Chart
Jul 27 0980, Tue
2:15 pm LMT −0:40:44
Tunis, Tunisia
36°N48' 010°E11'
Geocentric
Tropical
Placidus
True Node

Chart 22: Death by Hanging
27 July 980, 2:15 p.m. LMT, Tunis, Tunisia, 36N48 10E11

Had Frankland been aware of the existence of Pluto, he also would have noticed that it is the most angular planet in the chart and therefore highly significant. Pluto closely conjoins the MC and tightly squares Uranus in the 1st house.

If we apply Frankland's rate of 1° per year of life, added to 0° Aries, to calculate his *Age along the Zodiac*, we find that at age 52 the *Age Point* at 22° Taurus makes a partile square from the 6th house to natal Venus, which rules the cusp of the 6th house of bodily injury. Taurus on the cusp of the 6th house symbolizes the neck and throat area.

If we calculate Frankland's *Point of Life* (one 30° zodiacal sign per each 7 years of life), at age 52 we arrive at 12° 51' of Scorpio, which lies in the 12th house of undoing, conjoins natal Neptune and the South Lunar Node in the 12th house, and applies to square natal Chiron in Aquarius.

If we calculate Frankland's *4/7° measure* at age 52, we arrive at 29° 43' Aries, which is 135° (sesquisquare) from Uranus in Sagittarius in the 1st house, activating the natal Uranus-Pluto square.

All three of Frankland's measures stimulate the stressful Grand Cross formed by the planets and sensitive points in the fixed signs Taurus, Leo, Scorpio, and Aquarius, and also involve the unfortunate 6th and 12th houses.

A Tragic Day in the Life of the Pope

Pope Francis was born on 17 December 1936 at 21:00 in Buenos Aires, Argentina, Rodden Rating AA (chart 23).

On 19 August 2014, the pope's nephew Emanuel Horacio Bergoglio had a tragic car accident in which the pope's 8-month-old and 2-year-old grandnephews and their mother were killed. The car Emanuel was driving crashed into a truck on the highway. Pope Francis was 77¾ years old at the time. His *Age along the Zodiac*, therefore, was at 17° 45' Gemini. Let's look at his birth chart, with Placidus houses, as used by Frankland.

At the time of the family tragedy, Pope Francis's *Age along the Zodiac* was closely conjunct his natal 12th house cusp of sorrow and misfortune. At the same time, it was departing from a square to natal Saturn in the 8th house of death and applying to square Neptune in Virgo in the 2nd house. Saturn was opposite to Neptune in the zodiac, and their midpoint was at 17° 44' Gemini.

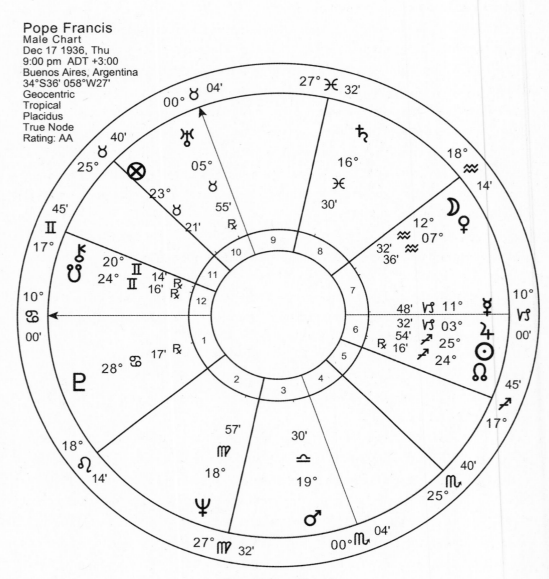

Pope Francis
Male Chart
Dec 17 1936, Thu
9:00 pm ADT +3:00
Buenos Aires, Argentina
34°S36' 058°W27'
Geocentric
Tropical
Placidus
True Node
Rating: AA

Chart 23: Pope Francis
17 December 1936, 9:00 p.m. ADT, Buenos Aires, Argentina, 34S36 58W27

The driver of the car was the pope's nephew. Siblings are signified by the 3rd house, and the children of siblings (nephews) by the derived 5th from the radical 3rd, which is the radical 7th house, in this case ruled by Saturn. The pope's *Age Point* at 77.75 years of age was intensifying the natal Saturn-Neptune opposition, which was in square aspect to the natal 12th house cusp, thus carrying the natal promise of loss or grief involving the child of a sibling because Saturn rules Capricorn on the cusp of the 7th house of nephews.

Traditionally, Saturn has an orb of 9°, and in the pope's chart, Saturn is part of a Grand Cross formation. In other words, natal Saturn in Pisces in the 8th house squares the cluster consisting of the 12th house cusp/Chiron/South Lunar Node in Gemini, which in turn squares natal Neptune in Virgo in the 2nd house, which squares the Sun-North Lunar Node conjunction in Sagittarius in the 6th house, forming a Grand Cross. Frankland repeatedly found that when an astrological direction interacts with any of the points (or midpoints) of a natal Grand Cross, "a most drastic or eventful time" is indicated.

Having identified the natal factors being accented by his symbolic measures, Frankland would then have looked for real-time-based astrological influences. In this case, the following were in effect at the time of the accident:

- Pluto was transiting 11° Capricorn, conjunct the pope's natal Mercury, ruler of his 3rd house and placed in the 7th house of nephews. The 3rd house is the nephew's turned 9th house of local travel.
- Chiron was transiting conjunct the pope's natal Saturn in 16° Pisces.
- The secondary progressed Moon was at 17° Sagittarius, opposite the Saturn/Neptune midpoint.
- The Partial Solar Eclipse of 23 October 2014 was at 0° 24' Scorpio, conjunct the pope's IC.

Princess Diana's Tragic Accident

Lady Diana Spencer was born on 1 July 1961 at 7:45 p.m. BST in Sandringham, England (chart 24), and she died from the injuries sustained in a car crash at age 36.168 on 31 August 1997 in Paris, France. How would Frankland have viewed her chart?

Frankland would have begun his analysis by studying the big picture and the overall patterns in the chart. In the case of Princess Diana, the most outstanding features are a stellium of planets in the 2nd house in opposition to a stellium in the 8th house. This cluster of oppositions includes the 8th-ruler Moon opposing Uranus, a symbol of sudden and unexpected events, in the 8th house. The Moon-Uranus opposition is involved in a close T-square with Venus, ruler of the 5th house of love affairs and the 10th house of public standing. In addition, there is a whole-sign Grand Cross involving the fixed signs (Taurus, Leo, Scorpio, and Aquarius). This fixed Grand Cross further calls our attention because of the presence of the Ascendant-ruler Jupiter at 5° 05' Rx of the fixed sign Aquarius.

Frankland would have cautioned Princess Diana that the period during which the opposing clusters of planets in the 2nd and 8th houses became stimulated by directions or transits would be an intensely stressful, eventful, and difficult time. Specifically, the *Point of Life* would activate Jupiter in 5° Aquarius by opposition around age 29, close to her Saturn return, and would continue to stimulate the two opposing stelliums until about age 36½, when the *Point of Life* would reach the final Pluto-Chiron opposition in 6° Virgo-Pisces.

Having identified the period from ages 29 to 36½ as quite active and potentially problematic, Frankland would have considered the *Age along the Zodiac*, or *Age Point*, which ranges from 29° Aries to 6½° Taurus during this period. At age 29, Diana's *Age Point* squares the Placidus 8th house cusp, initiating concerns about 8th house issues between ages 29 and 36½.

At age 31, the *Age Point* at 1° Taurus activates Mars, the contrary-to-sect malefic, in the 8th house by a trine aspect. Natally, Mars conjoins Pluto and squares the cusp of the Placidus 12th house.

At age 35, the *Age Point* at 5° Taurus activates Jupiter in the 2nd house, the ruler of the 1st and 12th houses, by square aspect and thereby stimulates the natal Jupiter-Neptune square.

Finally, at age 36, the *Age Point* at 6° Taurus activates Pluto in the 8th house by trine, and in doing so activates the natal Pluto-Chiron opposition as well as the natal Mars-Pluto conjunction.

Frankland regarded major transits as "excitants" and would have been especially concerned about natal Pluto at age 36, because a Partial Solar Eclipse occurred on 2 September 1997 at 9° 34' Virgo within orb of Pluto's birth position in the 8th house. Furthermore, the symbolic direction of natal Mercury by the arc of the *Age Point*, 36° at age 36, places directed Mercury at 9° 12' Virgo when Diana turned 36 years old, in partile conjunction with the Partial Solar Eclipse, which took place just three days after her fatal accident.

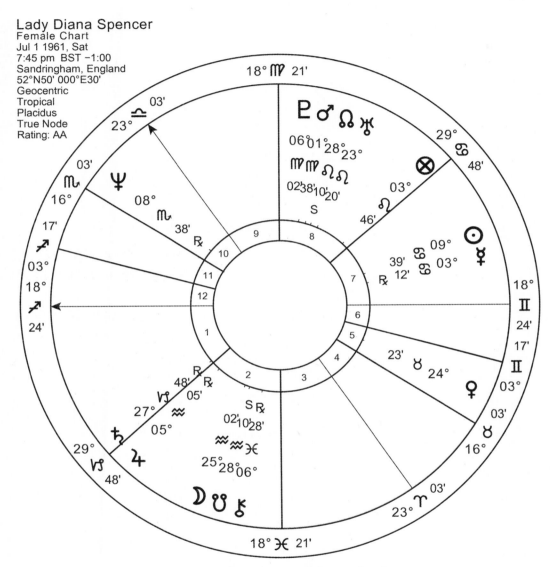

Chart 24: Diana Spencer, Princess of Wales
1 July 1961, Sandringham, England, 52N50 0E30

Considering the *4/7° Age along the Zodiac* measure:

At age 35, the *4/7° Age Point* lies at 20° Aries.

At age 36, the *4/7° Age Point* lies at 20° 27' Aries.

Neither of these makes a direct hit to any planet or point in Diana's chart, but if we consider the 90° midpoint modal sort of her natal chart,[1] the following active midpoints are symbolically consistent with a serious accident:

- Uranus/Ascendant midpoint at 20° 52' Libra
- Mercury/Neptune midpoint at 20° 55' cardinal
- Pluto at 21° 02' cardinal (sesquiquadrate to the *4/7° Age Point*)
- Pluto/Chiron midpoint at 21° 15' cardinal (sesquiquadrate to the *4/7° Age Point*)

An investigation found that the driver of Diana's vehicle was traveling (Mercury) at high speeds under the influence of alcohol and prescription drugs (Neptune) at the time of the fatal accident (Uranus, Pluto, Chiron).

The *4/7° Age along the Zodiac* on the day of Diana's demise at age 36.168 was at 20° 40' Aries (36.168 × 4/7 = 20.667). The natal Ascendant represents her body and life force. Directing the Ascendant by this arc, we arrive at a directed Ascendant of 9° 04' Capricorn, which closely opposes her natal Sun and also activates the following natal midpoints by 8th harmonic aspects within a 1° orb in the midpoint modal sort:

- Saturn/Ascendant midpoint at 8° 06' Capricorn
- Uranus at 8° 20' cardinal
- Venus/Uranus midpoint at 8° 52' Cancer
- Directed Ascendant at 9° 04' Capricorn
- Moon/Uranus midpoint at 9° 11' cardinal
- Venus at 9° 23' cardinal

---

1. By way of review, the midpoint modal sort (aka 90° midpoint sort) groups together the zodiac signs by modality (cardinal, fixed, mutable). Thus, it compresses the 360° dial into 90°. All four signs of each modality are stacked upon one another. In doing so, it groups together the POINTS, PLANETS, and MIDPOINTS that are in conjunction, square, or opposition to one other. The modal sort is especially useful for finding any 8th harmonic aspects (SEMISQUARE or SESQUISQUARE) to midpoints in a chart. For example, in Diana's chart, her natal Uranus lies at 23° 20' Leo (fixed), which makes a hard minor aspect to 8° 20' of the cardinal signs, so that Uranus at 8° 20' cardinal appears in her modal sort.

- Sun at 9° 39' Cancer
- Moon/Venus midpoint at 9° 43' Aries
- Moon at 10° 02' cardinal

The natal T-square involving the 8th-ruler Moon, Uranus in the 8th house, and Venus in the 5th house squaring the natal Moon-Uranus opposition is a central feature of this group of midpoints. Unlike Frankland, who advocated the use of midpoints but was limited in his ability to calculate them rapidly, astrologers today have the advantage of using computer software that can show us midpoints at a glance and allow a quick assessment of chart factors that are being activated by various symbolic directions.

The Passing of Queen Elizabeth II

Queen Elizabeth II was born in London on 21 April 1926 at 2:40 a.m. GDT, Rodden Rating AA (chart 25). She became queen at age 25 upon the death of her father, King George VI, on 6 February 1952. The queen's health issues were prominent in the news during 2021–22, and several commentators wondered whether she would meet her end at age 96 in 2022.

In fact, Elizabeth II died surrounded by family at Balmoral Castle on the afternoon of 8 September 2022, some 140 days after her April 21st birthday. In an amazing astrological "coincidence," the secondary progressed Moon of her son Charles was at 21° 22' Capricorn, exactly conjunct the queen's natal Ascendant, at the time of her demise, which occasioned his ascension to the throne. Queen Elizabeth II was about 96.4 years old at the time of her passing.

If Frankland had been consulted about the queen in early 2022, what might he have forecast for the coming year?

As usual, Frankland would have begun by looking for significant patterns in the birth chart. Queen Elizabeth II has a notably angular Saturn Rx conjunct the MC and in a T-square formation with Mars and Jupiter in Aquarius and the Moon and Neptune in Leo. This is an example of Marc Edmund Jones's *Bucket* shape chart pattern, with Saturn at the "handle" as the high-focus planet. Saturn, the malefic contrary-to-sect in this night chart, is also the Ptolemaic timelord of the *seven ages of man* during this period of the queen's life (ages 68 onward). Natives with a dominant Saturn are typically responsible, disciplined, systematic, reality-oriented, conscientious, status-conscious, and focused on societal norms and long-term accomplishments.

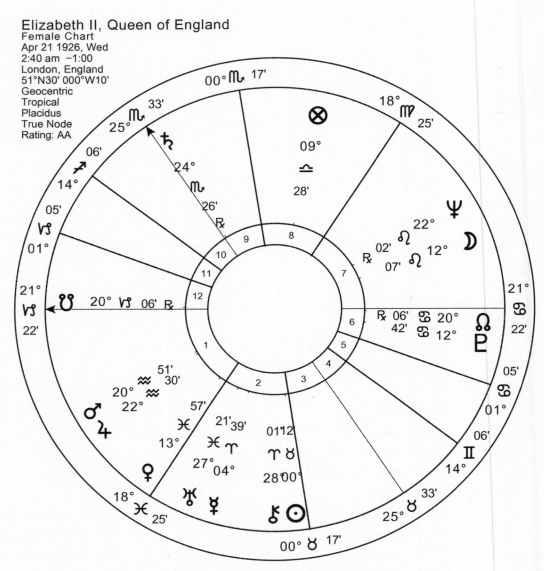

Elizabeth II, Queen of England
Female Chart
Apr 21 1926, Wed
2:40 am −1:00
London, England
51°N30' 000°W10'
Geocentric
Tropical
Placidus
True Node
Rating: AA

Chart 25: Elizabeth II, Queen of England
21 April 1926, 2:40 a.m. GDT, London, England, 51N30 0W10

Frankland paid close attention to eclipses and would have noticed immediately that the Total Lunar Eclipse at 25° 16' Taurus on 16 May 2022 would fall almost exactly opposite the queen's natal Saturn and conjunct the 4ᵗʰ house cusp of endings, about a month before her birthday. Given the fact that Saturn, the contrary-to-sect malefic, rules both her natal Ascendant (body and life force) and her 12ᵗʰ house of undoing, this Lunar Eclipse is of ominous portent.

Do any of Frankland's symbolic measures highlight this difficult natal T-square configuration?

The *Point of Life* at age 96 ranges from about 21.5° to 26° of Taurus, activating Queen Elizabeth's natal Saturn at 24° 26' Scorpio Rx by opposition and conjoining the cusp of her 4ᵗʰ house of endings. On the day of her passing, 8 September 2022, the *Point of Life* was at 23° 04' Taurus, within orb of conjoining natal Saturn and squaring natal Neptune, Mars, and Jupiter. In the midpoint modal sort, this *Point of Life* activates the following fixed midpoints: Mars/Saturn at 22° 39' fixed, Mars/MC at 23° 12', Saturn/Neptune at 23° 14' fixed, Jupiter/Saturn at 23° 28' fixed, and Mercury/Pluto at 23° 41' fixed. The Saturn/Neptune midpoint especially is associated with the dissolution of structure, organic decomposition, and the unhampered progress of a disease. In the queen's 2022 solar return for London (chart 26), this *Point of Life* (at 23° 04' Taurus in the 12ᵗʰ house of the return) squares return Saturn at 23° 36' Aquarius, with Saturn ruling the 8ᵗʰ house of death in the solar return chart.

The queen's *Age along the Zodiac* at age 96 lies at 6° Cancer, which does not closely aspect any natal planet or house cusp in her chart but does conjoin significant cardinal midpoints in her midpoint modal sort. Specifically, natal Mars lies at 5° 51' cardinal, the Mars/Chiron midpoint at 5° 59' Aries, and Mars/Neptune at 6° 27' Aries. The Mars/Neptune midpoint is associated with weakness, lack of energy, and poor health.

The queen's *4/7 Age along the Zodiac* at age 96 lies at 24° 51' Taurus, also activating her natal Saturn at 24° 26' Scorpio Rx by opposition and conjoining the cusp of her 4ᵗʰ house of final endings.

Do the queen's Birth Numbers correlate with her age at the time of her passing?

Born 21-04-1926, Queen Elizabeth's *Single Digits Birth Number* is 2 + 1 + 4 + 1 + 9 + 2 + 6 = **25**, which reduces to **7**.

Her *Additional Single Digits Birth Number* is found by adding **25** to the year of birth, 25 + 1926 = 1951, and reducing the result, 1 + 9 + 5 + 1 = **16**, which further reduces to **7**. Then we add together 25 + 16 + 7 = **48** as her *Additional Single Digits Birth Number*, which further reduces to **12** and **3**.

The queen's *Double Digits Birth Number* is 21 + 4 + 1 + 9 + 2 + 6 = **43**, which reduces to **7**.

Her *Additional Double Digits Birth Number* is found by adding **43** to the year of birth, 43 + 1926 = 1969, and reducing the result, 1 + 9 + 6 + 9 = **25**, which further reduces to **7**. Then we add together 43 + 25 + 7 = **75** as her *Additional Double Digits Birth Number*, which further reduces to **12** and **3**.

Combinations of these Birth Numbers (3, 7, 12, 16, 25, 43, 48, 73) with each other or with the queen's day of birth (the 21st of April) indicate potential significant years in her life.

In this case, her *Additional Double Digits Birth Number*, **75**, added to her day of birth, **21**, gives a total of **96** (75 + 21 = 96), her age at the time of her passing.

Of course, Birth Numbers are not significant in and of themselves, but they become important when other astrological factors give prominence to a particular year of life. In this case, the Lunar Eclipse on 16 May 2022 falling on the IC opposite natal Saturn was a powerful "excitant." Frankland also paid attention to transiting stations of planets closely "hitting" natal positions by bodily conjunction or aspect to another planet. In 2022 the following stations of transiting planets "excited" the queen's natal placements, especially her natal T-square:

- Transiting Pluto at 28° 35' Capricorn SRx on 29 April 2022 squares natal Chiron at 28° 01' Aries.

- Transiting Saturn at 25° 15' Aquarius SRx on 4 June 2022 squares natal Saturn at 24° 26' Scorpio Rx and the natal IC at 25° 33' Taurus.

- Transiting Neptune at 25° 26 Pisces SRx on 28 June 2022 trines natal Saturn and the natal MC.

- Transiting Uranus at 18° 55' Taurus SRx on 24 August 2022 squares natal Mars at 20° 51' Aquarius.

- Transiting Neptune at 22° 38' Pisces SD on 4 December 2022 makes a quincunx to natal Neptune at 22° 02' Leo Rx in the 8th house.

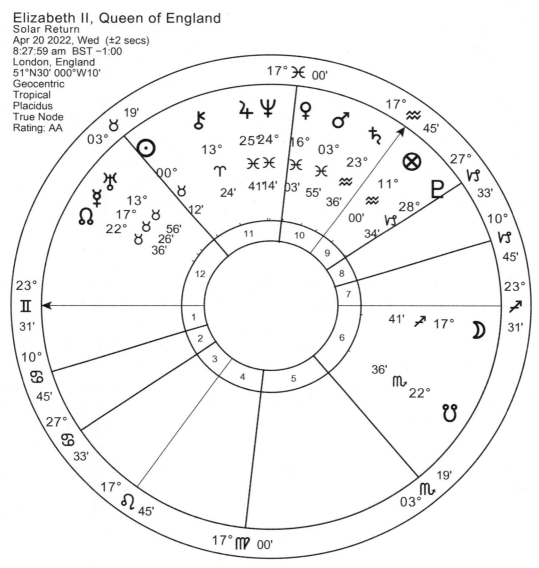

Chart 26: Elizabeth II, Queen of England, Solar Return 2022
20 April 2022, 8:27:59 a.m. BST, London, England, 51N30 0W10

Finally, the dominant primary direction of 2022 (calculated by the method of Placidus semi-arc with 0° latitude at the Naibod rate) was the square of Saturn to its natal position by primary motion, which perfected on 28 June 2022 well within orb of her demise in September. Saturn is especially prominent at age 96 because it is the timelord of this Ptolemaic period of the queen's life, is the apex of her natal T-square and conjoins the MC of her birth chart, and is the most elevated and angular planet and lies "at the bendings" (in square to the lunar nodes) in the 2022 solar return chart. Frankland notes that astrological influences have added weight and produce more profound effects during years that coincide with important totals related to the Birth Numbers. Thus, in 2022, primary directed Saturn square natal Saturn coincided with her Birth Number totals and was profoundly influential, presaging her demise at age 96.

Novelist Mary Ann Evans (aka George Eliot)

George Eliot, one of England's most notable novelists of the nineteenth century, was born Mary Ann Evans on 22 November 1819 at 5:00 a.m. LMT in Nuneaton, England, Rodden Rating AA (chart 27). A brilliant woman and gifted author, she adopted the pen name George Eliot for her works of fiction to distinguish them from her scholarly writings and her translations of German philosophical and theological texts. Her first major scholarly work was the English translation of David Friedrich Strauss's provocative *Das Leben Jesu kritisch bearbeitet* (*The Life of Jesus, Critically Examined*, 1846), which caused a sensation in both Germany and England because David Strauss argued that miracles attributed to Jesus in the Bible were nothing more than embellished fictional accounts with little basis in fact, designed to create the myth of godlike powers. To the great dismay of her father, Eliot's scholarly work caused her to question her own Anglican religious upbringing and to view herself as an atheist in her early 20s.

Eliot's mother died in February 1836 when Mary Ann was 16 years old. When she questioned her Christian religious teachings in her early 20s, her father apparently threatened to kick her out of the house, but to appease him she continued to attend church services and to care for him at home until his death in 1849, when she was 30 years old. Eliot's father also apparently believed that his daughter was not physically attractive enough to secure a husband, and so, recognizing her keen intelligence and fondness for learning, he sought to provide her with the best education and access to books that he could afford.

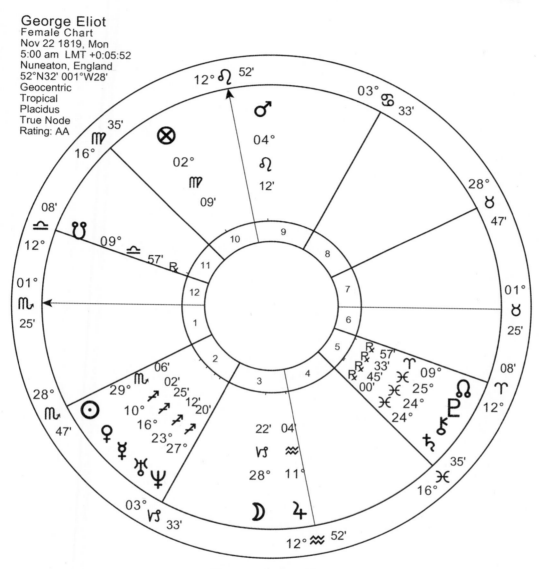

Chart 27: George Eliot
22 November 1819, 5:00 a.m. LMT, Nuneaton, England, 52N32 1W28

In 1850 Eliot moved to London to pursue her goal of becoming a writer. The following year she met the well-known philosopher and critic George Henry Lewes, and by 1854 (at age 34) she and Lewes decided to openly live together, a scandalous act in Victorian society. She and Lewes lived together "out of wedlock" until his death on 28 November 1878, when Mary Ann was 59 years old. Two years later, on 16 May 1880, she married John Cross, 20 years her junior. The newlyweds honeymooned in Venice, where John Cross allegedly jumped from the hotel balcony into the Grand Canal, which he survived. They returned to England, where Mary Ann developed a throat infection, which, coupled with her chronic kidney disease, eventuated in her death on 22 December 1880 at the age of 61.082 years.

Frankland would have begun by assessing the overall patterns in Eliot's chart. Like Queen Elizabeth II, George Eliot has a general Bucket shape chart but with Mars in Leo in the 9th house as her "handle," or high-focus planet. With Ascendant-ruler Mars in Leo, she is likely to express herself in a dramatic, independent, contentious, and self-assured manner. In the 9th house, the energy signified by Mars is directed into higher learning, philosophy, religion, travel, foreign interests, linguistic pursuits, translation, writing, publishing, social justice, etc.

There are two stelliums in mutable signs, Sagittarius and Pisces, disposed by Jupiter and in square to each other. The dispositor Jupiter lies in Aquarius tightly conjunct the IC as her most angular planet. Jupiter opposes the "handle" planet Mars and rules Sagittarius in her 2nd house of income and Pisces on the cusp of her 5th house of creative endeavors.

This chart also contains what modern astrologers call a Kite pattern. Specifically, Jupiter opposes Mars, Jupiter sextiles both Venus and Rahu (the North Lunar Node), and Mars trines both Venus and Rahu. As the focal planet of this Kite pattern, Jupiter points to an area where the native can channel the talents symbolized by the Grand Trine (in this case, Mars trine Venus trine Rahu). Jupiter lies at the end of the 3rd house of communication and rules the 5th house of creative activity.

In addition, the tension inherent in the Mars-Jupiter opposition (between the 9th and 3rd houses) can be productively directed to planets in sextile to Jupiter, namely, Venus in the 2nd house and Rahu in the 5th house. The planet Venus is conjunct Mercury (writing), which closely squares the 5th house cusp of creativity. The planet Mars disposes the

North Lunar Node in the 5th house and occupies the 9th house of religion, philosophy, languages, and publishing, from which it opposes Jupiter, the focal planet of the Kite pattern. The Capricorn Moon, which rules the 9th house, applies to conjoin Jupiter in Aquarius, oppose Mars in Leo, and sextile the Scorpio Sun, ruler of the Midheaven.

Thus, George Eliot has a highly integrated natal chart. Citing the astrological literature, Celeste Teal explains in her book *Identifying Planetary Triggers* (2000) that natives who achieve great prominence, as opposed to more ordinary or less notable individuals, have birth charts in which "the planets form very tight aspects and nearly all are interwoven into one complex pattern … as if every fiber of the[ir] being has evolved to possess but one primary intention" (Teal 2000, 6).

Frankland cited the chart of George Eliot as a key example of the *Point of Life* indicating the year of death of the native, especially when hard aspects of Saturn or Uranus are involved. He noticed immediately that the two stelliums in mutable signs were in square aspect, the closest and most troublesome of which was the mutually applying square between Uranus at 23° 12' Sagittarius and Saturn at 24° 00' Pisces Rx. Seeing Jupiter as the dispositor of both stelliums on the IC, the 4th house cusp of final endings, he would have warned her of the risk of serious illness, injury, or death at age 61, when the *Point of Life* passes from 21° 26' to 25° 43' of Sagittarius, conjoining Uranus and activating its natal square with Saturn.

In addition, at age 61 the *Age along the Zodiac* lies at 1° Gemini in the 8th house of death and quincunx the natal Ascendant at 1° 25' Scorpio. Furthermore, at age 61 the *4/7 Age along the Zodiac measure* lies at $61 \times 4/7 = 34.857°$ from 0° Aries, which is 4° 51' Taurus, in square to Ascendant-ruler and 6th house ruler Mars (the body and its illnesses), which triggers the Bucket and Kite patterns into action.

Frankland's measures also highlight other important events in George Eliot's life. At age 16 when her mother died, Eliot's *Point of Life* was in the 8th house opposite natal Venus, a general symbol of important women in her life. At age 22, when she was studying and translating German philosophers and theologians, her *Point of Life* had just entered her 9th house of religion, languages, and philosophy. During this period, she rejected the dogmas of her early training in Christianity and espoused atheism. At age 34, when she and George Henry Lewes scandalously decided to live openly as an unwed couple in staid Victorian society, her *Age along the Zodiac* was at 4° Taurus squaring natal Mars in the 9th house, and her *Point of Life* was at about 26° Leo in the 10th house of public reputation and applying closely to trine natal Neptune, which is disposed by Jupiter, ruler of the Pisces 5th house cusp of romance. Modern astrologers often link Neptune to scandals and to euphoric romantic experiences. George Henry Lewes died when Eliot was 59 years old and her *Age along the Zodiac* was at 29° Taurus, exactly conjunct the cusp of the 8th house of death and opposite her natal Sun, which is a general signifier of the husband in a woman's chart.

Chapter 10
MIDPOINTS AND AREAS OF LIFE

In predictive work, Frankland begins by carefully studying the natal chart to determine the character of the native, the strengths and weaknesses of the natal planets, the houses that are most or least emphasized, and the regions of the birth chart that are influenced by major aspects and planetary configurations. When symbolic measures highlight such regions, operative influences can more easily stimulate the planetary aspects found there into manifestation. In this way, the natal promise gets fulfilled at various stages of life. The period of an area of life that is beneficial will be more favorable for the native and will reduce the severity of any adverse operative influence in effect at that time.

To quote Frankland in *Astrological Investigations* (1926), "By considering the age or period of life through which the Native is passing, when such [operative] Influences are directed, one can estimate the strength or weakness of the Native's position to receive such influences" (Frankland 1926, 57). In other words, the various areas of life, as indicated in the birth chart by significant planetary placements and configurations, will become sensitized by symbolic measures (Birth Numbers, *Point of Life, Age along the Zodiac*, etc.) during specific periods in the native's life span.

The more such areas of life are highlighted by Frankland's symbolic measures, the more likely and easily operative influences during those periods will result in the manifestation of the natal promise. Frankland summarizes this idea as follows: "The more points of importance there may be at a given age when Influences operate the more weighty their effect" (Frankland 1926, 59). In other words, the symbolic measures highlight, emphasize, sensitize, and intensify certain regions of the chart (areas of life), and the real-time-based operative influences trigger the natal promise of those "ripened" regions into manifestation.

Thus, before an operative influence is judged, it is imperative to examine carefully the area of life through which the native is passing. To illustrate, Frankland compares operative influences to strong winds, and areas of life to the place through which the wind is blowing. A powerful wind is more dangerous to a person standing on the edge of a cliff than to someone safely sheltered in a well-secured edifice.

Frankland relates his discussion of beneficial and adverse areas of life coinciding with various astrological operative influences to a passage from Matthew 13:3–9 in the New Testament (King James Version):

Behold, a sower went forth to sow;

And when he sowed, some seeds fell by the way side, and the fowls came and devoured them up:

Some fell upon stony places, where they had not much earth: and forthwith they sprung up, because they had no deepness of earth:

And when the sun was up, they were scorched; and because they had no root, they withered away.

And some fell among thorns; and the thorns sprung up, and choked them:

But others fell into good ground, and brought forth fruit, some an hundred-fold, some sixtyfold, some thirtyfold.

Who hath ears to hear, let him hear. (Matthew 13:3–9 KJV)

George Bernard Shaw and Areas of Life

Frankland begins his chapter about "areas of life" with a brief discussion of the chart of writer George Bernard Shaw, who was born on 26 July 1856 at 00:55 a.m. LMT in Dublin, Ireland, Rodden Rating A (birth data from the family bible, according to Astro.com). He has the Sun in Leo, Moon in Taurus, and Ascendant at 23° 36' Gemini (chart 28).

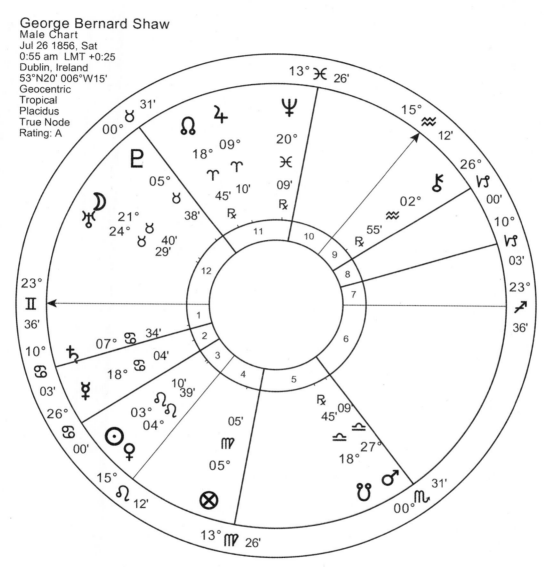

Chart 28: George Bernard Shaw
26 July 1856, 00:55 a.m. LMT, Dublin, Ireland, 53N20 6W15

Frankland begins by explaining that an adverse operative influence, which is active at the same time that the native is passing through a beneficial period or "area of life," will have a much milder impact than the same adverse influence acting during a stressful period or area of life. The *Point of Life* symbolic measure (one sign per 7 years equals 30° divided by 7 years, or 4.2857° per year—in fraction form, 4 2/7° per year) is a useful way to identify important areas of life. As the *Point of Life* advances around the birth chart, starting at 0° Aries, it will encounter the various planets and their aspects, highlighting areas that will be neutral, beneficial, or adverse to the native.

George Bernard Shaw at Age 23

For example, in George Bernard's chart, at age 23 his *Point of Life* was passing through the region from 8° 34' to 12° 51' Cancer. It was separating from a recent conjunction with natal Saturn and was in square to natal Jupiter, highlighting the stressful Saturn-square-Jupiter aspect in his birth chart—an area of life that is related to Saturn and Jupiter, the aspects they form with other planets, and the houses they occupy and rule. Saturn (restriction), in its fall in Cancer, rules the 9th house of publishing and forms a sextile with natal Pluto (intensity). Jupiter (expansion) rules and occupies his 11th house of hopes and ambitions and is the ruler, by exaltation, of Cancer on the 3rd house cusp of writing. In addition, Jupiter receives trines from natal Sun and Venus. During Shaw's early to mid-20s, he began to write several novels but was frustrated because more than half of his writing was rejected by publishers. According to Astro.com, "He and his mother moved to London in 1876 and he began writing a series of five novels, 1879–1883, of which only two were published" (Astro-Databank, "Shaw, George Bernard").

Operative influences during the period around age 23 included:

- Secondary progressed Sun in Leo was separating from a square to natal Uranus in Taurus.
- Secondary progressed Sun was approaching a sextile to natal Mars within two years. Mars rules the natal 6th house (illness, tedious labor) and the sign Aries, intercepted in the natal 11th house (hopes, ambitions, awards).
- Secondary progressed Saturn was separating from a square to natal Jupiter.
- Secondary progressed Jupiter was retrograde.

- Solar arc directed Ascendant was square the secondary progressed true lunar nodes.

Thus, the majority of operative influences were adverse and occurring during a stressful period or "area of life." The result was frustration in his literary endeavors.

George Bernard Shaw at Age 29

Things changed dramatically for Mr. Shaw at age 29 when his *Point of Life* traversed the region from 4° 17' to 8° 31' Leo, activating his natal Sun and Venus, which were at birth both applying to trine his natal Jupiter in Aries, thus intensifying this natal trine between benefics. With this favorable "area of life" symbolically intensified by his *Point of Life*, Shaw was hired as a reviewer for the *Pall Mall Gazette* and advanced professionally at this time.

Also in 1885, Shaw (age 29) met drama critic William Archer, who persuaded him to redirect his literary talents away from his unprofitable production of novels and instead devote himself to writing criticism of music, painting, and drama, at which he became immensely successful. At this time (1885, age 29), his secondary progressed Ascendant was exactly conjunct his natal Mercury (writing) in the 2nd house of income, and his progressed Mars (directed effort) was in trine to his progressed Midheaven. By Placidian primary direction, Neptune (music, theater) had advanced in the sky in the hours after birth to a position in sextile to that of natal Jupiter (fortune, expansion). Thus, a confluence of beneficial operative influences coincided with a favorable area of life when he established his reputation as a first-rate critic.

The Exaltations of Planets

A note about Mercury, the winged messenger of the gods, in Shaw's birth chart is in order. Mercury rules Shaw's Ascendant (his basic motivations in life) and his 5th house of creative endeavors. Natal Mercury closely squares the Moon's true nodes, a configuration called "*at the bendings*," which stresses issues signified by this planet in the life of the native. The winged planet occupies Cancer in the natal 2nd house of income. Cancer is found on the cusps of the 2nd (income) and 3rd (writing) houses. In addition, Cancer is the exaltation sign of Jupiter, and Mercury at 18° 04' Cancer lies quite close to the exaltation degree of Jupiter, which is the 15th degree of Cancer. Although Frankland doesn't emphasize them, the traditional exaltations of planets can be quite useful in chart delineation and predictive work. For reference, here is a list of exaltation degrees from the traditional literature of Western astrology. (This entire list of exaltations is from al-Biruni's *Book of Instruction in the Elements of the Art of Astrology*, section 443, page 258, of the 1934 translation by R. Ramsay Wright.) Note the difference between cardinal and ordinal numbers; for example, the 15th degree of Cancer spans the region from 14° 00' to 14° 59' of Cancer.

Sun: 19th degree of Aries (18° 00'–18° 59')
Moon: 3rd degree of Taurus (02° 00'–02° 59')
Mercury: 15th degree of Virgo (14° 00'–14° 59')
Venus: 27th degree of Pisces (26° 00'–26° 59')
Mars: 28th degree of Capricorn (27° 00'–27° 59')
Jupiter: 15th degree of Cancer (14° 00'–14° 59')
Saturn: 21st degree of Libra (20° 00'–20° 59')
North Lunar Node: 3rd degree of Gemini (I prefer to use the true lunar nodes.)
South Lunar Node: 3rd degree of Sagittarius

George Bernard Shaw Wins the 1925 Nobel Prize for Literature at Age 69

Oddly, Frankland, in his 1926 text *Astrological Investigations*, does not mention Shaw's 1925 Nobel Prize for Literature, which made me wonder whether his book went to press before the Nobel Prize was announced in November of 1926 or whether he was unable to find evidence for its occurrence in his new symbolic measures. Most likely Frankland's book was already printed by the time of the announcement.

In fact, on 11 November 1926, the Nobel committee announced that the 1925 Nobel Prize for Literature would go to George Bernard Shaw, for writing "which is marked by both idealism and humanity, its stimulating satire often being infused with a singular poetic beauty" (Nobel Prize Outreach AB 2023). Shaw, then 69 years old, was initially planning to refuse the prize, but his wife convinced him to accept it for the honor of Ireland. He compromised, deciding to accept the prize but to refuse the financial award, because "I can forgive Nobel for inventing dynamite, but only a fiend in human form could have invented the Nobel Prize" (National Gallery of Ireland). Shaw eventually directed the funds from the award into a literary project. Can we find evidence in Shaw's birth chart, using Frankland's symbolic measures, of such a major award at age 69?

Shaw's *Point of Life* at age 69 was passing through the final 4 2/7° of Capricorn. In doing so, it was intensifying the natal Placidus 9th house cusp of publishing and foreign interests as well at the square from natal Mars to the early degrees of the 9th house.

At age 69, Shaw's *Age along the Zodiac* (1° per each year of life) fell into 9° of Gemini, exactly sextile his natal Jupiter at 9° 10' Aries, with Jupiter ruling and occupying the 11th house of "friendship, trust, hope, confidence, the praise or disparaise of anyone" and the "favourites" of the king; also, "Jupiter doth especially rejoyce in this House" (Lilly 1647, 56). In addition, Jupiter receives favorable trines from the Sun and benefic Venus in the natal chart.

Regarding the *4/7° per year measure*, at age 69 we calculate it to be 69 × 4/7 equals 39.428°, or 39° 36'. Advancing from 0° Aries by this amount takes us to 9° 36' Taurus, which will exactly sextile the cusp of the 2nd house of income during the year. The Nobel Prize carried a sizable cash award.

As for operative influences, during this period there were several eclipses that hit key points in Shaw's birth chart:

- 8 February 1925—A Partial Lunar Eclipse at 19° 35' Leo closely trined his natal true lunar North Node.

- 20 July 1925—A Solar Annular Eclipse at 27° 36' Cancer conjoined the cusp of his 3rd house of writing and squared his natal Mars.

- 4 August 1925—A Partial Lunar Eclipse at 11° 30' Aquarius conjoined his MC and sextiled his natal Jupiter.

- 14 January 1926—A Total Solar Eclipse at 23° 21' Capricorn conjoined the cusp of his 9th house of publishing and foreign interests and trined his natal Moon and Uranus in Taurus.

- 28 January 1926—A Lunar Appulse Eclipse at 8° 06' Leo occurred in his natal 3rd house of writing and closely trined his natal Jupiter in Aries in the 11th house of "the praise or disparaise of anyone."

A Modern Example (Anonymous)

In the spring of 2022, I was discussing Frankland's work with a friend and fellow astrologer who asked me to demonstrate some of these "new measures" in his chart. He gave permission to use his birth chart in this book. To keep his information private, I will state only that when he turned 38 years old in early September of 2021, we apply Frankland's techniques to his chart (chart 29).

Looking for potentially difficult areas of life, we identified Mars in the 9th house widely square Saturn in the 12th house, with Mars being his out-of-sect malefic. When this Mars is activated, problems may arise.

In addition, natal Pluto in the 12th house conjunct Saturn across the sign boundary, with Saturn widely square Mars, looked like another potential problem area.

At age 38 (he had turned 38 about six months earlier), the *Age along the Zodiac* (1° for each year of life, starting at 0° Aries) would have been at 8° Taurus, which trines his natal Sun in the 10th house, indicating a period that favors career matters. My friend acknowledged that his professional life had been going well at that time.

Influenced by the findings of Alfred Witte of the Hamburg School, Frankland also stressed the importance of midpoints in astrological prediction. The Solar Fire program has a useful report called the "midpoint modal sort" based on modulus 90° with an orb of one degree. This report lists all the midpoints as they fall in sequence from 0° 0' to 29° 59' in each zodiac sign according to modality, that is, whether the sign is cardinal, fixed or mutable, and also lists the points that are in semisquare or sesquisquare to chart points and midpoints of the particular mode.

In other words, the midpoint modal sort allows the astrologer to find any of the eightfold or 8th harmonic aspects (conjunction, waxing and waning semisquares, waxing and waning squares, waxing and waning sesquiquadrates, and the opposition) to the midpoints in a chart. The modal sort is sometimes referred to as the cardinal/fixed/mutable sort. The 8th harmonic is related to concrete, tangible events.

As Harding and Harvey explain in *Working with Astrology* (1990):

We are looking for the actual midpoint between each pair of planets and then looking to see if that point is conjunct, semisquare, square, sesquiquadrate, or opposite any other planet. Any multiple of the 45° aspect, in fact, which will pull together the combined energies of the planets we find. (Harding and Harvey 1990, 21)

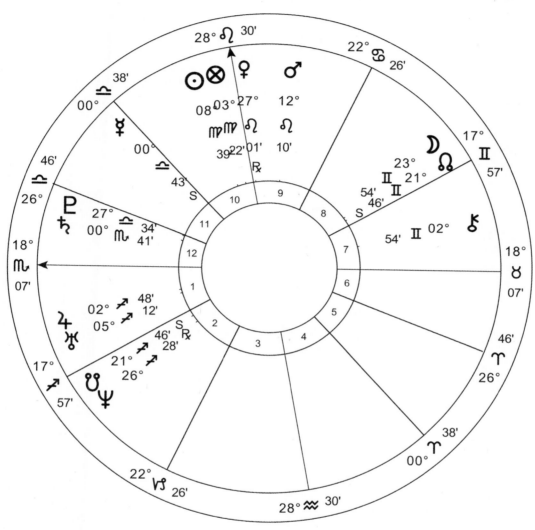

Chart 29: A Modern Example (Anonymous)

In Alfred Witte's experience, the significations of a planetary pair are likely to manifest when a transit, direction, or progression aspects that midpoint by 0°, 45°, 90°, 135°, or 180°.

Looking at the fixed midpoints within a tight orb around **8° Taurus** in the midpoint modal sort report for my friend's chart, we find the following the modulus angles of points in semisquare or sesquisquare to chart points and midpoints of the fixed mode:

- Moon/true North Lunar Node at 7° 50' fixed mode
- Pluto/Asc at 7° 50' fixed mode
- Moon at 8° 54' fixed mode

In this man's natal chart, the Moon and true North Node lie in the 8th house, the Moon rules the 9th house, and Pluto occupies the 12th house. Hence, this period could be somewhat problematic (8th and 12th house emphasis) and might involve long-distance travel (9th house).

Frankland also considered *4/7° Age along the Zodiac*, in which we take the age of the native, multiply by 4, and divide by 7. In this case, age 38 × 4 equals 153, which divided by 7 equals 21.71°, to be directed from 0° Aries. Thus, his *4/7° Age Point* at age 38 is 21.71° Aries, or **21° 43' Aries**, which closely aspects his natal true lunar nodes with favorable soft aspects. The midpoints closest to this value in Solar Fire's midpoint modal sort under cardinal signs are the following:

- Mercury/Mars 21° 27' cardinal
- Sun/Uranus 21° 56' cardinal
- Neptune/Asc 22° 17' cardinal

Mercury rules the 8th house and occupies the 11th house in this man's chart. The Sun rules and occupies the 10th house, again emphasizing career issues. Neptune is a mysterious planet having to do with fog, floods, and the oceans. In this chart, Neptune opposes the Moon in the unfortunate 8th house. During the summer of 2021, transiting Neptune was passing through 22° Pisces and closely squaring his natal true lunar nodes. In addition, on 19 August 2021, Uranus turned stationary retrograde at 14° 47' Taurus opposite his natal Mars, suggesting a sudden or unexpected disruptive event.

The **Point of Life** is based on a rate of 7 years per zodiac sign, measured from 0° Aries. In this chart, age 38 corresponds to 12° 51' Virgo, with each year of life encompassing 4 2/7° on the ecliptic.

The *Point of Life*, at 12° 51' Virgo, lies in the 10th house, again highlighting career issues. By aspect, the *Point of Life* is separating from a semisextile to Mars in the 9th house, which is a stressful configuration because the signs Virgo and Leo are in aversion.

Looking up the midpoints connected to 12° 51' Virgo in the midpoint modal sort under mutable signs, we find:

- Chiron/true North Node at 12° 20' mutable
- Neptune/MC at 12° 29' mutable
- Pluto at 12° 34' mutable
- True North Node/Part of Fortune at 12° 34' mutable

The involvement of the true lunar nodes suggests a fateful event that lies outside the native's control. The activation of Neptune and Pluto, with Pluto in the 12th house conjunct Saturn, is of concern. The *Point of Life* would have passed these positions earlier in the summer of 2021 because it arrived at 12° 51' Virgo on his birthday in September.

I asked my friend if the summer before his birthday in September of 2021 had been particularly stressful. He replied that he had been living in New Orleans at the time, where he experienced Hurricane Ida, which was quite destructive in Louisiana. The building he lived in suffered some damage, but he made it through okay. Not long afterward, he decided to relocate from New Orleans to a different part of the country. The symbolism of the destructive force of Pluto, the turbulent seas of Neptune, the fateful nodes of the Moon, the 8th, 9th, and 12th house emphasis, etc., seemed to fit what he had lived through.

Frankland viewed these symbolic measures as highlighting and intensifying certain areas of the chart (areas of life) that could then be triggered into manifestation by real-time-based directions, progressions, and transits. In this case, the station made by Uranus in August of 2021 opposite his natal Mars and the square of transiting Neptune to his natal true lunar nodes appeared to serve as triggers to the disruption in his life caused by Hurricane Ida.

Rudolph Valentino

One of Frankland's examples, which he used to illustrate areas of life, is that of actor Rudolph Valentino. According to Astro.com, Valentino's birth data are rated AA. He was born on 6 May 1895 at 15:00 MET (3:00 p.m. Standard Time) in Castellaneta, Italy (chart 30).

Frankland focuses on two significant events.

When Valentino was 11 years old, his father died of malaria. (I was unable to find the exact date of his father's death.)

Valentino himself died on 23 August 1926 at the age of 31, after a period of illness that began on 15 August 1926 with appendicitis and gastric ulcers, followed by surgery, peritonitis, pleurisy, and ultimately death. He was 31.3 years old at the time of his demise.

Valentino's Birth Numbers

Valentino was born on 6 May 1895. The date 6/5/1895 reduces to 6 + 5 + 1 + 8 + 9 + 5, or **34** as his *Single Digits Birth Number*, which further reduces to 3 + 4, or **7**.

Adding 1895 to his *Single Digits Birth Number* (34) gives 1895 + 34 = 1929, which reduces to 1 + 9 + 2 + 9, or 21, which further reduces to 2 + 1, or **3**. Thus, his *Additional Single Digits Birth Number* becomes 34 + 21 + 3 = **58**, which further reduces to 5 + 8, or **13**, and then to 1 + 3, or **4**.

Potentially significant ages based on these Birth Numbers are **34** and **58** and combinations of these numbers with each other or with their reduced forms, that is, **4, 7,** and **13.**

None of these ages appear to be directly relevant to the two events we are examining, namely, the death of Valentino's father at age 11 and his own demise at age 31. However, combinations of these numbers are revealing:

4 + 7 = 11, his age when his father died

58 + 7 − 34 = 31, his age at his own demise

34 − 12 = 21, his age when he achieved public notoriety

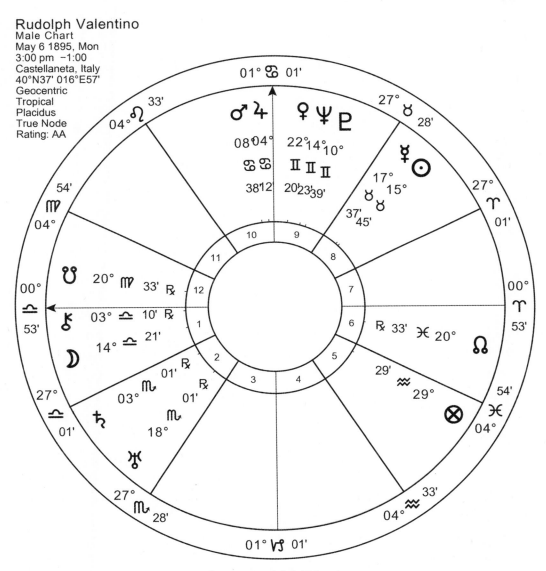

Chart 30: Rudolph Valentino
6 May 1895, 3:00 p.m. Standard Time, Castellaneta, Italy, 40N37 16E57

Age 21 was a highly significant year (May 1916–May 1917) for Valentino. Living in New York City at the time and working as a dancer, he achieved celebrity in the notorious Bianca de Saulles divorce trial. Bianca, having learned that her husband was involved in a love affair with Valentino's dance partner, cultivated a relationship with Valentino, who testified on Bianca's behalf. Valentino's testimony enraged Bianca's soon-to-be ex-husband, John de Saulles. After the divorce was finalized in December of 1916, de Saulles used his political connections to have Valentino arrested on trumped-up vice charges, together with a madam by the name of Mrs. Thyme.

At age 21, Valentino's *Point of Life* was traveling between 0° and 4° 17' Cancer, conjoining his natal MC and Jupiter (public status), squaring his natal Chiron on the Ascendant (being wounded), and semisquaring his natal Sun-Mercury conjunction in the 8th house, with Mercury ruling the 12th house of confinement.

Professionally, in 1916 the 21-year-old Valentino appeared as an actor in the serial *Patricia*, after which he decided to try his luck in Hollywood.

At age 11, when his father died, Valentino's *Point of Life* was traveling from 17° 08' to 21° 26' Taurus over the course of the year. During this period, his *Point of Life* conjoined natal Mercury in the 8th house of death and opposed natal Uranus in Scorpio.

In Valentino's birth chart, the 4th house is ruled by Saturn, signifying his father, and the 9th house (the derived 8th from the 4th) represents the death of the father. Valentino's 9th house has Taurus on the cusp and Venus as its ruler. Natal Venus receives a stressful quincunx from Uranus in Scorpio within about a 4° orb, symbolizing the unexpected or unusual loss of the father.

Valentino's primary directions at age 11 (Placidus semi-arc, Ptolemy key, zero latitude) connected Venus with Uranus. Specifically, on 1 January 1907, primary directed Uranus perfected a sesquisquare to natal Venus, ruler of the father's 8th house of death in Valentino's chart. Thus, Uranus was stimulated by the symbolic *Point of Life* at this age, and Uranus was also active in the real-time measure, represented by the primary direction involving Venus.

Valentino's Demise at Age 31

During the year when Valentino died, his *Point of Life* (at age 31) ranged from 12° 51' to 17° 09' Leo, squaring both his natal Sun and Mercury in Taurus in the 8th house of death and activating his natal Mercury-Uranus opposition. Thus, by Frankland's symbolic *Point of Life measure*, Valentino was passing through a difficult period or area of life. Any adverse operative influence of similar signification would be particularly intensified and deleterious at this time.

His *Age along the Zodiac* at age 31.3 was at 1° 18' Taurus in the 8th house and opposite to natal Saturn within an orb of less than 2°. His secondary progressed Saturn on the day of his demise was at 1° 08' Scorpio, almost exactly opposite his symbolic *Age Point*.

In addition, the primary direction active in August of 1926 (Placidus semi-arc, Ptolemy key, zero latitude) was primary directed Pluto sesquisquare his natal Ascendant, exact on 22 August 1926—clearly an adverse operative influence, occurring as he was traversing a particularly stressful area of life.

The Value of Midpoints: Christa McAuliffe

Christa McAuliffe was a American teacher and private citizen who became an astronaut in the ill-fated flight of the NASA spacecraft *Challenger*. Born in Boston on 2 September 1948 at 10:13 p.m. EDT (chart 31), Christa and her fellow astronauts died when the *Challenger* exploded shortly after takeoff around 11:40 a.m. EST on 28 January 1986. She was 37.4 years old at the time.

The cause of the disaster was traced to a circular O-ring gasket that was supposed to seal the right rocket booster. Several engineers had warned that the O-rings would become less elastic in the record below-freezing temperatures forecast for the launch and might not function properly.

NASA management decided to proceed despite the scientific evidence being proffered by the booster rocket engineers. News reports prior to the launch cited the warnings of the engineers who were strongly recommending against the launch. The concern was that the extremely cold temperatures would stiffen the rubber O-ring seals, allowing rocket fuel to leak from the booster joints, ignite, and cause an explosion.

Let's consider Frankland's symbolic measures in McAuliffe's chart at age 37.4.

Christa's *Age along the Zodiac (Age Point)* was at 7° 24' Taurus, separating within a 1° orb from a conjunction to her true North Lunar Node in the natal 12th house, a semisextile to the natal 12th house cusp, and a quincunx to her natal 6th house cusp.

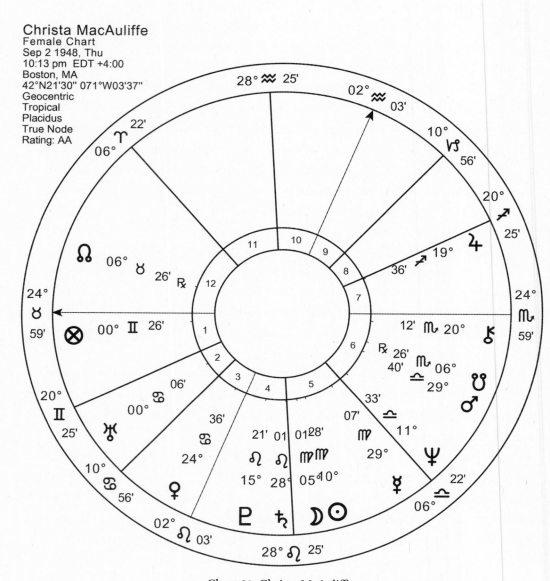

Chart 31: Christa McAuliffe
2 September 1948, 10:13 p.m. EDT, Boston, Massachusetts, 42N22 71W04

At age 37.4, the *Age Point* at 7° 24' Taurus (a fixed sign) was tightly conjunct the Venus/Chiron midpoint at 7° 24' fixed and the Mars/Pluto midpoint at 7° 31' fixed in the midpoint modal sort. Venus rules Christa's Ascendant and 6th house cusp, and Chiron is often active at times of wounding or bodily harm. Mars/Pluto is associated with overwhelming force, violent assaults, crises, injuries, accidents, and sudden ruin through the misuse of power.

At the time of the *Challenger's* explosion on 28 January 1986, transiting Saturn was at 7° 42' Sagittarius, receiving a close quincunx from her *Age Point* at 7° 24' Taurus. In addition, transiting Pluto was at 7° 20' Scorpio, in almost exact opposition (within 04' of arc) to her *Age Point* on that date.

Christa's *Point of Life* at age 37.4 was at 10° 17' Virgo, closely conjunct her natal Sun, which rules her 4th house of endings and 5th house of creative endeavors. Her natal Sun squares Jupiter, ruler of her 8th house, as well as the 8th house cusp.

This *Point of Life* at 10° 17' Virgo (a mutable sign) closely conjoins the Uranus/Chiron midpoint at 10° 09' mutable in the midpoint modal sort. Uranus is linked to sudden disruptive events, and Chiron signifies the "wounded healer."

At the moment of the *Challenger* disaster on 28 January 1986, transiting Venus (ruler of Christa's natal 1st and 6th houses) was at 10° 37' Aquarius in close quincunx to her *Point of Life* and natal Sun, ruler of her 4th house of endings. In addition, the transiting Moon was at 11° 02' Virgo in square to transiting Chiron at 9° 25' Gemini Rx.

Christa's *4/7° Age Point* at age 37.4 lay in a cardinal sign at 21° 22' Aries (4 × 37.4° / 7 = 21.371°), where it conjoined, within a 1° orb, the Mars/Neptune midpoint at 20° 36' cardinal, the Neptune/MC midpoint at 21° 48' cardinal, the Mercury/Pluto midpoint at 22° 14' cardinal, and the Jupiter/Asc midpoint at 22° 17' cardinal in the midpoint modal sort. The prominence of Neptune relates to situations marked by illusion, foggy thinking, over-idealization, unrealistic expectations, and the failure to realistically assess a situation. Alfred Witte associated Mars/Neptune with destruction and denial. Jupiter in Christa's chart rules her 8th house of death, and the Ascendant signifies her body and life force. Mars rules her 12th house of misfortune and occupies her 6th house of bodily injury.

Frankland routinely directed chart points and planets by the *4/7° Age Point* measure. Because Christa was born at night, Saturn is her out-of-sect malefic, capable of doing much harm. If we symbolically direct Saturn by 21° 22', we arrive at 19° 23' Virgo, which closely squares her 8th-ruler Jupiter at 19° 36' Sagittarius within 13' of arc, indicating the risk of death around age 37.4.

Midpoints and 0° Aries (the *Aries Point*)

Frankland's *Age along the Zodiac*, *Point of Life*, and *4/7° Age Point* are essentially symbolic directions whose point of departure in the birth chart is 0° Aries, which is considered analogous to the native's moment of birth. Astrologers today often refer to 0° Aries of the tropical zodiac as the *Aries Point*, which, in Uranian astrology, is shorthand for *0° of all the cardinal signs* and is regarded as a point that links the inner symbolism of the birth chart with its manifestation and involvement in the outer world. It is not surprising, then, that Frankland's symbolic directions of the *Aries Point* to the planets and midpoints of the birth chart indicate important events in the life of the native.

As mentioned previously, we can take advantage of modern computer sorts of midpoints, such as the 90° midpoint modal sort in Solar Fire, to make full use of Frankland's methods. In doing so, we regard Frankland's symbolic measures as indicating a directed *Aries Point* at a given age and then look in the midpoint modal sort to see which natal planetary pairs are being activated by the directed *Aries Point* at that time.

The basic interpretation of such planetary pictures can be found in Alfred Witte's *Rules for Planetary Pictures* (1930s). A summary of Witte's key midpoint meanings appears in the article "Astrology Topics: The Meaning of Midpoints" at CafeAstrology.com. The book *The Combination of Stellar Influences* by Reinhold Ebertin is also useful in this regard.

Not included in these references are midpoints involving Chiron, which are useful in predicting hurts and injuries, using Frankland's methods. In mythology, the centaur Chiron was a teacher and healer who could not heal his own wound, which was accidentally inflicted by the arrow of Heracles. Chiron was also emotionally wounded in infancy when his own mother abandoned him because of his physical appearance, being half-human and half-horse. Symbolically, Chiron represents core wounds that persist and need healing. When Chiron is activated by symbolic directions, the native often faces situations involving emotional pain or physical injury.

A friend of mine has natal Chiron at 4° Leo in partile square to Venus at 4° Taurus. When he turned 29 years old, his *Point of Life* at 4° 17' Leo highlighted this natal Chiron-Venus square. At that time he became involved in a serious relationship and moved in with his partner, but the relationship was marked by considerable emotional pain and he had difficulty fully experiencing the joy of living with someone he loved.

Chiron and Actor Christopher Reeve

An example in which Chiron symbolizes physical injury is that of actor Christopher Reeve, who played Superman in the movies. On 27 May 1995, Reeve was thrown from a horse during an equestrian competition and broke his neck, leaving him paralyzed.

Frankland would have begun his delineation by looking at the big picture and the prominent patterns in the chart. Reeve's nativity is outstanding for its stellium of five planets in Libra (chart 32). In addition, Libra receives a whole-sign square from Uranus in Cancer at the cusp of the unfortunate 12th house, with Uranus in close square (by degree) to the natal Saturn-Neptune conjunction in Libra in the 3rd house of short trips. In addition, Libra receives a square from Chiron (injuries and emotional pain) in Capricorn in the 5th house of romance, children, theater, and recreational events. Chiron also squares (by degree) his natal Sun-Mercury conjunction in early Libra. The Sun rules his natal Ascendant, which symbolizes the body and life force of the native.

Reeve's Leo Ascendant is conjunct both the true South Lunar Node and Pluto, which lie in his 1st house. The planet Jupiter rules the 5th house of sporting events and the 8th house of life-threatening illness and lies in the 10th house in Taurus, in partile square to the Moon's true nodes—a condition known as "being at the bendings." According to astrologer Kevin Burk in his *Complete Node Book* (2003):

> A planet that is *"at the bendings"* must be given careful consideration, because that planet, and the issues associated with it, will tend to take center stage repeatedly in the individual's life. (Burk 2003, 212; italics mine)

As far back as the second century CE, Claudius Ptolemy, in book 3, chapter 12, of the *Tetrabiblos*, linked the position of the Moon "at the nodes or her bendings" to injuries, illnesses, paralysis, and dangers such as falling from a height.

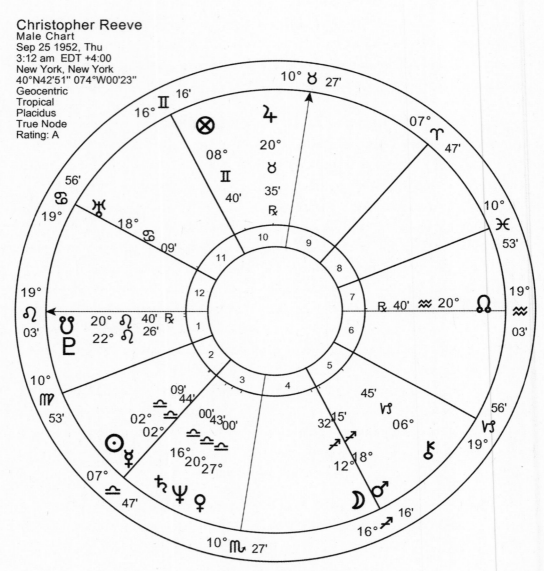

Chart 32: Christopher Reeve
25 September 1952, 3:12 a.m. EDT, New York, New York, 40N43 74W00

The "bendings" refers to the fact that at these points the Moon is changing direction in its movement along the lunar orbit around the Earth from north to south, or vice versa. The bendings of the Moon are analogous to the solstice points of the Sun, at which the Sun appears to stand still and change its direction of motion along its apparent orbit around the Earth above or below the equator from north to south, or vice versa. The summer solstice is the day of maximum daylight. The winter solstice is the day of maximum darkness. In Reeve's chart, Jupiter occupies the ecliptic position at which the Moon's orbit is at its maximum northern latitude above the ecliptic, and after which the Moon begins its descent to the south.

With such a strong emphasis on Libra and the squares from Uranus and Chiron to this sign in Reeve's chart, Frankland would have expected the ages from 42 to 49 to be difficult and potentially harmful (the Sun rules the Ascendant, Reeve's body and vitality), especially the beginning of that period (ages 42–44), when the square of Chiron to Sun-Mercury became activated, and later (ages 46–47), when the square from Uranus became highlighted by the symbolically directed *Point of Life*. The early part of the Libra period looks especially challenging because around age 42, transiting Uranus opposes its natal position and, in addition, transiting Neptune squares its natal position.

By way of review, Frankland in *New Measures in Astrology* (1928) advised that if one sign is dominant, owing to a stellium of planets, the astrologer should note carefully the nature of the sign (Libra, a cardinal air sign in this case) and the natal houses it affects (here, Libra spans the end of the 2nd house and the first 22 degrees of the 3rd house of local travel, and contains the 3rd house cusp). He would then pay close attention to the ages signified by the sign, according to Alan Leo's comparison of the human life span with the orbit of Uranus.

In Alan Leo's scheme, Libra is assigned to ages 42–49. Frankland also took note of the 7-year periods governed by the signs in square to the dominant sign. In Reeve's case, these would be Cancer (ages 21–28) and Capricorn (ages 63–70), which form a T-square with Libra. Of these 7-year periods of signs in square aspect to the dominant stellium, Frankland writes:

Watch these years carefully. If there be any adverse directions they are detrimental, and certainly cause bodily changes that require care. (Frankland 1928, 38)

Notably, about four weeks prior to the accident that left Christopher Reeve paralyzed, primary directed Saturn (Placidus semi-arc, Naibod rate, 0° latitude) perfected a semisquare from his 1st house to natal Neptune in the 3rd house. Challenging Saturn-Neptune aspects are often associated with severe illnesses of long duration, especially so here because Saturn rules his 6th house of illness. Saturn traditionally signifies falls, and Ebertin specifically links Neptune to paralysis.

Born on 25 September 1952 at 3:12 a.m. in New York City, Reeve was 42.67 years old at the time of this accident. At this age we find the following:

The *Point of Life* is at 2° 52' Libra at age 42.67.

The natal Sun at 2° 09' Libra and natal Mercury at 2° 44' Libra are in square aspect to natal Chiron at 6° 45' Capricorn in the 5th house of sporting events.

Reeve's *Point of Life* closely conjoins the natal Mars/Uranus midpoint at 3° 12' Libra, a midpoint that commonly signifies accidents.

The *Age along the Zodiac (Age Point)* is at 12° 40' Taurus at age 42.67.

The natal midpoint closest to this *Age Point* is Mars/Chiron at 12° 30' Taurus, which links the forceful nature of Mars with the wounding of Chiron.

The *4/7° Age Point* is at 24° 23' Aries at age 42.67.

The natal midpoints within a 1° orb of the *4/7° Age Point* are Chiron/MC at 23° 36' cardinal and Venus/Neptune at 23° 52' Libra in the modal sort.

Natal Neptune lies in Reeve's 3rd house of local travel and squares Uranus (accidents) in Cancer at the cusp of the 12th house.

Further Reflections on Frankland and Alfred Witte

Both Frankland and Witte were developing their seminal ideas during the period from about 1913 to 1928. After studying Frankland's case examples, I have the impression that he must have been aware of Witte's findings about midpoints. Like Witte, Frankland placed a strong emphasis on 0° Aries in the birth chart, and, by 0° Aries, he had in mind 0° of all four cardinal signs, that is, the 0° points of the cardinal Grand Cross. Also, like Witte, Frankland explicitly stresses the importance of the midpoints of the cardinal Grand Cross, as he notes in *Astrological Investigations* (1926):

When some strong direction is formed between or on the points of the square, a most drastic or eventful time is indicated. (Frankland 1926, 45)

For Witte, 0° Aries was second in importance only to the MC, which he regarded as the most significant point in the horoscope. Frankland began measuring his symbolic directions commencing from 0° Aries rather than from the Ascendant, MC, or other significant planets or points in the birth chart. Both Witte and Frankland viewed 0° Aries (the *Aries Point*, or Earth Point) as indicating one's relationship with the outer world and external states of being that are available to public view.

For Frankland, the most important midpoints involve personal factors, especially the Sun, Moon, and ruler of the Ascendant. These include:

- The Sun/Moon midpoint as a focus of personal energy. Harding and Harvey describe the Sun/Moon midpoint as the "inner marriage," or *conjunctio*, of the alchemists.
- The Sun/Ascendant ruler midpoint.
- The Moon/Ascendant ruler midpoint.
- The midpoints involving the Ascendant ruler and other "vital points," but Frankland does not specify which vital points he has in mind; most likely he means the Ascendant and MC, and perhaps the planetary rulers and cusps of the houses.

Witte regarded the most personal factors to be the Sun, Moon, MC, and Ascendant. Thus, all of these midpoint combinations were highly significant. In addition, the lunar nodes and the *Aries Point* were of major importance. Witte divided these significant chart factors along a spectrum from inner and personal to external and impersonal.

According to Witte, the MC represents the "I" of the native, *the most personal and important point in the birth chart*; one's soul, ego, and aims in life. Witte also considered the MC to be related to the time (the "when") of an event, and the Ascendant to its location (the MC signifies "at this time" and the Ascendant, "at this place"). These attributions make sense because the MC is the point at which the native's meridian meets the ecliptic, or path of the Sun. The meridian is the great circle that passes through the birthplace and the North and South Poles, dividing the celestial sphere into eastern and western hemispheres. The meridian circle intersects the equator vertically at an equatorial degree called its "right ascension," which is a measure of time on Earth. In other words, the MC shows *when* (at what moment) you were born.

The luminaries are also strongly personal factors. The Sun signifies the life force and body of the native; the Moon represents the emotions and the mind.

The Ascendant denotes one's immediate personal connections, acquaintances, and surroundings; the "you" as others see you, the environment from which you come; and the place or location (the "where") of an event. Associating the Ascendant with location makes sense, because the Ascendant is the point where the eastern horizon of the native, which depends on the latitude of the birthplace, meets the ecliptic, or path of the Sun. In other words, the Ascendant depends on *where* (at what location) you were born.

In Witte's spectrum from innermost to most external significant chart factors, the lunar nodes signify less immediate and more indirect connections, such as joining with others publicly or in the community rather than on a strictly personal level. This might involve working with others on the job, in groups, at school, at conferences, etc. Witte's keywords for the lunar nodes include unions, connections, fellowship, junctions (joining with others), communications, terminations, limits, and boundary relations (connecting across borders). In Ebertin's view, the North Node, or Dragon's Head, represents the urge to join with others, as in associations and alliances. Thus, the lunar nodes can refer to meetings, societies, and group membership but also to blood ties and family relationships.

In his hierarchy, Witte considered 0° Aries to signify the most impersonal and indirect form of contact with others. The *Aries Point* symbolizes one's connections with the outside world in the most general sense. Witte viewed the Cardinal Cross as representing the Earth, and 0° cardinal (the Earth Point) as signifying our relationship to this world in the most general terms, perhaps as beings who happen to inhabit the Earth for a span of years.

Although Frankland does not appear to use the following midpoints very often in his case examples, a few significant ones from Witte's writings are worth noting:

- The MC/0° Aries midpoint combines our most personal point (MC) with our connections in the external world, the "I," or soul, embodied on Earth.
- The MC/Asc midpoint combines the "I" and aims of the native with their immediate personal connections, acquaintances, and surroundings, thus joining the native's most personal aims with those of others. Ebertin notes that this midpoint indicates important periods in one's life.

- The MC/lunar node midpoint combines the soul of the native with the desire to associate with others. Witte's keyword for this midpoint is soul union. The MC represents the soul, or "I," of the native, and the Moon's node signifies the desire to join in fellowship with others. Traditionally, the MC signifies what we choose to do, that is, the actions in which we purposefully engage the external world.

Chapter 11
THE 12 HOUSES

An understanding of the significations of the twelve houses is essential to identifying areas of life when doing predictive work. Frankland used Placidus houses in which each of the twelve quadrant houses is determined by the passage of two planetary hours. He also took the Placidian house cusps seriously, regarding them as important "sensitive points" in the birth chart.

Prior to the introduction of Placidus houses in the mid-1600s, the predominant system of domification was that of Regiomontanus. When the Latin texts of Placidus were translated into English in the eighteenth century, British astrologers were captivated by his brilliance as an astronomer and mathematician and decided to abandon the Regiomontanus system in favor of that of Placidus, who writes:

> The twelve houses or mansions in heaven, authors divide several ways, but they all disagree. Rejecting the opinion of them all, we [Placidus], with Ptolemy, distinguish them by the two temporal hours [aka "planetary hours"]; for so it is, that there is proportional and equal division, not indeed of the heavenly and aerial space, but of the successive influx of the stars and houses; and the Mundane rays appear equal and proportional. But it is our opinion, that the division of the houses, by great circles passing through the common sections of the horizon and meridian, and the twelve equal divisions of the equator, which late authors [Regiomontanus] make use of, are, of all, the most remote from and abhorrent to natural truth. (Placidus, *Primum Mobile,* Cooper translation, 1814, 20)

Because an understanding of the significations of the houses is so important, this section begins with descriptions by Alan Leo, Sepharial (Walter Gorn Old), and William

Frankland from the first three decades of the 1900s regarding their interpretations of the houses. It then proceeds with a brief summary of Firmicus Maternus's fourth-century view of the astrological houses, William Lilly's seventeenth-century description of the houses, and some comments about additional significations from Jyotish, the astrological tradition of India.

Alan Leo on the Significations of the Twelve Houses (1907)

Regarding the combining of the cusps of houses, Frankland, writing in 1926, recommends that his readers study the significance of the twelve astrological houses as described by Alan Leo in his book on horary astrology. To this end, I have quoted Alan Leo's comments verbatim from his *Astrological Manuals No. VII: Horary Astrology*, 1st edition, 1907.

> *The First House,* or the **Ascendant,** represents the person asking the question, to be known in future as the "Querent." It does not matter who asks the question, whether it be the person who is erecting the map for himself, or whether it be erected for him by another, the First House always represents, or symbolises, the *Querent.* The sign ascending, and its lord or ruler, in addition to any planets placed therein, must all be studied in connection with any matters relating to this house. In a secondary sense also Saturn and Mars should be considered.

> *The Second House* is concerned with all matters of money, possessions, earnings and movable property. Its nature is determined by the sign upon the cusp and its lord or ruler. In a secondary sense Jupiter and Venus also should be considered.

> *The Third House* concerns relatives, kindred, travel, papers, correspondence, etc. Its nature is determined by the sign upon the cusp, its lord, and in a secondary sense, the Sun and Moon.

> *The Fourth House* is concerned with the home and domestic affairs, mines, land, and property or estate, things lost, the end of life, and the final upshot of the question asked or undertaking proposed. Its nature is determined by the sign on the cusp, its lord, and in a secondary sense the Moon and Uranus.

The Fifth House concerns love affairs, courtships, children, schools, all places of pleasure and speculation. The sign on the cusp, its lord, and in a secondary sense Venus and the Sun show the nature of this house.

The Sixth House concerns phenomenal magic, sickness servants, inferiors, and labour. Its nature, strength or weakness is shown by the sign on the cusp, its lord, and in a general sense Mercury.

The Seventh House concerns marriage, partnerships, engagements, unions, and appointments. It is governed by the sign on the cusp, its lord, and in a secondary sense the Moon and Venus.

The Eighth House concerns deaths, legacies, wills, and the goods or possessions of partners or immediate associates. It is governed by the sign on the cusp, its lord, and in a secondary sense Saturn and Mars.

The Ninth House concerns long journeys, voyages, the publication of books, foreign affairs, legal matters, religious questions, and science. It is governed by the sign on the cusp, its lord, and in a secondary sense Jupiter.

The Tenth House concerns profession, honour, ruling powers, rank, those in authority, business affairs, official and social standing. It is governed by the sign on the cusp, its lord, and in a secondary sense Saturn and Mars.

The Eleventh House concerns friends, acquaintance, hopes and wishes, the deliberations of rulers, governing bodies, associations and public companies. It is governed by the sign on the cusp, its lord, and in a secondary sense the Sun and Saturn.

The Twelfth House concerns secrets, romances, intrigues, imprisonments and confinements, misfortunes and unseen troubles. It is governed by the sign on the cusp, its lord, and in a more general sense, Venus and Jupiter. (Leo 1907, 7–8; bold highlighting mine)

Sepharial on the Twelve Houses (1914)

The influential astrologer Walter Gorn Old (20 March 1864–23 December 1929) wrote under the pseudonym *Sepharial*. The following quaint, and sometimes idiosyncratic, comments are quoted from his *Manual of Occultism* (1914):

The Kabala of the Houses

shows them to be divided into four groups, viz. :—

Individual, 1st,   5th,   9th;
Possessive, 2nd,   6th,   10th;
Relative,   3rd,   7th,   11th;
Terminal,   4th,   8th,   12th.

Of these, among the Individual group, the 1st is *external* and relates to the person or body of the man; the 5th is *intermediate* and has relation to the psychic nature or soul; and the 9th is *internal* and is related to the spiritual nature or individuality. Hence all the Houses are either physical (1st, 2nd, 3rd and 4th), psychic (5th, 6th, 7th and 8th), or spiritual (9th, 10th, 11th and 12th).

The close study of these intimate relationships of the Houses and their correspondence with the signs of the zodiac is the most profound work of the astrologer. *It is the foundation of the whole art of correct foreknowledge.* [italics mine]

For practical purposes we may brief the dominations and significations of the Houses as follows :—

Significations of the Houses

The **1st House** governs the body, personal appearance, physical well-being, and accidents happening to the person.

The **2nd House** governs the personal property, money in hand, personal effects.

The **3rd House** rules the personal relations, the tie of consanguinity, brothers and sisters; also means of communication, whether by vehicle, letter post, telegraph or other means whatsoever. It denotes cables, bridges, telegraph wires, viaducts and other means of connection; writings, letters.

The **4th House** governs the end of the physical life, the grave; material products, mines, farming produce; land, houses, freeholds, leases, tenancies and hence landlords.

The **5th House** is the extension of the 1st and governs the psychic nature; progeny; passions, pleasures, love affairs; hence theatres, places of amusement, sport, etc.; the younger generation and such things and persons as tend to their well-being.

The **6th House** is an extension of the 2nd; it governs the food, clothing, servants, personal comforts, relative possessions generally; also the work or profession in which the subject engages; whatever contributes to the well-being of the subject's possessions.

The **7th House** is an extension of the 3rd; it governs the tie of conjugality, the marriage partner; persons in contract; rivals (as opposing the 1st House).

The **8th House** is an extension of the 4th; it governs the dissolution of the vital forces; death, matters relating to the dead; wills, legacies, etc., and (being the 2nd from the 7th) dowry or personal property of the marriage partner.

The **9th House** is an extension of the 5th; it governs the spiritual nature; "the far-off land," whether it be that across the ocean or beyond the veil, teleological subjects, theology, philosophy; publications; the law, lawyers; insurances; dreams, visions and other-world experiences.

The **10th House** is an extension of the 6th; it denotes the ambitions, success, attainments of the subject; honour, credit, public esteem; the father or mother. (The 10th is always of the same sex as the 1st, and in a female horoscope denotes the mother.)

The **11th House** is an extension of the 7th, and denotes the tie of friendship; congeners; associates; syndicates, companies, leagues, clubs, associations of which the subject is a member; his confederates and supporters.

The **12th House** is an extension of the 8th, and denotes privation, confinement, restraint; the hospital, prison or other place of detention; sequestration, exile; ambushes, plots, secret enemies; the occult.

It will be seen that many other interpretations apply to the House by *reflection*. Thus the 1st being the subject of the horoscope and the 7th his wife; the 3rd his relatives and the 9th his wife's relatives, the latter house comes to mean brothers- and sisters-in-law, *i.e.* marriage relatives.

The 10th being the father and the 4th the mother (in a male horoscope), the 7th is the maternal *grandfather* and the 1st the maternal *grandmother*.

The 6th being the uncles or aunts on the mother's side (*i.e.* maternal aunts or uncles), the relatives of the mother, the 5th (progeny) from the 6th (*i.e.* the 10th House) will denote maternal *cousins*. Similarly with all those relations which "a man may not marry," as expounded in the Book of Common Prayer. (Sepharial 1914, 23–26)

Frankland on the Twelve Houses (1926)

In chapter 2 of *Astrological Investigations* (1926), Frankland gives his own account of the 12 astrological houses. He writes:

The twelve Celestial Houses. These relate to the Material or Mundane affairs of life.

THE 1ST HOUSE. Its symbolism—i.e., the sign upon the House, the Planet in the House, and ruler of the House [cusp], and aspects thrown thereto (this applies to all the houses), all have the effect of inclining the Native to certain things, they give the disposition. They incline the life in certain directions. The 1st House gives the key to the setting of the whole twelve Houses, therefore it is tremendously important. Likewise the degree upon that House [cusp] is important, not so much in itself, but that it is the key to the pattern of all the other houses. The Disposition to things in life is bound to have far-reaching effects.

THE 2ND HOUSE. Generally called the Financial House. It is the House concerned with possessions, not only in the actual sense of money or stock, etc., but also of the ability to acquire, to earn, and on the other hand the claims likely to be made upon the possessions, the avenues of expenditure, losses, etc. These matters are not confined entirely to this House, but are chiefly affected by the House. For example, a very adverse Horoscope in regard to health is bound to affect the Finance, but the condition of the 2nd would show how much resource there was.

THE 3RD HOUSE. Often termed the House of Relations or the Relative House, that which relates whether mentally, as in correspondence, reports, etc., or physically, as in journeys from one place to another, in short measure, such as locally. This House is connected with Kindred. It is the House that shows the relation one has to certain people, objects or places, etc. It typifies the neighbour-hood, the things within easy access, mental or material.

THE 4ᵀᴴ HOUSE. Connected with Home, life, environment, and immedi-ate surroundings. This house is also closely connected with parentage, and in a general sense indicates that from which we spring, that which surrounds us, our immediate setting and the condition of the final departure. It represents the Mid-night from which the Day is born and the Midnight of the Day's return.

THE 5ᵀᴴ HOUSE. This is called the House of Pleasure, enterprise and chil-dren. It gives us a clue to that which we create, whether physically, socially, or any other way. Through the 5ᵗʰ House we may find much happiness or misery of our own begetting, consciously or unconsciously. A house often lightly dealt with, but one that would repay earnest study and thought.

THE 6ᵀᴴ HOUSE. This is generally termed the House of Service and also of Sickness, etc. It will stamp its character upon one's work or service, or upon the kind of service one is likely to obtain, also upon the bodily condition, because it is the body that gives service to us or to the Mind or Soul within. Therefore one could study this house profitably not only in regard to outside service received from others, but in regard to what *bodily service* we may acquire or develop for ourselves physically, and in a deeper sense, the service one may give to others and to life in general.

THE 7ᵀᴴ HOUSE. This is called the House of Marriage or Partnerships. This is the house of Union, the direct link with others, from public affairs to the most intimate bond with those with whom one links one's life. The symbolism of this House will stamp its character upon all such partnerships. This House will either greatly oppose the Native or will greatly assist him. It is the House of every type of Partnership.

THE 8ᵀᴴ HOUSE. This is generally called the House of Death, Wills, and Legacies, or all things connected with Death. I have always found this House affected at the time of Death. Any planet in this House and the Ruler of the House [cusp], and sign upon the House, will directly or indirectly share in bring-ing about the termination of earthly existence. They will also give an index to anything in the nature of benefits or otherwise, in connection with the death of others that may occur during the course of one's life. The conditions existing in this House, however, go deeper than this. They give a clue to the Influences that will either prove a barrier to consciousness of other planes of being while in this life or conversely may lead one to the consciousness of other phases of existence, just as finally they help to provide the means of exit from the material life to planes beyond. *A most mysterious House.*

THE 9ᵀᴴ HOUSE. This House is termed the House of Travel, Philosophy and Religion. Strong Influences in this House have bearing upon all such matters. It is the House which has the possibility of taking one far afield, whether physically, as in ordinary travel; mentally, as in Philosophy, etc., or spiritually, as in Religion. The whole Horoscope would show the type of person, and therefore largely determine which of the three would be most evident. However, this House will either incline to distant fields of activity or will tend to negative such according to the character of its sign and Planets therein. Many Planets in the 9th Sign Sagittarius would give the inclination to such things, but in the 9th House would give more chance to actual expression, particularly in regard to actual physical travel.

THE 10ᵀᴴ HOUSE. This is generally termed the House of Profession, Position and Standing or Attainment, etc. The Influence of this House certainly characterizes the conditions that are likely to obtain in regard to Position and Profession, but other factors help to determine the actual profession. The links with Mercury, for instance, incline the Mind to certain professions, as also do planets with the Sun. Therefore personally I consider the 10th House more in regard to conditions obtaining in Profession, Business or Position, rather than as actually determining the Profession. As this is the highest point of the Nativity, Planets, Signs, affecting that House, either help to uplift the Native, or make it more difficult to rise in life, according to the Nature of the Planet.

THE 11ᵀᴴ HOUSE. This is generally termed the House of Hopes, Wishes and Friendships. It does seem that in this House are the keys to many of the ambitions and aspirations of life from a Mundane point of view. Just as the Sign Aquarius will eventually give much experience of Human Nature and Life in its Inner Significance, so will the 11th House provide the mundane or material experience of others through the acquaintances and friendships made. Good Planets in this House, or Planets well placed and well aspected, give sunshine to the Nativity as it were, in that the actual experiences of Human Life through others will prove very hopeful, happy and encouraging, while this House badly influenced is apt to give disillusion in regard to Human Nature in actual contact or experience.

THE 12TH HOUSE. This has been termed the House of Mystery, of undoing, confinement, etc. I always think of this House, with its tenants, as a House with the blinds drawn. The Figures are more or less shadows. You can surmise, rather than actually know the doings and effects of the House. It may not always produce or reveal its mystery, but it suggests possibilities of hidden experiences. It reminds one perhaps of things that lie deep and latent, or of callings and periods of time when the veil is placed before the eye of publicity. It conjures up matters connected with hospitable work, or with periods of confinement in hospitals, institutions, etc. I have heard it said that there is less mystery than is supposed in this House, but if it presents nothing of this to me, when strongly tenanted, then I incline to the idea that the nature is either not sufficiently strong to bring things from the deeps into expression, or they are so veiled that my knowledge fails to penetrate them. One should also note whether Planets occupying this House are quick of motion, as by progression such would naturally pass into the 1st House, while the slower Planets like [Pluto,] Neptune, Uranus, Saturn, or Jupiter, would remain near the position occupied at Birth.

In regard to the influences of Houses, there is one point that might be considered. The difference in influence between the sign upon the House [cusp] and the Planet in the House. For instance, Capricorn upon the 11th House [cusp] is more likely to give reserve and aloofness from friendships, that is fewer friendships, etc., than say Saturn in that House, whereas Saturn in the House would give a Saturnine friendship. If Saturn were in the House, but Venus ruled it, then there might be the *inclination* to friendships, but delay, or Saturnine friends, while Saturn ruling the House but Venus in the House would rather incline to aloofness from friends, but probably won over by merry, bright or Venusian friendship.

This applies in a general sense to all the Houses. For instance, a fruitful sign and [fruitful] Ruler of the 5th House [cusp] would be more likely to give children, or *benefit* from children, than say Jupiter actually *in that House*. The Ruler of the House [cusp] lies more at the *Root* of the matter than does the Planet in the House, though the Planet in the House may be quicker in its expression. (Frankland 1926, 21–28; bold highlighting mine)

Firmicus Maternus and the Twelve Places (*Topoi*)

Next, I have summarized the descriptions of the 12 "places" (*topoi*) by Julius Firmicus Maternus in his *Matheseos* from the fourth century CE. These ancient significations are often helpful in delineating the impact of an aspect. The following comments are based on my translation of the Latin version of Maternus's *Matheseos* edited by Kroll and Skutsch.

Firmicus Maternus entitles this chapter "On the Rulerships of the Twelve Places" (*De duodecim locorum potestatibus* in Latin) and follows the original tradition of calling the 12 divisions "places" (from the Greek *topoi*) rather than houses. Reflecting on these fourth-century descriptions can enhance our appreciation of the root meanings of the houses.

1st **Place: Life and Spirit of the Native.** Often called the "Helm" of the chart, the 1st Place is the frame and substance of the entire nativity.

2nd **Place: Gates of Hades,** presumably inactive (*piger* in Latin) because it is averse (not connected by aspect) to the rising sign. It signifies increase related to the hope and possessions of the native.

3rd **Place: [Moon] Goddess,** which beholds the rising sign by sextile aspect. It signifies siblings, friends and travel.

4th **Place: Imum Caelum,** or **Bottom of Heaven,** which is joined to the rising sign with maximum strength by square aspect. It signifies our parents' property, movable foundations, and any hidden or stored resources that belong to them.

5th **Place: Good Fortune,** which signifies the number and gender of children. It is a place associated with benefic Venus and is strongly connected to the rising sign by a trine aspect. Sometimes the degree of the Mid-heaven is found opposite to this place.

6th Place: Bad Fortune, associated with malice and the malefic planet Mars. It signifies physical defect (*vitium* in Latin) and illness. This place is inactive and averse to the rising sign, which it does not behold by any aspect. Sometimes the malice of the 6th Place is diminished when a planet placed in the 6th receives a fortunate aspect from one in the 10th Place.

7th Place: Descendant, an angular place, which signifies the quality and number of marriages. Because the Descendant lies directly opposite the rising degree, it is connected violently (*violenta* in Latin) to the Ascendant. By a violent connection, Firmicus Maternus means that a planet on the western horizon, conjunct the Descendant, has the potential to harm the native, whose body and vitality are signified by the Ascendant. A modern example is the chart of President John F. Kennedy, relocated to Dallas, Texas, where he was assassinated. If he were born in Dallas, JFK's birth chart would have Chiron, a symbol of bodily injury, on the Descendant in an almost exact opposition to the rising degree.

8th Place: signifies the **quality of death.** This Place is inactive and averse to the Ascendant because it does not behold the rising sign by any aspect.

9th Place: Sun-god. It signifies sects, travels and religion. The 9th Place is powerfully and favorably connected to the rising sign by trine.

10th Place: Medium Caelum, or **Middle of Heaven,** is joined to the rising sign with maximum strength by square aspect. It signifies all the actions of the native, life and spirit, the homeland, all constant practical experience, even the arts and that which is conferred upon us through the arts. Mental disorders can also be discerned here.

11th Place: Good Spirit or **Good Daemon.** The degree of the Mid-heaven is often found in this place. It is a fortunate place that is associated with the benefic planet Jupiter and is joined to the rising sign by a sextile aspect.

12th Place: Evil Spirit or **Bad Daemon.** This place shows the quality of our enemies and the substance of our slaves. Like the 6th, it also signifies bodily defects and illnesses. The 12th is inactive because it is averse to the rising sign, unable to behold it with any aspect. The 12th is also unfortunate because of its association with the malefic planet Saturn. (Maternus 1897)

The Houses in Jyotish

This section includes some keywords for the houses from the astrology of India, which inherited much of the Hellenistic tradition and further developed it, using whole signs as houses. These meanings from Jyotish are often useful in astrological forecasting, as they may indicate house-related matters not found in the Western astrological tradition.

Some of the Jyotish house meanings resemble those of the ninth-century Persian Muslim astrologer Abu Ma'shar, who associated each house with a visible planet, starting with Saturn, the outermost and slowest, and proceeding in Chaldean order, from slowest to fastest. The planet associated with each house, according to Chaldean order, is indicated in italics in parentheses.

House 1 (*Saturn*): The body, physical stature, complexion, disposition, state of health, well-being of the native, span of life, energy, vitality, life force, character, direction in life.

House 2 (*Jupiter*): Resources that sustain the life and body of the native, money matters, earnings through self-effort, wealth, possessions, the lower part of the face (eyes, nose, mouth, teeth, tongue, oral cavity, vocal cords, etc.), the native's voice and speech, oratorical ability, the food that nourishes us, our eating habits, our nurturing in early childhood, family support, close family relatives, the birth of siblings and other additions to the family.

House 3 (*Mars*): Younger siblings, short trips, local movement and travel, one's neighbors and neighborhood, mental ability, communications, writing skills, news, rumors, courage, confidence, valor, prowess, physical fitness (because Mars is the con-significator of the 3rd house according to the Chaldean order of planets). As the 12th from the 4th, the 3rd house can signify leaving home, a change of residence, separation from parents in childhood, dissolution of domestic happiness, etc.

House 4 (*Sun*): The native's roots, mother, home, domestic happiness, land, buildings, real estate, houses, education, vehicles and conveyances, farming, agriculture, buried or hidden treasure, resources within the earth, one's private life (the darkest place in the chart, at the Bottom of Heaven), old age, the longevity of the 9th house father or guru.

House 5 (*Venus*): Children, progeny, conception of offspring, abortion or miscarriage, knowledge, intelligence, scholarship, intellectual capabilities, devotion to the gods, spiritual practices, karma from past lives, love affairs, attractions, courtship, pleasures, sports, gambling, enjoyments, playfulness, banquets, cultural activities; mental intelligence and creative, artistic, or literary endeavors; envoys, agents, and ambassadors.

House 6 (*Mercury*): Sickness, injuries, illness, disease, wounds, accidents, painful incidents, bodily injuries and ailments, debts, obstacles, enemies, difficulties, litigation, disappointments, worry, mental upset, troubles, subordinates, service, servants, pets, small animals, power over enemies, separation from a spouse or the dissolution of a 7th house partnership (as the 12th from the 7th).

House 7 (*Moon*): Spouse, sex partner, coitus, sexual union, marriage, any sexual relationship, divorce, partners and associates in general, trade, contracts, agreements, private business, the marketplace, social relationships, breaks in journeys, opponents, competitors, adversaries, open enemies, thieves, others with whom the native has dealings, danger to the life or physical well-being of the native (via the 7th house cusp's opposition to the Ascendant).

House 8 (*Saturn*) Longevity; death, its nature and quality; legacies, wills, hidden aspects of life, mystery, the unknown, knowledge of the hidden laws of nature, astrology, bringing concealed matters to light, sudden gains or losses, upheavals, unexpected changes, crises, accidents, danger, fear, depression, serious illness, surgery, unexpected gains or losses, the partner's finances, taboo behaviors, fearful situations, difficult routes, psychological problems, mental anguish.

House 9 (*Jupiter*): The father (as teacher and guru), gurus, teachers, higher education, religious pilgrimages and devotions, faith, churches, the clergy, spiritual interests, mystic initiations, divination, philosophy, legal disciplines, lawyers, legal advisers, higher knowledge, wisdom, enlightenment, long journeys, travel abroad or over long distances, communications with those at a distance, contact with foreigners, imports and exports, extramarital affairs.

House 10 (*Mars*): Profession, career, the kind of work you do in the world, leadership, success, government service, administrative or executive positions, the source of livelihood, public status, fame, recognition, applause, renown, reputation, honors, political power, judges, those in authority, distinguished persons, the father as an authority figure, the illness of one's children (as the 6th from the 5th), the loss of a friendship or older sibling (as the 12th from the 11th).

House 11 (*Sun*): Older siblings, friends, social groups, hopes and wishes, acquisition, gains or profits, income from career, the support of benefactors, the favor of those in power, fulfillment of desires, rewards, fame, recognition, awards, longevity of the 4th house mother (as the derived 8th from the 4th); release from confinement, hospitalization or imprisonment (as the derived 12th from the 12th).

House 12 (*Venus*): Detachment, expenditures, discharge of debts, decrease of wealth, termination of employment, losses of any kind, sorrow, grief, misfortune, renunciation, insomnia, defects, mental anguish, self-undoing, the end of a cycle (which began at the 1st house), confinement, imprisonment, hospitalization, death of a child (8th from the 5th), illness of a partner (6th from the 7th), risk to the native's health and well-being (12th from the 1st), exile, emigration, foreign travel, living far from home, secret enemies, activities done in secret, sexual pleasures of the bedroom (because Venus is the con-significator of the 12th house according to the Chaldean order of planets). A basic tenet of Jyotish is that *the 12th house to any house signifies the negation or dissolution of the significations of that house.*

William Lilly and the Twelve Houses (1647)

The seventeenth-century British astrologer William Lilly had a major impact on the practice of astrology in the English-speaking world. Here is a quotation from book 3 of *Christian Astrology* (1647) in which Lilly delineates the houses with respect to how the native will be able to acquire wealth. I have updated Lilly's spelling to modern English.

CHAP. CXV.
From whence, or by what means the Native shall come to an Estate
or to Poverty.

[...]

The nature of the Signs are as follows.

Fiery [signs] signify profit by such things as are made by fire, or by rapine and contention: *Earthly*, from the profits of the earth: *Airy*, Windmills, gifts of Magistrates: *Watery*, by Watermills, Fishponds, Navigations.

[The nature of the Planets.]

Saturnine profit is from the earth, Corn, Metal, usury of Moneys: *Jovial*, from public office, or Church-preferment: *Martial*, from contentions, and works done by fire: *Solar*, from Kings, Princes and their gifts: *Venereal*, from Women: *Mercurial*, by Wit, Industry, Merchandise, Journeys, Embassages [embassies, or messages sent by an embassy].

The Nature of the HOUSES.

First House.

Signifies Wealth acquired by the Native's proper industry.

Second House.

It shows Wealth and Substance [which] are necessary to support the Life of man, and also Household-stuff, gain procured by the Native's own labour.

Third House.

Signifies brothers, sisters, Kinsmen, near neighbors, short Journeys. Hospitality, sudden News or Novelties.

Fourth House.

It hath Signification of the Father, of Lands, of Patrimony, immovable Goods, Buildings, Foundations, Fields, Pastures, Villages, Treasure obscured anywhere, all manner of Mines, or profit out of the Bowels of the Earth, Husbandry.

Fifth House.

Children male and female, Gifts, curious Apparel, Banquets, Plays, all pleasant things.

Sixth House.

Any thing which portends or signifies Sorrow or Care, hurts of the Body or [its] Members, Servants, small Cattle; Uncles and Aunts on the Father's side; Sickness, Medicine or Physick; Bees, Doves, Geese, Hens, Swine.

Seventh House.

Hath signification in Marriages, Women, Partnership, Lawsuits, Foreign Affairs, public Enemies, Thefts, Rapines, all manner of Wars, &c., Seditions.

Eighth House.

Death of people, Dowry or Joynture of the Wife [Jointure refers to an estate settled on a wife to be taken by her in lieu of dower], Estate of Women, unexpected Inheritances, Poisons, deadly Fears [elsewhere, Lilly writes "anguish of mind"], Legacies.

Ninth House.

Religion, or Godliness, Sects of Religion, Dreams, long Journeys or Voyages, Churchmen, and things appertaining to the Church, Epistles, Wisdom, Science, Learning, Scholarship, Embassages [embassies, or messages sent by an embassy].

Tenth House.

Government, Kingdoms or Principality, Office, Power, Command, Honour, public Magistrates, public Administrations in the Commonwealth, Trade, the several kinds of Professions, it peculiarly [particularly] denotes the Mother, the Native's proper Vocation.

Eleventh House.

Happy conclusion of any Business, Friendship, support of Friends, profit arising by Office or Preferment, Hope, Comfort, Promotion by commendation of Friends.

Twelfth House.

This is *malus Daemon* [evil Daimon, evil spirit], hath signification of sad events, it's the house of Sorrow, Anguish of mind, Affliction, Labour, Poverty, Imprisonment, private Enemies, Impostors [deceivers, swindlers, cheats], greater Cattle who are fierce and hard to be ruled, Harlots, Horses, Cows, Oxen Bulls. (Lilly 1647, book 3, 554–59)

Robert Zoller on Delineating the Houses

Frankland views the planets as principles of human nature, the zodiac signs as molding or characterizing influences, and the twelve houses as representing the material or mundane affairs of life. He used the Placidus house system. In delineating the houses, Frankland first considered whether any planet was tenanting a house, because planetary occupants of a house have an immediate and direct impact on the expression of the affairs of the house. Second, he looked at the planetary ruler of the cusp of the house which lies at the root of the house's affairs and disposes any bodies within the sign on its cusp. Third, he took into account planets that became associated with the house by secondary progression at a given time in life.

Frankland's approach is consistent with that of the seventeenth-century French astrologer Morinus, who taught that the location of a planet in a house functions as a stronger and more immediate determinant than house rulership. As real estate agents often say, the most important factor in the sale of a house is "location, location, location." Back in the 1990s, I recall discussing this point with Rob Zoller at a conference in New York City. Based on his studies of medieval authors and Morinus, Rob further elaborated his understanding of the basic principles of house delineation. Fortunately, I still have my notes from that discussion and will summarize them here.

Rob began by stating that first and foremost one has to study the natal potential of the chart, because prediction consists of timing when the natal potential is likely to manifest in the life of the native. The natal potential indicates *what* can happen or *what* is possible, and the timing shows *when* it is likely to happen.

The condition of each planet is affected by three factors: planets can be (1) dignified or debilitated by their location on the zodiac circle, (2) fortified or afflicted by aspects from other planets, and (3) strengthened or weakened by their house position with relation to the horizon or meridian axis. Planets in angular houses are the strongest and most evident in their expression. Planets in the cadent houses will generally be weak in expressing what they promise and will need assistance. Planets in succedent houses will be intermediate between angular and cadent houses in their ability to manifest the natal promise.

Rob then explained the order in which he approached the delineation of houses:

1. First, study any planets in the house. According to Morinus, the ruler of a house occupying its own house takes precedence; otherwise, the planet closest to the cusp is predominant in determining the native's experience of the affairs of that house.

2. Second, consider the natural signifier of the affairs of the house, which may or may not be a planet that occupies or rules the house. In Jyotish, such natural or universal signifiers are called "karakas." Someone may have Sagittarius on the cusp of the 8th house, for example, so that Jupiter rules the 8th house of death. Nonetheless, Saturn, a natural signifier of death, will also need to be taken into account when delineating the 8th house affairs of this native.

3. Consider the ruler of the cusp of the house and its placement in the birth chart. Frankland emphasizes that when the ruler of a house cusp occupies a different house, it links the significations of the two houses in the life of the native. Zoller relies on Jean-Baptiste Morin's teaching that the favorable or adverse matters signified by a house emanate from the planetary ruler of the house. William Lilly believed that the ruler of a house being closely conjunct the cusp of another house (within 5°) will connect the meanings of the two houses.

4. For example, in the chart of Christa McAuliffe, her MC-ruler Saturn (her livelihood) technically lies within the boundaries of her 4th Placidus house (home and roots) but tightly conjoins the 5th house cusp (children, creative endeavors). She worked as a teacher of American history and English to high school children, which captures the significations of the 10th (career), 4th (one's roots), and 5th (children) houses.

5. Study the *almuten* of the cusp of the house, which is the planet with the most essential dignity at the cusp. Frankland did not use almutens.

6. Take into account the lots or Arabic parts related to the house under consideration. Frankland used the Part of Fortune and also created his own lots, or "sensitive points," by combining the longitude of two house cusps, or sometimes two house cusps plus the position of a related planet.

7. For example, Frankland calculated his *Lot of Life-Threatening Illness* by adding the longitudes of the cusps of the 6th (illness) and 8th (death) Placidus houses. He would then direct his lots, or sensitive points, by one of his new symbolic measures, such as the *4/7 of a degree per year measure.*

Directions and Progressions Involving House Cusps

Frankland paid attention to secondary progressed planets entering natal houses. He also symbolically directed planets to house cusps, and vice versa. Regarding secondary progressions, British astrologer R. C. Davison published a book in 1955 called *The Technique of Prediction* detailing his extensive research on this topic. The following comment about directing cusps of houses is from the 2nd edition of Davison's text:

A scrutiny should be made of any directions involving the intermediate house cusps. In the writer's experience, the Placidean system of house division gives the best results in this connection. Cuspal directions generally operate most powerfully when a planet comes by [secondary] progression to the cusp of the house which it occupied at birth. The affairs governed by that house will then assume a more than usual prominence in the native's life and the cuspal directions will thus emphasize the importance of other directions in force which involve the house or the corresponding sign. (Davison 1971, 97)

Significators and Con-significators of Houses

Strictly speaking, the seven visible planets "rule" the *signs* of the zodiac, but they do not "rule" the *houses* of the horoscope. Rather, the planet that rules the sign on the cusp of a house becomes a "significator" of the matters related to that house. As Sue Ward explains in the textbook for her *Traditional Horary Course* (2021):

The planet ruling the sign on the cusp of any house does not, in fact, become the ruler of that house; it becomes the significator of the matters represented by that house.... It is thus misleading to use the term "house ruler." Nevertheless, it is a phrase that you will often encounter, but if you are clear about the difference, you will not confuse signs with houses. (Ward 2021, 75–76)

As Ward points out, many astrologers use the term "house ruler" or the phrase "rules the house" as a kind of shorthand to refer to the *planet that rules the sign on the cusp* of a house, but it is important to bear in mind that planets rule zodiacal signs rather than houses.

The concept of astrological houses derives from the ancient Hellenistic practice of assigning topics to each sign of the zodiac according to the order in which the sign rose to the eastern horizon of the birth chart. The sign that rose first, or in 1st *place*, was called the Ascendant and signified the body and life force of the native. The sign that rose second, or in 2nd *place*, was viewed as a significator of the native's finances and resources, and so on around the horoscope wheel. For example, the sign that rose tenth, or in 10th *place*, signified the native's profession and actions in the world. Planets ruled the signs, and each sign became a signifier of certain topics, depending on the sign's *place* with respect to the eastern horizon.

We might imagine the horoscope as a carousel in an amusement park, with 12 uniquely decorated wooden horses, each one representing a different area of life. The horse in 1st *place* would be in the Ascendant, the next one in sequence would signify matters of the 2nd *place*, and so on. Each horse's *place in the sequence* would determine which area of life that horse signifies.

The principle that "place in the sequence determines signification" allowed our astrological forebears to correlate other ordered sequences with the astrological "houses" or "places." Such correlations produce systems of "con-significators" or "co-significators" of the houses.

For example, astrologers who assigned the start of the zodiac to the sign Aries assigned Aries to the 1st place, Taurus to the 2nd place, and so on, ending with Pisces assigned to the 12th place. William Lilly included this system of con-significators in his *Christian Astrology* (1647), but, as Sue Ward points out, "This consignification by sign is used exclusively in medical matters referring as it does to anatomical correspondences" (Ward 2021, 75). It is not clear when astrologers started to use Aries as the first sign of the zodiac. In ancient Hellenistic astrology, the Thema Mundi places the sign Cancer on the Ascendant at the eastern horizon and Aries in the 10th place.

Tradition also assigns the visible "planets" in Chaldean order, from Saturn to the Moon, to the twelve *places* of the horoscope. Abu Ma'shar uses these planet-to-place correlations to explain the significations of the twelve houses. The pairing goes like this:

Saturn–1st and 8th places
Jupiter–2nd and 9th places
Mars–3rd and 10th places
Sun–4th and 11th places
Venus–5th and 12th places
Mercury–6th place
Moon–7th place

In this system of planetary con-significators of *places*, or houses, each planet, owing to its placement in the sequence of celestial bodies in our solar system, lends its natural signification to the analogous *place*, or house, of the horoscope. In Jyotish, for example, Venus is a significator of the fun and leisure of the 5th house and also the pleasures of the bedroom of the 12th house, which William Lilly associates with "harlots."

In addition to the traditional planetary con-significators of houses, there are other systems that pair the planets with their preferred zodiac signs and also with the houses, or *places*, in which they "rejoice." Non-luminary planets each rule two signs; and those of the nocturnal sect prefer their signs of the negative polarity, whereas those of the diurnal sect prefer their signs of the positive polarity. In other words, Venus prefers or "rejoices in" Taurus, Mars prefers or "rejoices in" Scorpio; Jupiter, in Sagittarius; and Saturn, in Aquarius. Androgynous Mercury prefers or "rejoices in" Virgo, a sign of negative polarity in which Mercury is exalted.

The houses of "joy" of the planets are as follows: Mercury (our mental faculties) "rejoices" in the 1st house, which signifies the head. The Moon rejoices in the 3rd house, which is the *place* of the Moon goddess. Venus (the goddess of love) has her joy in the 5th house of pleasure, pregnancy, and entertainment. Mars (the god of war) rejoices in the 6th house of servitude and bodily ailments. The Sun finds joy in the 10th house of the Sun god. Jupiter (good fortune) rejoices in the 11th house of benefactors, hopes, and wishes. Finally, Saturn (the greater malefic) rejoices in the 12th house of misfortune and undoing. A joyful planet, by sign or by house, can more freely and easily express its essential nature.

Joyful Jupiter Wins $35 Million in the Lottery

In an online article about tertiary progressions, astrologer Lesia Valentine discusses the chart of a woman who won $35 million in the lottery on 26 October 1996 when she was 46.5 years old. The birth data of the winner were reported as 24 April 1950, 4:45 a.m. EST, Methuen, Massachusetts. I cast the chart in Solar Fire with Placidus houses (chart 33).

Although Frankland apparently did not use these traditional concepts in his work, this chart illustrates the usefulness of the con-significations, joys, and dignities of the planets. Ascendant-ruler Mars lies in the 6th house, where it rejoices and closely trines Mercury, which rules the signs on the cusps of the 6th house, containing Mars, and the 2nd house of income. Mercury, in turn, closely sextiles the Moon in its own sign of Cancer in the 4th house, sextiles Venus in Pisces, where Venus is exalted, and widely trines the Midheaven. Jupiter lies in its own sign of Pisces and occupies the 11th house of benefactors, where it rejoices. Benefic Jupiter closely trines Uranus, suggesting sudden, unexpected good fortune, and also sextiles the Sun, which is the most angular planet in the chart and is con-significator of the 11th house. The Sun rules Leo on the cusp of the 5th house of speculative gains.

At 46.5 years old, this woman's *Age along the Zodiac* was at 16.5° Taurus in the 1st house, within orb of a trine to the MC, a sextile to Venus, a sextile to the IC, and a square to Pluto in Leo in the 5th house of sudden, unexpected good fortune. Her *4/7 Age along the Zodiac* was at 26° 34' Aries and not aspecting any natal planet or house cusp, but in the midpoint modal sort it activates the midpoints Moon/Asc at 25° 34' cardinal, Pluto/North Lunar Node at 26° 26' cardinal, Mars/Jupiter at 27° 04' cardinal, and Sun/Moon at 27° 32' cardinal. The Sun/Moon midpoint is an extremely sensitive personal point and, when activated, usually indicates a highly significant period in one's life. The Moon's North Node is a principle of expansion and material gain, and here it is paired with Pluto, which Charles Carter describes in *The Principles of Astrology* (1939) as an indicator of "the openings and endings of chapters in the life" (Carter 1939, 60).

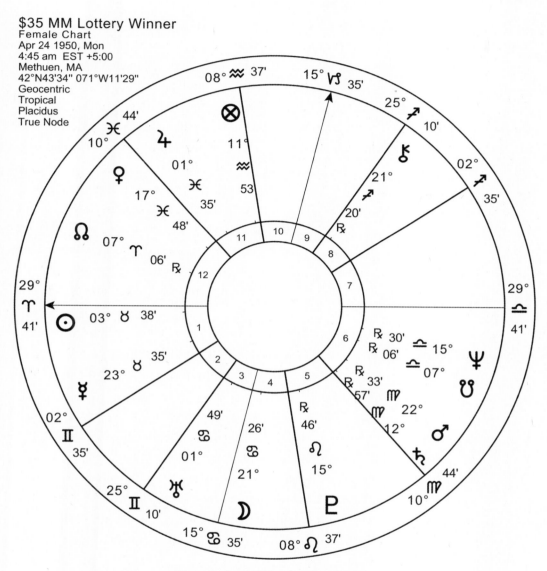

$35 MM Lottery Winner
Female Chart
Apr 24 1950, Mon
4:45 am EST +5:00
Methuen, MA
42°N43'34" 071°W11'29"
Geocentric
Tropical
Placidus
True Node

Chart 33: $35 Million Lottery Winner
24 April 1950, 4:45 a.m. EST, Methuen, Massachusetts, 42N44 71W11

Frankland would also have been impressed by natal Jupiter applying extremely closely to trine natal Uranus within 14 minutes of arc. Directing by the *Age along the Zodiac measure* of 1° for each year of life, he would have studied the birth chart to see when the natal Jupiter-Uranus trine would "ripen" and be ready to manifest. Because Jupiter is 46° of ecliptic longitude from the MC, he would have told the client that around age 46 her symbolically directed MC would conjoin her natal Jupiter, triggering the Jupiter-Uranus trine's natal promise. If there were a concurrent astrological operative influence in effect during the same period of her life, a sudden windfall would be a sure thing.

Two significant primary directions did perfect in her chart in 1996. By Placidus semi-arc with zero latitude at the Naibod rate, primary directed Mercury, which rules Gemini on the cusp of the 2nd house of income, conjoined exalted Venus in Pisces on May 3rd of 1996. Eight months later, directed Jupiter in Pisces in the 11th house conjoined the Midheaven on January 3rd of 1997. She won the lottery on October 26th of 1996, between the dates when these two favorable directions perfected and within orb of each.

As for "excitants" to these primary directions (Mercury to Venus, and Jupiter to MC), transiting Venus in Virgo opposed natal Venus on October 18th and perfected a trine to natal Mercury on October 23rd of 1996, and transiting Jupiter conjoined the natal MC on November 16th of 1996.

The secondary progressions in effect when this woman won the lottery were progressed Moon opposite Neptune on October 23rd, square the MC/IC axis on October 26th, trine Pluto on October 31st, and semisquare Jupiter on November 26th. The MC/IC axis represents her public status and her domestic situation. Natal Pluto occupies her 5th house of good fortune and speculative gains. Jupiter natally trines Uranus (unexpected good luck) and by primary direction is conjunct the Midheaven during this period.

Finally, this woman's Birth Numbers identify age 46 as a potentially significant period:

Her *Single Digits Birth Number* (for 24 April 1950) is **25**, which reduces to **7**. Her *Additional Single Digits Birth Number* is found by adding 25 + 1950 = 1975, which reduces to 22, and then to 4; and 25 + 22 + 4 = **51**, which reduces to **6**.

Her *Double Digits Birth Number* (for 24 April 1950) is **43**, which reduces to **7**. Her *Additional Double Digits Birth Number* is found by adding 43 + 1950 = 1993, which reduces to 22, and then to 4; and 43 + 22 + 4 = **69**, which reduces to **15** and then to **6**.

The sum of her *Single Digits Birth Number* (25) and the reduced forms of her *Additional Double Digits Birth Number* (15 and 6) is 25 + 15 + 6 = **46**, which is her age when she won the lottery.

House Relationships between Zodiac Signs

An ancient technique considers the "house," or "place," relationship between the signs of the zodiac. For example, Valens in the second century notes in his *Anthologies* that a sign in the 8th place in zodiacal order from another sign bears a destructive relationship toward the initial sign. The 8th place signifies death, and modern astrologers associate it, along with signs in 6th place relationship, with the *quincunx* configuration. Sophia Mason, in her 1985 book *Delineation of Progressions*, has found that the quincunx can signify a situation in which you need to provide a service or make a demanding adjustment, at personal cost, such as caring for a sick or confined person; providing childcare; dealing with change in a relationship, such as a separation or death; or assuming too many responsibilities and feeling stretched thin.

Valens gives several examples of use of this principle to delineate aspects between signs and their rulers. For example, Sagittarius lies in the 8th place from Taurus, indicating that Sagittarius is potentially destructive toward Taurus, and configurations involving the rulers of those signs, that is, Jupiter and Venus, can signify death through too much pleasure-seeking, such as excessive eating or overindulgence in wine or sex, or via cerebral hemorrhage, which can be a consequence of such behavior. Jupiter signifies excess, and Venus represents one's appetites and desires. The death, however, is likely to be tranquil, and the life, one of luxury, because Venus and Jupiter are benefic planets.

Chapter 12
COMBINING CUSPS OF HOUSES
TO PRODUCE SENSITIVE POINTS

Frankland was practicing astrology in London during the early decades of the 1900s. At that time many astrologers regarded Placidus cusps as the most sophisticated method of house division, consistent with the classical teachings of Claudius Ptolemy. Convinced that the cusps of houses were especially powerful points, Frankland used the Placidus cusps to develop one of his "new measures" in astrology. He wrote the following in *New Measures in Astrology* (1928):

> The degrees on the cusps of houses should be of great importance if the division of houses are of importance. (Frankland 1928, 25)

> As a few minutes of birth time would alter the degrees on the cusp of the houses, it is clear that measurement of areas, periods, or years of events by cusps of houses will be confined to those cases where the time of birth is accounted for. When the time of birth is doubtful these measurements cannot be used, until the time has been ascertained or rectified. (Frankland 1928, 25)

Having clarified the importance of an accurate birth time, Frankland went on to describe his "new measure" that consisted of **sensitive points** produced by **combining house cusps,** that is, **adding together the zodiacal longitudes of the cusps of particular houses,** and sometimes also adding the position of a symbolically relevant planet:

> I offer a simple calculation to determine **when the houses are more *ripe for effect*.** (Frankland 1928, 23; italics and bold highlighting mine) ... **Add the cusp of the 4th house or ascendant to the cusp of any house required, such as the 2nd**

for finance, etc. *To the degree thus obtained, add a degree for each year of life.* [In his books Frankland implies that his preferred practice was to add the cusps of the other houses *to the cusp of the 4th* to produce sensitive points related to those houses.] (Frankland 1928, 25; italics and bold highlighting mine)

The **cusp of the 4th house seems to be very strong in its influence,** and its addition to other cusps plus years [of life] is very interesting. (Frankland 1928, 32; bold highlighting mine)

In other words, to study the significations of a particular house, add the cusp of that house to the longitude of the IC (4th cusp). Then direct the sensitive point obtained through the chart at a rate of 1° of longitude for each year of life. Alternatively, you can direct it at the rate of 4/7° of longitude for each year of life, which also produces impressive results.

The suggestion is here made that by a process of combination of two cusps a point is established that is important in regard to such houses. There is nothing illogical in this. We combine their influence when determining the influence of aspects from one house to another.

Once the cusps of houses are correctly established as to degree, then I suggest it is possible to *establish important points by* the simple method of *adding the cusps of two houses together.*

For instance, the cusp of the **6th house plus** the cusp of the **8th** may be taken as **a point for dangerous illnesses,** for this is combining the 6th and 8th house influence. (Frankland 1928, 27; italics and bold highlighting mine)

As the **cusps of [the intermediate] houses are generally reckoned in degrees only,** with the exception of the ascendant and mid-heaven, **this method only furnishes sensitive *years.***

Its value lies in that once the **sensitive years are established,** then it can readily be seen whether there is the combined influence of operative activity. This combination would make that particular year an eventful one.

The part of the year most eventful can then be determined by excitants. [Frankland regarded transits, including eclipses and planetary stations, as important "excitants" when predicting the specific timing of an event.] (Frankland 1928, 28–29; bold highlighting mine)

Any student may make the calculations without elaborate tables of logarithms, semi-arcs, trigonometry, etc., and, although the mathematical formula may be of exceeding value to the deeper student, and where detailed accuracy is necessary or desired, yet **this simple method will prove very valuable to those content to find important years.**

If one of these points of importance is found to accord with directions of similar nature, then the year is of great importance for such affairs.

Then examine that point in the light of suitable **transits** or **excitants** to ascertain the part of the year most propitious. (Frankland 1928, 31–32; bold highlighting mine)

In other words, Frankland viewed transits as triggers for the manifestation of the significations of primary directions, secondary progressions, and transits of the heavy, slow-moving planets. Thus, transits could pinpoint a fairly narrow range of dates in which a more ponderous, symbolically similar aspect might manifest. For example, if the native were passing through a period characterized by a progressed aspect between Mars and Saturn, then the transits of Mars during this period would be highly likely to correlate with symbolically related events in the native's life.

This method of calculation is commended for its simplicity combined with value, though of itself it is not so important as the measurements of signs and planetary bodies.

It will be found that **in many instances an adjustment of a degree or two on cusps of houses will yield these points.**

This would be **like rectifying the birth time a few minutes,** and in how many cases is the time known so accurately? [For simplicity in calculation, Frankland rounded the cusps of the intermediate houses to the nearest degree. His goal was to identify broad periods of influence rather than specific dates.] (Frankland 1928, 32; bold highlighting mine)

Unless the [birth] time is fairly accurately known—within, say, half an hour—house influence is better left alone; though its exclusion tremendously depletes the possibilities of judgment.

If known within the half-hour, then with a little skill the exact cusps of the houses can be determined, and repays the trouble that may be entailed. (Frankland 1928, 37)

Numerous examples could be shown that sufficiently demonstrate the fact that **the cusps of houses and their degrees are of importance,** and that **when they are totalled together give a point. This point, moved forward at a degree per year, reaches degrees that are beneficial or adverse. Such years are ripe for events of the nature of such houses, should there be suitable directional influence at the time.** (Frankland 1928, 31; bold highlighting mine)

The **angular houses**—1st, 10th, 7th, and 4th—are considered most important.

They certainly are from one point of view, in that they are expressive, less obscure in their working—yet every house is just as important, though the effects are less visible.

For example, the **10th house** is allied to **honour, position, matters obtaining in profession,** and, from an outward point of view, how important the position or **standing in life** is. (Frankland 1928, 33; bold highlighting mine)

Cases of **honour and upliftment** to the highest point.

Take Cusp of 1st,

plus Cusp of 10th,

plus Jupiter's position (Frankland 1928, 30; bold highlighting mine)

Ramsay MacDonald's *Point of Honour and Upliftment*

As an example of this last statement, Frankland considers the chart of British politician Ramsay MacDonald, born on 12 October 1866 in Lossiemouth, Scotland, at 8:30 a.m. GMT, Rodden Rating AA (chart 34). MacDonald became prime minister of the United Kingdom on 22 January 1924 (at age 57.285 years) and again from 1929–35. In his chart, calculated with Solar Fire, we see the following:

MacDonald's Ascendant is at 9° 02' Leo.

His MC is at 11° 25' Aries.

His natal Jupiter is at 23° 21' Capricorn.

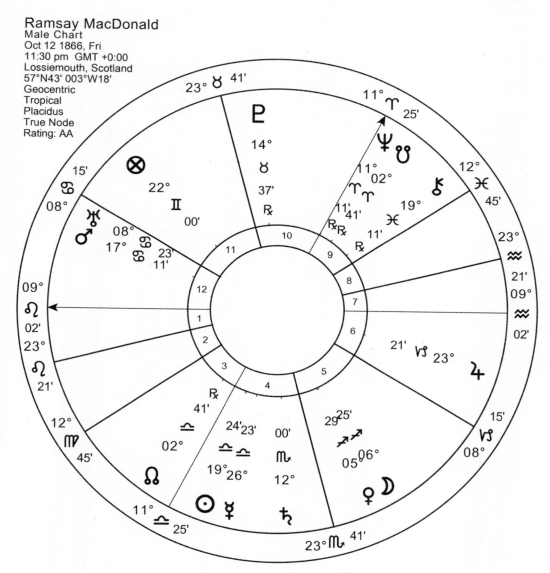

Chart 34: Ramsay MacDonald
12 October 1866, 11:30 p.m. GMT, Lossiemouth, Scotland, 57N43 3W18

Adding these three longitudes together (Asc + MC + Jupiter), we calculate his sensitive *Point of Honour and Upliftment* to be at 13° 48' Gemini.

If we add 57.285° (one degree for each year of life) to 13° 48' Gemini, we arrive at longitude 73.8° + 57.285°, which equals 131.085° and is equivalent to 11° 05' Leo. In other words, at age 57.28 MacDonald's directed *Point of Honour and Upliftment* lies in his natal 1st house, almost exactly trine his MC, which lies at 11° 25' Aries.

Interestingly, natal Saturn (the out-of-sect malefic in MacDonald's nocturnal chart) lies at 12° 00' Scorpio and casts its square to 12° 00' Leo in the 1st house. MacDonald became prime minister in January of 1924 as the directed *Point of Honour* was closely applying to trine his natal MC at 11° 25' Aries.

By the end of 1924, the directed *Point of Honour* would conjoin the square from Saturn in 12° 00' Leo. By that time, as a result of a bungled prosecution of a communist newspaper editor and other factors, MacDonald suffered an adverse vote in the House of Commons. The Conservatives regained a majority, and MacDonald resigned on 4 November 1924, as his directed *Point of Honour* conjoined malefic Saturn's square aspect at 12° 00' Leo.

The Directed *Point of Life* in MacDonald's Chart

At age 57.285, MacDonald's directed *Point of Life* was in early Sagittarius, conjunct his natal Moon and Venus, which are applying to trine his natal Ascendant. To calculate the directed *Point of Life* more precisely:

At age 57, the directed *Point of Life* was at longitude 244.286°, or 4° 17' Sagittarius.

At age 58, the directed *Point of Life* was at longitude 248.571°, or 8° 34' Sagittarius.

Doing the math, we see that at age 57.285 (when MacDonald became prime minister), his directed *Point of Life* was at 5° 30' Sagittarius, exactly conjunct his natal Venus and applying to soon conjoin his natal Moon (at 6° 25' Sagittarius).

Benito Mussolini's Point of Honour and Upliftment

According to his birth certificate, Benito Mussolini was born on 29 July 1883 at 14:00 LST in Dovia di Predappio, Italy (chart 35). (Frankland used a birth time of 1:54 p.m. in Milan, which is slightly different from the currently accepted 2:00 p.m. birth chart of Mussolini.)

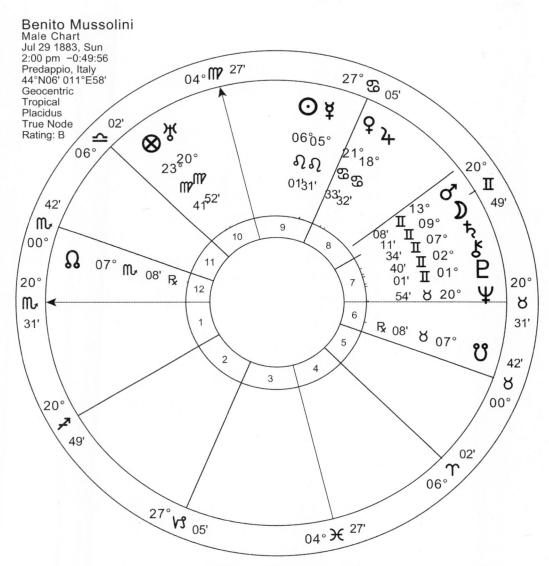

Chart 35: Benito Mussolini
29 July 1883, 2:00 p.m. LST, Dovia di Predappio, Italy, 44N06, 11E58

Using Frankland's formula, we would calculate Mussolini's *Point of Honour and Upliftment* by adding together the longitudes of the following points:

Asc at 20° 31' Scorpio

MC at 4° 27' Virgo

Jupiter at 18° 32' Cancer

Summing these three longitudes, we arrive at 13° 30' Leo as his *Point of Honour and Upliftment*. Mussolini became prime minister of Italy in 1922 at the age of 39½. Hence, we must add 39.5° to his *Point of Honour* to arrive at its directed position in 1922:

13° 30' Leo (*Point of Honour*) + 39.5° (at age 39.5) equals 23° 00' Virgo, which conjoins the Part of Fortune at 23° 41' Virgo in his 10th house of career.

Mussolini's birth time was officially recorded as 2:00 p.m., but this time may be rounded rather than the precise time of birth. If he had been born a few minutes earlier, as in the 1:54 p.m. chart used by Frankland, then his directed *Point of Honour* would have been conjunct natal Uranus in the 10th house and separating from favorable sextiles to natal Venus and Jupiter in Cancer—symbolism also consistent with his unexpected rise to power in Italy in 1922.

At age 39½, Mussolini's *Point of Life* (calculated at a rate of 7 years per sign, starting at 0° Aries) would have been at 19° 17' Virgo, which is sextile to the Jupiter-Venus conjunction in Cancer (separating from the sextile to Jupiter and applying to the sextile to Venus).

Because Mussolini's precise time of birth may be somewhat different from what is recorded on his birth certificate, we might consider a range of dates. At age 39, his directed *Point of Life* was in the 10th house at 17.14° of Virgo, and at age 40 it was at 21.42° Virgo, having crossed over Uranus in the 10th house and sextiled Venus in Cancer—marking age 39 as a highly significant year in his professional life.

Frankland's slightly earlier birth time for Mussolini placed the directed *Point of Life* conjunct the dictator's natal Uranus at age 39½. Frankland commented about such a conjunction in *New Measures in Astrology* (1928):

When a sensitive area of both house and sign coincides, then the power is increased. Take again the case of Mussolini. The point of upliftment plus his years just brings him to the degree of Uranus in the 10th house at that year of life. The same year, measured by sign at 7 years per sign, also brings him exactly to this degree of Uranus, thereby giving a very sensitive area, so that an operative influence at that time would have very powerful effect. This is further increased by the point being so powerful at birth (Uranus in the 10th house sextile Jupiter, sextile Venus, and sextile to the ascendant)

In such a case as this the point is almost causative—that is, it requires very little stimulus for effects. (Frankland 1928, 50–51)

In summary, Frankland developed his system using Placidus houses, and he regarded the cusp of each house as a sensitive point that embodied the significations of that house. A particular house becomes "ripe for effect" when one of the sensitive points, derived from the house cusp, becomes activated by a direction, progression, or transit.

Frankland described several ways to calculate the sensitive house-derived points:

- Adding the ecliptic longitude of a house cusp to the degree of the Ascendant (1st house cusp). For example, the 1st house cusp plus the 2nd house cusp would identify a sensitive point related to the meanings of the 2nd house (finances, income, etc.).

- Adding the ecliptic longitude of a house cusp to the degree of the IC (4th house cusp). For example, the 9th house cusp plus the 4th house cusp would identify a sensitive point related to the meanings of the 9th house (travel, publishing, religious activities, astrology, higher learning, etc.).

- Adding the cusps of any two houses to produce a sensitive point related to the combined meanings of the two houses. For example, the 11th house cusp (friends) plus the 7th house cusp (marriage) would produce a sensitive point regarding friendship that leads to marriage. Another example: the 6th house cusp (illness, injury) plus the 8th house cusp (death) identifies a sensitive point whose meaning is a dangerous (potentially fatal) illness or bodily injury.

After combining two house cusps, a relevant planet can also be added to the mix. For example, the house-related *Point of Honour and Upliftment* has this formula: 1st house cusp (the native) plus 10th house cusp (worldly status) plus Jupiter (good fortune). Charles Emerson (1923–92), one of the founders of the National Council for Geocosmic Research (NCGR), may have been influenced by Frankland when he developed his own *Point of Death*, which has this formula: longitude of Mars plus longitude of Saturn minus the MC degree.

The house cusps themselves are sensitive points that carry the meanings of the houses they represent. The planetary rulers of the signs on the house cusps have a similar significance. House cusps and their rulers can be directed to other points in the chart, and they can also receive the influence of directions and aspects of other planets to them.

Directions of house cusps (or planets or other points in the chart) to midpoints can be highly significant.

Serious Illness in the Life of Yusuf Islam (aka Cat Stevens)

The popular singer Yusuf Islam, aka Steven Demetre Georgiou and commonly known by his stage name, Cat Stevens, says that he was born at noon BST in London, England, on 21 July 1948, Rodden Rating A (chart 36). Birth times given as exactly on the hour are often rounded from the precise time, so the cusps of the chart presented here may be accurate to within a few degrees. Let's test Frankland's methods by studying some notable events in Yusuf/Cat Stevens's life.

On 20 February 1968 (at age 19.4), Yusuf/Cat Stevens was diagnosed with life-threatening tuberculosis and spent three months in King Edward VII Hospital in Midhurst, England. He then needed nine more months of convalescence at home. The period of recuperation from illness lasted from about age 19.4 to age 20.4. During this time, he wrote songs and pursued spiritual interests.

On 8 February 1976 (at age 27.45), he nearly drowned while swimming off the coast of Malibu, California. Struggling to survive his near-death experience, he bargained with God that "if you save me, I will work for you." Soon thereafter, a wave appeared and carried him safely back to shore. About six months later, on his 28th birthday (21 July 1976), he received a copy of the Qur'an, the holy book of Islam, as a gift from his brother David.

Cat Stevens
Male Chart
Jul 21 1948, Wed
12:00 pm BST −1:00
London, England
51°N30' 000°W10'
Geocentric
Tropical
Placidus
True Node
Rating: A

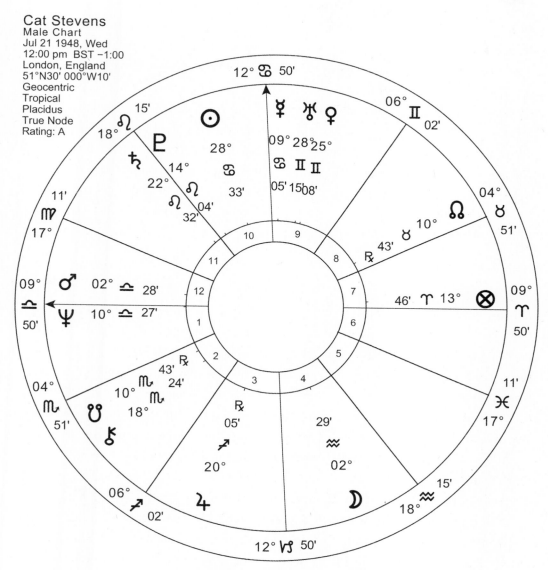

Chart 36: Yusuf Islam (Cat Stevens)
21 July 1948, 12:00 p.m. BST, London, England, 51N30 0W10

Yusuf/Cat Stevens's *Age along the Zodiac*

During Yusuf/Cat Stevens's illness from ages 19.4 to 20.4, his *Age along the Zodiac* ranged between 19.4° and 20.4° of Aries, making a trine to Jupiter Rx in Sagittarius in the 3rd house, coinciding with his concerns about health and his spiritual interests. Jupiter, a planet associated with religion and spirituality, rules his natal 3rd house, the ancient house of the Moon goddess, and also rules his 6th house of illness. The beneficial trine to Jupiter correlates with his survival of a life-threatening bout of tuberculosis.

At age 27.45, when he nearly drowned, his *Age along the Zodiac* was at 27.45° Aries; and at age 28, when he received the gift of a Qur'an, his *Age along the Zodiac* was at 28° Aries. These *Age Points* are sextile to Uranus in Gemini in the 9th house of religion and also square to his Sun in Cancer in the 10th house of career. The symbolism of a major shift in the direction of his career, simultaneous with a strong interest in a new religion, is apparent.

Yusuf/Cat Stevens's *4/7° Age Point*

During Yusuf/Cat Stevens's illness from ages 19.4 to 20.4, the *4/7° Age Point* ranged between 11.09° and 11.66° of Aries and was not applying closely to any point or stellar body in his chart. It is, however, separating from an opposition to Neptune in Libra near the Ascendant and from a quincunx to the South Lunar Node in Scorpio. These recent past influences could be references to his nagging cough in the period prior to February of 1968 and the factors that made him prone to contracting tuberculosis, namely, excessive drinking, smoking, lack of sleep, and fast living while on the road as a pop musician.

At age 27.45, when he almost drowned, and at age 28, when he received his first Qur'an, his *4/7° Age Point* would have been at 15.69° and 16° of Aries, respectively. These *4/7° Age Points* do not closely aspect any point or stellar body in the natal chart.

If we direct the planets in Yusuf/Cat Stevens's chart by 15.69° (the arc at the time of the swimming accident), we find that the natal Moon arrives at 18° 10' Aquarius, almost exactly square natal Chiron at 18° 24' Scorpio. The Moon rules his 10th house of career, which was impacted dramatically and for the remainder of his life by the near-death experience, a psychological wound, at age 27.45.

Yusuf/Cat Stevens's *Point of Life*

From ages 19 to 20, Yusuf/Cat Stevens's *Point of Life* ranged from about 21½° to 30° of Gemini. During this period of recuperation and convalescence from life-threatening tuberculosis, his *Point of Life* conjoined Venus and Uranus in Gemini in the 9th house of religion, semisextiled the Sun in Cancer in the 10th house of career, and sextiled Saturn in Leo in the 11th house of friendships.

At age 27, his *Point of Life* ranged from about 25° 42' Cancer to 0° Leo. Here it conjoined his Sun in Cancer in the 10th house of career. Yusuf/Cat Stevens's swimming accident had a major impact on the direction of his career. When he received his first Qur'an at age 28, his *Point of Life* was just entering Leo and would soon sextile Mars in Libra in the 12th house and oppose the Moon in Aquarius in the 4th house, perhaps symbolizing his turning away from his childhood religion to follow a new path in his spiritual quest. In the old Hellenistic texts, the 12th place belongs to the Bad Daemon or Evil Spirit and is associated with mental anguish related to spiritual issues.

Combining Houses and Rectifying Yusuf/Cat Stevens's Chart

Frankland calculated a house-derived *Point of Dangerous Illness* by adding the longitudes of the cusps of the 6th and 8th houses:

6th cusp: 17° 11' Pisces

8th cusp: 04° 51' Taurus

Adding the two cusps produces 22° 02' Aries as the *Point of Life-Threatening Illness*. For simplicity in calculation, Frankland would have rounded the 6th house cusp in Yusuf/Cat Stevens's chart to 17° Pisces and the 8th house cusp to 5° Taurus, which, when added together, would produce a sensitive point at 22° Aries.

If we direct the *Point of Dangerous Illness* at 22° Aries by the *Age Point* to age 20, we arrive at 12° Taurus, which does not closely aspect any natal planet in his chart.

If we direct 22° Aries (the *Point of Dangerous Illness*) by the *4/7° Age Point* of about 11.5° when he was recuperating from tuberculosis, we arrive at 3.5° Taurus, which does not closely aspect any natal planet.

If we direct 22° Aries (the *Point of Dangerous Illness*) by the *Age Point* at age 27.5, when he almost drowned, we arrive at 19.5° Taurus, which is separating from an opposition to Chiron but does not aspect any other natal planet.

If we direct 22° Aries (the *Point of Dangerous Illness*) by the *4/7° Age Point* at age 27.5, we arrive at 7.7° Taurus, which does not aspect any natal planet.

The *Point of Dangerous Injury or Illness* does not appear to be working for a birth time of exactly 12:00 noon. It could be that this method is not always effective or, more likely, that the birth time is off by a few minutes. Using the chart cast for exactly noon, we may have calculated this house-based point with inaccurate house cusps. The symbolic directions just described would be more appropriate if he had been born around 12:07 p.m. instead of noon.

At 12:07 p.m., for example, the cusp of the 6th house would be 18° 35' Pisces, and the cusp of the 8th house would be 6° 13' Taurus. The "rectified" *Point of Dangerous Injury or Illness* would then calculate to 24° 48' Aries instead of 22° 02' Aries. With this rectified value, the following directions would be in effect:

- At age 19.4, when Yusuf/Cat Stevens was diagnosed with tuberculosis, the "rectified" *Point of Dangerous Illness*, symbolically directed by his *Age along the Zodiac*, would arrive at 24.8° + 19.4°, which equals 14.2° of Taurus (14° 12' Taurus) in the 8th house, tightly square to Pluto in Leo, an aspect that could readily symbolize danger of death.

- At age 27.45, when he nearly perished in the Pacific Ocean, the "rectified" *Point of Dangerous Illness*, symbolically directed by his *Age along the Zodiac*, would arrive at 24.8° + 27.45°, which equals 22.25° of Taurus (22° 15' Taurus), closely square to Saturn (a natural symbol of death) in Leo from the natal 8th house of near-death experiences.

- At age 27.45, his *4/7° Age Point* lies at 15.69° Aries. If we symbolically direct his "rectified" *Point of Dangerous Illness* by 15.69°, we arrive at 24.8° + 15.69°, which equals 10.49° Taurus (10° 29' Taurus), almost exactly conjunct his North Lunar Node in the 8th house of death. The Moon's North Node tends to amplify and expand the significations of the points or planets that it contacts.

Because these symbolic directions are so descriptive of the events that occurred during these periods of life, I suspect that Yusuf/Cat Stevens was probably born around 12:07 p.m. BST.

Frankland would have further examined such a preliminary rectification of the birth time by first checking whether the overall "pattern or plan" of the rectified chart correlated with the course of life of the native. Next, he would have checked well-documented events against important transits ("excitants") to vital points in the nativity. Transiting Mars, in particular, can promote activity in the areas of the chart that it contacts and also trigger the manifestation of long-acting operative influences (directions, progressions, etc.). Frankland comments in *Astrological Investigations* that the process of rectification by transits is "very tedious work."

A Note on Frankland's Quick and Easy Method of Combining Cusps

Frankland was interested in a rapid and effective method of forecasting. To this end, he rounded the values of the house cusps to the nearest degree. He also had a quick method for combining zodiac signs. Let me illustrate with the example from Yusuf/Cat Stevens:

6th house cusp: 17° 11' Pisces is rounded to 17° Pisces

8th house cusp: 4° 51' Taurus is rounded to 5° Taurus

Frankland then gives Pisces the value of 11 (by subtracting 1 from the ordinal number of the sign, with Pisces as the 12th sign) and Taurus the value of 1 (by subtracting 1 from the ordinal number of the sign Taurus, which is the 2nd sign). Thus, Pisces plus Taurus equals 11 + 1, or 12, which is a complete cycle of the zodiac that corresponds to sign 0, or Aries. The addition of the two cusps by this simple method is 17° + 5° equals 22°, and sign 11 + sign 1 adds up to sign 12, which is equivalent to sign 0, or Aries.

To use this method of addition, assign numerical values to the signs as follows:

0 or 12 = Aries (a complete cycle of the zodiac)

1 = Taurus

2 = Gemini

3 = Cancer

4 = Leo

5 = Virgo

6 = Libra

7 = Scorpio

8 = Sagittarius

9 = Capricorn

10 = Aquarius

11 = Pisces

If the sum is 12 or more, simply subtract 12 to find which of the 12 signs is indicated. The following table listing the zodiac longitude of the beginning of each sign may also be helpful.

ECLIPTIC LONGITUDES OF 0° OF EACH ZODIAC SIGN			
Sign	Longitude of the Initial Degree	Sign	Longitude of the Initial Degree
Aries (0)	0°	Libra (6)	180°
Taurus (1)	30°	Scorpio (7)	210°
Gemini (2)	60°	Sagittarius (8)	240°
Cancer (3)	90°	Capricorn (9)	270°
Leo (4)	120°	Aquarius (10)	300°
Virgo (5)	150°	Pisces (11)	330°

Combining Cusps in the Chart of William Ewart Gladstone

To illustrate Frankland's quick method of addition of cusps to produce sensitive points, let's look at one of his examples, the chart of British politician William Ewart Gladstone, who was born 29 December 1809 in Liverpool, England, at about 8:00 a.m. (the break-fast hour).

Gladstone served four terms as prime minister of the United Kingdom under Queen Victoria between 1868 and 1894. He originally wanted to become a priest in the Church of England, but his father dissuaded him. Instead, Gladstone became a candidate for election to Parliament in December of 1932, shortly before he turned 23 years old. His *Point of Life*, in 8° 34' Cancer at age 23, was separating from an opposition to his natal Sun, applying to sextile Uranus at his MC in Scorpio, and also applying to trine natal Pluto in Cancer in the 2nd house of finance. One of his early positions in government was connected with the treasury.

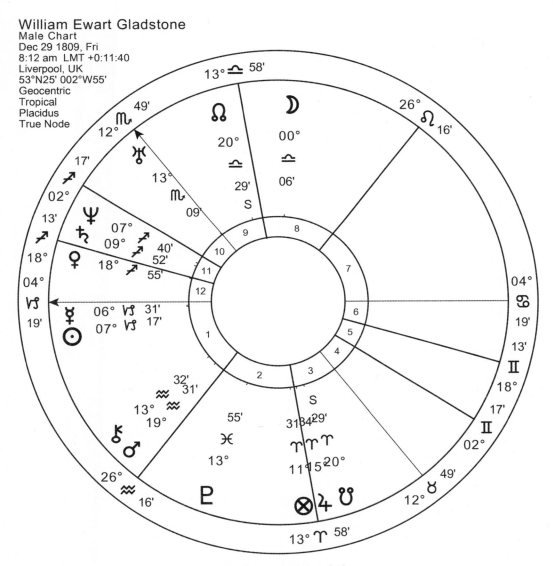

Chart 37: William Ewart Gladstone
29 December 1809, 8:12 a.m. LMT, Liverpool, England, 53N25 2W55

Interestingly, Gladstone's natal 10th house ruler Mars (career) is sextile 9th house ruler Venus (the priesthood), and Mars is trine the North Lunar Node in the 9th house. Besides ruling the 9th house cusp of religious matters, Venus also rules the 4th house, which signifies his father. Perhaps natal Uranus conjunct the MC, which became activated by a sextile from his *Point of Life*, which was at 13° Cancer when he turned 24 years old, correlates with the dramatic shift in his career path from religion to politics in his early 20s.

Alan Leo gives Gladstone's birth time as 8:00 a.m., and Astro.com lists it as 8:15 a.m. LMT, Rodden Rating C. Frankland appears to have used a birth time for Gladstone closer to 8:12 a.m. LMT, which is the chart used in this text (chart 37).

Gladstone (born on 29 December 1809) died of cancer on 19 May 1898 at 88.4 years of age. Frankland calculated two distinct house-related sensitive points related to death:

A. The 6th house cusp (illness) plus the 8th house cusp (death) as a *Point of Serious Illness*.

B. The 4th house cusp (final endings) plus the 8th house cusp (death) as a *Point of Fatal Illness at the End of Life*.

We can show Frankland's simple method in tabular form for sensitive point A, a *Point of Serious Illness*:

A. 6TH + 8TH HOUSE CUSPS (*Point of Serious Illness*)			
	Sign	**Degrees**	**Minutes**
6th House Cusp	Gemini (2)	18°	13'
8th House Cusp	Leo (4)	26°	16'
Sum	Libra (6)	44° (30° + 14°)	29'
Converting	**Scorpio (7)**	**14°**	**29'**
Age 88.4		88° (60° + **28°**)	24'
88.4° =	+ 2 signs	28°	24'
Add 88.4° to 14° 29' Scorpio	Capricorn (9)	42° (30° + **12°**)	53' (= 29 + 24)
Converting	**Aquarius (10)**	**12°**	**53'**

In this table, the sum of the 6th and 8th house cusps is 14° 29' Scorpio. Then, adding 88.4° to symbolically direct this sensitive point at the rate of 1° for each year of life, we arrive at 12° 53' Aquarius, which is conjunct Gladstone's natal Chiron and square to his natal Uranus at the time of his death.

Let's do a similar calculation for sensitive point B, a *Point of Fatal Illness at the End of Life*:

B. 4TH + 8TH HOUSE CUSPS (*Point of Fatal Illness at the End of Life*)			
	Sign	**Degrees**	**Minutes**
4th House Cusp	Taurus (1)	12°	49'
8th House Cusp	Leo (4)	26°	16'
Sum	Virgo (5)	38° (30° + 8°)	65' (1° + 5')
Converting	**Libra (6)**	**9°**	**5'**
Age 88.4	2 signs	28°	24'
Add 88.4° to 9° 5' Libra	Sagittarius (8)	37° (30° + 7°)	29'
Converting	**Capricorn (10)**	7°	**29'**

The sensitive point generated by adding together the 4th and 8th house cusps lies at 9° 5' Libra. We direct this point to age 88.4 by adding 88.4° and arrive at 7° 29' Capricorn, which was conjunct Gladstone's natal Sun in the 1st house and semisextile his natal Neptune in Sagittarius when he succumbed to terminal cancer.

Note also that the Sun, to which this symbolic direction arrives, rules his 8th house of death and is closely conjunct Mercury, which rules his 6th house of illness. In addition, Neptune, which receives a stressful semisextile from the directed 4th + 8th house–related point, is conjunct natal Saturn, ruler of the Ascendant.

I have repeatedly found that with directions, whether they be symbolic or real-time based, the semisextile behaves much like the quincunx and relates symbolically to 6th and 8th house issues. As with the quincunx, the signs involved in the semisextile aspect are in aversion.

Justin's Bieber's Facial Paralysis

In early June of 2022, singer Justin Bieber was diagnosed with paralysis of the right side of his face due to a syndrome first described in 1907 by James Ramsay Hunt. The symptoms are due to an infection of the facial nerve near the ears by the varicella-zoster virus, the cause of chickenpox and shingles. Bieber was scheduled to give a concert on 7 June 2022 in Toronto, Canada, but had to cancel due to illness.

In early June of 2022, Justin Bieber was 28.26 years old (chart 38). His Frankland measures were:

Age along the Zodiac (Age Point): 28.26° Aries (28° 16' Aries)

4/7° per year measure: 16.15° Aries (16° 09' Aries)

The *Point of Life* at ages 28 to 29 ranges from 0° to 4° 17' of Leo.

At age 28.26, the *Point of Life* is at about 1° 07' Leo (0.26 × 4° 17').

When Bieber became ill in early June of 2022, his *Point of Life* was at 28° 16' Aries in his natal 5th house of entertainment (concerts) and closely quincunx his natal Pluto, which is stationary and conjoins the Ascendant. At the same time, his *4/7° per year measure* at 16° 09' Aries conjoined his 5th house cusp of entertainment and concerts. In the midpoint modal sort (mod 90), the *4/7° per year measure* at 16° 09' Aries (cardinal) is closely connected to the natal midpoints Chiron/Lunar Node, Saturn/Pluto, and Saturn/Ascendant—the combination of which symbolically describes a period of illness or injury associated with intense effort, feelings of restriction, and isolation from other people.

Bieber's *Point of Life* at age 26.26 lies at about 1° 07' Leo in the 8th house and is applying to the position of a Solar Eclipse at 2° 01' Scorpio on 25 October 2022. Bieber's *Point of Life* at age 28 ranges from 0° to 4.17° of Leo in his 8th house and forms a quincunx to natal Saturn, his contrary-to-sect malefic. With natal Saturn in his 3rd house, one might expect difficulty with his ability to communicate at this time.

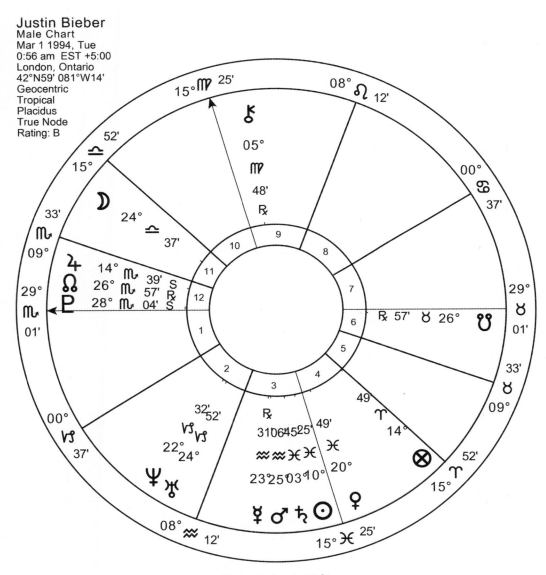

Chart 38: Justin Bieber
1 March 1994, 00:56 a.m. EST, London, Ontario, Canada, 42N59 81W14

Symbolically Directing Justin Bieber's 6th House Cusp of Illness

One of Frankland's methods of directing house cusps appears in *New Measures in Astrology* (1928):

> Add the cusp of the 4th house or ascendant to the cusp of any house required, such as the 2nd for finance, etc. *To the degree thus obtained add a degree for each year of life.* (Frankland 1928, 25, italics mine)

Frankland appears to favor beginning with the 4th house cusp, to which he added the cusp of the house in question. He also rounded figures to the nearest degree to make calculating easier. Here are the calculations done to the exact degree:

Bieber's 4th house cusp is at 15° 25' Pisces and his 6th house cusp at 9° 33' Taurus. Adding the degrees of these cusps, we obtain 15° 25' + 9° 33' = 24° 58'.

Adding the whole signs, we arrive at Pisces (330) + Taurus (30) = Aries (360); or, using the numerical equivalents of signs, 11 + 1 = 12.

Thus, at age 28, we direct by adding 28° to the sum of the 4th and 6th house cusps:

24° 58' Aries + 28° = 22° 58' Taurus as a sensitive point, which lies in his 6th house and is in close square to natal Mercury, ruler of the 10th of career. (Bieber canceled his concerts at this time due to illness.)

House Cusps of Stanley Conder, Boy Explorer

An example that Frankland often cited is that of Stanley Conder, the "boy explorer" who drowned in Canada in 1910 at the age of 15½. Based on Frankland's description of the chart and information in Alan Leo's *1001 Notable Nativities*, I have reconstructed a reasonable approximation of the birth chart of Conder, as used by Frankland (chart 39). However, I was unable to find biographical information about Stanley or his exact place of birth.

The boy explorer apparently drowned in Canada at the age of 15½. Frankland notes that, in the boy's natal chart, the danger from water is symbolized by the Sun in Libra, the sign of its fall, in the 9th house (long journeys) and in square to Jupiter, the 12th house ruler (misfortune) in the water sign Cancer. The fallen Sun rules the 8th house of death and squares the ruler of the 12th house of undoing.

In addition, natal Venus rules the 4th house of endings and occupies the 8th house of death, from which Venus squares Neptune, the god of the seas. Neptune occupies the unfortunate 6th house of illness and accidents.

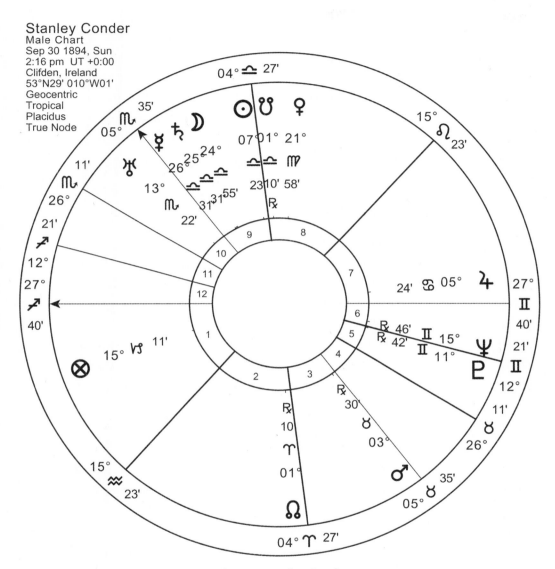

Chart 39: Stanley Conder
30 September 1894, 2:16 p.m. UT, Clifden, Ireland, 53N29 10W01

At age 15½, the boy's *Age along the Zodiac* (calculated by counting at the rate of 1° per year, starting at 0° Aries) is at 15° 30' Aries, in sextile to Neptune in the 6th house and in square to the Part of Fortune.

According to Frankland, we can also count the *Age along the Zodiac* backward, or in reverse zodiacal order, which takes us to 14½° Pisces, a point in square to natal Neptune at 15° 46' Gemini Rx in the 6th house within an orb of slightly more than 1°. This orb is at the outer limit of those customarily used by Frankland, but in *Astrological Investigations* (1926) he notes that such symbolic directions do not precisely time events; rather:

> Aspects formed by this method [*Age along the Zodiac*] to other parts of the Nativity, *while in themselves not necessarily giving events,* yet give added weight, when combined with other factors. (Frankland 1926, 78)

Frankland rarely uses this method of symbolic directing "backward" by counting the *Age along the Zodiac* in reverse zodiacal order. Today we would call this a "neo-converse" direction, because the astrologer is measuring the arc of direction in the reverse order of the natural zodiac, thus directing the horoscope backward in time.

A more useful "new measure" related to dangerous illness and the risk of death is found by adding together the cusps of the 6th (illness) and 8th (death) houses. In my reconstruction of Stanley Conder's chart, this involves:

6th house cusp equals 12° 21' Gemini.

8th house cusp equals 15° 23' Leo.

Their sum is 27° 44' Libra.

In his book, Frankland rounded the house cusps to whole degrees and arrived at the sum of 28° Libra, a value that is 16' of arc greater than the sum of the cusps in my reconstructed chart.

Stanley drowned at age 15½, so we must add 15.5° (1° per year of life) to 27° Libra 44', which directs *the Point of Danger to Life* to 13° Scorpio 14', a point that is conjunct his natal Uranus at 13° 22' Scorpio and closely applying to a semisquare to Chiron (the wounded healer), which lies at 28° 34' Virgo in the 8th house.

Stanley Conder was born at the end of September and died at age 15½, which means that his passing occurred in late March or early April of 1910. The following table lists the **transits of the outer planets** for that period in 1910.

CONDER'S OUTER PLANET TRANSITS, MARCH–APRIL 1910			
Date = 1910	**Transiting Planet**	**Aspect**	**Natal Planet**
March 28	Neptune 16° Can 32'	Stationary direct	
March 29	Pluto 24° Gem 55'	Trine	Moon
April 3	Uranus 24° Cap 55'	Square	Moon
April 6	Saturn 24° Ar 55'	Oppose	Moon
April 11	Saturn 25° Ar 31'	Oppose	Saturn
April 18	Jupiter 7° Lib 23' Rx	Conjunct	Sun
April 19	Saturn 26° Ar 31'	Oppose	Mercury
April 20	Saturn 26° Ar 42'	Semisquare	Pluto

Notice that at age 15½, transiting Uranus (activated in the natal chart by his *directed Point of Danger to Life*) squares his natal Moon. Then transiting Saturn opposes his natal Moon and goes on to oppose his natal Saturn. Next, his Ascendant-ruler Jupiter conjoins the Sun, which rules his 8th house of death. This is followed by transiting Saturn opposing natal Mercury, ruler of the 6th house of illness, and then forming a semisquare to Pluto, which lies on the cusp of the 6th house.

The Transit of Mars to Conder's Natal Chart

Not included in the list of transits of the outer planets in 1910 just presented is that of transiting Mars, which on 1 April 1910 conjoined his natal Pluto at 11° 42' Gemini, activating the natal Pluto-Neptune conjunction and its quincunx to natal Uranus. Mars often acts as a trigger to outer planet configurations.

Solar Arc Directions in Conder's Chart

Here are Conder's **solar arc directions** for the first six months of 1910 as calculated in Solar Fire:

Stanley Conder–Male Chart
Sep 30 1894, 1:51 p.m., +0:25
53°N29', 010°W01'
Geocentric Tropical Zodiac
Placidus Houses, True Node

- Directed Mercury at 11° 42' Scorpio *quincunx* natal Pluto on 11 February 1910. (Mercury rules the 6th house of bodily ailments in Conder's chart, and Pluto is a general signifier of the afterlife. Pluto conjoins the cusp of his 6th house. The quincunx is a configuration that links planets 6 or 8 whole signs apart and has 6th and 8th house significance.)

- Directed Uranus at 28° 34' Scorpio *sextile* natal Chiron on 20 February 1910. (Uranus indicates sudden, unexpected events. Chiron is often activated when there are unexpected injuries to the body.)

- Directed Neptune at 01° 10' Cancer *square* the natal true lunar nodes on 29 April 1910. (Planets square to the true lunar nodes often indicate crises and fateful events.)

- Directed Venus at 7° 23' Libra *conjunct* natal Sun on 13 May 1910. (Venus rules the 4th house of end-of-life matters, and the Sun rules the 8th house of death.)

Stanley Conder and Alan Leo's Zodiac Signs as Periods of Life

If we apply Alan Leo's concept of zodiac signs corresponding to stages of life, then Stanley Conder at age 15½ was in his Gemini phase (ages 14–21). Gemini is a difficult sign for this native because it contains a Pluto-Neptune conjunction, which falls on the cusp of the 6th house of illness and receives a stressful quincunx from Uranus in Scorpio.

Uranus is powerful in this chart because it occupies the angular 10th house, and it has an adverse influence because Uranus in Scorpio is disposed by Mars, the out-of-sect malefic in this diurnal chart. Mars lies in its detriment in Taurus and is strong because it conjoins the angular 4th house cusp.

A sensitive point in early Gemini (ages 14–21) would be 7° 23' Gemini, which is the trine from the Libra Sun, lord of the 8th house of death. The Sun is in its fall in Libra.

At age 15, Stanley Conder's directed *Point of Life* (calculated by equating each zodiac sign with 7 years of life, commencing from 0° Aries) would be at 4° 17' Gemini, and at age 16 it would be at 8° 34' Gemini. Thus, at age 15½ years when he drowned, his directed *Point of Life* would have been at 6° 26' Gemini, closely approaching the trine from his fallen Sun, ruler of the 8th house of death.

Valerie Percy and the Charts of Twins

On 18 September 1966 at about 5:15 a.m., Valerie Jean Percy, who had a twin sister, was found beaten and stabbed to death in her bed in her family's Kenilworth mansion. Valerie's father was running for the US Senate at the time. According to the birth certificates of the twin sisters, Valerie was born on 10 December 1944 at 5:25 p.m. PWT in Oakland, California (chart 40), just 2 minutes before her sister Sharon.

Valerie and her surviving twin, Sharon, have quite similar birth charts, a significant difference being that Valerie's Ascendant lies at 13° 39' Gemini, whereas Sharon, born 2 minutes later, has her Ascendant in a different degree, namely, 14° 10' Gemini. Born at 5:25 p.m. PWT in Oakland, California, Valerie was murdered at 21.77 years of age. Her twin, Sharon, born at 5:27 p.m. PWT, is still living and has led a productive public life.

Can Frankland's method of combining house cusps to generate sensitive points help differentiate the birth charts of these twins?

Frankland would have begun by looking at the major themes in the chart. In Valerie's chart (and in that of her sister, because they were born just two minutes apart), Frankland would immediately have noticed the angular Uranus conjunct the Ascendant opposite the angular Mars-Sun conjunction at the cusp of the 7th house. Such a configuration shows the natal potential for sudden, unexpected danger to the life or health at some point during the life of the native. This natal Mars-Uranus opposition is more pronounced in Valerie's chart, which has an earlier Ascendant degree, because the planets involved are closer to the horizon.

Taking a broad view of the planetary placements *by sign* in the chart, Frankland would have noticed that 8th house ruler Saturn and the North Lunar Node in Cancer oppose 1st house ruler Mercury, 12th house ruler Venus, and the South Lunar Node in Capricorn, in a T-square formation involving Chiron, Neptune, and the Moon in Libra. The activation of the T-square at some point in Valerie's life could be quite dangerous because it involves the Ascendant-ruler Mercury, and the Ascendant is afflicted by a Uranus-Mars opposition at birth.

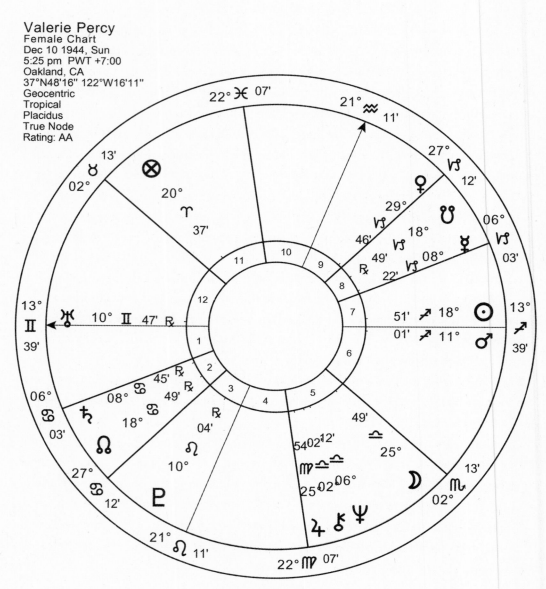

Valerie Percy
Female Chart
Dec 10 1944, Sun
5:25 pm PWT +7:00
Oakland, CA
37°N48'16" 122°W16'11"
Geocentric
Tropical
Placidus
True Node
Rating: AA

Chart 40: Valerie Percy
10 December 1944, 5:25 p.m. PWT, Oakland, California, 37N48 122W16

Frankland would have observed that the *Point of Life* traversing Aries from age 0 until age 7 could be a difficult period because it highlights this natal T-square. The next challenging period would run from age 21 until age 28, when the *Point of Life* passes through Cancer (in square to Aries), highlighting the natal 8th house ruler Saturn opposing Ascendant-ruler Mercury and squaring the natal Chiron-Neptune conjunction—ages 21 to 22 being an especially dangerous period.

In his quick assessment of birth charts, Frankland estimated the future positions of the slow planets, especially Uranus and Neptune, on the basis of their cycles—roughly 84 years for Uranus and 164 years for Neptune. Thus, Uranus opposes its birth position around age 42 and squares it around ages 21 and 63. Neptune's orbit is more erratic, so estimates of its position are less precise. Neptune opposes its natal position around age 82 and squares it around age 41, give or take a few years.

Highlighting the period around ages 21 to 22 is the fact that Uranus squares its natal position at this time. In Valerie's chart, the square from transiting Uranus would activate the natal opposition between Uranus and the Mars-Sun conjunction across the horizon axis. Mars opposing Uranus on the Ascendant can symbolize the risk of an accident or unexpected violence.

Neptune during this same period would be roughly semisquare its natal position around age 21. Because Neptune closely squares natal 1st-ruler Mercury on the 8th house cusp, at age 21 Neptune would be approximately semisquare both natal Mercury and the 8th house cusp—a potentially dangerous transit.

The *Point of Life* at age 21.77, when the murder took place, lies at 3° 18' Cancer, opposite the natal 8th house cusp and in square to the natal Chiron-Neptune conjunction in Libra, which is part of the natal T-square involving Saturn in Cancer opposite Mercury in Capricorn. Natal Neptune also closely squares the 8th Placidus house cusp.

Thus, both twins were in danger of death around ages 21–22. Are there any distinguishing features between the two charts?

Frankland believed that the Placidus house cusps were especially sensitive points with regard to the significations of the houses. He also found that combining house cusps, by adding together their zodiacal longitudes, could produce sensitive points related to the combined meanings of the houses. In this case of a murder that went unsolved, he might have combined the cusp of the 8th house of death with the cusp of the 12th house of mysterious enemies who do the native harm. The following table compares these factors in the charts of Valerie and her twin sister.

SENSITIVE *POINT OF DEATH BY SECRET ENEMY*			
Twin	**8th Cusp**	**12th Cusp**	**8th + 12th House Cusps (*Point of Death by a 12th House Secret Enemy*)**
Valerie (b. 5:25 p.m. PWT)	6° Cap 03'	2° Tau 13'	8° Aqu 16'
Sharon (b. 5:27 p.m. PWT)	6° Cap 30'	2° Tau 52'	9° Aqu 22'

Essentially, Frankland calculates a sensitive point, similar to a lot or Arabic part, that combines the significations of both houses. Here, the *Point of Death by a 12th House Secret Enemy*, resulting from the addition of the 8th and 12th cusps of the natal houses, helps to distinguish the two birth charts:

Valerie, born at 5:25 p.m., has her *Point of Death by a 12th House Secret Enemy* at 8° 16' Aquarius, **applying** at birth to quincunx 8th house ruler Saturn and to semisextile Ascendant-ruler Mercury, which conjoins the 8th house cusp. Applying aspects generally refer to the future one is moving toward. Valerie is the twin who was mysteriously murdered.

Sharon, born at 5:27 p.m., has her *Point of Death by a 12th House Secret Enemy* at 9° 22' Aquarius, **separating** from a quincunx to Saturn and separating from a semisextile to Mercury, because the planetary positions between the two charts are essentially the same. Separating aspects generally refer to the past, which one is moving away from. Sharon is the twin who survived and had to grieve the murder of her sister.

Chapter 13
AVERAGE POSITIONS AND MIDPOINTS

William Frankland's birth chart does not appear in Astro.com, nor have I been able to find it via google searches of the internet. However, from various comments Frankland made about his own chart in his books, I was able to reconstruct his natal chart.

In appendix A of his book *The Moment of Astrology* (1994), Geoffrey Cornelius describes the horary chart that made Frankland famous in 1926, and he comments that the astrologer was originally from Burnley, England, but moved to London about 10 years earlier. A google search revealed the GPS coordinates of Burnley, England, to be latitude 53.7894° (53° N 47') and longitude -2.255° (02° W 15'). Solar Fire gives the coordinates of Burnley as 53° N 48', 02° E 14'.

In his books, Frankland gives the following clues about his own birth chart.

Using Placidus houses, the cusp of his 8th house is at 7° Aries, and the cusp of the 6th house is at 20° Aquarius. He rounded the intermediate house cusps to the nearest degree.

His natal Moon lies in 26° Virgo.

His natal Saturn is retrograde in 29° Pisces. His secondary progressed Saturn retrograded to perfect an opposition to his natal Moon in September of 1908 when he was 29.93 years old, about 6 months after his Saturn return at age 29.5. Frankland commented that his natal Moon-Saturn opposition correlated with a difficult childhood and early life.

In *New Measures in Astrology* (1928), Frankland states that in his birth chart "Virgo rises with Uranus, Mercury, Venus, and Moon in that sign" (Frankland 1928, 37–38).

Using the above data, we can look in the ephemeris for the late 1800s and find that William Frankland was born early on Thursday morning, 26 September 1878, in Burnley,

England. The Sun had not yet risen. It was a Mercury day, during a Moon hour, the 11th hour of the night. Using Solar Fire, I calculated that the figure that most closely matches Frankland's description of his own chart has a birth time of 4:26 a.m. UT (chart 41).

Frankland erected his own chart using an ephemeris and astronomical tables of the early 1900s. A modern computer-generated chart varies slightly from the one he described. For example, Solar Fire places his Moon at 27° 08' Virgo, whereas Frankland had it at 26° Virgo. In addition, Solar Fire places Frankland's 8th Placidus house cusp at 7° 06' Aries and his 6th house cusp at 20° 37' Aquarius. (Elsewhere in his text, Frankland explains that the cusps of the intermediate houses are generally reckoned in degrees only; hence he lists only the rounded degrees of the 6th and 8th house cusps and omits the number of minutes.)

Regarding his own life, Frankland mentions the following significant incidents, which he uses to illustrate his methods of symbolic direction:

- A dangerous illness at age 18.5
- A dangerous illness at age 30.5

If we consider these serious illnesses from the point of view of annual profections (which Frankland did not use), then at age 18 his profected Ascendant was in Pisces, which activated Saturn Rx in Pisces in the 7th house opposite his 1st house planets, especially his natal Moon, Mars, and Sun.

The Moon is a general signifier of the body, and the Sun of one's vitality. Mars in this case rules Frankland's 8th house of near-death experiences. Saturn rules his 6th house of illness and, as the out-of-sect malefic in a night chart, can be especially harmful in its hard aspects (square and opposition). It is not surprising, then, that Frankland suffered a dangerous illness when his natal Saturn was activated by the annual profected Ascendant at age 18 and again, 12 years later, at age 30.

Instead of discussing annual profections, Frankland uses his two illnesses to illustrate one of his "new measures in astrology." Because the 6th house deals with illness and the 8th house with death, he argues that the sum of the cusps of the 6th and 8th houses will produce a symbolically significant point in the zodiac symbolizing the serious illness of the native. This "point of illness" can then be symbolically directed to other factors in the birth chart.

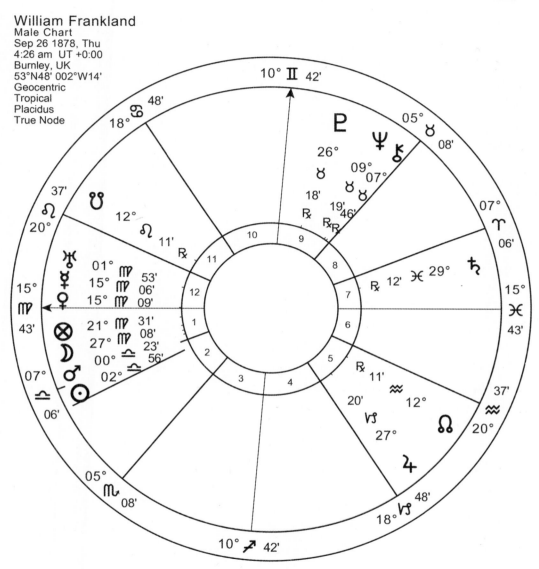

William Frankland
Male Chart
Sep 26 1878, Thu
4:26 am UT +0:00
Burnley, UK
53°N48' 002°W14'
Geocentric
Tropical
Placidus
True Node

Chart 41: William Frankland
26 September 1878, 4:26 a.m. UT, Burnley, England, 53N48 2W14

To illustrate with Frankland's chart:

The 6th house cusp is at 20° 37' Aquarius, which is equivalent to zodiac longitude 320:37°.

The 8th house cusp is at 7° 06' Aries, which is equivalent to zodiac longitude 7:06°.

The *sum* of the degrees of the two cusps equals zodiac longitude 327:43°, equivalent to *27° 43'Aquarius*, which is identified as *a sensitive point symbolic of serious illness* in his chart. Illnesses are likely to occur at ages when this sensitive point is symbolically directed to relevant factors in his birth chart.

Frankland uses the formula one degree along the ecliptic equals one year of life, so that 18.5 years old is equivalent to an arc of 18.5°, and 30.5 years old is equivalent to an arc of 30.5°. Because he was born at the end of September and does not give the specific dates of his illnesses, I assume he meant by 18.5 and 30.5 years old that they occurred at some point between mid-March and mid-April during the years following his birthdays at ages 18 and 30.

Frankland's Illness at Age 18.5

27° 43' Aquarius (the *Point of Illness*) + 18.5° equals 16° 13' Pisces, suggesting that an illness might occur when 16° 13' Pisces, the directed *Point of Illness*, activated some factor in Frankland's birth chart. The *Point of Illness* is directed at a rate of one degree for each year of life. At age 18.5, his directed *Point of Illness* was almost exactly opposite his natal Ascendant, which represents his body and state of health.

Frankland's Illness at Age 30.5

27° 43' Aquarius (the *Point of Illness*) + 30.5° equals 28° 13' Pisces, suggesting that an illness might occur when the directed *Point of Illness*, 28° 13', activates some relevant factor in Frankland's birth chart. The *Point of Illness* is directed at a rate of one degree for each year of life. At age 30.5, the symbolically directed *Point of Illness* opposed his natal Moon and was applying to conjoin his natal Saturn. In fact, the directed *Point of Illness* was almost exactly square the Moon-Saturn **midpoint** (at 28° 10' Gemini) when he fell dangerously ill. Symbolic directions to midpoints are quite useful with this technique.

Frankland Moves to London

According to Geoffrey Cornelius, in 1916 Frankland decided to leave Burnley and relocate to London. He turned 38 years old in September of 1916, and his directed *Point of Life* at this age would have ranged roughly from 13° to 17° Virgo, highlighting his natal Mercury, Venus, and Ascendant—all three in 15° Virgo. His secondary progressions in 1916 were as follows:

• Progressed Mercury semisquare natal Mars in February of 1916
• Progressed Venus sextile natal Uranus in March
• Progressed Mercury sextile natal Ascendant in April
• Progressed MC sextile natal Mercury in July
• Progressed MC sextile natal Venus in August
• Progressed Asc sesquisquare natal Pluto in September
• Progressed Sun quincunx natal MC in October

Mercury rules Frankland's natal Ascendant and MC. Venus rules his natal 9th house (long trips, astrology) and his natal 2nd house (income). The *Point of Life* during this period gave added weight to progressions and directions involving Mercury, Venus, and the natal Ascendant.

The Importance of Midpoints and Average Positions

In his writings, Frankland frequently mentions the importance of **midpoints** in predictive work. Interestingly, the astrologer most commonly associated with midpoints, Alfred Witte, founder of the Hamburg School of Uranian Astrology, was also born in 1878, about seven months earlier than William Frankland. To be precise, Witte was born on 2 March 1878 in Hamburg, Germany, and died on 4 August 1941.

The following is a quote from Frankland's *Astrological Investigations* (1926) about the importance of midpoints in chart delineation and prediction:

> Planets occupying the Mid-Point (within a few degrees) between the Luminaries, or Mid-point between the Ruler [of the Ascendant] and Luminaries or Vital points, would be in a sensitive place. The Nature and Position of such planets should be well considered. (Frankland 1926, 43)

Midpoints and the Astrologer Who Died at Age 46

One of Frankland's examples of the use of midpoints with his symbolic measures in *Astrological Investigations* is the chart of an astrologer who was born on 20 July 1824, presumably in England at about 6:30 p.m. (chart 42). Frankland tells us that this person has the Sun at 28° Cancer and a stellium of planets in Cancer, including Venus, Jupiter, and Mercury, all of which are conjunct the Sun.

When we cast the chart described by Frankland, we find the natal Sun by modern calculation at 27° 52' Cancer, receiving a square from the *Point of Life* in Aries at age 27.87. Because the Sun rules the Placidus cusp of the 8th house of death and anguish of mind, this native may find the period around age 27 to be particularly challenging. Applying Frankland's idea of the "ripple effect" of planets according to Ptolemy's *seven ages of man*, the next ripple of the *Point of Life*'s square to the natal Sun will occur 19 years later, when the native is about 46 years old.

Across the wheel from the stellium in Cancer lies the Ascendant in Capricorn with Uranus at 13° and Neptune at 7° of Capricorn. The *average position of the planets* in Cancer is 24° 44' Cancer. The *average position* of Uranus and Neptune is 10° 28' Capricorn. The midpoint of the average positions of these opposing clusters of planets lies at 17° 35' Libra. Frankland notes that the *Point of Life* traversing mid-Libra will be an adverse period because the *Point of Life* will then be squaring, and thus intensifying, the natal Cancer-Capricorn opposition.

In fact, this astrologer died when he was 46 years old, which corresponds to the directed *Point of Life* lying at 17° 08' Libra when he reached that age. In *Astrological Investigations* (1926), Frankland comments that "Uranus at 46 [years of age] has moved to the planets in Cancer. Neptune at 46 has moved into Aries" (Frankland 1926, 45).

Interestingly, this person's demise occurred around the time that his directed *Point of Life* (17°–21.5° Libra at age 46) was traversing his natal/solar return Uranus midpoint at 17° 54' Libra, squaring the solar return true South Lunar Node at 19° 03' Capricorn, and opposing Neptune at 21° 49' Aries in the solar return. Alfred Witte, in his rules for planetary pictures, links the combination of Uranus with Neptune to incapacitation, funerals, and death. In addition, the astrologer under discussion was passing through his Mars period (ages 41–56), according to Ptolemy's *seven ages of man*.

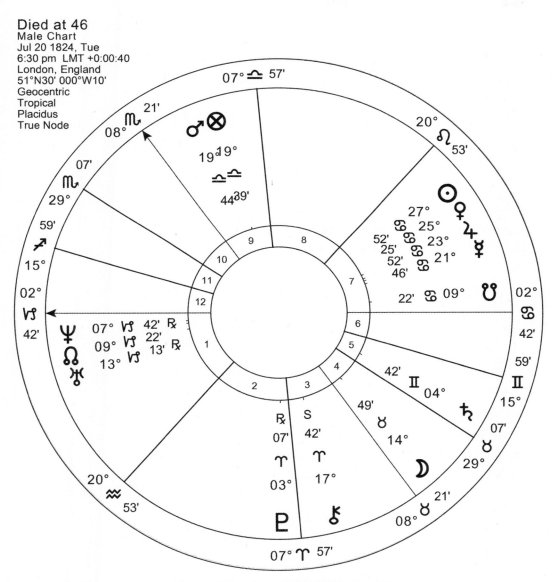

Died at 46
Male Chart
Jul 20 1824, Tue
6:30 pm LMT +0:00:40
London, England
51°N30' 000°W10'
Geocentric
Tropical
Placidus
True Node

Chart 42: Astrologer Who Died at Age 46
20 July 1824, 6:30 p.m. LMT, London, England, 51N30 0W10

Even without looking at an ephemeris, Frankland would have seen in the natal chart that this native's early to mid-40s would be a difficult time of life. Knowing that transiting Uranus opposes natal Uranus during the same period that transiting Neptune is squaring its natal position, Frankland would have estimated that around age 42, Uranus would be in Cancer and Neptune in Aries, in a Grand Cross formation with natal Mars in Libra, natal Chiron in Aries (if he had known about the existence of Chiron), and the natal Cancer-Capricorn oppositions.

Frankland also attended to the average, or *mean*, positions of clusters of planets in each sign. The average natal position of Uranus and Neptune was around 10° Capricorn in this chart, and the average natal position of the man's stellium in Cancer was about 25° Cancer. There is a difference of 15° (half a sign) between degrees within their signs of these two positions. Because it takes Uranus about 3.5 years to traverse half a sign, the period around age 42 plus 3.5 years equals 45.5 years of age, which would be especially problematic.

Furthermore, the midpoint modal sort in Solar Fire for this man's chart reveals that both of the malefics, Mars and Saturn, fell at 19° 43' Libra in the list of midpoints, corresponding to roughly age 46.5 years. This occurs because natal Mars lies at 19° 44' Libra, and natal Saturn is almost exactly sesquisquare to Mars from its position at 4° 43' Gemini. The directed *Point of Life* arrived at 19° 43' Libra when the native was 46 years and 7.5 months old, that is, around early March of 1871. Frankland does not tell us in which month this astrologer died.

This example highlights the importance Frankland placed on knowing basic astronomical facts about the orbits of the slower planets. In this way, since he didn't have access to an ephemeris, he could look at a natal chart and estimate the positions of the transits of the ponderous planets. For example, knowing that the tropical orbit of Uranus is about 84 years, he would know that transiting Uranus forms hard aspects to its natal position around ages 21, 42, and 63. Therefore, he would look for other evidence of major life changes or disruptive events around these ages.

Similarly with Neptune, Frankland knew that the tropical orbit of Neptune is about 164 years, so that the opposition of transiting Neptune to its natal position occurs around age 82 (half the orbit) and the transiting square at about age 41 (a quarter of the orbit). Because the orbit of Neptune is irregular, these ages are approximate and the exact aspect may perfect a few years before or after. For example, Neptune typically perfects a square to its birth position between 38 and 45 years of age.

The ponderous planet Saturn has a tropical orbit of about 29.42 years, so that it forms hard aspects to its birth position every 7.36 years. Thus, transiting Saturn opposes its natal position around age 14.7 (which can be rounded to age 15) and forms a square to its natal position around age 7.4 and again around age 22. With these facts in mind, Frankland would have eyeballed the chart of the astrologer who died in his mid-40s and known immediately that he experienced a Saturn opposition to its natal position at about age 44 (the initial opposition around age 15 plus Saturn's orbit of about 29 years means that the opposition repeats around age 15 + 29, which equals 44). Thus, at age 46, when the stressful transits of Uranus and Neptune were activating the Grand Cross, it would be apparent that transiting Saturn was at the same time passing through the natal 12th house—a difficult combination of astrological influences that interact quite stressfully with the natal chart.

Everyone experiences these challenging aspects of transiting Saturn, Uranus, and Neptune to their natal positions at roughly the same time during their late 30s and early to mid-40s. We call this the period of the mid-life crisis. What characterizes this span of time for each individual, however, depends on how these universal astrological influences interact with the particular pattern of the native's birth chart.

The Importance of Mean Positions of a Related Group of Planets: Deborah Houlding's Mutable T-Square

In the March 1999 issue of *The Traditional Astrologer*, Deborah Houlding gave an account of a personal experience with serious illness. Deborah's first symptom was hearing loss in one ear, which occurred when she departed an airplane after landing in Australia while on a lecture tour. Being an astrologer, she carefully noted the time: 5:03 p.m. AEST. After several consultations with doctors over a period of months, she was finally diagnosed in the autumn of 1998 (at age 36.41) with a benign acoustic neuroma, which was successfully removed surgically.

According to AstroDatabank, Deborah was born on 14 May 1962 at 8:30 a.m. BST in Mansfield, England (chart 43). At the time she first noticed the hearing loss, she was 35.875 years old. At that age:

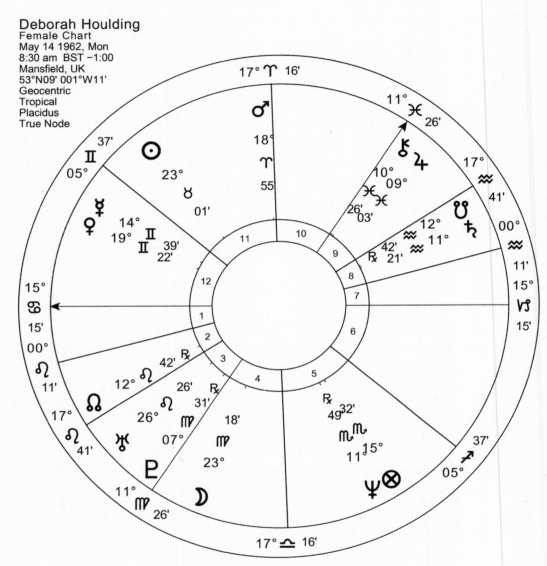

Deborah Houlding
Female Chart
May 14 1962, Mon
8:30 am BST −1:00
Mansfield, UK
53°N09' 001°W11'
Geocentric
Tropical
Placidus
True Node

Chart 43: Deborah Houlding
14 May 1962, 8:30 a.m. BST, Mansfield, England, 53N09 1W11

- Her *Age along the Zodiac* was 35.875°, which converts to 5° 53' Taurus.
- *4/7 of her Age along the Zodiac* was 20.5°, or 20° 30' Aries.
- Her *Point of Life* at age 35.875 was at 3° 45' Virgo.

If Frankland were examining this chart, he would have immediately noticed the mutable T-square involving the planets in Gemini, Virgo, and Pisces. He found repeatedly that "when some strong direction is formed between or on the points of the square, a most drastic or eventful time is indicated" (Frankland 1926, 45).

Frankland paid close attention to midpoints, but also to the *mean positions* of all the planets involved in a particular Grand Cross or T-Square formation. For example, in this chart there are six planets (Mercury, Venus, Pluto, Moon, Jupiter, Chiron) in the mutable signs. Frankland would have estimated the *mean position* of all six planets in the mutable signs to be about 14°. If we calculate it precisely, we arrive at a mean position of 14° 04' of the mutable signs. Thus, a direction, progression, or major transit to around 14° of mutable signs is likely to trigger the challenging natal mutable T-square into action.

In this nativity, the Sun in the favorable 11th house and in sextile to the Ascendant would traditionally be considered *hyleg*, that is, the "giver of life." By Frankland's *4/7° measure* at the time that Deborah noticed her first symptom of hearing loss (an arc of 20.5°), the directed Sun would arrive at 13° 31' Gemini, applying within orb to conjoin the mean position of all the planets in the mutable T-square. This directed Sun to the mean position of the mutable planets would perfect at age 36, when the benign tumor was finally diagnosed.

Uranus often signifies unexpected or surprising events. In this case, Uranus directed by the *4/7° measure* at age 35.875 (an arc of 20.5°) arrived at 16° 56' Virgo, in close square to the Mercury/Venus midpoint in Deborah's 12th house of chronic and hard-to-diagnose illness. Mercury and Venus occupy her 12th house, which is ruled by Mercury.

Also during this period, the *Age along the Zodiac* lay at 5° 53' Taurus and was quincunx the natal 6th house cusp, indicating the possibility of illness. In addition, the *Point of Life*, which passes through Virgo from ages 35 until 42, was activating her T-square and approaching natal Pluto, which opposes Jupiter-Chiron, in a little over a year. Jupiter in this chart rules the 6th house of illness. Prior to conjoining natal Pluto, the *Point of Life* would square the 6th and 12th house cusps (5° 37' mutable), which corresponds roughly to September of 1998.

No doubt Frankland would have cautioned Deborah to follow up on any medical symptoms she noticed around age 36, especially in the late summer and early autumn of 1998 when the *Point of Life* was closely squaring her natal 6th and 12th house cusps on its way to conjoining natal Pluto.

Another interesting point is that if we were to relocate Deborah's natal chart to the airport in Australia, her relocated natal 8th house cusp would be at 25° 08' Gemini. If we then directed the relocated natal Ascendant by the *4/7° Age Point* at 35.875 years of age, it would arrive at 15° 38' Cancer, closely conjunct her natal Ascendant, indicating a strong 8th house signification at that time.

4th and 8th Harmonic Aspects of the *Point of Life*

Frankland found that significant events were indicated by the hard aspects of directions, progressions, and transits made by the more ponderous planets, that is, the slowest bodies, such as Saturn, Uranus, and Neptune. (Pluto had not yet been discovered in 1926.) He also noted that the *Point of Life* makes a major hard (4th harmonic) aspect to its current position every 21 years (conjunction, square, opposition).

In Deborah Houlding's chart, seeing that the *Point of Life* conjoined Pluto at age 36, thereby *activating the earliest planet in the mutable Grand Cross*, Frankland would have advised her to be aware of the potential for difficult and stressful periods especially at ages 15, 36, 57, 78, and 99 (the *4th harmonic aspects*), and also, but to a lesser extent, at ages midway between these (the *8th harmonic aspects*, i.e., semisquares and sesquisquares), that is, around ages 25.5, 46.5, 67.5, and 88.5. In practice, I have also found that a *quincunx* can trigger a Grand Cross formation, as can be seen in the next case example.

The Mutable Grand Cross of the Grieving Mother from Madrid

A 47-year-old woman engaged in psychotherapy to deal with complicated grief following the death of her 15-year-old son in a hospital shortly after a motorcycle accident two years prior. The woman was born on 10 September 1965 at 4:30 p.m. CET in Madrid, Spain (chart 44). This case was presented at an international astrology conference. To protect the woman's privacy, the exact date of the son's demise was not given.

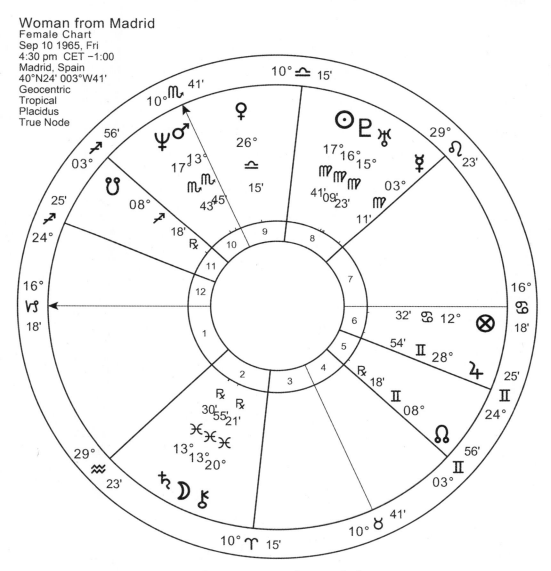

Chart 44: Woman from Madrid
10 September 1965, 4:30 p.m. CET, Madrid, Spain, 40N24 3W41

Frankland would have immediately noticed the mutable Grand Cross formed by the stellium of planets in Virgo opposing the cluster in Pisces, all squaring the lunar nodes in Gemini and Sagittarius. The planet in the earliest degree of this Grand Cross is Mercury at 3° 11' Virgo at the cusp of the natal 8th house of death. With Mercury ruling the 5th house of children and squaring the lunar nodes, which straddle the 5th/11th house axis, Frankland might have wondered whether at some point in the woman's life she would become concerned about the mortality of one of her children. The 5th house ruler Mercury *"at the bendings"* (in square to the lunar nodes) indicates the natal potential for some type of crisis involving 5th house issues.

When might this natal Mercury, which functions as the entrance to the mutable Grand Cross, be triggered? The *Point of Life* traverses the first four degrees of Virgo at age 35, semisquares this position at age 45.5, and squares it at age 56. We know that this woman's son died when she was 45 years old, which is consistent with the semisquare of the *Point of Life* to natal Mercury at that age. Let's look at Frankland's other symbolic measures at age 45:

- The *Point of Life* at age 45 ranges from about 13° to 17° Libra. Thus, it is square to the Ascendant and quincunx to the Moon-Saturn conjunction, which lies at 13° Pisces and is part of the mutable Grand Cross involving the 2nd, 5th, 8th, and 11th houses.

- The *Age along the Zodiac* is at 15° Taurus, which is opposite to the Mars/Neptune midpoint in Scorpio at the cusp of the 10th house. The natal 10th house, ruled by Mars, is the derived 6th house of bodily injury from the 5th house of children.

- The *4/7° Age along Zodiac* is at 25.7° Aries (25° 43' Aries), which opposes natal Venus, which conjoins the contra-antiscion of Mercury, ruler of the natal 5th house of children. Venus rules the natal 4th house, which is the derived 12th house (hospitalization, undoing) of the 5th house of children.

Frankland found that the symbolic directions need a real-time operative influence to indicate the manifestation of an event. If we calculate this native's primary directions for the year 2010 (when she turned 45 years old), we find that primary directed Mars (Placidus semi-arc, 0° latitude, Naibod key) conjoined natal Uranus in the 8th house in

September near her birthday. In October of 2010, primary directed Jupiter (ruler of the natal 12th house, which is the derived 8th from the 5th) sesquisquared natal Uranus in the 8th house.

Midpoints and the Demise of Garry Hoy

Canadian lawyer Garry Hoy worked for the law firm of Holden Day Wilson in Toronto, Canada. To demonstrate the unbreakable nature of the glass windows of the Toronto-Dominion Centre, his practice was to hurl his body at one of the windows, always bouncing back into the room. On 9 July 1993, however, Mr. Hoy attempted to show a group of students how unbreakable the windows were. As usual, he leaped forcefully against a window. As promised, the glass did not break, but in this instance the window frame gave way and Mr. Hoy plunged several stories to his death.

Several sources give Garry Hoy's birth date as 1 January 1955, time unknown. I wondered whether Frankland's measures would indicate the risk to his life at age 38.52, when he fell out of the window. Because his birth time is unknown, the chart here is cast for midday, with the Sun on the 1st house cusp (chart 45).

Without an accurate birth time, we cannot use measures that rely on the cusps of the houses. Eyeballing the chart, however, we can see certain natal configurations that could relate to a fatal accident at some time in Hoy's life:

- Pluto (lord of the underworld) in Leo squares Saturn and Venus in Scorpio.
- A group of planets in Capricorn oppose the Jupiter-Uranus conjunction in Cancer, and this opposition squares the Moon in Aries and Neptune in Libra in a cardinal Grand Cross configuration.
- The Moon in Aries squares the Moon's nodes. Let me remind the reader that Ptolemy, in book 3, chapter 12, of the *Tetrabiblos*, linked the position of the Moon at the nodes or its bendings to injuries, illnesses, paralysis, and dangers such as a falling from a height.

Were any of these configurations highlighted by Frankland's measures when Mr. Hoy was 38 years old, the year of his demise?

At age 38, Hoy's *Point of Life* ranges from 12° 51' to 17° 09' Virgo, which trines his natal Mercury and does not adversely interact with any of his natal planets. However, as he approaches age 39, his *Point of Life* becomes within orb of an opposition to natal Mars.

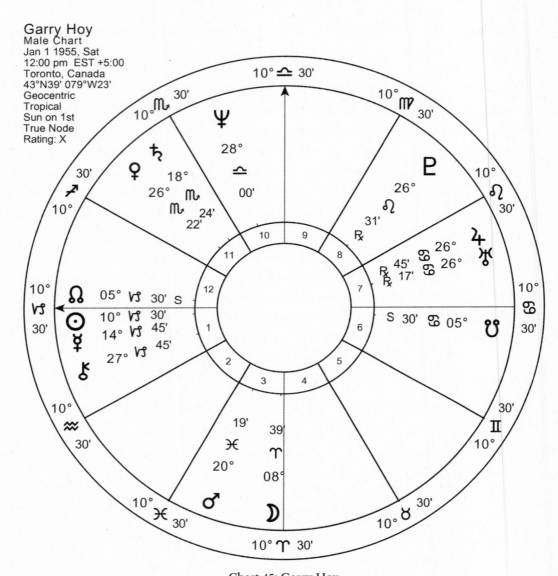

Garry Hoy
Male Chart
Jan 1 1955, Sat
12:00 pm EST +5:00
Toronto, Canada
43°N39' 079°W23'
Geocentric
Tropical
Sun on 1st
True Node
Rating: X

Chart 45: Garry Hoy
1 January 1955, 12:00 p.m. EST (time unknown), Toronto, Canada, 43N39 79W23

At age 38.52, Hoy's *Age along the Zodiac* was at 8° 31' Taurus, which is almost exactly semisextile to his natal Moon at midday, which is part of his cardinal Grand Cross. Because we don't know his time of birth, we cannot rely on this aspect in our interpretation.

At age 38.52, Hoy's *4/7° Age Point* lies at 22° 01' Aries, which falls in the midst of his natal cardinal Grand Cross and is closely quincunx the Saturn/Uranus midpoint at 22° 20' Virgo. Saturn is associated with falls, and Uranus with accidents and sudden unexpected occurrences.

Following Frankland's reasoning in the previous example of the astrologer who died at age 46, we can calculate the average positions of the groups of planets involved in the Cancer-Capricorn oppositions:

In Capricorn, the average position of the Sun, Mercury, and Chiron is 17° 40' Capricorn. (Chiron is included because it is often active in cases of bodily injury.)

In Cancer, the average position of Jupiter and Uranus is 26° 31' Cancer.

The midpoint of the average positions of the groups of planets in Capricorn and in Cancer is 22° 06' Aries.

Thus, the *4/7° Age Point*, at 22° 01' Aries at the time of his death, was almost exactly conjunct the midpoint of the average positions of the two sets of planets in opposition to each other in Cancer and Capricorn.

In many ways, Frankland's symbolic measures and use of midpoints and average positions of groups of planets constitute a remarkable technique. Even without an exact birth time, Frankland's methods can identify significant periods in the native's life by considering clusters of planets in different signs and how they relate to one another. In this case, there is a group of planets in Capricorn opposing another group in Cancer. The "influence" of each cluster of planets appears to center around the average position of the planets in each group. Then, by calculating the midpoint of the average positions of the opposing clusters, Frankland's symbolic measures are able to approximate the age of the native when the effects of this opposition will manifest.

Chapter 14
ASPECTS AND ORBS:
THE KNATCHBULL TWINS

The twin grandsons of British Lord Mountbatten were born in London, 20 minutes apart, on 18 November 1964—Nicholas Knatchbull at 3:40 p.m. GMT and Timothy Knatchbull at 4:00 p.m. GMT, Rodden Rating AA. Both boys were on an outing with their grandfather in Mullaghmore, Ireland, when, on 27 August 1979, the Irish Republican Army (IRA) bombed the family gathering. Lord Mountbatten and 14-year-old Nicholas (born at 3:40 p.m.) died instantly. Timothy, born 20 minutes later than his identical twin, survived the explosion but was blinded in one eye. A 15-year-old friend, Paul Maxwell from Enniskillen, was also killed in the incident. Timothy went on to write a book about his experience, *From a Clear Blue Sky: Surviving the Mountbatten Bomb* (published 19 October 2009), for which he won the Christopher Ewart-Biggs literary award in 2011 at age 46.

I am grateful to Maria Blaquier for drawing my attention to the charts of the Knatchbull twins. Because they were born 20 minutes apart, the natal angles and house cusps will be fairly unique for each chart. Frankland developed his system using Placidus houses. At 3:40 p.m. GMT, the Ascendant was 17° 50' Taurus, the MC was 20° 51' Capricorn, and the 8th house cusp was 14° 51' Sagittarius. Twenty minutes later, at 4:00 p.m. GMT, the Ascendant was 25° 54' Taurus, the MC was 25° 35' Capricorn, and the 8th house cusp was 20° 01' Sagittarius. Let us apply Frankland's methods to the birth chart of Nicholas (chart 46), who died in the bombing.

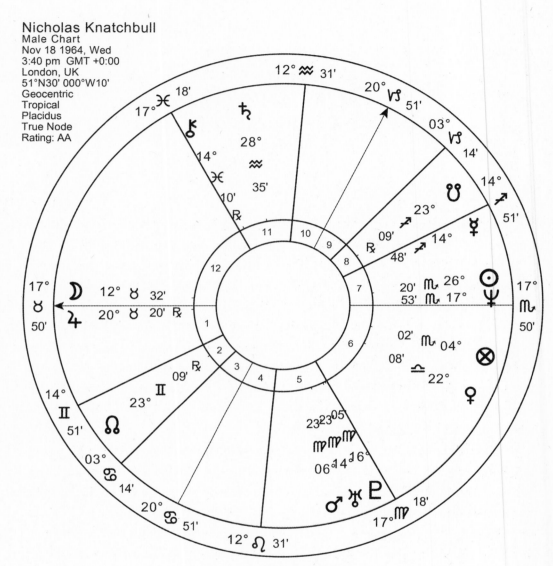

Chart 46: Nicholas Knatchbull
18 November 1964, 3:40 p.m. GMT, London, England, 51N30 0W10

Frankland often began by studying the numerology of the birth date. In this case, the deceased twin, Nicholas, was born on 18 November 1964:

Adding the single digits of the birth date produces $1 + 8 + 1 + 1 + 1 + 9 + 6 + 4$, which equals **31** as his *Single Digits Birth Number*, which reduces to $3 + 1$, or **4**.

Because the month and day are double-digit figures, we must also calculate the *Double Digits Birth Number*: $11 + 18$ equals 29, which we add to the sum of the digits of the year 1964. The result is **49** as his *Double Digits Birth Number*, which further reduces to $4 + 9 = $ **13** and then to $1 + 3 = $ **4**.

Frankland also calculated *Additional Birth Numbers* by adding the principal Birth Numbers to the 4-digit year of birth:

$1964 + $ **31** equals 1995, which reduces to $1 + 9 + 9 + 5$, or **24**, which further reduces to $2 + 4$, or **6**. Then, **31** $+$ **24** $+$ **6** $= $ **61** as the *Additional Single Digits Birth Number*, which reduces to $6 + 1 = $ **7**.

$1964 + $ **49** equals 2013, which reduces to $2 + 0 + 1 + 3$, or **6**. Then, **49** $+$ **6** equals **55** as the *Additional Double Digits Birth Number*, which reduces to $5 + 5 = $ **10** and then to $1 + 0 = $ **1**.

Potentially significant ages, based on these Birth Numbers, are **31, 49, 55,** and **61** and combinations of these Birth Numbers with each other or with their reduced forms, that is, **1, 4, 7, 10,** and **13**.

Frankland also believed that combinations of these numbers and their reduced forms could highlight important years. For example:

- $31 + 13 = 44$, the age at which Timothy published his book about the bombing
- $10 + 4 = 14$, the age at which Nicholas died in the incident
- $31 + 10 + 4 + 1 = 46$, the age at which Timothy won the Christopher Ewart-Biggs literary award

I remain somewhat skeptical of Birth Numbers. Frankland, however, felt that we must first carefully examine the birth data, which consists of a set of numbers indicating the day, month, and year of the nativity:

Examine the way it [the birth date] is built, just as you might examine the stones upon which you build. (Frankland 1926, 30–31)

Judging the Overall Tenor of the Chart

Frankland would have next studied the birth chart, looking for patterns and prominent features that reveal the natal promise.

Nicholas was born with an exalted Moon in Taurus conjunct Jupiter and the Ascendant—a fortunate configuration. The Ascendant-ruler Venus lies in her own sign of Libra, made prominent by a close square to the MC.

Natal Moon and Jupiter at the Ascendant are opposed by the Sun and Neptune in Scorpio. Neptune, which can signify dissolution, exactly conjoins the 7th house cusp, giving it special prominence in the life of the native as the most angular planet in the chart.

Broadly speaking, the Moon-Jupiter-Ascendant in Taurus cluster opposes Sun-Neptune in Scorpio and forms a square to natal Saturn in Aquarius. This is a potentially stressful T-square pattern, formed when two or more planets in opposition both aspect a third "focal," or "apex," planet by square aspect. This natal T-square can be triggered by operative influences affecting any of the fixed signs at some point during the life of the native.

In addition to the T-square, this birth chart contains a Grand Cross pattern involving the mutable signs. The cluster of planets in Virgo (Mars, Uranus, Pluto) are a potentially violent and explosive combination. Uranus tightly opposes Chiron in Pisces and tightly squares Mercury and the 8th house cusp in Sagittarius, which in turn oppose the true lunar North Node in Gemini. An operative astrological influence affecting any of the mutable signs can trigger this Grand Cross into action at some point during the life of the native.

Frankland's Symbolic Measures in Nicholas's Chart

The *Age along the Zodiac (Age Point)* begins at 0° Aries and proceeds at a rate of 1° per each year of life. Around age 6, the *Age Point* at 6° Aries makes a quincunx to Mars at 6° 23' Virgo in Nicholas's chart. I do not know what occurred in his life at this early age. Perhaps a childhood injury or illness?

The next aspect formed by the *Age Point* occurs around age 14, when it traverses 14° Aries and forms a stressful semisextile to Chiron in Pisces, a quincunx to Uranus in Virgo, and a trine to both Mercury and the 8th house cusp in Sagittarius. (The semisextile and quincunx are stressful because the signs involved are in aversion, and the quincunx in particular links signs that bear a 6th or 8th house relationship to one another.)

The close trine of the *Age Point* to both Mercury and the 8th house cusp is a generally harmonious aspect. In this case, however, the activation of Mercury simultaneously triggers the tight square of Mercury to the Chiron-Uranus opposition, with Uranus being part of a potentially dangerous stellium with Mars and Pluto. In addition, Mercury rules the 6th house and almost exactly conjoins the 8th house cusp—Frankland regarded the combination of the 6th (bodily injury) and 8th (death) houses to have a potentially life-threatening significance.

Natal Mercury lies at 14° 48' Sagittarius, which corresponds to age 14 + 48/60 = 14.80 years old. The bombing occurred on 27 August 1979 when Nicholas (born 18 November 1964) was 14.77 years old.

If we consider the *Point of Life* (one zodiac sign for each year of life, starting at 0° Aries), at age 14 it was traversing the region from 0° to 4.3° of Gemini. At age 14.77 (when the bombing occurred) the *Point of Life* would have been at 3° 18' Gemini (4.3° × 0.77), within orb of a square to natal Mars at 6° 23' Virgo, thus triggering the natal mutable Grand Cross.

On page 72 of *Astrological Investigations* (1926), Frankland states that he uses the *Point of Life* to identify important areas of life that will be activated within a one-year period. Thus, he uses an orb of about 4° for aspects made by the *Point of Life*, that is, the period of about a year before and after the specific *Point of Life* at a given age.

If we consider the *4/7° measure* (4/7° along the zodiac is equivalent to one year of life), then at age 14, the *4/7° measure* is 14 × 4/7°, or 8° of Aries, on Nicholas's birthday in 1978, which does not closely aspect any planet or point in his chart.

Frankland also symbolically directed each point in the chart by the *4/7° measure*. In this case, we would add 8° to each chart point to calculate the direction. Hence, at the time of Nicholas's solar return in 1978, when he turned 14 years old, the following were in effect:

- Directed Moon conjoined natal 8th house ruler Jupiter.
- Directed Mars conjoined natal Pluto.
- Directed Neptune conjoined the natal Sun.

- Directed Mercury conjoined the Moon's true South Node in the 8th house.
- The directed natal Placidus 8th house cusp conjoined the Moon's true South Node in the 8th house.
- Directed Saturn opposed natal Mars.

The symbolism of all of these symbolic directions is consistent with Nicholas's death in the explosion at age 14.

Rectifying the Birth Chart

Frankland often mentions rectifying a birth chart by means of his symbolic measures. Glancing at the *4/7° symbolic directions* at the time of the bombing, we see that the major difference between the charts of Nicholas, who died, and his brother Timothy, who survived the explosion, lies in the house cusps rather than the positions of the planets at birth. Specifically, Nicholas had natal Mercury almost exactly on the 8th house cusp, and these two points, together with the squares from natal Uranus and Chiron, were directed almost exactly to the true South Lunar Node (Ketu) on the day of the incident.

If Nicholas had been born at 3:39:32 p.m. GMT (a matter of 28 seconds before his recorded birth time of 3:40 p.m. GMT), then the symbolic direction of the 8th house cusp to Ketu would have been exact. Most likely 3:40 p.m. GMT is rounded to the nearest minute, so that an actual birth time of 3:39:32 p.m. GMT is entirely feasible.

In contrast, Timothy, who was born 20 minutes later at 4:00 p.m. GMT, would not have had natal Mercury conjunct the natal 8th house cusp, nor would he have experienced the directed 8th house cusp arriving at Ketu at the time of the explosion. It appears that the symbolic direction of the Placidus natal 8th house cusp to the true South Lunar Node at the time of the bombing spelled the difference between life and death for the identical twins.

Summary of Orbs

After experimenting with Frankland's techniques in many charts and reading about Charles E. O. Carter's experiences with Frankland's method, I have found that the following orbs are generally effective:

- To assess the natal promise of the birth chart, use Al-Biruni's classical orbs: Sun, 15° before and after its position; Moon, 12° before and after; Saturn and Jupiter, 9° before and after; Mars, 8° before and after; and finally, Mercury and Venus, 7° before and after. In addition, any planet within 5° of conjoining a Placidus house cusp is strongly linked to the significations of that house, and planets within 3° of a major aspect to the horizon or meridian axis are strongly emphasized in the chart.

- For the *Point of Life measure* (one zodiac sign per 7 years, or 4 2/7° per year), use an orb of 4°, which corresponds roughly to one year before and after the aspect becomes exact. Frankland's interest in using symbolic directions was to identify important years or periods of life.

- For the 1° per year *Age along the Zodiac (Age Point) measure*, use an orb of 1° (which corresponds to one year) before and after the aspect becomes exact.

- For the *4/7° per year measure*, use an orb of about ½°, which corresponds to about one year before and after the aspect becomes exact.

Bearing in mind that Frankland's symbolic measures (the *Point of Life, Age along the Zodiac,* etc.) act like slow-moving bodies in traditional directions, Alan Leo's advice about orbs in progressed charts in *The Progressed Horoscope* (1983) is also worth noting:

Strong directions formed by slow moving bodies extend their influence over considerable periods of time and are liable to produce effects whenever similar lunar directions, transits or eclipses coincide. But it is not safe to go to the extreme and affirm that such directions do not act unless stimulated to do so in this way, for experience does not justify this idea. (Leo 1983, 58, italics mine)

Chapter 15
THE *4/7° AGE POINT*

Frankland's second book, *New Measures in Astrology* (1928), presented his research, conducted with the aid of Protheroe Smith, on a "new measure" that was not included in his *Astrological Investigations*, published in 1926. To quote directly from page 72 of his 1928 text:

> The new measure here suggested is that **four-sevenths of a degree (zodiacal) equals one year of human life.**
>
> This proportion of four-sevenths is very much supported by occult facts.
>
> The numbers 4 and 7 are of great occult significance. (Frankland 1928, 72; bold highlighting mine)

Years later, in his book *Forecasting by Astrology* (1982), British astrologer Martin Freeman, who does not cite Frankland in his bibliography, wrote:

> Seven is made up of the sum of trinity and quaternity (3 + 4 equals 7), the Qualities (cardinal, fixed and mutable) and the Elements (fire, earth, air and water). (Freeman 1982, 23)

To avoid having to write out "4/7 of a degree equals one year of life," I often abbreviate this symbolic measure as the *4/7° Age Point*.

Unlike the symbolic measures discussed in his first book (i.e., *Age along the Zodiac* and the *Point of Life*), Frankland appeared to regard the *4/7° Age Point* not only as a symbolic measure but also as an "operative influence." In other words, you can use his new *4/7° measure* not only to highlight areas of life but also to symbolically direct all the points and planets in a chart. In this way, you can identify potentially significant years or ages in life, and also find when a particular natal promise might become a reality, similar to the way we use primary directions and secondary progressions.

A Case from Frankland's Files

Frankland illustrates his new "operative influence" with a case from his own practice, of a woman born on 10 July 1877, with about 12° Taurus rising and 17° Capricorn on the MC. He does not give the time or place of birth of his client, but from the cusps and planetary positions of the chart in his book, she appears to have been born in Southern Ireland, close to midnight. Here is a computer-generated reconstruction of the chart, almost identical to the one used by Frankland (chart 47).

Frankland tested his *4/7° measure* against two notable events in this client's life:

- She married at age 28.
- Her parents died when she was 39 years old.

At age 28, when this woman wed, 4/7° × 28 equals 16°; hence, we must direct the points and planets in her chart by an arc of 16°, which produces these symbolic directions:

- Directed Moon arrives at 6° 11' Leo and conjoins natal Venus (goddess of love) at 6° 19' Leo. The Moon rules her 4th house of home and domestic life.
- Directed Venus arrives at 22° 19' Leo and conjoins natal Uranus (at 22° 48' Leo) in the 5th house of love and romance. Venus-Uranus contacts often signify sudden attachments and love at first sight.
- Directed Saturn (commitment) arrives at 6° 16' Aries, where it trines natal Venus (marriage) in the 4th house (domestic life).
- Directed Jupiter (good fortune) arrives at 12° 11' Capricorn, where it sextiles the 7th house cusp of marriage at 11° 43' Scorpio from the 9th house of religious ceremonies.

At age 39, when this woman's parents died, 4/7° × 38 equals 22.28°, or 22° 17' of arc. Directing the points and planets in her birth chart by this amount produces the following symbolic directions:

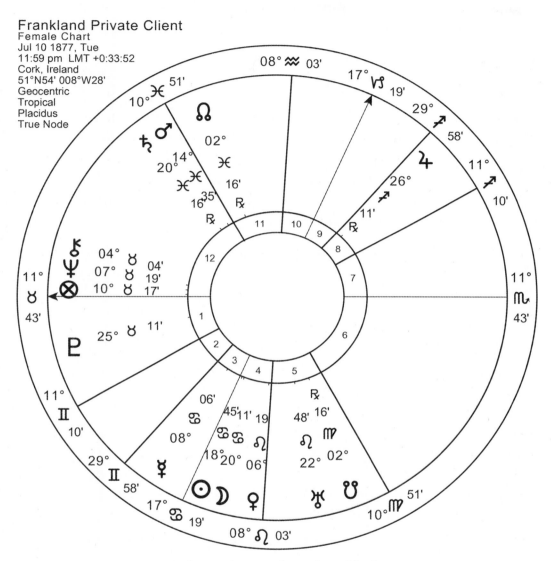

Frankland Private Client
Female Chart
Jul 10 1877, Tue
11:59 pm LMT +0:33:52
Cork, Ireland
51°N54' 008°W28'
Geocentric
Tropical
Placidus
True Node

Chart 47: Private Client of Frankland
10 July 1877, 11:59 p.m. LMT, Cork, Ireland, 51N54 8W28

- Directed Jupiter, ruler of the 8th house of death, arrives at 18° 25' Capricorn, opposite her natal Sun (a father symbol) at 18° 35' Cancer in the 4th house of parents.

- Directed Uranus arrives at 15° 05' Virgo, opposite her natal Mars in the 12th house of grief, sorrow, and mental pain and suffering.

- The natal Sun and Moon are closely conjunct in the 4th house, with the Moon ruling the cusp of the 4th house. Rather than direct each luminary individually, we can direct their midpoint, which lies at 19° 28' Cancer here. Adding the age-arc of 22.28° to the Sun/Moon midpoint, we arrive at 11° 44' Leo, which forms a tight square to her Ascendant/Descendant axis. Frankland was a strong proponent of using midpoints in predictive work.

In his research, Frankland repeatedly found that the *4/7° measure*, when used to symbolically direct points and planets in the birth chart, produced symbolic directions that were clearly related to events in his clients' lives.

Frida Kahlo and the *4/7° Symbolic Measure*

Let's take an example from the life of Frida Kahlo to further illustrate this concept.

Artist Frida Kahlo was born on 6 July 1907 at 8:30 a.m. LMT in Coyoacan, Mexico, Rodden Rating AA (chart 48).

On 22 October 1913, 6-year-old Frida contracted polio, which left her with one leg shorter than the other. She was bedridden for nine months while recuperating from the illness. When she was finally able to get out of bed, she had already turned 7 years old.

Frida apparently suffered sexual exploitation at the age of 13 at the hands of her female gym teacher. In an extended set of interviews between 1949 and 1950 with Mexican psychology student Olga Campos, Frida confided that she had her first sexual experience with her gym and anatomy teacher, Sara Zenil. Eventually, Frida's mother discovered letters referring to the sexual relationship and pulled Frida from the school.

Twelve years after contracting polio, on 17 September 1925, Frida suffered a serious accident while riding on a wooden bus when it was hit by an electric trolley car. A metal handrail from the trolley pierced her body. Frida survived but sustained multiple injuries that would plague her for the rest of her life. She was 18.2 years old on the day of the accident.

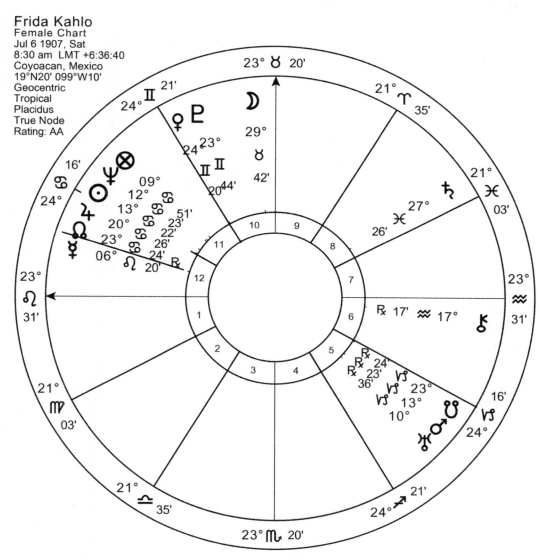

Frida Kahlo
Female Chart
Jul 6 1907, Sat
8:30 am LMT +6:36:40
Coyoacan, Mexico
19°N20' 099°W10'
Geocentric
Tropical
Placidus
True Node
Rating: AA

Chart 48: Frida Kahlo
6 July 1907, 8:30 a.m. LMT, Coyoacan, Mexico, 19N20 99W10

Frankland would have glanced at Frida's chart and immediately identified areas of concern:

- Her cluster of planets in Cancer opposes a group of planets and the true lunar South Node in Capricorn, near the cusps of the unfortunate 12th and 6th houses. Because the *Point of Life* begins at 0° Aries and proceeds through each sign in 7 years, the first seven years of Frida's life might be difficult, especially with regard to 6th and 12th house issues (illness, confinement, etc.).

- Saturn, ruler of the 6th house of illness in Pisces in the 8th house, squares Venus in Gemini. Frankland did not know of the existence of Pluto, but its presence so close to Venus is another potentially problematic factor.

Frida's Symbolic Measures at Ages 6 and 7

At age 6, Frida's *Point of Life* moves between 25.7° and 30° of Aries. The only aspect it forms during this period is a semisextile to Saturn in Pisces in the 8th house. Although a "minor" aspect, the semisextile is stressful because the signs involved are inconjunct (in aversion), and such aspects often signify problems with health, more so in this case because Saturn rules the 6th house and occupies the 8th house.

At age 7, the *Point of Life* passes from 0° to 4.28° of Taurus, forming no major aspect to planets or points in her chart.

At ages 6 and 7, her *Age along the Zodiac* traverses 6° and 7° of Aries, making a trine to Mercury at 6° 20' Leo in the 12th house.

At age 13, when Frida was sexually exploited at school, her *Age along the Zodiac* was in 13° Aries, in a T-square configuration with her natal Sun-Mars opposition and within orb of a square to natal Neptune. At the same time, her *Point of Life* was traversing the region from about 25.7° to 30° of Taurus, where it sextiled Saturn in Pisces in the 8th house and conjoined the Moon (ruler of her 12th house) at the end of Taurus in the 10th house. Her *4/7° Age Point* at age 13 was at 7.4°, which directed her natal Mars-Sun opposition to connect closely with natal 8th house ruler Jupiter at that time.

Charles E. O. Carter's Extension of the Use of *Age along the Zodiac*

In Frankland's books, there are many examples in which he applied his *Age along the Zodiac* (one zodiacal degree per year of life) to symbolically direct from either (a) 0°

Aries or (b) one of his symbolic "house measures" (sensitive points like lots or Arabic parts, or the Sahams of Jyotish), which are determined by adding together the cusps of two houses and sometimes also adding the longitude of a relevant planet.

An example of the latter would be Frankland's *Point of Honour and Upliftment*, which he obtained by adding the cusp of the 1st house plus the cusp of the 10th house plus the zodiacal position of Jupiter. Frankland would then symbolically direct this natal *Point of Honour and Upliftment* to a particular age of the native by adding one degree to its position for each year of life.

Charles Carter, in his book *Symbolic Directions in Modern Astrology* (1929), suggested extending Frankland's principle of directing at a rate of 1° (zodiacal) for each year of life to any planet or stellar body in the chart. After all, Frankland was using this measure to symbolically direct from *0° Aries* and from his *sensitive house-related points*, so why restrict it to just these factors? After testing this method of directing, Carter advocated the use of both the 1° per year and the 4 2/7° per year measures "in connection with the Sun, Moon, planets, and angles, while at the same time by no means gainsaying the value of 0° Aries, which is, of course, the zodiacal analogue of the mundane ascendant" (Carter 1929, 26–27). Because the Sun travels roughly 1° per day, this symbolic *1° per year of life measure* produces values close to those found by solar arc directions, usually within roughly a 1° orb.

Another suggestion of Charles Carter was to use the cardinal point *0° Capricorn* as analogous to the natal MC to create a system of symbolic directing similar to the *Point of Life* but applied to the native's career. Carter writes in *Symbolic Directions in Modern Astrology* (1929):

> 0° Aries may be used for all practical purposes as a kind of zodiacal ascendant, and may be progressed [directed] in a similar manner, nor is it improbable that in the same way 0° Capricorn may be used as a zodiacal analogue of the Midheaven. (Carter 1929, 27)

Let's apply the symbolic *1° for each year of life measure* to Frida's chart at age 7.

At age 7, after Frida spent 9 months in bed recovering from polio, her directed Sun would have conjoined natal Jupiter, ruler of the 8th house of life-threatening conditions.

At the same time, directed Mars (which opposes the Sun at birth) would have opposed her natal Jupiter, ruler of the 8th house.

Frida's directed Jupiter, at age 7, would have exactly trined natal Saturn in Pisces in the 8th house, perhaps symbolizing her ability to recover from polio rather than succumb to the disease.

Frida Kahlo's Bus Accident

At age 18.2, Frida was severely injured when a trolley collided with the bus in which she was a passenger. We can make the following comments about her chart using Frankland's methodology:

- Frida's *Point of Life* at age 18 was moving from about 17° to 21½° of Gemini, and was not aspecting any natal planets or points in her chart.
- Her *Age along the Zodiac* was at 18.2° of Aries, approaching a square to 8th house ruler Jupiter that would perfect in about 2 years and would be more likely to highlight age 20 as a difficult period.
- Her *4/7 Age Point* was at 10.4° Aries, tightly square to natal Uranus at 10.6° Aries, thus strongly intensifying her natal Uranus-Mars conjunction in Capricorn, which closely opposes her natal Neptune-Sun conjunction in Cancer, with these signs ruling her 6th and 12th houses. The symbolism of this natal configuration is consistent with a significant accident endangering her life.

In Frankland's case examples, he appears to regard his symbolic measures as activating whole zodiacal signs and any planets and house cusps contained within those signs. In this sense, he is using a combination of both Whole Sign and Placidus houses in his predictive work.

If we direct the various planets in Frida's chart by the *4/7° Age Point* at age 18.2 (at 10.4° Aries), we find directed Uranus opposite natal Jupiter (ruler of the 8th house), and the directed Ascendant-ruler Sun conjunct the lunar nodal axis, with directed Mars conjunct the natal true lunar South Node (Ketu) near the cusp of the 6th Placidus house of bodily injury.

Although Frankland appears not to have used annual profections, we can see that at age 18 Frida's profected Ascendant was in Aquarius, ruled by Saturn in the 8th house and at birth in square to Venus, ruler of her 3rd house of local transportation (by car, bus, trolley, etc.).

Astrologer Pat Harris and the *4/7° Measure*

Pat Harris is a prominent British astrologer who became the focus of a particularly nasty period in the modern revival of traditional horary astrology. In 1995 Pat was invited to submit an article for publication in the May 1995 edition of the newsletter of the British Astrological Association.

Pat was learning horary astrology at the time and had recently done a reading for a friend, Christeen Skinner, about a question of professional reputation. Specifically, Christeen had asked whether appearing as an astrologer as part of a BBC documentary about belief systems would be damaging to her professional reputation. Apparently, Christeen wondered whether the BBC production would be presented impartially.

The horary question was asked on 9 February 1995 at 1:57 p.m. GMT (1W19, 51N04). Pat cast the chart and proceeded to interpret it, but did not follow the standard technique of identifying the querent (Christeen) with the Ascendant. Instead, perhaps because Pat had become so involved in helping her friend formulate the question, Pat read the chart as if she herself were the querent and placed her friend Christeen in the 11th house. She then interpreted the chart from this point of view, telling Christine that there would be no damage to her reputation and, in fact, the BBC appearance would bring her more clients. The horary reading turned out to be spot-on. Christeen benefited from the BBC documentary, just as Pat had foreseen.

Unfortunately for Pat, however, a particularly nasty and arrogant subgroup of astrologers populated the horary community in England and the US at the time. This mean-spirited clique, like the church inquisitors of old, launched a vicious attack in print against Pat for not having used the Ascendant to signify the querent. How could such heresy be permitted in the traditional horary community of 1995? Such ideas must be eradicated and the perpetrator burned at the stake (literally, of course, in the twentieth century)! Poor Pat, who was but a student of horary at the time, was cast out of the horary course in which she had enrolled for her "substandard" performance. A noted horary astrologer of the period, Olivia Barclay, exclaimed in the same newsletter that she had never seen a chart so badly judged. Apparently, this clique of malicious and supercilious astrologers had not read Geoffrey Cornelius's book *The Moment of Astrology* (1994).

Would Frankland have foreseen this petty attack on Pat's public image with his symbolic measures? Let's take a look.

Pat Harris
Female Chart
May 20 1953, Wed
11:58 am BST −1:00
Bradford, UK
53°N48' 001°W45'
Geocentric
Tropical
Placidus
True Node
Rating: A

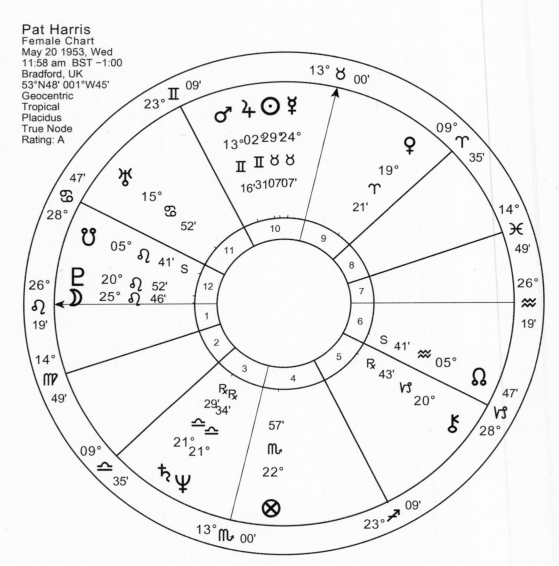

Chart 49: Pat Harris
20 May 1953, 11:58 a.m. BST, Bradford, England, 53N48 1W45

According to AstroDatabank, Pat Harris was born on 20 May 1953 at 11:58 a.m. GDT in Bradford, England, Rodden Rating A (chart 49). Pat's Leo Ascendant is ruled by the Sun in the 10th house of public standing. The Sun is afflicted by a square from the 12th house (hidden enemies) Pluto (lord of the underworld), indicating that she might be maliciously attacked by secretive, backstabbing enemies at some point in her life.

Venus rules Pat's 10th house of career and public reputation and occupies Aries (its sign of debilitation, ruled by aggressive Mars) in the 9th house of astrology and publication. Venus is also part of a cardinal Grand Cross made up of oppositions from Saturn and Neptune and squares from Uranus and Chiron. The triggering of this Grand Cross could initiate a difficult period in her life.

At the time that her now-famous horary chart was published in May of 1995, Pat was 42 years old. Thus, by Frankland's measures:

- At age 42, Pat was in the Mars period of Ptolemy's *seven ages of man* (ages 41–56). At this time the houses occupied and ruled by Mars become prominent. The closest aspects of Mars in the natal chart are the semisextile to the MC and the quincunx to the IC.
- Her *Point of Life* was at 0° Libra, triggering the cardinal Grand Cross involving Libra, Aries, Cancer, and Capricorn.
- Her *Age along the Zodiac* was at 12° Taurus, within a 1° orb of the natal MC and therefore highlighting her career and public image.
- Her *4/7° Age Point* was at 24° Aries.

Pat's *4/7° Age Point* at 24° Aries is making no close "hits" in her natal chart in 1995, but Frankland also directed the natal points and planets by the arc of 24° as part of his assessment. Hence, the symbolic directions active by the *4/7° measure* in May of 1995 are:

- Directed Venus (ruler of the 10th house) at 13° 13' Taurus, conjunct the natal MC at 13° 00' Taurus. The ruler of the 10th house conjunct the 10th house cusp by direction indicates a highly significant year for career matters. The placement of directed Venus on the natal MC, a powerful angle, strongly activates the natal cardinal Grand Cross.

- Directed Venus at 13° 13' Taurus semisextile natal Mars at 13° 16' Gemini. Mars is also the dispositor of natal Venus. The semisextile and quincunx are stressful configurations involving signs in aversion.

- Directed South Lunar Node at 29° 31' Leo square the natal Sun at 29° 07' Taurus. In other words, the natal Sun is *at the bendings* with respect to the directed lunar nodes, which is usually symbolic of a crisis involving the planet, in this case the Sun, which rules the Ascendant and occupies the 10th house (her reputation).

- Directed Moon at 19° 26' Virgo (ruler of the 12th house of secret enemies) quincunx natal Venus at 19° 21' Aries (ruler of the 10th house).

- Directed Uranus at 9° 42' Leo trine the natal 9th house cusp at 9° 35' Aries.

It seems clear that Frankland would have pinpointed 1995 as an important year, perhaps one of crisis, with respect to 10th and 1st house issues. Pat's career, public reputation, and sense of identity will be major themes at age 42.

A Modern Example: George Michael

According to Astro.com, singer George Michael was born on 25 June 1963 at 6:00 a.m. GDT in Finchley, England, Rodden Rating A (chart 50). At age 53, he died of heart failure at his home in England, on Christmas Day in 2016. The birth date was verified by his official birth certificate, and the time of birth is that given by the singer's office. Birth times exactly on the hour are suspect, and after studying his directions, progressions, and transits, I suspect that he was born several minutes before 6:00 a.m. GDT.

George Michael's Birth Numbers

Let's begin with George Michael's Birth Numbers, as Frankland would calculate them:

25 June 1963 produces the sum 2 + 5 + 6 + 1 + 9 + 6 + 3, which equals **32** as his *Single Digits Birth Number*, which reduces to 3 + 2 = **5**.

25 June 1963 produces the sum 25 + 06 + 1 + 9 + 6 + 3, which equals **50** as his *Double Digits Birth Number*, which reduces to 5 + 0 = **5**.

Next, we add each of these Birth Numbers to the year of birth to calculate *Additional Birth Numbers*:

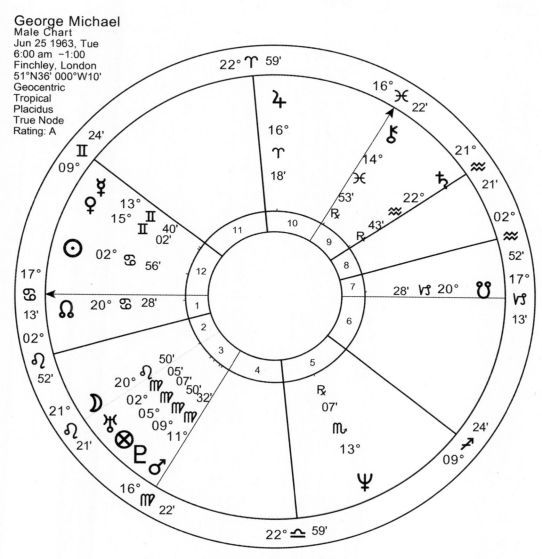

Chart 50: George Michael
25 June 1963, 6:00 a.m. GDT, Finchley, London, England, 51N36 0W10

32 + 1963 = 1995, which reduces to 1 + 9 + 9 + 5, or **24**, which further reduces to 2 + 4, or **6**. Then **32** + **24** + **6** = **62** as his *Additional Single Digits Birth Number*, which reduces to 6 + 2 = **8**.

50 + 1963 = 2013, which reduces to 2 + 0 + 1 + 3, or **6**. Then **50** + **6** = **56** as his *Additional Double Digits Birth Number*, which reduces to 5 + 6 = **11** and further to 1 + 1 = **2**.

Potentially significant ages, based on these Birth Numbers, are **32, 50, 56,** and **62** and combinations of these Birth Numbers with each other or with their reduced forms, that is, **2, 5, 8,** and **11**.

Here we must use combinations involving *subtraction* to generate significant ages, for example, 32 − 2 = 30. When George Michael turned age 30, he released his second solo album, *Five Live*, in 1993, an important year for his career. In addition, Michael's lover Anselmo Feleppa died in March 1993.

Age 50 refers to the year 2013. On 16 May 2013, George Michael injured his head when he fell from a moving car and needed to be airlifted to a hospital. This event ought to be symbolized in his directions, progressions, and transits of 2013, which would be given extra weight because they occurred during a Birth Number age.

The year of George Michael's death at age 53 can be generated from his Birth Numbers and their reduced forms by a combination of addition and subtraction: 50 + 5 − 2 = 53.

George Michael's *Point of Life* and *Age along the Zodiac*

In 2013, when he turned 50 years old, Michael's *Age along the Zodiac* was at 20° Taurus and his *Point of Life* was at 4° 17' Scorpio. The *Age along the Zodiac* advances at a rate of 1° per year and was within orb of a square to his natal Moon (at 20° 50' Leo) when he had the car accident. His natal Moon lies on the cusp of his 3rd house (local travel) and is afflicted by an opposition from Saturn. His *Point of Life* at this time was in orb of a sextile to his natal Part of Fortune in his 3rd house, perhaps reflecting the fact that he survived the car accident and was able to be airlifted to a hospital.

When Michael turned 53 in 2016 (the year of his death), his *Age along the Zodiac Point* was at 23° Taurus, and his *Point of Life* was at 7° 08' Scorpio, closely sesquisquare his natal Saturn, ruler of his 8th house of death. By aspecting Saturn, the *Point of Life* was animating his natal Moon-Saturn opposition, which is dangerous to his life because Saturn rules the 8th house and the Moon rules his Ascendant (his body, vitality, and health).

George Michael's Sensitive *Point of Life-Threatening Illness*

Frankland assessed danger to life by adding the longitudes of the cusps of the 6th and 8th houses, which he advanced at the rate of one ecliptic degree for each year of life. Let's do the math in the 6:00 a.m. chart for George Michael. If he had been born a few minutes earlier, the point of dangerous illness would be a degree or two earlier than we are about to calculate.

The 6th house cusp equals 09° 24' Sagittarius.

The 8th house cusp equals 02° 52' Aquarius.

Adding the 6th and 8th house cusps, we get 12° 16' Libra as his *Point of Dangerous Illness*, based on a 6:00 a.m. time of birth.

Adding 53° (for his birthday at age 53) to 12° 16' Libra, we get 5° 16' Sagittarius, which is sesquisquare his natal Moon (at 20° 50' Leo), thereby activating his natal Moon-Saturn opposition.

If Michael were born about five minutes before 6:00 a.m., this *Point of Dangerous Illness* would have been at about 2°–3° of Sagittarius when he turned 53, in close square to his natal Uranus (at 2° 05' Virgo). In addition, his *Point of Dangerous Illness* at that age would have been in close quincunx to his natal Sun in the 12th house.

George Michael's *4/7° Age Point*

At age 30, George Michael experienced career success with the release of his second album. He also suffered a major loss, namely, the death of his lover. At age 30, this *Age along the Zodiac* would have been at 0° Taurus, and by the *4/7 of a degree measure*, the *4/7° Age Point* would have been at 4 × 30 / 7 equals 17.125°, or 17° 08' Aries.

In Michael's birth chart, the *4/7° Age Point* (17° 08' Aries) is separating from a conjunction to Jupiter (ruler of the natal 6th house of illness) in the 10th house of career and is almost exactly square to his horizon. The square to the 7th house cusp is consistent with a stressful major event involving an intimate partnership.

Frankland paid close attention to midpoints. The *4/7° Age Point* at 17° 08' Aries is in close aspect to Michael's natal Mars/Saturn midpoint at 17° 07' of cardinal signs, in square to his natal Ascendant at 17° 13' Cancer, and in semisquare to his natal Uranus at 2° 05' Virgo. Here is the list of midpoints near 17° 08' Aries in Michael's natal chart, generated by Solar Fire's midpoint modal sort, modulus 90°, cardinal points:

CARDINAL MODE MIDPOINT SORT FOR GEORGE MICHAEL	
Midpoint or Stellar Body	**Cardinal Degree**
Saturn/Pluto	16° 17'
Jupiter	16° Aries 18'
Jupiter/Ascendant	16° 46'
Uranus	17° 05'
Mars/Saturn	17° 07'
Ascendant	17° Cancer 13'
Moon/Mercury	17° Cancer 15'
Moon/Chiron	17° 52'

The midpoint symbolism, activated by his *4/7° Age Point*, certainly fits the life events Michael experienced at age 30. Saturn rules his 8th house of death and his 7th house of partnerships. Jupiter rules his 6th house, which is the derived 12th of the 7th of partners, but Jupiter also rules his 10th house of career. Uranus signifies sudden, disruptive events. Mars/Saturn is a combination of both traditional malefics.

Michael's solar return at age 30 had transiting Saturn in the first degree of Pisces opposite transiting Mars in the first degree of Virgo, forming a T-square to his natal Sun at 2° 56' Cancer. In addition, transiting Uranus conjoined transiting Neptune in 20° of Capricorn, conjunct his natal true South Lunar Node at 20° 28' Capricorn in the natal 7th house of partnerships.

Hence, the symbolic time measure, the *4/7° Age Point*, coincided with extremely difficult real-time operative aspects, which were linked symbolically to his lover when he was 30 years old.

An Example from Alexandre Volguine

In his book *The Technique of Solar Returns* (1976), the Russian-born astrologer Alexandre Volguine discusses the case of a man from Nice, France, whose mother died in 1936. The man was born on 14 January 1909 at 00:37 a.m. UT (chart 51), and his mother passed on 22 May 1936, about four months after he turned 27 years old. Let's see how Frankland might have approached this chart.

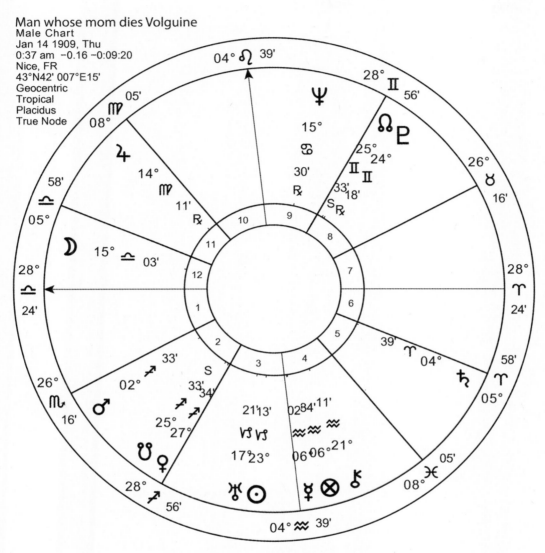

Man whose mom dies Volguine
Male Chart
Jan 14 1909, Thu
0:37 am −0.16 −0:09:20
Nice, FR
43°N42' 007°E15'
Geocentric
Tropical
Placidus
True Node

Chart 51: Man Whose Mother Died
14 January 1909, 00:37 a.m. UT, Nice, France, 43N42 7E15

Frankland would have calculated the Birth Numbers of the man from Nice. He was born on 14 January 1909, which contains a two-digit number in the day field.

Thus, 14/1/1909 produces the sum 1 + 4 + 1 + 1 + 9 + 0 + 9, which equals **25** and reduces to 2 + 5, or **7**. His *Single Digits Birth Numbers* are **25** and **7**.

His *Additional Single Digits Birth Number* is generated by adding **25** to his year of birth, 1909, which results in 1934 and reduces to 1 + 9 + 3 + 4 = **17** and then to 1 + 7 = **8**. Then 25 + 17 + 8 = **50** as his *Additional Single Digits Birth Number*, which reduces to 5 + 0 = **5**.

Next, adding the 14 as a double-digit number:

14 + 1 + 1 + 9 + 0 + 9, which equals **34** and reduces to 3 + 4, or **7**. His *Double Digits Birth Numbers* are **34** and **7**.

His *Additional Double Digits Birth Number* is generated by adding **34** to his year of birth, 1909, which results in 1943 and reduces to 1 + 9 + 4 + 3 = **17** and then to **8**. Then 34 + 17 + 8 = **59** as his *Additional Double Digits Birth Number*, which reduces to 5 + 9 = **14** and further to 1 + 4 = **5**.

Potentially significant ages, based on these Birth Numbers, are **25, 34, 50,** and **59** and combinations of these Birth Numbers with each other or with their reduced forms, that is, **5, 7,** and **14**.

Frankland also generated relevant numbers by combining the ones he initially calculated. He usually added together the various Birth Numbers, but in some cases, subtracting Birth Numbers also identified significant ages, for example:

25 + 7 equals 32.
25 − 7 equals 18.
34 + 7 equals 41.
34 − 7 equals 27.

Thus, significant ages for this man might be 7, 18, 25, 27, 34, and 41. Symbolic measures and operative influences active at these ages will be given extra weight in our judgment of the chart. For example, the man's mother died when he was 27 years old, one of his Birth Number combinations.

In Ptolemy's *seven ages of man*, age 27 falls in the Sun period (ages 22–41). The Sun's aspects in this man's chart, within the classic orb of 15°, include:

- Sun square Moon

- Sun conjunct Mercury

- Sun conjunct Uranus

- Sun sextile Mars

- Sun trine Jupiter

- Sun sextile Saturn

- Sun opposite Neptune

- Sun quincunx Pluto, which is the Sun's closest aspect in this chart (1° orb)

Several of the Sun's aspects are soft and favorable in this chart. The most difficult aspects are the Sun conjunct Uranus, Sun opposite Neptune, and Sun quincunx Pluto in the 8th house. In his birth chart, the Sun rules the 10th house (career, honors, the mother) and occupies the 3rd house (siblings, short trips, communications, the Moon goddess).

At age 27, the man's *Age along the Zodiac* was at 27° Aries, near the 7th house cusp, in trine to both the Ascendant-ruler Venus in the 2nd house and the true South Lunar Node, and in sextile to Pluto in the 8th house.

At age 27, his *Point of Life* was in the range from 25° 43' to 30° Cancer, and formed a quincunx to both his true South Lunar Node and his Venus in Sagittarius, thus intensifying Venus and the true lunar nodes. The *Point of Life* at age 27 was in square to the horizon (Asc/Dsc axis).

In the man's birth chart, Venus rules the Ascendant and the 12th house (grief, sorrow). Venus (a general signifier of women) opposes Pluto (radical transformation) in the 8th house of death. The *Point of Life*'s intensification of this natal Venus-Pluto opposition across the 2nd and 8th houses, with Venus ruling the natal 12th house, fits symbolically with the loss of his mother.

By Frankland's *4/7 of a degree measure*, at age 27 we calculate 27° × 4 divided by 7 equals 15.428° of Aries, that is, 15° 26' Aries. In this man's birth chart, this *4/7° Age Point* forms a Grand Cross with Neptune at 15° Cancer in the 9th house, the Moon at 15° Libra in the 12th house, and Uranus at 17° Capricorn in the 2nd house. In Frankland's research, a Grand Cross configuration, like this one, correlates with "a most drastic or eventful time" in the life of the native. Thus, the *4/7 of a degree measure* indicates the likelihood of a momentous event occurring in this man's life around age 27.

Now let's consider relevant operative influences in 1936. We begin by locating the mother and her derived houses in the man's birth chart:

The 10th house represents the mother, who is ruled by the Sun because Leo is on the man's MC.

The derived 12th house of the mother is the radical 9th house with Gemini on the cusp (ruled by Mercury) and Neptune contained therein. Both Pluto and the true North Lunar Node conjoin the radical 9th house cusp, which is the mother's derived 12th house.

The derived 6th house (mother's illness) from the 10th house of the mother is the radical 3rd house with Sagittarius on the cusp, ruled by Jupiter.

The derived 8th house (mother's death) from the 10th house of the mother is the radical 5th house with Pisces on the cusp, ruled by Jupiter.

Thus, Jupiter rules both the mother's illness and her demise.

The following are some of the real-time-based operative influences in effect within orb and intensified by Frankland's symbolic measures at the time of his mother's passing:

On 25 May 1936 (the mother died on 22 May 1936), **transiting Neptune** turned **stationary direct** at 13° 59' Virgo, almost exactly conjunct the man's natal Jupiter, which rules his mother's 6th and 8th houses (illness and death). Stations of transiting planets, especially the ponderous planets, are powerful, long-lasting influences.

On 10 February 1936, **primary directed Venus** (Placidus semi-arc, 0° latitude, Ptolemy key) sesquisquared natal Neptune in the radical 9th house, the mother's derived 12th house of undoing.

On 18 March 1936, **primary directed Jupiter** (Placidus semi-arc, 0° latitude, Naibod key) perfected a quincunx to natal Uranus.

On 23 April 1936, the **primary directed Sun** (Placidus semi-arc, 0° latitude, Naibod key) conjoined natal Venus on the cusp of the radical 3rd house (the mother's derived 6th house of illness).

On 15 May 1936, **primary directed Uranus** (Placidus semi-arc, 0° latitude, Ptolemy key) squared the natal MC (representative of the mother, as cusp of the radical 10th house). The man's mother passed on 22 May 1936.

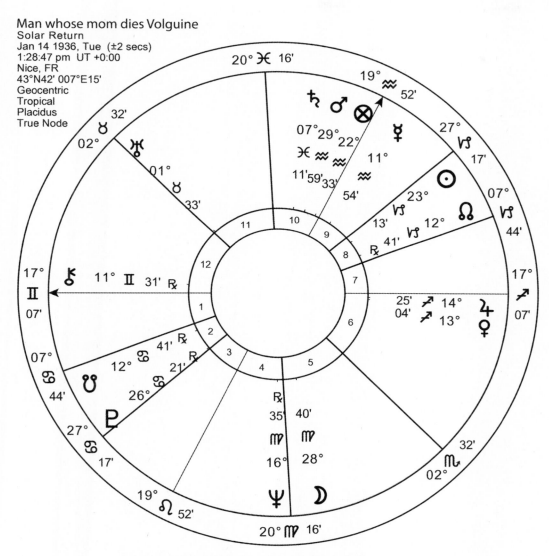

Chart 52: Man Whose Mother Died, Solar Return 1936
14 1936, 1:28:47 p.m. UT, Nice, France, 43N42 7E15

On 19 June 1936, a **Solar Eclipse** at 27° 43' Gemini conjoined both the lunar nodal axis and Pluto in the radical 8th house, almost exactly opposite Venus (ruler of the mother's illness) in the 2nd house. Eclipses powerfully stimulate the planets and areas of the birth chart with which they make contact.

On 24 July 1936, **primary directed Mars** (Placidus semi-arc, 0° latitude, Ptolemy key) squared the MC (the 10th house cusp, which represents the mother).

In this man's solar return for 1936 (chart 52), his *Point of Life* at age 27 (in the range from 25° 43' to 30° Cancer) conjoined return Pluto in Cancer at the cusp of the return 3rd house, which is the mother's derived 6th house of illness. By activating return Pluto, the *Point of Life* is intensifying the quincunx that return Pluto makes to return Mars in the 10th house of the mother in the solar revolution chart.

Return Mars is conjunct return Saturn (across a sign boundary), and Saturn in the 10th house of the mother rules the return 8th and 9th houses, the 9th house being the derived 12th house of the mother (10th house). Both malefics in the 10th house of the solar return indicate a potentially difficult year for the native's mother, represented by the 10th house. By annual profection (which Frankland does not mention) at age 27, Capricorn rules the profected Ascendant, and Saturn (ruler of the return 8th house of death and of the return 9th house, which is the turned 12th house of the mother) is lord of the year. The Sun in the solar return chart occupies the 8th house, suggesting that themes of death and human mortality will be predominant this year.

A Boy's Father Dies by Suicide

The noted French astrologer Denis Labouré posted a video about solar returns on You-Tube on 14 March 2017 in which he discussed the case of a young man whose father died by suicide when the boy was 11.84 years old. The video is titled "Cours d'astrologie gratuit: La révolution solaire par Denis Labouré."

According to Labouré, the boy was born on 6 February 1984 at 5:44 p.m. CET in Villeurbanne, France (chart 53). His father died by suicide on 11 December 1995 while suffering from a psychotic depression with mystical and paranoid delusions. Let's apply Frankland's measures to this example.

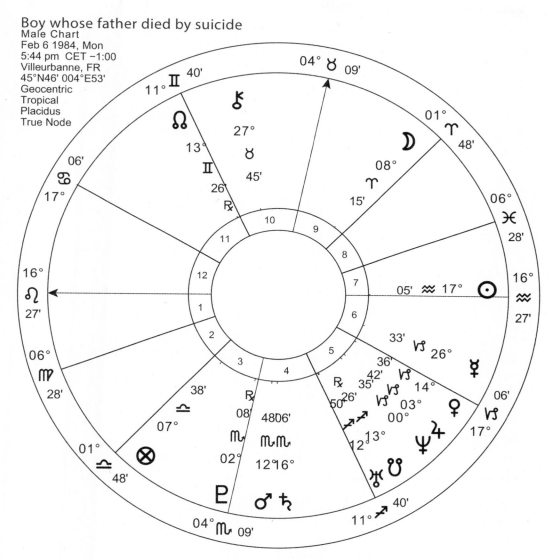

Boy whose father died by suicide
Male Chart
Feb 6 1984, Mon
5:44 pm CET −1:00
Villeurbanne, FR
45°N46' 004°E53'
Geocentric
Tropical
Placidus
True Node

Chart 53: Boy Whose Father Died by Suicide
6 February 1984, 5:44 p.m. CET, Villeurbanne, France, 45 N46 4E53

Eyeballing the chart, it is not hard to anticipate his father's difficulties. The 4th house signifies the father. In the boy's chart, Pluto conjoins the 4th house cusp, and both traditional malefics, Mars and Saturn, occupy the 4th house. Mars, the contrary-to-sect malefic, rules the 4th house cusp and is afflicted by Saturn. Mars is also quincunx Raju, the Moon's true North Node, which conjoins the 11th house cusp, which is the father's derived 8th house of death. The Sun rules the Ascendant and conjoins the cusp of the 7th house, which is the father's turned 4th house cusp of endings. The radical Ascendant and 7th house cusp, as well as the Sun, receive a square from Saturn in the 4th house.

The Boy's Birth Numbers, According to Frankland

The boy's day and month of birth are single digits, so we only need to calculate and reduce a single-digit Birth Number.

A birth date of 6 February 1984 produces the sum 6 + 2 + 1 + 9 + 8 + 4, which equals **30** and reduces to 3 + 0, or **3**. The boy's *Single Digits Birth Numbers* are **30** and **3**.

Frankland also calculated *Additional Birth Numbers* by adding the primary number (30 in this case) to the year of birth, reducing it, and then combining the results.

Thus, 30 + 1984 (year of birth) equals 2014, which reduces to 2 + 0 + 1 + 4, or **7**. Then adding 7 to 30 gives **37** as his *Additional Birth Number*, which reduces to 3 + 7 = **10** and then to 1 + 0 = **1**.

Potentially significant ages, based on these Birth Numbers, are **30** and **37** and combinations of these Birth Numbers with each other or with their reduced forms, that is, **1**, **3**, and **10**.

Frankland then calculates combinations of this set of Birth Numbers to generate ages that are potentially significant if corresponding astrological influences coincide:

10 + 1 = **11**, the boy's age when his father died.

3 + 30 = **33**, the boy's age when Denis Labouré discussed his birth chart in the YouTube video.

The Boy's Symbolic Measures

At the time of his father's demise, the boy was 11.84 years old, which corresponds to the following:

- **11° Aries 50'** as his *Age along the Zodiac* (*Age Point* at 1° per year)
- **6° Aries 46'** as *4/7° Age along the Zodiac*
- **20° Taurus 44'** as his *Point of Life* (which ranged from 17.14° to 21.43° of Taurus at age 11)

The *Age along the Zodiac* lies at 11° 50' Aries in the boy's 9th house and applies to trine Uranus in Sagittarius in the 5th house and to quincunx Mars in Scorpio in the 4th house. The quincunx to Mars, ruler of the 4th house, suggests that the boy will have to deal with some stressful situation regarding home, family, and his father around age 11. The closest midpoint related to this degree (11° 50' Aries) is that of Moon/Venus, which can be stressful because the Moon rules the natal 12th house and Venus rules the natal 3rd house, which is the derived 12th house of the father.

The *4/7° Age Point* at 6° 46' Aries is also in the 9th house, opposing the Part of Fortune and semisextile the natal 8th house cusp. Semisextiles are difficult aspects because they involve whole signs in aversion to each other.

The *Point of Life* at 20° 44' Taurus (ranging from about 17° to 22° of Taurus at age 11) lies in the boy's 10th house. It is separating from an opposition to Saturn in the 4th house and a square to the Sun in Aquarius, which perfected about the time he turned 11 years old. The closest midpoints related to this degree (20° 44' Taurus) are Mars/Chiron and Moon/Jupiter. Mars signifies his father in this chart, and Chiron often indicates some type of wound, physical or emotional. Moon/Jupiter is significant because the Moon rules the radical 12th and Jupiter rules the radical 8th—houses associated with misfortune and endings.

Frankland often directed relevant points in the chart by his symbolic measures, especially by the *4/7 of a degree of longitude per year of life measure*. For example, in this chart, the father's 8th house of death is the radical 11th house, ruled by Mercury. Natal Mercury lies at 26° 33' Capricorn, so we would add the *4/7° measure* (6° 46') to the position of the father's derived 8th house ruler: 26° 33' Capricorn + 6° 46' = 3° 19' Aquarius.

Thus, natal Mercury (ruler of the father's house of death) symbolically directed at age 11.84 forms a semisextile to Jupiter (ruler of the radical 8th house of death), a square to the meridian axis (the IC signifies the father), and an almost exact square to the Pluto/

IC midpoint (which lies at 3° 08' Scorpio). Pluto (Hades) rules the afterlife, and the IC represents the father.

Frankland often added together the ecliptic longitudes of house cusps to derive a point related to the combined meanings of the two houses. For example, the 4th house cusp signifies the father, and the radical 9th house cusp (the derived 6th from the 4th) represents the father's illness. The 4th house cusp at 4° 09' Scorpio, when added to the longitude of the 9th house cusp at 1° 48' Aries, gives a result of 5° 57' Scorpio as the *father's Point of Illness*. Mars, as ruler of both the radical 4th and radical 9th house cusps, thus signifies both the father and his illness.

We can add the native's age, and also 4/7 of his age, to symbolically direct the father's *Point of Illness* to a particular year of life. When his father died, the boy's *4/7 Age Point* was at 6° 46' of longitude, which, when added to the father's *Point of Illness*, takes us to 12° 33' Scorpio, almost exactly conjunct natal Mars, ruler of the 4th house cusp of the father and of the 9th house cusp of his illness. Thus, Frankland's symbolic directions would predict significant illness for the father around the time this native is 11.84 years old.

The Boy's Operative Influences in December of 1995

Frankland emphasized that his symbolic measures served to highlight and intensify areas of the birth chart, whose natal promise could then be more easily triggered into manifestation by real-time-based configurations such as primary directions, secondary progressions, transits, eclipses, stations of a transiting planet, etc. In his second book, *New Measures in Astrology*, published in 1928, he regarded his new *4/7 of a degree per year measure*, when used as a symbolic direction, as another type of operative influence capable of identifying important years in the life of the native.

In this case, a review of the traditional primary directions in effect around December of 1995 in the boy's chart reveals that primary directed Saturn conjoined the natal IC (4th house cusp of the father) on 4 November 1995. Primary directions proceed at the rate of one equatorial degree crossing the MC for each year of life, so this conjunction of Saturn to the 4th house cusp was in effect for a long time and was active as an "operative influence" at the time of the father's suicide.

As for transits, a Solar Eclipse occurred on 24 October 1995 at 0° 17' Scorpio, conjunct natal Pluto and the 4th house cusp. Prior to the Solar Eclipse, there was a Lunar

Eclipse on 8 October 1995 at 14° 54' Aries, forming a quincunx to the Mars/Saturn mid-point in Scorpio and a square to Venus in Capricorn near the cusp of the 6th house. Venus rules the turned 12th house of the father and conjoins the radical 6th house.

On 2 December 1995, just 9 days before the father's death by suicide, the ponderous planet Uranus, transiting at 27° 50' Capricorn, perfected a semisquare to its natal position. Transiting Uranus had conjoined natal Mercury (ruler of the father's derived 8th house of death) in late September of 1995 and was still within orb of that conjunction at the time of the father's death.

This example illustrates well how the confluence of symbolic measures with operative influences correlate with major events in the native's life.

Chapter 16
FRANKLAND'S MEASURES
WITH UNKNOWN BIRTH TIMES

While writing this book, I happened to watch a documentary about the history of ancient Rome in which the life of Emperor Hadrian was mentioned, together with significant dates from his life. It occurred to me that these dates would be a good test for the symbolic measures of astrologer William Frankland.

Hadrian (Publius Aelius Hadrianus), one of Rome's so-called "five good emperors," was born on 24 January 76 CE in Italica, Hispania Baetica, the first Roman settlement in present-day Spain. The Roman ruins of Italica are located near modern-day La Algaba, which lies north and a bit west of Seville in southern Spain.

Hadrian's mother, Domitia Paulina of Gades, was a wealthy noblewoman, and his father, Publius Aelius Hadrianus Afer, a wealthy Roman soldier and senator who had been born in Italica to a family with strong ties to Roman nobility, including Emperor Trajan.

Historians tend to agree on the following facts about the life of Emperor Hadrian:

Hadrian was born in Italica on 24 January 76 CE (Julian calendar).

His parents died in 86 CE, when Hadrian was 10 years old. As a result, he was sent to Rome as the ward of future Emperor Trajan and family friend Acilius Attianus.

Hadrian was fascinated by Greek culture, architecture, and standards of beauty.

In 98 CE, at age 22, Hadrian cemented a positive relationship with Emperor Trajan and became his favorite to become heir to the throne.

In 101 CE, at age 25, he was elected liaison between Emperor Trajan and the Roman Senate.

Also at age 25, Hadrian wedded Vibia Sabina in an arranged marriage, most likely for the political advantage of Trajan's wife, Plotina. Hadrian was apparently unhappily married to Vibia Sabina, and the couple never produced any offspring.

In the years before becoming emperor, Hadrian established himself as a powerful and gifted military leader.

In 117 CE, when Hadrian was 41 years old, Emperor Trajan fell ill and died, after allegedly naming Hadrian as his heir. (Trajan's wife Plotina's signature was on the succession documents, not Trajan's.)

Hadrian ruled as emperor from 117 to 138 CE.

In 122 CE, at age 46, Hadrian began an extended tour of the Roman Empire.

Late in 123 CE, at age 47, in what is now Turkey, Hadrian met Antinous, an intelligent and handsome pubescent Greek youth from Bithynia, who later became Hadrian's lover and constant companion. Hadrian offered the boy the opportunity to travel to Rome to receive the training and education needed to become his page. Historians give the birth date of Antinous (born in what is now Bolu, Turkey) as around November (some say November 27th) of either 110 or 111 CE (Julian calendar). Thus, he would have been about 12 or 13 years old when he first met the emperor.

In 126 CE, at age 50, Hadrian ended the tour of his empire and returned to Rome, where he reconnected with Antinous and invited the teenager to reside at his villa in Tivoli. At some point during the next couple of years, Hadrian (age 50–52) and Antinous (now around 16 or 17 years old) became romantically involved.

In 128 CE, at age 52, Hadrian began another imperial tour, which would last for 7 years, with Antinous as his traveling and hunting companion.

Around 28 October 130 CE (Julian calendar), Antinous (now about 19 years old) somehow fell into the Nile River and drowned after attending a festival with Emperor Hadrian in Egypt. (Such deaths are not uncommon among 19-year-old boys partying on spring break.) The emperor, then 54.74 years old, was devastated by the loss of his young lover.

After October of 130 CE, the inconsolable Hadrian surrounded himself with images of Antinous and had a city built in his honor. He also had the youth deified so that he could be worshiped as a god. The cult of the beautiful teenage god spread throughout the Roman Empire and lasted for about 200 years.

In 132 CE, Hadrian (now 56 years old) named a group of stars near the constellation Aquila (the Eagle) after the deified boy Antinous. This asterism remained in star charts for centuries and was even mentioned by Tycho Brahe. Claudius Ptolemy, writing in the year 150 CE in his *Almagest*, describes Antinous as a group of six stars that are a subdivision of the constellation Aquila, located above the constellation Sagittarius in the sidereal zodiac.

Grieving and angry about the death of Antinous, Hadrian, at the age of 56 in 132 CE, savagely put down a Jewish rebellion in a manner uncharacteristic of the peaceful and enlightened way in which he had ruled prior to 130 CE. Roman soldiers killed more than half a million Jews to quell the uprising.

Hadrian died on 10 July 138 CE (Julian calendar) at the age of 62.

Because Hadrian's time of birth is not certain, I will work with a *sunrise* chart cast with Whole Sign houses in the tropical zodiac at Hadrian's birthplace near Seville in modern Spain (chart 54). The Moon at midday on 24 January 76 CE would have been at 1° 19' Aquarius (tropical zodiac) and traveling fast, at about 15° per day, so that his natal Moon would have been in either late Capricorn or early Aquarius.

I chose to work with Hadrian's chart in the *tropical* zodiac because Frankland did his research on tropical charts, and his measurements commence at the ecliptic position of the vernal equinox. The ancient literature, however, contains a birth chart for Emperor Hadrian in the writings of Antigonus of Nicaea and Hephaestion of Thebes. This chart appears to be cast in the sidereal zodiac, with Aquarius rising and the Sun, Moon, and Jupiter all in Aquarius, and Mercury and Saturn in Capricorn in the 12th place. For those interested in viewing this sidereal chart, a close approximation can be calculated using the following data: 24 Jan 0076, 6:56 a.m. LMT, LaAlgaba, Spain, 37N28, 005W01, Raman ayanamsa.

Hadrian's Birth Numbers

Frankland would have begun by calculating Hadrian's Birth Numbers. An interesting twist is that Hadrian was born when the Julian calendar was in effect, which gives us a chance to see how a change in official calendar system might affect the Birth Number technique.

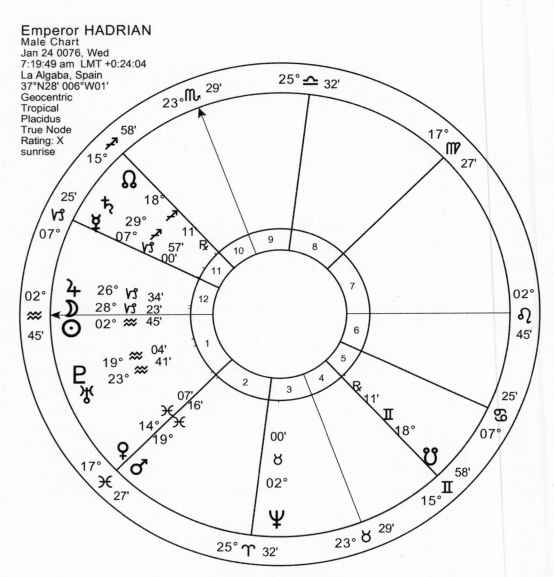

Emperor HADRIAN
Male Chart
Jan 24 0076, Wed
7:19:49 am LMT +0:24:04
La Algaba, Spain
37°N28' 006°W01'
Geocentric
Tropical
Placidus
True Node
Rating: X
sunrise

Chart 54: Emperor Hadrian
24 January 76, 7:19:49 a.m. LMT (sunrise chart), La Algaba, Spain, 37N28 6W01

Hadrian's *Julian* birth date is 24 January 76. This produces the following Birth Numbers:

Adding single digits, 1/24/0076 => 1 + 2 + 4 + 7 + 6, which is **20** and reduces to 2 + 0, or **2**, so his *Single Digits Julian Birth Numbers* are **20** and **2**.

His *Additional Single Digits Julian Birth Numbers* are generated by adding the **20** to his year of birth: 20 + 76 equals **96**, which reduces to 9 + 6, or **15**, which further reduces to 1 + 5, or **6**. Then 20 + 15 + 6 = **41** as his *Additional Single Digits Birth Number*, which reduces to 4 +1 = **5**.

By this method, we have *Single Digits Birth Numbers* **20** and **41**, which reduce to **2** and **5**.

Because 24 consists of two digits, we must also calculate his *Double Digits Julian Birth Numbers*: 1 + 24 + 7 + 6 equals **38**, which reduces to 3 + 8, or **11**, which further reduces to 1 + 1, or **2**, so his *Double Digits Birth Numbers* are **38, 11,** and **2**.

For additional numbers, we add the **38** to the year 0076, which gives 0114, which reduces to 1 + 1 + 4, or **6**. Then 38 + 6 = **44** as his *Additional Double Digits Birth Number*, which reduces to 4 + 4 = **8**.

Hence, his *Double Digits Birth Numbers* are **38** and **44**, which reduce to **2, 8,** and **11**.

Thus, we have as Hadrian's Birth Numbers **20, 38, 41,** and **44**, which reduce to **2, 5, 8,** and **11**.

Frankland would look at combinations of these Birth Numbers to identify ages at which important events might occur in the native's life, *provided* there were other astrological factors operating during those years that forecast the event. For example, in the year 98 CE, at age 22 (*Birth Number* 20 + 2 = 22), Hadrian proved himself to be a loyal ally of Emperor Trajan and became the favorite heir to succeed him as emperor of Rome. In April of 98 CE, transiting Jupiter was traveling through Sagittarius and made a station at 17° 51' Sagittarius, almost exactly conjunct his North Lunar Node in Sagittarius.

Summing Birth Numbers 2 + 8 + 44, we arrive at 54, Hadrian's age when he suffered the loss of his beloved Antinous. Loss and death often correlate with Saturn transits. Around the time of Antinous's death (late October 130 CE), Saturn semisquared its natal position on 23 November 130 CE, squared natal Pluto on 2 January 131 CE, and stationed retrograde on 2 March 131 CE at 21° 45' Scorpio Rx in close square to both natal Pluto and natal Uranus (whose midpoint is at 21° 22' Aquarius). In addition, on 30

November 130 CE, transiting Uranus (sudden disruptions) at 26° 34' Libra (the sign of the love goddess Venus) squared natal Jupiter (associated with long-distance travel) in Capricorn.

Hadrian's Dominant Signs and *Point of Life*

Frankland identified the native's dominant sign, if there was one, early in his delineation of a birth chart. Hadrian's chart has clusters of planets in both Capricorn and Aquarius. These two Saturn-ruled signs therefore play a dominant role in his life. In addition, Pisces is occupied by two of his personal planets, Venus and Mars, and will strongly impact the nature of his interactions with others, including his intimate relationships.

With a large number of planets in Aquarius in the chart, we would expect notable difficulties in his life as the *Point of Life* moves through Taurus and squares Aquarius. This occurs from ages 7 to 14. The *Point of Life* squares natal Pluto and Uranus between ages 11 and 13, the period just after his parents died and he was sent to Rome as ward of the future emperor.

When Hadrian was about to turn 21 years old, the *Point of Life* opposed natal Saturn before it entered the sign Cancer (ages 21–28). Once in Cancer, the *Point of Life* would oppose natal Mercury at about age 22, trine natal Venus and Mars in Pisces around ages 24–26 (his arranged marriage occurred when he was 25 years old), and oppose natal Jupiter around age 27, before moving into Leo at age 28.

In Leo (ages 28–35), the *Point of Life* would oppose the natal Sun at age 28 and then oppose natal Pluto and Uranus around ages 32–34.

In Virgo (ages 35–42), the *Point of Life* would trine natal Neptune at age 35, trine natal Mercury at age 36, oppose natal Venus and Mars at ages 38–40, and trine natal Jupiter but also square natal Saturn at age 41 (when he became emperor).

If we calculate the measure of *4/7 of a degree per year of life* at age 41.5, when Hadrian became emperor, the result is 23.71° of arc. Adding this arc to 0° Aries takes us to 23° 42' Aries, which is closely sextile to natal Uranus at 23° 41' Aquarius.

In Libra (ages 42–49), the *Point of Life* would trine the natal Sun at age 42, square natal Mercury at age 43, trine natal Pluto and Uranus (his first encounter with Antinous at age 47) at ages 45–47, and then square natal Jupiter and sextile natal Saturn at age 48.

In Scorpio (ages 49–56), the *Point of Life* would oppose natal Neptune and square the natal Sun at age 49; sextile natal Mercury at age 50; trine natal Venus at age 52 (Hadrian, having recently initiated an intimate relationship with Antinous, began a tour of the empire with the youth at his side); trine Mars, square Pluto, and sextile the true North Lunar Node at age 53; square natal Uranus at age 54 (Antinous died unexpectedly at this time); and sextile natal Jupiter at age 55 (Hadrian deified Antinous not long after he died).

In Sagittarius (ages 56–63), the *Point of Life* would sextile Hadrian's natal Sun at age 56 (at this time he created the asterism Antinous), square natal Venus at age 59, sextile natal Pluto and square natal Mars at age 60, sextile natal Uranus at age 61, and conjoin natal Saturn at age 62. Hadrian died at age 62.4 while the *Point of Life* was crossing over natal Saturn within an orb of less than one degree. Frankland might have added together Birth Numbers to get a result indicating age 62 as follows: $41 + 11 + 8 + 2 = \mathbf{62}$.

The Asterism of Antinous

Though not particularly relevant to the techniques of William Frankland, the history of the cluster of stars named Antinous in the constellation Aquila is of general interest to astrologers. During the period following the drowning of Antinous (in October of 130 CE), probably around the time of the flooding of the Nile in 131 CE, a new star—perhaps a supernova—was observed in the constellation Aquila (the Eagle) in the vicinity of the known star Delta Aquilae near the center of Aquila and above the zodiacal constellation Sagittarius.

In 1999 astronomers discovered Nova V1494 Aquilae near the fixed star Delta Aquilae in the center of Aquila. Nova V1494 Aquilae may have been the new star observed in Aquila during the year following Antinous's death. Hadrian's response was to declare a group of six stars within Aquila to be the asterism Antinous. According to Claudius Ptolemy (150 CE), the asterism Antinous was made up of the six stars Eta, Theta, Delta, Iota, Kappa, and Lambda Aquilae, which lie above the constellation Sagittarius in the zodiac belt.

The historian Lucius Cassius Dio (c. 155–c. 235 CE) discussed Emperor Hadrian in book 69 of his *Roman History*:

> In Egypt also he rebuilt the city named henceforth for Antinous. Antinous was from Bithynium, a city of Bithynia, which we also call Claudiopolis; he had been a favourite of the emperor and had died in Egypt, either by falling into the Nile,

as Hadrian writes, or, as the truth is, by being offered in sacrifice. For Hadrian, as I have stated, was always very curious and employed divinations and incantations of all kinds. Accordingly, he honoured Antinous, either because of his love for him or because the youth had voluntarily undertaken to die (it being necessary that a life should be surrendered freely for the accomplishment of the ends Hadrian had in view), by building a city on the spot where he had suffered this fate and naming it after him; and he also set up statues, or rather sacred images, of him, practically all over the world. Finally, he declared that **he had seen a star which he took to be that of Antinous,** and gladly lent an ear to the fictitious tales woven by his associates to the effect that **the star had really come into being from the spirit of Antinous and had then appeared for the first time.** On this account, then, he became the object of some ridicule, and also because at the death of his sister Paulina he had not immediately paid her any honour. (Dio 1925, book 69, p. 11; bold highlighting mine)

Emmett Till: Another Unknown Birth Time

At the time of his demise, Emmett Louis Till was a 14-year-old African American boy from Chicago, who at age 6 was stricken with polio, from which he recovered with a slight stutter. His parents were separated because his father, Louis Till, was abusive toward his mother. Louis enlisted in the army in 1943, and a few weeks before Emmett's 4th birthday in 1945, Louis was executed for murdering an Italian woman and raping two others.

In the summer of 1955, Emmett was spending time with relatives in Mississippi. Unaccustomed to the violent racism of the American South, teenage Emmett allegedly flirted with a white woman in her family's grocery store. Whether he did or not is unclear, because the woman later recanted part of her testimony. On 28 August 1955, in response to the woman's complaint, her husband and brother-in-law kidnapped and savagely beat young Emmett, gouging out his eye, shooting him in the head, and tossing his dead body in the river. When the corpse was recovered, the body was so disfigured that it could only be identified by the ring Emmett was wearing, which bore his initials.

Local authorities wanted to bury the mutilated corpse ASAP, but Emmett's mother, Mamie Bradley, asked that her only son's body be returned to Chicago. She was so shocked by the condition of her son's remains that she decided to have an open-casket funeral to expose to the world what the racists had done to her son. The image of the murdered boy went viral and had a major impact on the civil rights movement.

The two murderers went on trial in September of 1955 and were found not guilty by a local jury. Protected against being charged twice for the same crime after a verdict of not guilty, the murderers admitted their guilt a year later in a 1956 *Look* magazine interview. The woman in the grocery store also eventually recanted part of her testimony.

Emmett Till was born in Chicago, Illinois, on 25 July 1941, time unknown (chart 55). Astrologers are at a disadvantage when discussing nativities with unknown birth times because the cusps of the houses are uncertain and the position of the Moon can vary as much as 15 degrees in the course of a day.

One way to cast a chart for such a birth is to use a sunrise chart, as we did with the nativity of Emperor Hadrian. Another alternative is to cast a chart for midday, which gives the mean positions of all the planets. In the midday chart, we can put the Sun on the Ascendant and use equal houses from the Sun so that the house cusps are at angles that form major aspects, plus the quincunx and semisextile, to the Sun. I will use this latter method with Emmett Till's chart.

Let's begin with Emmett's Birth Numbers:

Till's birth date is 25 July 1941: 25-7-1941.

The single digits add up to **29**, which reduces to **11** and **2** as his *Single Digits Birth Numbers*.

The double-digit method gives a sum of **47**, which also reduces to **11** and **2** as his *Double Digits Birth Numbers*.

Now let's calculate Till's *Additional Birth Numbers*:

29 + 1941 = 1970, which reduces to **17** and then to **8**. Then 29 + 17 + 8 = **54** as his *Additional Single Digits Birth Number*, which reduces to **9**.

47 + 1941 = 1988, which reduces to **26** and then to **8**. Then 47 + 26 + 8 = **81** as his *Additional Double Digits Birth Number*, which reduces to **9**.

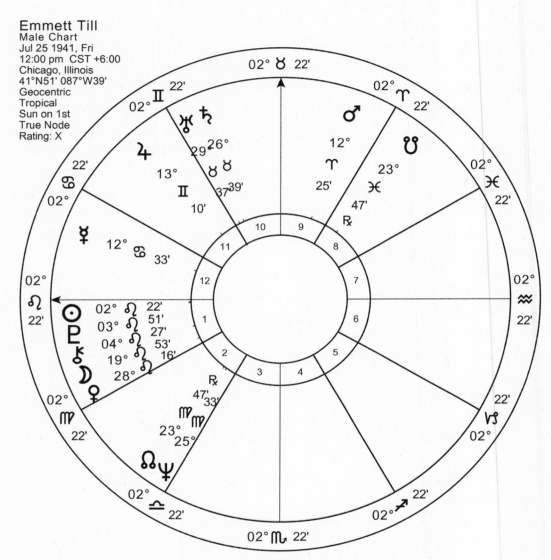

Chart 55: Emmett Till
25 July 1941, 12:00 p.m. CST (midday chart), Chicago, Illinois, 41N51 87W39

Thus, in Frankland's system, Emmett Till's Birth Numbers are **29, 47, 54,** and **81,** which reduce to **2, 9,** and **11.** None of these numbers seem particularly relevant to his murder at age 14; however, the combination produced by serial subtraction, 54 − 29 = 25, and then 25 − 11 = 14, gives his age at the time of the fatal racist incident.

Because Emmett had such a short life span, we will need to pay special attention to minor aspects made by Frankland's symbolic measures, such as semisextiles, semi-squares, sesquisquares, and quincunxes, which may correlate with early life events. His birth time is unknown, so we cannot use the house cusps for predictive work.

Till's overall chart pattern indicates certain potential difficulties. Natal Mars in Aries closely squares natal Mercury in Cancer, stressfully linking the planet of action and aggression with the signifier of speech and communications. This square is alleviated somewhat by benefic Jupiter in Gemini sextile to Mars, but Jupiter is also semisextile to Mercury. His persistent stammering caused by polio at age 6 may correlate with this natal Mars-square-Mercury aspect.

In this midday chart, the Moon lies at almost 20° Leo. On Till's day of birth, the Moon traveled slightly more than 13°, that is, within the range 13.5°—26.5° Leo. If he were born late in the day, the natal Uranus-Saturn conjunction in Taurus would have been in square to his natal Moon by secondary progression during much of his life.

Perhaps Till's most difficult configuration is the stellium of planets in Leo, which receive a whole-sign square from the Saturn-Uranus conjunction in Taurus. Natal Saturn and Uranus both closely square natal Venus, and these squares will be active by secondary progression during a good part of his life, indicating the potential for serious and unexpected problems involving matters related to Venus.

The close conjunction of Till's Sun with natal Pluto may describe his abusive father, who committed rape and murder, but may also reflect his own natal potential to be exposed to violence at various times in his life. The centaur Chiron, the wounded healer, is also an essential player in his natal Sun-Pluto-Chiron configuration in Leo. Perhaps Chiron's wound that will not heal relates to Emmett becoming a symbol of the wound of racism that has pervaded American society since the founding of the United States of America.

Emmett Till's *Point of Life*

Beginning at 0° Aries, Emmett's *Point of Life* advances through the zodiac at a rate of one sign every seven years. While traversing Aries, the *Point of Life* makes trine aspects to the cluster of planets in Leo. This should be a generally favorable period, except when difficult natal configurations become activated.

During his first couple years of life, Till's *Point of Life* was highlighting the natal Sun-Pluto-Chiron conjunction by trine. During this period, his mother separated from his father, who then joined the army and ended up being executed for murder when Emmett was about 4 years old. Around age 3, the *Point of Life* conjoined natal Mars and semisquared the natal Saturn-Uranus conjunction, which was in square to natal Venus.

At age 6, Emmett contracted polio, which created a persistent stammering problem. The *Point of Life* at this age was traversing the final 4° of Aries and would enter Taurus when he turned 7 years old. At the end of the sign Aries, the *Point of Life* semisextiled (an inconjunct configuration) his natal Saturn-Uranus conjunction in Taurus and trined natal Venus at the end of Leo. In doing so, it highlighted the difficult square between natal Venus and Saturn-Uranus. The *Point of Life* was also within orb of a square to the natal Sun (a symbol of health and vitality), which by progression was in semisquare to the lunar nodal axis.

The period from age 7 to 14, by Frankland's methods, was likely to be highly challenging for Emmett. The *Point of Life* was traversing Taurus and squaring his stellium in Leo. At the end of Taurus, the *Point of Life* would conjoin the natal Saturn-Uranus conjunction. Any directions, progressions, or transits of a similar nature at this time would be greatly intensified.

Fixed Stars in the Chart of Emmett Till

Among his forecasting techniques, Frankland included directions, progressions, and transits of the Moon's nodes, fixed stars, Part of Fortune, sensitive points, and critical degrees. In Emmett Till's birth chart, two potentially unfortunate fixed stars influence his natal Saturn-Uranus conjunction.

Caput Algol (the Head of the Medusa) lies at 25° 21' Taurus, conjunct natal Saturn at 26° 39' Taurus within an orb of slightly more than one degree. At the time of Emmett's murder in 1955, Algol was at 25° 33' Taurus. We allow the *Point of Life* a one-year orb of influence, equivalent to 4 2/7°. At age 13, his *Point of Life* arrived at 25° 43' Taurus, highlighting his natal Saturn (at 26° 39' Taurus), which was afflicted by Algol, until shortly after he turned 14. In other words, the position of Saturn plus the orb of 4 2/4° takes us to 0° 56' Gemini as the period when the *Point of Life* places an emphasis on natal Saturn. Symbolically, Algol is associated with misfortune, violence, murder, and beheading.

There is also a close conjunction of the fixed star Alcyone of the Pleiades (the Seven Weeping Sisters) at 29° 10' Taurus with natal Uranus at 29° 37' Taurus. Just before Till turned 14 years old, the *Point of Life* would have highlighted this natal Alcyone-Uranus conjunction.

Vivian Robson associates Alcyone-Uranus contacts with accidents, troubles through women, losses through fire or enemies, heavy losses at the end of life, and a violent death. In Till's chart, Alcyone is closely square to natal Venus, which lies at 28° 16' Leo. Robson links Alcyone-Venus contacts to strong passions, disgrace through women, sickness, and loss of fortune. Adding to the difficulties represented by these Alcyone connections is the fact that Saturn conjoins Alcyone-Uranus and squares natal Venus. It would have been no surprise to Frankland that when Emmett turned 14 years old, he might encounter severe and potentially dangerous trouble through women.

At age 14, Till's *Point of Life* would enter Gemini, ruled by Mercury, which was afflicted at birth by a tight square from Mars in Aries. By secondary progression (in this midday chart), Uranus entered the sign Gemini shortly before Emmett turned 13 years old. When he was murdered on 28 August 1955, his progressed Uranus was at 0° 01' Gemini, and the *Point of Life* conjoined progressed Uranus shortly after he turned 14 years old on 26 July 1955, that is, about a month before he was murdered.

Other Operative Influences in Emmett Till's Chart

On the day of Till's murder, 28 August 1955, transiting Pluto in Leo was almost exactly square natal Saturn at the end of Taurus, and transiting Mars in the 1st degree of Virgo was square to progressed Uranus in the 1st degree of Gemini, which was being highlighted by the *Point of Life*, which entered Gemini at age 14.

Another "operative influence" within orb of the *Point of Life* at age 14 was the Total Solar Eclipse of 20 June 1955 at 28° 04' Gemini, almost exactly semisextile to the Saturn/Uranus midpoint (at 28° 08' Taurus). Semisextiles in progressions and directions are inconjunct formations, similar to quincunxes, because the signs involved are in aversion. The set of inconjuncts (semisextiles and quincunxes) tend to relate to 2nd, 6th, 8th, and 12th house issues. In the zodiac, the 12th house is a place of misfortune, sorrow, and undoing and is related to the Ascendant by semisextile.

At age 14, Emmett's *Age along the Zodiac* was at 14° Aries, making a semisquare to natal Uranus and highlighting the natal Saturn-Uranus conjunction that squared natal Venus. The *4/7° measure* at age 14 was at 8° Aries, which does not aspect any significant planetary positions. It is possible that if we knew the time of birth, the *4/7° measure* might indicate important symbolic directions involving house cusps.

For further study, I have tabulated all the non-lunar aspects in Till's midday chart (chart 55) from the 13th to 16th day after his birth, which correspond to ages 12 to 15. The aspects by transit on these days correspond to the secondary progressions during this age period, at a rate of one day equals one year of life. In this way, we can see which progressed influences are intensified by their co-occurrence with Frankland's symbolic measures. For example, progressed Mercury conjoins the natal Pluto-Chiron conjunction around the time of Till's murder. If we direct natal Mercury (at 12° 31' Cancer at midday) by 14° (his age converted to degrees), we arrive at 26° 31' Cancer, which sextiles natal Saturn (at 26° 29' Taurus), conjoins Algol, and also interacts with several sensitive midpoints: Venus/North Node, Saturn/Neptune, Uranus/North Node, and Venus/Neptune. Thus, symbolically directed Mercury triggers these sensitive factors in the birth chart at the time of Till's demise.

EMMETT TILL'S TRANSIT-TO-NATAL ASPECTS: AUGUST 6–8, 1941						
Planet in Transit	Aspect	Planet in Radix	Date Perfected	Age Progression (in Years)	Position 1	Position 2
Venus	SQ	Jupiter	6 Aug 1941	12.4	13° Vi 10' D	13° Ge 10' D
Mercury	CNJ	Sun	7 Aug 1941	12.8	02° Le 22' D	02° Le 22' D
Uranus	CNJ	GEMINI	7 Aug 1941	12.8	00° Ge 00' D	00° Ge 00' D
Saturn	SSq	Mercury	7 Aug 1941	13.5	27° Ta 33' D	12° Cn 33' D
Mercury	CNJ	Pluto	8 Aug 1941	13.5	03° Le 51' D	03° Le 51' D
Mercury	CNJ	Chiron	8 Aug 1941	13.9	04° Le 27' D	04° Le 27' D
NNode	Direct		8 Aug 1941	15.3	23° Vi 05' D	

Chapter 17
FRANKLAND'S STUDENT
L. PROTHEROE SMITH

At the end of 1926, a young man named L. Protheroe Smith scheduled an astrological consultation with William Frankland. The youth had been studying astrology for some time and had become frustrated because traditional predictive techniques did not seem to be working when he applied them to his own chart. He hoped that an experienced astrologer like Mr. Frankland could clarify his doubts and set him on the proper path of learning to predict effectively. As Mr. Smith wrote in the beginning of his foreword to Frankland's *New Measures in Astrology* (1928):

> Towards the end of 1926 I had my first interview with Mr. Frankland. It proved to be a startling one. My astrological complacency had been severely shaken during 1924 and 1925 by some events which were entirely unaccountable according to accepted methods of directing. The birth horoscope had shown the probability of such events at some time or another, but the recognised time factors had conspicuously failed.
>
> Having been a student for eleven years, I was naturally disappointed, not to say disgruntled, and I had made my way to Mr. Frankland's office intent on complaining bitterly to him of the inadequacy of our science, when a crisis of outstanding consequence could strike one unawares.
>
> But I had neither time nor opportunity to state my grievance and the nature of my mission. Mr. Frankland took the offending chart in his hand, looked at it for a few moments, and proceeded to describe the very events in question, their nature, and the time of their occurrence. (Frankland 1928, 7–8)

Curious about what might have transpired in Protheroe Smith's first consultation with Frankland, I reconstructed his birth chart from comments about it in *New Measures in Astrology*. Here is the data used to deduce his birth date and time.

Because Frankland was practicing in London, I assumed that Protheroe Smith was born in or near London.

The years 1924 and 1925 were difficult, and his confidence in astrology was severely shaken at that time.

Protheroe's father died when he was 5 years old, so I hypothesized a chart with Saturn or Uranus in the 10th house within about 5° of the MC or IC.

Protheroe had a severe illness at age 12¼.

He had gone through an extremely adverse period from ages 19 to 26. Thus, he must have been at least 26 years old when he visited Mr. Frankland at the end of 1926, which implied that he was born before the year 1900, probably in the late 1890s.

Protheroe noted that his natal Ascendant, directed symbolically by the *4/7° Age Point*, was square his 10th house ruler Jupiter when he was 5 years old—his age when his father died. Thus, the MC must have been in either Sagittarius or Pisces.

Jupiter also ruled his 11th house. Based on Placidus tables of houses for London, I deduced that early Sagittarius was on the MC and that late Capricorn or early Aquarius was on the Ascendant when he was born.

Protheroe wrote that the Moon ruled his 6th house, which implies that Cancer must have been on the cusp of the 6th house. In addition, at age 12¼ he had a serious illness, and at that time his natal true South Lunar Node was directed symbolically to the 6th house cusp by the *4/7° per year of age* measure. This meant that the true South Lunar Node was either in very late Gemini or very early Cancer at his birth, which suggested a birth date around the summer of 1899.

At the time of his severe illness, Protheroe noted, his natal Saturn was directed by the *4/7° measure* to the square of the 8th Placidus house cusp, which must have been in Virgo according to the tables of houses. Thus, at his birth Saturn must have been in Gemini or Sagittarius, in square to Virgo. The ephemeris confirmed that Saturn was in Sagittarius in 1899.

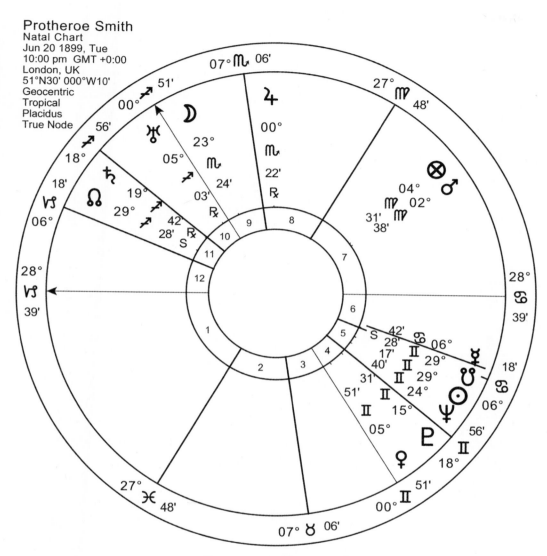

Chart 56: L. Protheroe Smith
20 June 1899, 10:00 p.m. GMT, London, England, 51N30 0W10

Protheroe commented that his natal Moon was directed to conjoin the MC by the *4/7° measure* when he fell ill at 12¼ years of age. Because the MC was in early Sagittarius, his natal Moon must have been within the last seven degrees of Scorpio.

Consulting the ephemeris for the summer of 1899, I deduced that Protheroe was born on 20 June 1899 at about 10:00 p.m. GMT, probably in London (chart 56). This is the chart that he most likely showed to William Frankland at their first consultation in December of 1926. Birth times recorded as exactly on the hour are often rounded from the actual time of birth, so he may have been born within several minutes of 10:00 p.m. If I were to rectify the chart using Uranus coming to the MC by primary direction at age 5 when his father died, the rectified birth time would be about 9:54 p.m.

A Fictionalized Account of
Protheroe's First Encounter with William Frankland

It was a cold December morning when Protheroe Smith made his way to the office of astrologer William Frankland in the West End of London. He had heard good things about Frankland's prowess as an astrologer and was eager for the consultation. At the appointed time, Frankland opened the door to the waiting room and invited Protheroe into his office.

"How can I be of assistance?" asked Frankland.

"The truth is," responded Protheroe, "that I am going through a crisis of faith. I became interested in astrology back in 1915 when I was 16 years old. The war was raging in Europe, and maybe I was looking for some spiritual guidance in a crazy world. Studying my birth chart helped me to see my life in a broader perspective. I have a copy of my chart with me today.

"The problem started when I was trying to learn predictive techniques and apply them to my natal chart. I spent a lot of time learning primary directions—the math was a killer. I also studied secondary progressions and transits. When I applied these techniques to my chart, however, sometimes they worked and sometimes they didn't. Events would occur without a corresponding progression, direction, or transit, and conversely major progressions, directions, or transits would take place and nothing special would happen in my life.

"This has been especially true during the past few years, in particular 1924 and 1925. A lot of bad shit was happening in my life then, but nothing was going on by primary direction, secondary progression, or transit to account for it, except for some general indications that some bad things might happen at some time in my life. What good is that? I was beginning to wonder if astrology is just a bunch of crap, and that's why I came to see you today."

At this point, Frankland interrupted and began to speak: "I went through something similar between 1922 and 1925, but never lost my confidence in astrology. During those years, like you, I became disillusioned with traditional predictive techniques, and for the same reasons. Sometimes they were impressively accurate in their symbolism and on target in timing events, but other times things would happen in my own life, or the lives of my clients, with no corresponding primary direction, progression, or transit. You're right about primary directions: they take forever to calculate. I've been hoping that some day we'll have a rapid calculator that will make the computations easier. Currently there are some analog machines that do basic adding and subtracting, but they are useless for astrologers. I suspect we'll have to wait until the 1940s when Uranus, which rules modern technology, enters into Gemini, a good mercurial air sign, for our engineers and scientist to develop useful computing machines.

"To get back to my frustration with traditional techniques, I began to experiment with new measures, that is, symbolic techniques, to see if they could be more reliable. I've written up my research into a book, which I hope to publish this year with the title *Astrological Investigations*. Not included in that book is yet another symbolic measure, which I'm testing at the moment and which could become the topic of a second book if I can verify its usefulness in a large number of charts. If you'd like, we can apply my new measures to your birth chart to test whether they are of value."

"I would love that," responded Protheroe, as he handed a copy of his chart to Frankland, adding, "My time of birth is taken from our family bible, which says 10:00 p.m., but I'm suspicious about being born exactly on the hour. My mother recalls the time as 10:00 p.m., but I may have been born a few minutes earlier or later."

"Let me stop you there and proceed with your chart," said Frankland. "I prefer to read the chart cold without knowing the details of your life. In that way, I can study your horoscope in an unbiased manner. You can fill in the details after I've had a chance to say what I see in the chart."

With that, Frankland picked up the paper on which Protheroe had drawn his chart, and spent a few minutes silently studying it, apparently doing some mathematical calculations in his head. Then he began to speak.

"Protheroe, the first thing that catches my eye is that your natal Uranus in Sagittarius lies close to the Midheaven in the angular 10th house. This powerful placement would have had a major impact on your early childhood, because Uranus opposes Venus in Gemini in the 4th house of home, family, parents, and early life. Venus happens to rule the 3rd house cusp, which is the derived 12th from the 4th, which signifies the dissolution or ending of 4th house matters, as does the 12th house from any house of the horoscope.

"Uranus is roughly 4° of ecliptic longitude away from the MC. By primary direction, Uranus would arrive at your MC around age 4, or maybe age 5 if you were born a few minutes earlier. This Uranus-Venus opposition coming to the powerful MC degree when you were 4 or 5 years old should correspond to some major disruption in your family life at that age."

Protheroe's jaw dropped as Frankland was speaking. "I can't believe what you just said. My father died unexpectedly when I was 5 years old!"

"I'm sorry to hear that," replied Frankland. "That makes even more sense because Venus rules Libra, which is intercepted in your 8th house, so the activation of Uranus opposite Venus triggered 8th house symbolism, in this case, an event related to a heightened awareness of human mortality. Traditionally, the 8th is a house of matters related to death and dying. You also have Jupiter in the 8th, and Jupiter rules the natal 11th, which is the turned 8th of the 4th, the death of a parent, especially of the 4th house father, although in India they use the 4th house for the mother."

"This is amazing," said Protheroe. "Please continue."

"If you don't mind," said Frankland, "let's apply my new measure to your chart. After studying hundreds of nativities, I've found that symbolically directing at a rate of *4/7° for each year of life* produces impressive results.

"Your father died when you were 5 years old, so we take 4/7 of 5 years: 4 times 5 equals 20, divided by 7 gives a tiny bit less than 3° (because 3×7 equals 21) as the arc of direction. To direct by this amount, we add about 3° to relevant points in your chart.

Let's start with your Ascendant, which is at 28° 39' Capricorn, and add 3°. The result is 1° 39' Aquarius at age 5. This point is within orb of a square to Jupiter, ruler of your father's derived 8th house. If you were born a few minutes earlier, as you suspect, this square would be closer to exact.

"We can also apply this *4/7° symbolic measure* to the cusp of the 8th house, which symbolizes your experience of matters related to death. The 8th house cusp lies at 27° 48' Virgo, and adding 3° brings us to 0° 48' Libra, which is within orb of a square to your natal Sun. I'm beginning to think that you may have been born a few minutes earlier than 10:00 p.m."

Protheroe continued to appear awestruck as Frankland read his chart with no prior knowledge of the youth's life.

Frankland added, "Remember what I said about the MC degree being really powerful? When planets arrive at the MC by direction or progression, major events tend to happen in the life. I notice that your Moon is close to the MC. In fact, they are only about 7½° apart, so when the Moon arrives at the MC by symbolic direction, an event related to the symbolism of the Moon could occur. Because your Moon rules the natal 6th house of illness, it could indicate you falling ill at that time. This is especially true because the true South Lunar Node is about 7° from the 6th house cusp, and by direction will conjoin the 6th house cusp in the same year of life that the Moon conjoins the Midheaven. Let's test my *4/7° measure* on these two directions. Moon to MC in 7½° corresponds to age 13.12, and true South Lunar Node to 6th house cusp in 7° corresponds to age 12.25. So by the *4/7° per year of life symbolic direction*, you may have suffered a significant illness when you were 12 or 13 years old."

Protheroe again looked startled. "This is [expletive deleted] amazing! I can't believe it. I became dangerously ill and underwent a period of confinement in September of 1911, when I was 12¼ years old."

"In that case," said Frankland, "since the Moon rules the 6th house and its contact with the MC is so powerful, you may have been born about 4 minutes earlier. The MC advances by 1° roughly every 4 minutes. Your rectified chart may have the MC in the very last degree of Scorpio rather than the first degree of Sagittarius. In addition, if you were born just a bit earlier, the cusp of the 8th house would be at about 26° Virgo instead of 27° 48' Virgo, and Saturn (ruler of the 12th house) at age 12½, by the *4/7° direction*, would square the cusp of the 8th house, which is symbolically consistent with a period of confinement due to a dangerous illness."

Frankland continued: "Another thing that stands out is the cluster of planets in Gemini in your chart. Alan Leo associates Gemini with ages 14 to 21, so this period should be highly significant in your life, and probably somewhat difficult because Uranus and Saturn in Sagittarius are opposing all those planets in Gemini. Stressful aspects from Saturn and Uranus tend to be especially difficult.

"In my *Point of Life* symbolic method, we equate each 30° sign of the zodiac with 7 years of life, similar to the way the planet Uranus spends about 7 years in each sign. Doing the math, 30° divided by 7 years means that each year of life corresponds to 4 2/7°. We draw an analogy between the birth of the tropical year at 0° Aries, the start of springtime, and the birth of the native. In other words, we start counting your life span from 0° Aries and count every zodiac sign as representing 7 years of your life.

"To get back to Gemini, which contains such a large number of planets and the true South Lunar Node, you were 14 years old when the *Point of Life* entered that sign. At age 15, the *Point of Life* was at 4 2/7° of Gemini, and at age 16 the *Point of Life* arrived at 8 4/7° of Gemini. This was probably a favorable period because you were born at night and the *Point of Life* conjoined natal Venus at age 15, Venus being the benefic of the nocturnal sect. With Uranus opposite Venus, you may have been surprised by an unexpected benefit at this age.

"After age 15, things probably became more difficult because the *Point of Life* conjoined Pluto, Neptune, and the true South Lunar Node and also encountered the opposition from Saturn. For example, at age 17 the *Point of Life* crossed over Pluto, at age 18 it opposed Saturn (this would have been a difficult period), at age 19 it conjoined Neptune (which was being opposed by Saturn), at age 20 it met up with the Moon's true South Node (often indicating a loss), and at age 22 it conjoined the cusp of the 6th house of illness.

"Meanwhile, Uranus in Sagittarius was opposing all those Gemini planets by the *Age along the Zodiac measure* and by the *4/7° symbolic direction*, which I've been testing lately. For example, if we focus on your late teens and early 20s, Uranus opposes Pluto in about 10.5°, which is equivalent to age 18 by the *4/7° measure*. Shortly thereafter, by the *Age along the Zodiac measure* (1° equals one year of life), Uranus opposes Neptune at about age 19½ and then moves on to oppose the Sun by symbolic direction at age 24 and oppose the true South Lunar Node (a point of loss and material deprivation) at about age 24½.

"Also making these years difficult is the square from Mars in Virgo to all the planets in Gemini. By the *Age along the Zodiac measure* (1° equals a year of life), Mars squares Pluto at age 13, squares Neptune at age 22, squares the Sun at around age 26½, and squares the true South Lunar Node at age 27. So for the past few years you've been going through a hell of a time having to deal with the triple whammy of symbolic oppositions from Saturn and Uranus and symbolic squares from Mars to all your planets in Gemini, the dominant sign in your birth chart. It's no wonder that you've been feeling so overwhelmed these past few years.

"Because Mercury disposits all the Gemini planets as well as Mars in Virgo, let's direct Mercury at the rate of 7 years per sign to Mars, which can act as a trigger to Uranus opposing Venus (possibly a breakup in an intimate relationship). Mercury lies in sextile to Mars, and they are about 56° apart. Dividing 56° by 4.286° per year (7 years per sign) directs Mercury to Mars at age 11.5. The Ptolemaic period of Mercury is 10 years, so you will feel a ripple effect beginning at about age 21.5.

"If we want to be more specific, we could direct Mercury to the square of Uranus, which lies at 5° 03' Virgo at a distance of about 58°. If we divide 58° by 4.286° per year, we get Mercury directed to the square of Uranus at age 13.5 years, with ripples every 10 years thereafter. In short, there may have been problems in a close relationship leading to a breakup (Uranus opposite Venus) between ages 21.5 and 23.5."

Looking at the expression on Protheroe's face, one could tell that he was astonished by Frankland's reading, which had been done simply by looking at the birth chart and doing simple calculations in his head.

"You are a godsend, Mr. Frankland," said Protheroe. "I didn't see any of these timings in my chart, and I can't tell you how grateful I am for your insights. You have restored my faith in astrology. A great burden has been lifted from my shoulders, and I can't wait to delve deeper into the subject. Do you give lessons? I'd love to learn more about your methods and, if possible, to participate in your research. I am amazed by what you were able to see in my chart, and I want to learn how to do it myself."

Frankland responded, "Thank you for your kind words and enthusiasm. As I mentioned earlier, I'm in the midst of a research project and need to test hundreds of natal charts with the new *4/7° symbolic measure* to ensure that it is reliable and a worthy topic for my next book. I can see that you are a dedicated student of astrology, and I would welcome your assistance and collaboration in this endeavor."

"It's a deal then," said Protheroe. "When do we start?"

"We've already started," said Frankland. "Let's schedule our next meeting."

Protheroe continued to meet with William Frankland to learn his techniques and assist him in the ongoing research. He even wrote the foreword to Frankland's next book, *New Measures in Astrology*, published in 1928, two years after their first encounter.

Boris Cristoff and the Proluna Method

Bulgarian astrologer Boris Cristoff became interested in the celestial art by the age of 10. He was born in Sofia, Bulgaria, on 22 September 1925 at about 9:08 a.m. GMT (chart 57). His family moved to South America when Boris was a child. His birth data has a Rodden Rating of A, and his calculated Ascendant is at 24° 52' Scorpio.

Cristoff was raised in Montevideo, Uruguay, after the family moved there in 1931. After graduating from university, he became a teacher of mathematics and languages, and in 1963 he began work as an astrologer. In 1982 Cristoff established a school of astrology in Montevideo and Buenos Aires, which resulted in his methods becoming well-known among Spanish-speaking astrologers.

According to Astro-Databank, Cristoff married in 1955, the year he turned 30 years old. If we apply Frankland's *4/7° per year measure* to his age, we get $4/7 \times 30 = 17.14°$, or 17° 8'. Adding 17° 8' to the position of his natal Venus (goddess of love and ruler of his 7th house cusp of marriage), we get 7° 27' Scorpio + 17° 8' = 24° 35' Scorpio, which closely conjoins his natal Ascendant of 24° 52' Scorpio. Thus, Frankland, after glancing at Cristoff's chart for under a minute, would have predicted the likelihood of marriage in 1955.

In the course of his lifetime, Cristoff wrote 32 books on astrology and did thousands of consultations. He made numerous accurate mundane predictions, one of which was of a worldwide pandemic in the year 2020. He died on 3 January 2017 before he could see his prediction come to pass.

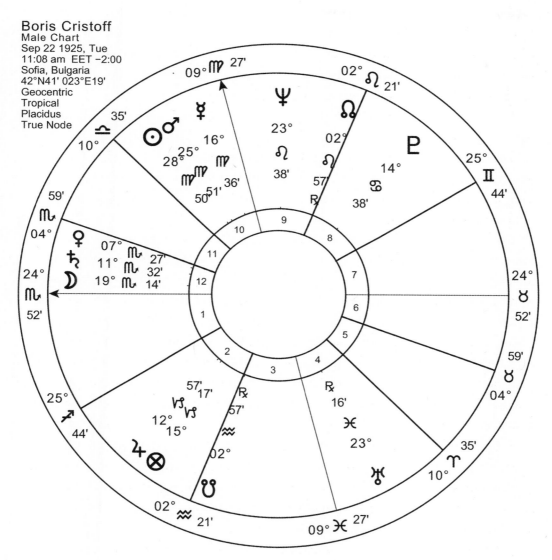

Boris Cristoff
Male Chart
Sep 22 1925, Tue
11:08 am EET −2:00
Sofia, Bulgaria
42°N41' 023°E19'
Geocentric
Tropical
Placidus
True Node

Chart 57: Boris Cristoff
22 September 1925, 11:08 a.m. EET, Sofia, Bulgaria, 42N41 23E19

Cristoff called his most popular predictive technique **Proluna** (**Progresión Lunar Natural** in Spanish, abbreviated PLN), and he first published it in 1963. Proluna is a type of symbolic direction at the rate of 7 years per astrological Placidus or Topocentric *house*, measured from the natal Ascendant. The similarities to Frankland's *Point of Life*, which was published 37 years earlier in 1926, are obvious.

Frankland's method, as distinct from Proluna, is a form of symbolic direction at the rate of 7 years per *sign* (rather than house), beginning at 0° Aries (rather than the natal Ascendant), and is rooted in the original writings of Alan Leo at the end of the nineteenth century. I do not know whether Cristoff was familiar with Frankland's books from the 1920s or the nineteenth-century works of Alan Leo in which he linked the orbit of Uranus to the human life cycle.

Cristoff's Proluna method of septenary (7-year) periods can be summarized as follows. The Proluna method begins at the degree of the natal Ascendant and calculates the distance in zodiacal longitude from the rising degree to the cusp of the 2nd house, which is equated to the first 7 years of life. The distance in longitude from the cusp of the 2nd house to the cusp of the 3rd house corresponds to ages 7 to 14, and so on around the wheel. An entire cycle of the zodiac requires 84 years (the period of the orbit of Uranus).

In addition to the Proluna method of symbolic direction (septenary periods of 7 years per house), Cristoff fine-tuned his predictive technique with symbolic directions at a rate of one month per house, one-twelfth of a lunar cycle per house, and finally two hours per house.

For readers who wish to experiment with Cristoff's Proluna method, let me present a very brief overview. As mentioned previously, the name Proluna is an acronym for the Spanish phrase **Progresión Lunar Natural**. As a symbolic direction, it is a type of "progression" that proceeds from the natal Ascendant and advances through the horoscope wheel at a rate of 7 years per Placidus house.

Lunar apparently refers to the similarities of the Proluna with the phases of the lunar cycle, which consists of four quarters of 7-day weeks. Cristoff was apparently impressed by the symbolic significance of the number 7 in the astrological literature, for example, the existence of just 7 visible planets and the *seven ages of man* by Claudius Ptolemy. In addition, the cycle of Uranus lasts 84 years, with Uranus passing through every sign in 7-year periods.

Impressed that the human life cycle corresponds roughly to the duration of the orbital period of Uranus (an idea found in the writings of Alan Leo at the beginning of the twentieth century), Cristoff paired each astrological house, starting from the Ascendant, with 7-year periods of human life:

House 1: ages 0–7, infancy
House 2: ages 7–14, youth
House 3: ages 14–21, adolescence
House 4: ages 21–28, early young adulthood
House 5: ages 28–35, middle young adulthood
House 6: ages 35–42, late young adulthood
House 7: ages 42–49, early mature adulthood
House 8: ages 49–56, middle mature adulthood
House 9: ages 56–63, late mature adulthood
House 10: ages 63–70, early senior adulthood
House 11: ages 70–77, middle senior adulthood
House 12: ages 77–84, late senior adulthood

Presumably, at each age the native participates in the area of life indicated by the associated house in a manner modified by the zodiac sign that the Proluna is traversing, as well as those planets that the Proluna encounters along the way.

Cristoff also associated the con-significators of the houses, described by Abu Ma'shar and William Lilly, with each of the 12 houses. The con-significators are simply the seven visible planets, starting at the Ascendant (the 1st house) with Saturn and continuing in Chaldean order from slowest to fastest:

House 1: ages 0–7, Saturn
House 2: ages 7–14, Jupiter
House 3: ages 14–21, Mars
House 4: ages 21–28, Sun
House 5: ages 28–35, Venus
House 6: ages 35–42, Mercury
House 7: ages 42–49, Moon
House 8: ages 49–56, Saturn

House 9: ages 56–63, Jupiter

House 10: ages 63–70, Mars

House 11: ages 70–77, Sun

House 12: ages 77–84, Venus

The element of the sign being traversed by the Proluna also plays a major role in the interpretation. *Fire* signs indicate a period of energy, creativity, action, adventure, enthusiasm, ambition, and individualism. *Earth* signs suggest practical, concrete accomplishments, tangible results, and material or economic matters, such as landing a job, building a home, buying a car, planning a wedding, starting a family, etc. *Air* signs highlight one's social interactions, relationships, associations, studies, travel, and communications with others. *Water* signs are connected with endings, and with joys and sorrows, occult interests, emotional and spiritual matters, empathic bonds, and even merging with others, as in sexual activity (which involves the exchange of bodily fluids).

The three qualities, or modalities, of the signs (cardinal, fixed, and mutable) are also taken into account. The Proluna traversing a *cardinal* sign indicates a period of action, high energy, new beginnings, and movement. *Fixed* signs have to do with establishing a firm and lasting foundation and maintaining the status quo. *Mutable* signs are dual and transitional in nature, marked by many choices and changes, including leaving the old behind and entering into something new.

Consider the example of the boy explorer Stanley Conder, which we discussed earlier in chapter 12. The young Conder died in Canada at the age of 15½ when his Proluna was traversing his 3rd Placidus house, which extended from 4° 27' Aries to 5° 35' Taurus. Because the cusp of the 3rd house corresponds to age 14 and the cusp of the 4th house to age 21, then at age 15.5 he was about 21.4 percent of the way through his 3rd house, whose size is 31° 08'. Thus, his Proluna at age 15.5 was at 11° 07' Aries.

The boy explorer's Proluna in Aries (cardinal fire) suggests a period of high energy, action, travel, exploration, and adventure. He was far from home, exploring Canada, at the time of his fatal accident, which occurred with his Proluna in the 3rd house, consignified by Mars, which also happens to rule the cusp of the Aries 3rd house. Mars, the warrior of the gods, is a planet of action, fighting, challenge, competition, and bravery in the face of danger. The closest aspect that the Proluna made around age 15.5 was a sextile to natal Pluto on the cusp of the 6th house of bodily injury.

The Proluna method is far more complex than this brief summary can cover. I have not extensively tested the Proluna and therefore cannot comment on its effectiveness from personal experience. Experimenting on the case examples in this text, however, I found Frankland's methods to be more convincing than the Proluna technique. On the other hand, the 1994 edition of Cristoff's book on the topic, published by Kier, has a total of 421 pages. Obviously, there is a lot more to Proluna than I have had time to experiment with.

Chapter 18
FORECASTING METHODS
OF WYNN AND ADAMS

Frustrated with cumbersome and time-consuming traditional techniques, William Frankland in England was not the only astrologer in the early decades of the twentieth century to seek quicker reliable methods of forecasting. In the United States, astrologer Sidney K. Bennett (aka Wynn) researched and popularized a novel technique for forecasting with solar returns. In a similar vein, Wynn's famous contemporary Evangeline Adams developed a streamlined method for doing horary astrology by combining the house cusps of the moment of the question with the natal planets of the querent. This chapter will consider the forecasting methods of Wynn and Adams in more detail.

Wynn's Key Cycle Progressed Solar Return

Like William Frankland in London, the US astrologer Sidney K. Bennett, aka Wynn, grew disillusioned with traditional predictive techniques such as primary directions and secondary progressions. To deal with this frustration, Wynn developed a method of progressing solar returns, which he called the Key Cycle, as an aid to prediction.

Sidney Bennett began to practice astrology professionally under the pseudonym Wynn, and his monthly publication, *Wynn's Astrology Magazine,* became quite popular in the 1930s and 1940s. On page 4 of his book *Your Future: A Guide to Modern Astrology* (1935), Wynn writes, "I was born in Chicago on February 10, 1892, at exactly 9 a.m. True Local Time," which is equivalent to 8:50:30 a.m. CST. For readers unfamiliar with True Local Time (TLT), let me quote an explanation by Carl Payne Tobey from Sydney Omarr's book *My World of Astrology* (1965), chapter 19:

True Noon or True Local Time is when the Sun is 90° or one quarter of a circle from the horizon at a point due east or west—in other words, halfway between the eastern and western horizon.... The rule for changing over from Standard Time to True Local Time is quite simple. One degree changes the time by four minutes. If you are east of the Time Zone Center, add four minutes per degree. If you are west of the Time Zone Center, deduct four minutes for each degree. (Omarr 1935, 135–36)

The GPS longitude of Chicago is 87° 37' 23.4372" West, and its Time Zone Center is at 90° 00' 00" West (CST, or Central Standard Time). The difference between these two longitudes is 02° 22' 36.57" degrees, which we must multiply by 4 minutes on the clock for each degree to find the difference between CST and True Local Time. Doing the calculation, we find a difference of 9.5 minutes between Wynn's true local time of birth and CST. In other words, Wynn's 9:00 a.m. TLT time of birth converted to CST is 8:50:30 a.m. CST.

Wynn, however, believed that birth times were usually recorded slightly after the actual moment of birth, and he often adjusted the recorded birth time accordingly. In his publications on the Key Cycle, Wynn cast his own birth chart for 8:49 a.m. CST, with an Ascendant of 8° 27' Aries and an MC of 4° 21' Capricorn, with the Moon at 25° 44' Cancer. In this text I will use Wynn's 8:49 a.m. CST birth chart with 8° 27' Aries rising, which is the one he used for himself.

While on a business trip to California in May of 1926, Wynn suffered a nearly fatal hit-and-run accident, which took him completely by surprise. He had studied the secondary progressions to his birth chart and was expecting to have a successful trip, which he believed was promised by some especially favorable progressed aspects in effect at the time. Unfortunately, Wynn was apparently unfamiliar with how to delineate secondary progressions, and he did so without reference to the condition or configuration of the planets in his birth chart. His unwitting error in astrological technique was costly, and he was almost killed in a vehicular accident around 9:00 p.m. in Merced, California, on 18 May 1926.

Wynn apparently had not read Leigh Hope Milburn's classic text *The Progressed Horoscope Simplified* (1928), in which she cautioned:

In estimating the influence of progressions and transits, it must be borne in mind that whatever aspects any [transiting or progressed] planet may make, whether favorable or unfavorable, it will stir into activity in *some* measure the influence denoted by its aspects in the nativity, even though the influence by progression is of a contrary nature to that in the nativity. (Milburn 1928, 28; italics mine)

In May of 1926, Wynn planned a business trip to California because he was expecting extremely favorable astrological influences related to his progressed Sun trine natal Moon on May 7th, progressed Moon trine natal Sun on May 21st, and progressed Sun conjunct natal Venus on May 29th. Instead, he was nearly killed in a hit-and-run car accident on 18 May 1926.

Wynn apparently ignored the condition and aspects of the Sun, Moon, and Venus in his birth chart (chart 58, inner wheel). Wynn's natal Sun lies in Aquarius, the sign of its detriment, and forms a stressful quincunx to his natal Moon in Cancer. In addition, his natal Sun rules the 6th house of bodily ailments and lies "at the bendings," in partile square to the true lunar nodes. Ptolemy, in book 3, chapter 12, of the *Tetrabiblos*, linked the position of the Moon "at the nodes or her bendings" to injuries and illnesses. Later astrologers found that any planet at the bendings was prone to being involved in some sort of life crisis. In Wynn's chart, natal Venus lies in the 12th house (confinement, hospitalization) opposite natal Saturn, which rules the 12th house and occupies the 6th house of illness.

Wynn also did not notice that the progressed MC at his birthplace (Chicago) formed a nearly exact square to his natal Uranus in May of 1926 (chart 58, outer wheel). The progressed MC square Uranus is a strong indicator of a sudden, unanticipated, and difficult life experience. His progressed MC also formed a partile trine to the natal Neptune-Pluto conjunction in Gemini, which is opposed by natal Mars at the cusp of the 9th house of travel. (In 1926, Wynn would have been unaware of the existence of Pluto. Sophia Mason, however, in her 1985 book *Delineation of Progressions*, specifically links Mars-Pluto oppositions to dangerous confrontations and serious vehicular accidents.)

Focusing only on the favorable aspects of the progressed Sun, Wynn also ignored the fact that in May of 1926 his progressed Sun in the natal 12th house opposed his progressed Saturn in the 6th house within an orb of slightly more than one degree. At the same time, his natal Saturn in Virgo in the 6th house was opposed by progressed Jupiter in Pisces, a sign that is ruled by Jupiter and is intercepted in the 12th house of undoing.

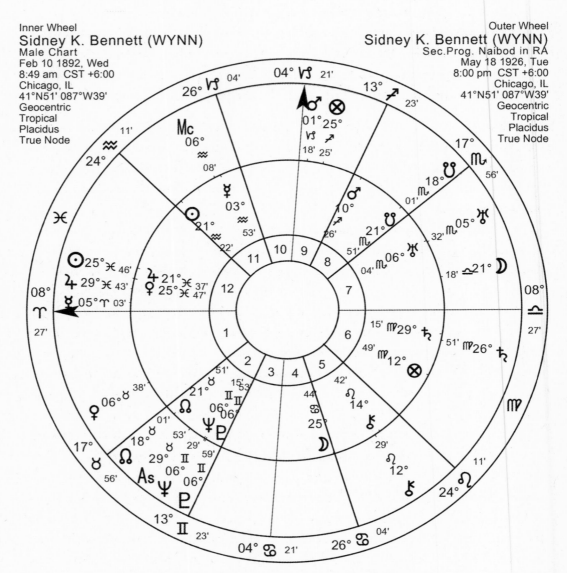

**Chart 58: Sidney K. Bennett (Wynn), Birth Chart,
with Secondary Progressions for 18 May 1926 in Outer Wheel**
Inner Wheel: 10 February 1892, 8:49 a.m. CST, Chicago, Illinois, 41N51 87W39
Outer Wheel: 18 May 1926, 8:00 p.m. CST, Chicago, Illinois, 41N51 87W39

Unaware of his erroneous understanding of how to delineate secondary progressions, Wynn became determined to find a more effective method of prediction. To this end, he studied the astrology of his May 1926 accident from many points of view. He had recently begun using solar returns, and found them to be useful but not entirely reliable. After much experimentation, Wynn devised a truly useful method for predicting events during a solar return year, based on the following observations of events in his own and his clients' lives:

- The solar return (SR) cast for the location of the event is more reliable than the return cast for the birthplace.

- Progressing the solar return angles and cusps to the actual date of the event is more effective than using the fixed return chart cast for the actual day of the annual return.

- The most effective method to progress the solar return cusps is to advance the SR MC at a rate such that, during one tropical year, the current solar return MC arrives at the exact position of the subsequent year's solar return MC. At this rate, at the birthplace, the SR MC advances roughly three zodiac signs per year. For example, if the SR MC this year were in Taurus, next year it would likely fall in Leo, three signs further along in the zodiac circle.

- The actual transits *at the time and place of the event* are more specific predictors than the directions or progressions of the birth chart.

- Natal or transiting planets that occupy the 1st house of the solar return chart progressed to the date and place of the event show what is coming into the life of the native at that time and place. The other house cusps of the Key Cycle chart are also relevant. Wynn developed his Key Cycle using Placidus houses.

- By studying a series of Key Cycle returns over the course of a year, or over a period of several years, the native can get a sense of the flow of life events, that is, the unfolding of the natal promise as revealed by both natal and transiting planets rising to the Ascendant or connecting with the various house cusps of the Key Cycle progressed solar return.

Chart 59 shows Wynn's Key Cycle progressed solar return for the date and place of his 1926 accident (inner wheel), with his natal positions superimposed (outer wheel).

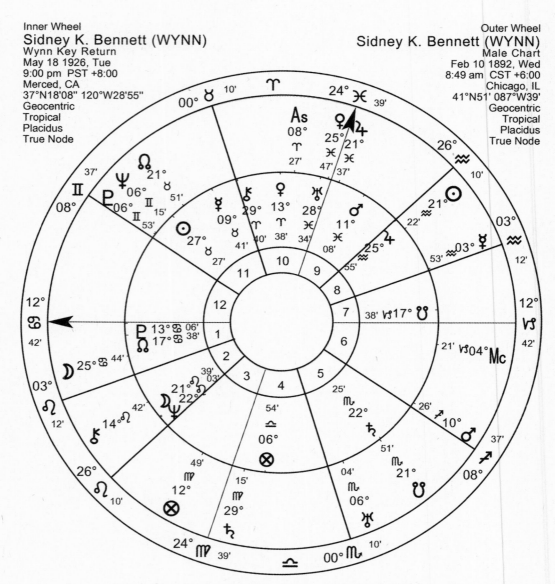

Inner Wheel
Sidney K. Bennett (WYNN)
Wynn Key Return
May 18 1926, Tue
9:00 pm PST +8:00
Merced, CA
37°N18'08" 120°W28'55"
Geocentric
Tropical
Placidus
True Node

Outer Wheel
Sidney K. Bennett (WYNN)
Male Chart
Feb 10 1892, Wed
8:49 am CST +6:00
Chicago, IL
41°N51' 087°W39'
Geocentric
Tropical
Placidus
True Node

Chart 59: Sidney K. Bennett (Wynn), Wynn Key Cycle Return
for 18 May 1926, with Birth Chart in Outer Wheel
Inner Wheel: 18 May 1926, 9:00 p.m. PST, Merced, California, 37N18 120W29
Outer Wheel: 10 February 1892, 8:49 a.m. CST, Chicago, Illinois, 41N51 87W39

In Wynn's Key Cycle progressed solar return chart for 18 May 1926 in Merced, California, transiting Pluto is rising to the Ascendant, indicating some type of dramatic event accompanied by much force. At the same time, natal Pluto lies at the cusp of the Key Cycle's 12th house (hospitalization). Transiting Mars lies in the 9th house (long-distance travel) and is closely square to his natal Mars (accidents), which lies at the cusp of the Key Cycle's 6th house cusp (bodily injury). Transiting Uranus is powerfully placed near the MC and is opposite natal Saturn at the IC. The Key Cycle's Ascendant-ruler Moon conjoins transiting Neptune (inattention) and opposes his natal Sun, ruler of the Key Cycle 3rd house of local travel.

Wynn's Key Cycle progressed solar return is a useful predictive tool, but my impression is that few astrologers today make use of it. In 1970 the American Federation of Astrologers republished Wynn's articles from the 1930s and 1940s about the Key Cycle technique from *Wynn's Astrology Magazine*. Solar Fire offers "Wynn's Key Return" as an option in its Returns menu, as does the program Meridian by Juan Saba.

The Man Who Drowned While on Vacation

For those wishing to calculate Wynn's Key Cycle return chart by hand or with the aid of a spreadsheet, let me give an example. In his discussion of the importance of the lunar nodes, William Frankland gives an example of a man who drowned at age 27 while swimming on the afternoon of 31 October 1908. The man was born on 13 January 1881 at 5:47:10 a.m. GMT in Hexham, UK (54N58, 002W06). I have reconstructed the chart from Frankland's description and his source material, including Alan Leo's *1001 Nativities*. Frankland does not specify the location of the drowning, so I will work with the birthplace solar return.

The solar return of 14 January 1908 (a leap year) occurred at 7:19:46 p.m. UT, with an MC of 13° 09' Taurus.

The solar return of 14 Jan 1909 occurred at 1:07:19 a.m. UT, with an MC of 5° 14' Leo.

The time elapsed between these two consecutive solar returns is 365 days, 5 hours, 47 minutes, and 43 seconds, that is, 365 days plus 5.7925 hours.

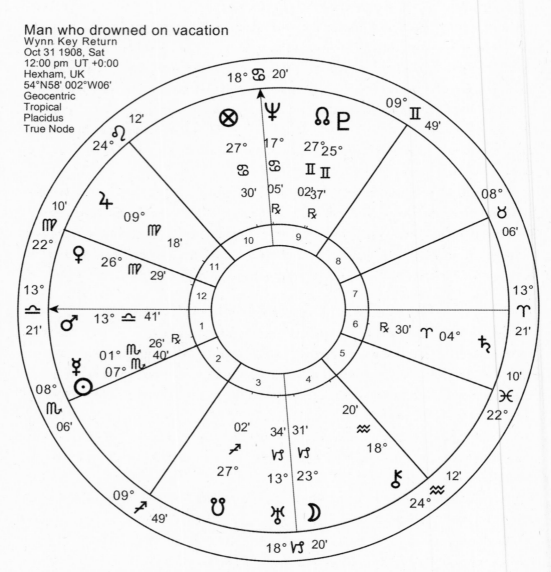

Chart 60: Man Who Drowned on Vacation, Wynn Key Cycle Return for 31 October 1908
31 October 1908, 12:00 p.m. UT (time unknown), Hexham, England, 54N58 2W06

Wynn decided to progress the MC at a rate that advances the annual MC from its position in the current solar return to its position in the next return exactly one tropical year later. This progression can be done by advancing the birth time of the current solar return, in this case by a mean amount of 5.7925 hours (or 347.55 minutes) divided by 365.242 days in a tropical year. These calculations are easily done in a spreadsheet:

347.55 minutes divided by 365.242 days in a year equals 0.951560882 minutes per day.

This person's solar return occurred on 14 January 1908, and he died on 31 October 1908, which is 291 days after his birthday in 1908.

291 days × 0.951560882 minutes per day equals 276.9042 minutes, or 4 hours 36 minutes and 54 seconds, which we must add to the "birth time" of the current solar return chart to determine the progressed solar return (Wynn Key Cycle return).

The 1908 solar return occurred at 7:19:46 p.m. UT, to which we must add 04:36:54, which produces a progressed time of 11:56:40 p.m. UT.

Wynn used the data for the solar return of 1908 but adjusted the birth time to 11:56:40 p.m. UT to calculate the progressed angles and cusps of the solar return progressed to 31 October 1908. His Key Cycle chart then uses these progressed SR cusps but inserts the transits of the date being studied. If the event occurred at a location other than the birthplace, he simply relocated the progressed solar return to the actual location. Chart 60 shows how Solar Fire renders the Wynn Key return for 31 October 1908 at the birthplace.

The cusps of the Wynn Key return chart are progressed from the 1908 solar return. The planets are the transits of the day of the drowning. Note transiting Mars rising at the Ascendant, with Neptune opposite Uranus conjunct the meridian axis. Transiting Mars is in partile square to transiting Uranus, a classic symbol of an accident. Transiting Venus lies in the 12th house and rules the 1st and 8th houses, and closely squares Pluto and the Moon's nodes. It is also noteworthy that the true lunar nodes are stationary on the day of the man's demise.

Wynn would also superimpose the natal chart around the Key return. For example, this man's natal Moon rules his natal 8th house and lies at 29° 04' Gemini, where it conjoins the North Lunar Node and Pluto and squares transiting Venus in the Key chart.

Wynn's Key Return of a Woman with Abnormal Liver Function Tests

A woman in her 70s had blood tests done as part of her routine medical care. The next day her doctor called to inform her that her liver function tests, which had always been in the normal range, were markedly elevated and that she would need further workup. She asked my astrological opinion about the matter, and fortunately she had noted the time at which the blood was drawn in the clinical laboratory. Among the techniques I used to answer her question was her Wynn Key Cycle chart for the time the lab technician drew her blood (chart 61). This chart represents a type of hybrid decumbiture chart that combines her progressed solar return Key Cycle MC and house cusps with the transits for the moment the diagnostic test was performed. In this Wynn Key Cycle chart, the Moon rules the woman's Ascendant and signifies the querent, her body and her health. Luna lies in the favorable 11th house and is exalted in Taurus. However, the Moon conjoins Uranus, Mars, and the North Lunar Node and also applies to square both the Sun and Saturn, in a T-square formation. Saturn rules and occupies the 8th house. In addition, a Total Lunar Eclipse at 25° 16' Scorpio on 16 May 2022 made a partile square to the Key Cycle chart's Sun and impacted the T-square involving the Sun, Saturn, Mars, Uranus, Moon, and North Lunar Node.

The most angular planets in the Key Cycle chart are Jupiter (ruler of the 6th house of illness) conjunct the MC, and Pluto (major change) on the 7th house cusp almost exactly opposite the Ascendant (her body and vitality). Venus, the benefic of the nocturnal sect of this chart, lies in the 1st house, which is a favorable indicator.

The nearly exact ecliptic position of Pluto on the western horizon opposite the Ascendant (the body) in this chart is quite striking. Pluto is a planet of transformation, regeneration, and bringing hidden matters to light. Its action is to cleanse, purge, destroy, and eliminate that which is no longer useful or needed. Major aspects of Pluto often correlate with life-altering crisis situations, and Pluto is likened to the phoenix rising from its ashes.

Overall, the Key Cycle chart for the moment of the blood draw suggests significant unanticipated (Uranus) health-related issues. The medical workup revealed a blockage as well as inflammation and infection in the bile duct and the incidental finding of a neuroendocrine mass in the pancreas that would need to be removed surgically. The woman's doctor told her that she was fortunate to have discovered the pancreatic mass early, while it was still a treatable condition.

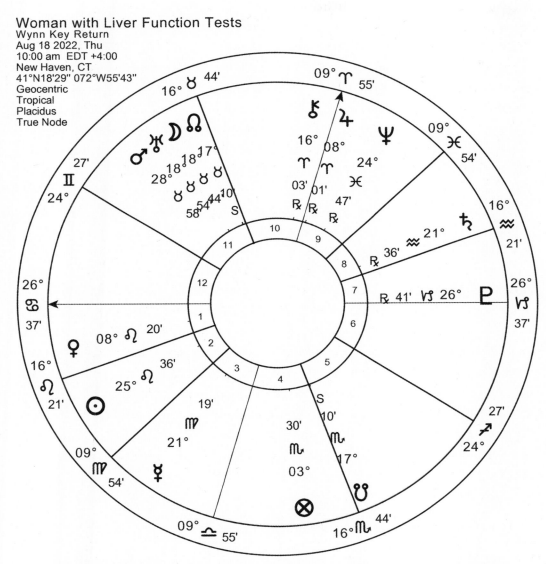

Chart 61: Woman with Liver Function Tests, Wynn Key Cycle Return for 18 August 2022
18 August 2022, 10:00 a.m. EDT, New Haven, Connecticut, 41N18 72W56

Symbolic Hybrid Charts in Western Astrology

Wynn's Key Cycle progressed solar return chart is a form of *symbolic hybrid chart*—a technique that dates back at least to the time of Vettius Valens in the second century CE. It is a hybrid chart because it combines the transits at the time of an event with the cusps of the progressed solar return in effect during a particular year.

Valens used the symbolic hybrid chart to study annual revolutions. Instead of the modern solar return, with cusps for the exact moment the Sun returns to its natal position, Valens used the Ascendant of the Moon's return during the solar month when the Sun returned to its natal zodiac sign. Into a chart whose houses were those of the lunar return during the annual solar month, Valens inserted the positions of the planets for the moment the Sun returned to its birth position by sign and degree. He felt that the combined symbolism of the Sun and the Moon was a better indicator of the start of a new annual cycle of life.

Evangeline Adams's New Horary Consultation Chart and the Accidental Ascendant

In the twentieth century, Evangeline Adams, a contemporary of William Frankland, used the symbolic hybrid method to generate consultation and horary charts for her clients. In her "new horary," Adams casts a chart either for the location and moment when the client enters her office (a consultation chart) or for the exact moment when the client asks a specific question (a "new horary" chart). Instead of inserting the positions of the transiting planets, she places the client's *natal* planets into the houses of the consultation or horary chart. Adams favored Placidus houses, and she called the Ascendant degree of this consultation or horary chart the "Accidental Ascendant." Adams describes her method in *The Bowl of Heaven* (1926):

> I consider the position of the heavens *in relation to the individual's own chart.* ... I have established after years of research and experimentation, that if I draw my conclusions from the position of the planets in combination with the chart of the individual at the moment I am asked to decide a given question, I will get my answer—and it will be the right answer. ... I note the degree that is rising at the moment my client enters. I then adjust his chart so the corresponding degree in

the chart will be an "Accidental Ascendant," and proceed to read the horoscope as if it were the radix. (Adams 1926, 18–19; italics mine)

For horary questions, Adams explains her method more specifically in *Your Place in the Sun* (1927):

Take the exact time the question is asked and work out for this time the Ascendant, or first house, as well as the cusps of the other eleven houses; just as you would if drawing a natal chart. Instead, however, of placing in this chart the planets as they appear in the heavens at the moment the question is asked, the querent's radical planets should be placed in this chart. The Astrologer should now proceed to read the chart in the same manner as if it were the radix, for the chart as it now stands might be considered the horoscope for the birth of the idea, just as the natal chart is the horoscope for the birth of the individual. (Adams 1927, 261)

Adams gives several examples of her "new horary" (a form of consultation chart) from her work with clients. One woman, whose natal Saturn fell in the 3rd house of the consultation chart, came to see Adams because she was concerned about her brother's ill health. The horary house placement of *natal* Saturn, a general signifier of worry and misfortune, often indicated the area of hardship, sorrow, restriction, or disappointment about which the client was most troubled.

Adams also found that *natal* planets, falling *in the 1st house of the "new horary" chart* and therefore rising toward the "Accidental Ascendant," symbolized that which was about to come into the life of the querent. For example, the natal Moon rising in the 1st house of the consultation chart often indicated travel, journeys, changes in domestic life, dealings with the public, etc. Natal Mars rising in the 1st house of the "new horary" chart warned of upcoming strife, conflict, quarrels, accidents, illness, surgery, and so on. On the other hand, the natal benefic planets, Venus and Jupiter, falling in the 1st house indicated impending good fortune of the nature of the planet in the immediate future. Natal Neptune rising in the horary chart suggested that some type of confusion, misinformation, deception, over-idealization, weakening, lack of clarity, blurring of boundaries, etc., was on the horizon. With natal Uranus rising in the horary, the client was cautioned to expect the unexpected.

Philip Payne and the Ill-Fated Flight of *Old Glory*

A compelling example of the significance of natal planets rising in the 1st house of Evangeline Adams's "new horary" chart is that of Philip A. Payne, managing editor of the *New York Mirror* newspaper, which made its debut on 24 June 1924. After Charles Lindbergh's successful transatlantic flight of the *Spirit of St. Louis* on 20 May 1924, "transatlantic fever" gripped the nation. Philip Payne saw in this phenomenon an opportunity to increase the circulation of the paper, and he convinced his boss, William Randolph Hearst, to sponsor a flight from the US to Rome, Italy. To further boost readership of the *New York Mirror*, Payne decided to tag along as a passenger.

Payne was a client of Evangeline Adams, and he consulted her about the advisability of a publicity stunt involving a flight to Rome. According to Adams, Payne's *natal* Saturn, Uranus, and Mars were all about to rise toward the Accidental Ascendant of the "new horary" chart, and she warned him accordingly of the potential for delays (Saturn), unexpected happenings (Uranus), and the risk of danger (Mars). Payne apparently ignored Adams's advice, decided to board the flight anyway, and was killed along with the pilot and copilot of the *Old Glory* aircraft, which took off from Old Orchard Beach, Maine, on 6 September 1927 at 12:23 p.m. EST. The event chart for the moment the plane became airborne had transiting Saturn conjunct the Ascendant, transiting Mars conjunct the MC, and the MC square the true lunar nodes.

Unfortunately, Adams does not tell us the date and time of the horary chart or give the birth data of her client Philip Payne. According to the 15 November 1926 issue of *Time* magazine, "Young like the sheetlets that he has built, Philip A. Payne is a managing editor at 32" (*Time* 1926, vol. 8, issue 20, p. 30). If Payne was indeed 32 years old at the time the article was written, then he must have been born between 15 November 1893 and 15 November 1894. Adams mentions that Payne's natal Saturn, Uranus, and Mars were close enough to fit into a single astrological house, and this condition is met between 17 November and 31 December of 1893. Checking the ephemeris for dates on which all three planets were transiting close to one another, I found a possible birth date for Payne to be around 12 December 1893, when Saturn was in 22° Libra, Uranus in 13° Scorpio, and Mars in 16° Scorpio. If Payne consulted with Adams on 11 July 1893 at 1:30 p.m. EDT to ask her advice about the flight to Rome, then his natal Saturn, Uranus, and Mars would have been rising in the 1st house of the "new horary" chart.

Adams's Gemini-Rising Chart for the USA

Evangeline Adams also used the symbolic hybrid chart in mundane forecasting. For the chart of the USA, she used the cusps of the Solar Eclipse in Philadelphia in August of 1776, closest to the date of the signing ceremony of the Declaration of Independence, and into the cusps of that eclipse chart she inserted the transits of the 4th of July. Adams's resulting symbolic hybrid USA chart for mundane forecasting was cast for about 3:03:30 a.m. LMT in Philadelphia on 4 July 1776. It is not an event chart, but rather a symbolic hybrid chart that depicts the transits of July 4th from the perspective of an important astrological event, namely, the point of maximum intensity of the Solar Eclipse closest to the official signing of the Declaration of Independence.

An alternative Gemini-rising USA chart popularized by Elbert Benjamine of the Church of Light takes the Descendant of the 1776 solar ingress into Cancer in Philadelphia as the Ascendant of the symbolic hybrid July 4th USA chart. Astrologers at the time believed that the USA was a country ruled by the sign Gemini.

Despite the symbolic hybrid chart's long and venerable history in Western astrology and its popularity in the first half of the twentieth century (Adams's horaries, the USA Gemini-rising charts, and Wynn's Key Cycle chart), few astrologers today appear to make use of it in forecasting.

Chapter 19
ATACIRS (SYMBOLIC DIRECTIONS)

This chapter is a bit technical but is included to put into historical perspective Frankland's methods of symbolic direction and offer additional food for thought.

Symbolic directions are especially popular in Spanish-speaking countries, where they are referred to in Spanish as *atacires* (from an Arabic word transcribed as *ataçir, atazir, al-tasyir*, or simply *tasyir*). Technically speaking, *atacir* refers to an astronomical method of calculating time spans associated with the distance between two bodies on the celestial sphere. This methodology was described in a 1277 CE text commissioned by Alfonso X el Sabio and used in the Middle Ages, especially in the practice of astronomical measurement of Al-Andalus. Atacirs were considered so useful that they appeared on astrolabes of the period. The twelfth-century astrologer Abraham ben Meir Ibn Ezra mentions atacirs in his writings.

The astronomical method of atacirs consisted of projecting the bodies of two planets or points on the celestial sphere onto the *celestial equator* and then measuring the *equatorial arc* between the projections of those two objects. The equatorial arc, or distance between the objects on the celestial equator, measured in *right ascension*, was then converted into an interval of time by some formula, commonly Claudius Ptolemy's practice of equating 1° on the *equator* with one year of life. For example, Alan Leo writes in *The Progressed Horoscope* (1983):

> The rules for working this system are so framed as to show how many *degrees of Right Ascension* pass across the meridian while a given direction is being formed; and these are then converted into years and months by means of the "measure of time," which is about one degree for each year of life. (Leo 1983, 26; italics mine)

Haly Abenragel in the Eleventh Century

Nowadays, the term *atacir* has come to refer to any symbolic direction that advances the various points or planets in a horoscope at a uniform rate around the wheel, along either the ecliptic or the celestial equator. This usage probably derives from the eleventh-century book *El Libro conplido de los iudizios de las estrellas* by Haly Abenragel (from *ibn Rijal*), who included a discussion in book 4, chapter 7, about directing the hyleg and other points at different uniform rates around the birth chart. As Alan Leo correctly noted, these rates were measured in terms of *equatorial arc* passing the meridian along the celestial equator.

In addition, Abenragel described annual profections at a rate of one sign (30° of ecliptic longitude) per year, which is equivalent to 2.5° per month. This measure appears to have been along the ecliptic rather than the equator. Thus, as 0° of the annual profected Ascendant sign is directed at a rate of 2.5° per month, the atacir (symbolic direction) will encounter sensitive points (such as planetary bodies or aspects), each of which will remain active until the atacir reaches the next sensitive point. For example, in a given year, if Virgo were the profected rising sign, with the square of Saturn lying at 5° Virgo and the trine of Venus at 10° Virgo, then about two months after the solar return, troubles related to Saturn would manifest and remain in effect until the atacir reached the benefic trine of Venus some two months later.

Haly Abenragel also made an important observation about atacirs that some modern astrologers ignore. He noted that the standard horoscope is cast with the positions of the bodies of the planets as they are projected onto the ecliptic, that is, onto the path of the Sun, which has 0° latitude because it lies on the ecliptic. In reality, however, the Moon and the planets are rarely found at 0° latitude on the ecliptic. Instead, they travel within a span that extends roughly 8° above or below the path of the Sun.

As a result, explains Abenragel, conjunctions and major aspects formed by atacirs along the ecliptic will vary in their ability to produce an effect, depending on whether the two celestial bodies involved are traveling in the same parallel of declination (i.e., the same small circle of declination on the celestial sphere, parallel to the celestial equator). If the two bodies are far apart in declination north or south of the celestial equator, then their ability to produce an effect is substantially diminished. An exception occurs, however, in the case of the opposition aspect, because the zodiacal positions of the planets will oppose each other on the ecliptic circle, and the actual positions of the planets, one being north and the other equally far south of the celestial equator, will oppose each other along a straight line drawn through the center of the celestial sphere.

Haly Abenragel comments that truly wise astrologers (*los sabios*, among whom he included Dorotheus and Abu Ma'shar) were aware of the need to assess both the ecliptic longitude and the parallel of declination of the celestial bodies involved in symbolic directions to determine their potency and potential effectiveness. Nonetheless, in reading case examples that use symbolic directions, one does not often see parallels of declination being taken into account, even though the traditional literature states that declination is an essential factor in judging the efficacy of an atacir contact.

Another feature of modern astrology in the Spanish-speaking world is that atacirs have multiplied like rabbits. No matter what concerns you, there is likely to be an atacir to cover it. The number of atacirs is so great that they are often referred to by numbers rather than names. For example, a traditional annual profection at a rate of 30° (one zodiac sign) per year is now simply called C-12. The "12" is derived from the division of the 360° of the zodiac circle by the number of degrees traveled per year. Because annual profections proceed at a rate of 30° per year, the 360° of the circle divided by 30° per year produces 12 equal partitions of the circle, each of which represents one year of life.

The formula for naming an atacir goes like this:

"**C-n**" stands for a 360° circle (**C**) divided into **n** parts, and each of the **n** parts is equivalent to one year of life. To find the number of degrees of the circle that are equivalent to one year of life, simply divide 360 by **n**.

Modern astrologers will recognize the similarity of this procedure to John Addey's generation of harmonic charts and the production of divisional charts, or *Vargas*, of Indian astrology.

Take C-1, for example. This notation refers to a circle (C) divided into 1 part, which is basically the entire undivided circle, and one full circle (360°) is equivalent to one year of life. This is just another way of referring to transits.

We have already seen that C-12 refers to a circle divided into 12 parts (like the 12 signs of the zodiac), and each part takes one year of life to traverse. Hence, the rate of this atacir is 360° divided by 12 equals 30° per year. Thus, C-12 refers to classical annual profections, which progress at a rate of one zodiac sign per year.

Consider C-630, which is a division of the circle into 630 equal parts, each part requiring a year to traverse. What is the size of these 630 equal partitions of the circle? We must divide 360° by 630 parts, which gives a result of 4/7°. Thus, C-630 is Frankland's symbolic measure of *4/7° for each year of life*. As mentioned previously in this text, 4/7° = 0° 34' 17.14", which is almost exactly the maximum angular diameter of the Moon at perigee, as viewed from Earth. Thus, the C-630 atacir (Frankland's *4/7° for each year of life*) symbolically directs points or planets at an annual rate equivalent to the maximum diameter of the Moon.

Another common symbolic direction is C-84, which divides the circle into 84 equal parts, each of which takes one year to traverse. C-84 is quite similar to the orbit of Uranus, which spends about 7 years in each zodiac sign. The size of each of the 84 equal partitions is 360° divided by 84, which equals 4 2/7° per each year of life. This is Frankland's *Point of Life* symbolic direction, sometimes referred to as the *septenary* measure because it divides each sign into seven parts. C-84 is similar to Boris Cristoff's Proluna, but differs in that the Proluna does not travel at a uniform rate around the zodiac. Instead, Proluna progresses at a uniform rate within each Placidus (or topocentric) house of the birth chart. Because the houses usually vary in length, the rate of progression depends on the size of the house being traversed.

Astrologers go a step further and assign specific significations to the various rates of progression around the wheel. Some of the meanings of the different rates of symbolic direction are quite silly yet imaginative, and may stretch credulity.

- **C-1, or 360° per year:** Transits, solar revolutions, planets traveling at the rates shown in the day-to-day ephemeris.

- **C-5, or 72° per year:** Love. C-5 divides the wheel into 5 equal 72° segments, each of which takes one year to traverse. Perhaps the association with love comes from 5 being the number of the 5th house, where Venus rejoices. (C-15 and C-25 apparently have similar meanings, maybe because 15 and 25 are multiples of 5?)

- **C-12, or 30° per year:** Annual profections, which indicate changes in the timelord of the year.

- **C-13, or 27.6932° per year:** Deaths and extreme situations, perhaps because 13 is considered an unlucky number, and the Death card is the 13th trump of the tarot. In the Bible, Judas, the 13th guest to the Last Supper, betrayed Jesus and hastened the Crucifixion. Judas then died by suicide.

- **C-16, or 22.5° per year:** Critical days, especially in one's health status (perhaps because it divides the circle into 16 parts, with 4 parts in each of the four quadrants of the horoscope wheel, much like the phases of the Moon).

- **C-25, or 14.4° per year:** This cycle progresses at a rate of 1° every 25 days, 14.4° per year, or 360° every 25 years. C-25 is allegedly related to Venus and the 5th house, where Venus rejoices, and is linked to issues such as romance, love affairs, children, pregnancy, fun, entertainment, creative projects, etc., perhaps because $25 = 5 \times 5$.

- **C-45, or 8° per year:** Deaths, suicides, murders, crises, vehicular accidents, and extreme situations. The C-45 rate of 8° per year divides the circle into 45 equal 8° segments, each of which takes a year to traverse. The 8th is the house of death, dying, anguish of mind, and crisis situations. The stressful semisquare aspect is one in which planets are 45° apart.

- **C-60, or 6° per year:** This atacir, popularized by Demetrio Santos, who directed the natal Ascendant at this rate, is apparently linked to significant changes in the direction of one's life, such as marriage, partnerships, important relationships, and so on. The C-60 rate of 6° per year divides the circle into 60 equal 6° segments, with a total of 5 such yearlong segments in each zodiac sign. Perhaps the meaning relates to the 5th house ($60 = 12 \times 5$) and to the similarity of the C-60 fivefold division of the circle to the 5 terms or bounds of each zodiac sign. Each change of bound by the primary directed Ascendant signifies a change in direction of one's life. Some sources mention that $60 = 3 \times 20$, that is, 60 years contains three Jupiter-Saturn cycles, which are key to mundane astrology.

- **C-72, or 5° per year:** Psychological development, illness, accidents, injuries, changes in one's health. C-72 divides the wheel into 72 equal 5° segments, with a total of 6 such segments in each sign of the zodiac. Perhaps the connection to illness is that $72 = 12 \times 6$. There are 12 houses, the 6th of which is the house of accidents, illness, and bodily infirmities. The connection to psychology is derived from the work of Bruno Huber in the 1960s. Huber was a Swiss astrologer who utilized a technique involving "Age Progression" and an "Age Point" that tracks one's psychological development. Huber's Age Point should not be confused with Frankland's *Age along the Zodiac* from the 1920s. The atacir C-144 (72 × 2) is allegedly related to illnesses that require hospitalization.

- **C-84, or 4 2/7° per year:** Frankland's *Point of Life* symbolic direction, sometimes referred to as the *septenary* measure because it divides each sign into 7 parts.

- **C-96, or 3.75° per year:** Limiting or extreme situations, natural deaths. C-96 divides the wheel into 96 equal 3.75° segments. Perhaps this signification derives from the fact that 96 = 12 × 8. There are 12 houses, the 8th of which is the house of death, the ultimate limiting situation. The 12th house is one of misery, confinement, bereavement, and undoing.

- **C-108, or 3.3333333° per year:** Travel, peace, calm, relaxation. C-108 divides the circle into 108 equal 3⅓° segments. The idea of travel may be based on the fact that 108 = 12 × 9. There are 12 houses, the 9th of which relates to long-distance travel but also to religion, philosophy, divination, astrology, publishing, etc.

- **C-120, or 3° per year:** Career, professional objectives. C-120 divides the horoscope wheel into 120 equal 3° segments, each of which takes a year to traverse. Again, the meaning may be based on the fact that 120 = 12 × 10. There are 12 houses, the 10th of which has to do with career, public standing, honors, authority, being the boss, etc.

- **C-132, or 2.72727272° per year:** Release from restrictive laws and situations. C-132 divides the circle into 132 equal 2 8/11° segments, each of which takes a year to traverse. Here, 132 = 12 × 11, and there are 12 astrological houses, the 11th of which is the house of the Good Daemon, our guardian angel and benefactor who helps us get out of tight spots.

- **C-144, or 2.5° per year:** Illness, confinement, unresolved issues from the past. This atacir apparently gets its meaning from the 12th house: 144 equals 12 × 12. In the C-144 atacir, each part measures 2.5°, the size of the classical 12th part, dodecatemoria, or *dwadashamsha* of the zodiac signs. In his book *Symbolic Directions in Modern Astrology* (1929), Charles Carter arrogantly commented about the C-144 atacir: "This System I call the Duodenary, preferring an English term, of Latin origin, to an Indian [term]" (Carter 1929, 27).

- **C-156, or 2.3076923° per year:** Deaths and other extreme situations. The meaning may be based on the fact that 156 equals 12×13, combining the significations of the unfortunate 12th house of dissolution and endings with the unlucky number 13 of the Death card of the tarot and the betrayal of Jesus.

- **C-360, or 1° per year:** Frankland's symbolic *Age along the Zodiac* symbolic measure, in which 1° of ecliptic longitude is equivalent to one year of life. C-360 divides the zodiac wheel into 360 1° segments, each of which takes a year to traverse.

- **C-600, or 0.6° per year:** The Naronic period, a division of the circle into 600 equal parts measuring 0.6°, each part requiring a year to traverse. According to Sepharial in *The British Journal of Astrology* (April 1929), C-600 is "useful in defining the periods of depression and expansion in any life within which the astronomical directions formed by planetary progress in more closely mathematical systems are found to gain additional significance when the two sets of indications agree." Translating Sepharial's words into comprehensible English, he appears to mean that when a C-600 "Naronic" symbolic direction coincides with a traditional primary direction or secondary progression, watch out!

- **C-630, or 4/7° per year:** Frankland's symbolic measure of *4/7° for each year of life*.

- **C-1440, or ¼° per year:** Introduced by Charles Carter, the C-1440 atacir divides the circle into 1,440 equal parts, each of which measures 0.25°. The chart is then directed at a rate of ¼° per year. According to Carter, C-1440 is symbolically related to worldly status, prosperity, serious illness, and sometimes death.

- **C-1728, or 0.2083333333° per year:** Divides the 360° circle into 1,728 parts, each measuring 0° 12' 30' of arc. Charles Carter calls the C-1728 atacir the *sub-duodenary measure*, based on 1/12 of the 12th part of a sign (Carter's duodenary measure C-144). The C-1728 (= 12×144) establishes an equivalence between 15° of zodiacal longitude and 72 years of human life. In his *Symbolic Directions in Modern Astrology* (1929), Carter comments that it [the sub-duodenary measure] is a "wonderful exemplification of Cosmic Symbolism" and "is of great value for rectification" (Carter 1929, 29).

A potential problem with the use of atacirs lies in selecting their orb of influence. As the number of divisions of the circle becomes larger, the corresponding orb must become smaller. Many astrologers use, as an orb of influence, the span of about one year before and after a direction becomes exact. Thus, for Frankland's *4/7° per year measure* (C-630), the orb of this atacir is then 0° 34', or about half a degree, before and after the direction perfects.

Given the ease with which we can assign meanings to an atacir, let's create a new one, tongue in cheek, based on the 1961 culturally significant novel by Joseph Heller, *Catch-22*, and the woo-woo type of reasoning demonstrated by Sepharial. C-22 divides the circle into 22 equal 16 4/11° segments, each of which takes one year to traverse. In numerology, 22 is a "master number" that connects you to the spiritual realm, gives you a sense of purpose, and helps you realize your most worthy ambitions. Unfortunately, 22 reduces to 4 (2 + 2), and 4 × 22 equals 88, which is close to the number 96 of C-96, an atacir that has to do with limiting or extreme situations. In addition, 96 − 88 = 8, which is the number of the 8th house of death, dying, and crises. The number 22 also appears in the term Catch-22, which has to do with a paradoxical situation from which there is no escape because of contradictory rules or regulations. Hence, the signification of our new atacir, C-22, is the ability to realize your most worthy ambitions only if you first become spiritually enlightened and totally devoid of any ambition.

Atacirs have played a significant role in predictive astrology for at least two millennia. Claudius Ptolemy in the second century proposed that we regard the passage of one *equatorial* degree over the Midheaven as equivalent to one year of life. Hellenistic astrology routinely made use of annual profections at a rate of one zodiacal sign per each year of life. Obviously, symbolic directions (atacirs) are worthy of study and experimentation, as discussed in Charles Carter's classic text *Symbolic Directions in Modern Astrology* (1929). On the other hand, we need to keep the usefulness of this technique in perspective and avoid assigning it powers that it does not possess.

In the next and final chapter of this volume, I will review the horary consultation done by William Frankland in 1926 that initially sparked my interest in his methods and led to my writing this book.

Chapter 20
FOUND BY THE AID OF THE STARS

The news of Saturday 27 February 1926 in Lancashire, England, featured the headline "Found by Aid of Stars: Coroner Told of London Astrologer's Guidance." A few days later, on the 1st of March, the same story about the body of a missing man being found with the aid of astrology was recounted in London's *Evening News*.

The story begins in Burnley, England, in October of 1925, when 63-year-old Edward Whitehead suffered a nervous breakdown, as a result of which he ceased working and stayed at home with his wife. On Thursday, 18 February 1926, he fell ill with stomach pains and remained in bed until about 4:00 a.m. Friday morning. He then mysteriously got up, dressed himself, walked out of his house, and disappeared. His wife became alarmed and notified the police that her husband had vanished in the early hours of Friday morning.

By Monday, February 22nd, despite searches by family and police, there was still no trace of Mr. Whitehead. His son-in-law had been active in the searches but had been unable to locate his wife's missing father. Whitehead's daughter knew of an astrologer, William Frankland, who himself was from Burnley but had moved to London about ten years earlier. She telegraphed Frankland, who called her by telephone, requesting Whitehead's date of birth and the time he went missing.

Frankland cast a horary chart (at 4:45 p.m. GMT, London) and sent his astrological findings to the family, with a detailed description of where the missing man might be found. The son-in-law followed the instructions given by the astrologer and discovered the body of his deceased father-in-law, Mr. Whitehead, drowned in a canal.

In his report, Frankland wrote that he had studied both the horary and the birth charts, including the secondary progressions of Mr. Whitehead. Frankland concluded that "there was probably death by water in a stream or canal; South and a little West; not exactly near the home but at no great distance; in a place where there are sheds, tools and boats, at a rather barren place" (Cornelius 1994, 343–44).

In his horary and predictive work, Frankland used derived houses, sometimes called "turning the chart." In this case, for example, the person who asked the question is represented by the 1st house and her father is signified by the 4th house. Deriving houses for the father involves viewing the radical 4th house, which signifies her father, as his 1st house. Then the radical 5th is the father's 2nd, the radical 6th is the father's 3rd, the radical 7th is the father's 4th, and so on around the wheel, up to the radical 3rd, which is the father's derived 12th house.

Frankland analyzed the horary chart as follows (chart 62). Because the daughter asked the question, she is signified by the 1st house, and her father is represented by Mars, ruler of the 4th house with Scorpio on its cusp.

Saturn occupying the 4th house of the father lies in close square to an angular Neptune (the god of the seas) in the 12th house of misfortune. Saturn also closely squares the horary Ascendant. These are ominous indications, further emphasized by the fact that the missing father at age 63 had recently entered the 7-year period of life that Alan Leo assigned to Capricorn, ruled by Saturn.

Mars, ruler of the 4th house in the chart, symbolizes the father and opposes the Moon without reception. The Moon, in turn, rules the radical 12th house of sorrow and undoing, and occupies the radical 11th house, which is the derived 8th from the 4th, signifying the death of the father. Gemini on the cusp of the radical 11th (the father's derived 8th) makes Mercury the signifier of the father's death. The Moon (ruler of the 12th house of grief and loss) is separating from a close trine to Mercury and transferring the light of Mercury (the father's death) to Mars (the father) by a very tight opposition aspect.

The prominence of Moon in Cancer opposing Mars (the father) from the father's derived 8th house of death suggests the involvement of active running water because Cancer is a cardinal (movable) water sign.

Mars in Capricorn in a succedent house suggests that the father is not too far from home and that he can be found in a southerly direction (the Tropic of Capricorn is the most southerly point of the Sun's path) and perhaps somewhat to the west (Mars is slightly to the west of the meridian).

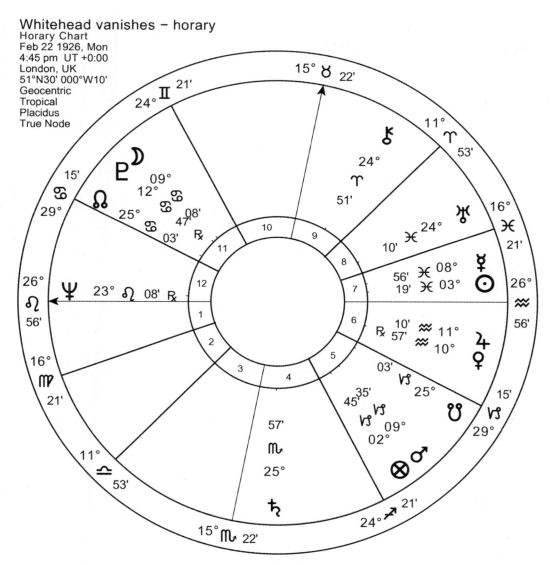

Whitehead vanishes – horary
Horary Chart
Feb 22 1926, Mon
4:45 pm UT +0:00
London, UK
51°N30' 000°W10'
Geocentric
Tropical
Placidus
True Node

Chart 62: Edward Whitehead Vanishes, Horary Chart
22 February 1926, 4:45 p.m. UT, London, England, 51N30 0W10

Capricorn, ruled by Saturn, suggests a Saturnian, commercial place, somewhat barren, perhaps a boat canal with sheds or tools nearby. Frankland was originally from Burnley and could match the symbolism of the chart to his recollection of the town's geography.

The astrologer feared that the missing man was deceased because the "directions then operative were very adverse and could prove fatal: Sun square Saturn, Sun square Jupiter, and others" (Cornelius 1994, 343–44). Frankland, here, is referring to the secondary progressed Sun being within orb of a square aspect (90°) to the natal positions of both Saturn and Jupiter at the time of the disappearance.

When Was Mr. Whitehead Born?

As an interesting aside, we can use this information to deduce the approximate birth date of Edward Whitehead. He was 63 years old when he disappeared on 18 February 1926. Hence, he must have been born roughly 63 years earlier. We can look in the ephemeris for a time about 63 years earlier when Jupiter and Saturn were traveling close together, and when the Sun by secondary progression in February 1926 would be in square to the natal positions of both Jupiter and Saturn.

Using Solar Fire software, I generated a monthly ephemeris for this period, shown in the following chart.

EPHEMERIS FOR SUN, JUPITER, AND SATURN: FEB. 1862–JAN. 1863			
Date	Sun	Jupiter	Saturn
Feb 18 1862	29° Aq 07'	25° Vi 22' R	20° Vi 51' R
Mar 18 1862	7° Pi 09'	1° Vi 56'	18° Vi 41'
Apr 18 1862	27° Ar 41'	18° Vi 33'	16° Vi 37'
May 18 1862	26° Ta 45'	17° Vi 30' D	15° Vi 51'
Jun 18 1862	26° Ge 26'	19° Vi 12'	16° Vi 38' D
Jul 18 1862	25° Cn 03'	23° Vi 02'	18° Vi 46'
Aug 18 1862	24° Le 45'	28° Vi 33'	22° Vi 00'
Sep 18 1862	24° Vi 48'	04° Li 58'	25° Vi 45'
Oct 18 1862	24° Li 22'	11° Li 26'	29° Vi 25'
Nov 18 1862	25° Sc 25'	17° Li 47'	02° Li 41'
Dec 18 1862	25° Sg 52'	22° Li 57'	04° Li 50'
Jan 18 1863	27° Cp 27'	26° Li 27'	05° Li 31' R

Jupiter and Saturn were traveling close to each other between February and August of 1862, after which they began to move significantly apart. We can conclude, then, that Mr. Whitehead was born in 1862 between February and August. During that period, Saturn remained within a few degrees of 18° Virgo.

The secondary progressed Sun could have squared Saturn's position at 18° Virgo when Mr. Whitehead disappeared in 1926 only if it had been at about 18° Gemini, which is the point that makes a 90° aspect to 18° Virgo.

Because the Sun travels about one degree every day, we must subtract an arc of 63° from 18° Gemini, which gives a date of birth in 1862 in the sign Aries (March 20–April 19). We can then work with our astrology software to find birth dates in which the secondary progressed Sun makes a square aspect, within an orb of 1°, to natal Jupiter and natal Saturn in February of 1926.

When the Sun transited Aries (March 20–April 19) in 1862, Saturn was traveling retrograde from 18° 32' to 16° 34' Virgo, and Jupiter was retrograde from 21° 40' to 18° 28' Virgo. Frankland wrote that the progressed Sun squared both natal Jupiter and Saturn at the time of the man's disappearance. Because the orb of influence of secondary progressions is generally taken to be about 1°, the earliest position of the progressed Sun would have been one degree before the earliest position of Saturn, that is, at 16° 41' Virgo minus one degree, or 15° 41' Virgo.

If the man were born on April 3, 1862, for example, his progressed Sun would have been in 15° Gemini at the time of his death, which is within about 1° of orb of squaring his progressed Saturn. Prior to that date, his progressed Sun would not have been in square to natal Saturn or Jupiter, so he must have been born on, or shortly after, 3 April 1862.

If he were born at sunrise on April 3rd, then transiting Pluto Rx in watery Cancer would have squared his natal Sun on 26 January 1926, turned stationary direct on March 27th, and again squared his natal Sun on 24 May 1926. Thus, he would have been under the influence of Pluto in Cancer (a water sign) square his natal Sun at the time of his death by drowning.

In addition, if he were born around 3 April 1862, his directed *Point of Life* at the time of his nervous breakdown would have been at about 2° of Capricorn, in square to his natal Neptune at 1° 45' Aries in the birth chart.

Frankland's *Point of Life* is calculated by allowing 7 years of life for each sign of the zodiac, counting from 0° Aries at birth. If we assume that the man's nervous breakdown occurred in October of 1925, when he was 63.5 years old, then his directed *Point of Life* at the time would have been at 2° 08' Capricorn. Transiting Neptune arrived at this degree of Capricorn on 12 April 1862—again suggesting that he was born in early April of 1862.

On the day of Mr. Whitehead's disappearance, transiting Mars at 12° 44' Capricorn was exactly opposite transiting Pluto at 12° 44' Cancer, and this opposition formed a close T-square with the natal Sun at 13° 13' Aries in the 3 April 1862 sunrise birth chart.

Frankland's comments about the birth chart, together with the astrological evidence, suggest that Mr. Whitehead was most likely born around the first two weeks of April 1862. Interestingly, Deborah Houlding built upon the report of this chart provided in Geoffrey Cornelius's book *The Moment of Astrology* to explore its deeper symbolism as part of a case study used in the STA Practitioners Level Horary Course, where she states:

> Geoffrey Cornelius reports that he was unable to find any birth records for an Edward Whitehouse that matched the reported age; however, my own subsequent research revealed parish records for a George Edward Whitehouse, who was born in Burnley on 23 March 1862 (making him 63 at the time of death, as stated). (Houlding, STA Practitioners Level Horary Course, https://sta.co/online_horary.html)

This quotation from Deborah Houlding is reproduced with permission of the School of Traditional Astrology (STA). According to Houlding, the birth record for Mr. Whitehead can be found online at "Baptisms at Holy Trinity in the Parish of Habergham Eaves [Burnley, Lancs.]." https://www.lan-opc.org.uk/Burnley/Habergham-and-Habergham-Eaves/holytrinity/baptisms_1858-1863.html.

EPILOGUE

We have reached the end of our survey of the astrological legacy of William Frankland and have explored his method of forecasting with a small set of symbolic measures, based on his many years of astrological research. Each of his techniques has been illustrated with case examples, some from Frankland's own writings and others from charts randomly selected to further test his methodology. Frankland was a master astrologer, and even if we don't end up using all of his measures, we will undoubtedly enrich our skills at chart interpretation by studying his techniques.

Frankland's approach to prediction can be summarized as a sequence of simple, logical, and orderly steps, which go roughly as follows:

1. Keep your eye on the big picture; don't get lost in the details. Consider the overall pattern of the chart. Which signs contain planets, especially clusters of planets? What are the whole-sign and degree-based aspects linking the planets? Do any significant chart patterns appear, such as T-squares, Yods, or Grand Crosses? What is the modality of crosses and T-squares (cardinal, fixed, mutable)? Which planets are strongest because of angularity?

2. Consider the age of the native at the time of the consultation.

2a. Does the native's age correspond to any of the **Birth Numbers** calculated by adding together the digits of the date of birth in the specific ways indicated by Frankland? If so, astrological factors active during corresponding years will be quite pronounced in their manifestation.

2b. Which planet is the timelord of the stage of life according to **Ptolemy's *seven ages of man?*** What is the condition of that planet in the birth chart? What role does that planet play in the current operative influences, such as directions, progressions, transits, etc.? Are the native's activities in accord or dissonant with the significations of the planet governing the stage of life? Does the natal condition of the current timelord of the stage of life benefit or challenge the native? Are current directions, progressions, or transits involving the timelord beneficial or adverse to the native?

2c. Each zodiac sign indicates a 7-year period. Which **zodiac sign,** in Alan Leo's system, is highlighted by Frankland's *Point of Life* at the native's current age? What is the significance of that sign in the native's birth chart in terms of the **areas of life** it influences and **any planets, chart points, or house cusps that fall within that sign?** Is the highlighted sign cardinal, fixed, or mutable? What other signs in the birth chart are aspected by the sign under consideration? In Alan Leo's scheme, each sign governs 7 years of life, beginning with Aries (which rules ages 0 to 7), followed by Taurus (which covers ages 7 to 14), and so on around the wheel. The focus here is on the 7-year period covered by each zodiac sign (and the signs in square or opposition to it), and the types of events that are likely to happen during those seven years.

2d. Although Frankland doesn't mention it, I would add the **Lord of the Profected Ascendant** as an important timelord influencing an entire year. The profected Ascendant begins with the natal Ascendant at age 0 (birth) and proceeds around the wheel at a rate of one zodiac sign per year. In the 2nd year of life (age 1), the ruler of the 2nd sign becomes timelord of the year; in the 3rd year of life (age 2), the ruler of the 3rd sign becomes timelord of the year; and so on, for the rest of the native's life.

2e. Frankland's examples do not include solar returns. Nonetheless, I have found that his symbolic measures (*Point of Life, Age along the Zodiac,* and the *4/7° measure*), and directions of the natal chart by the arc of these measures, often highlight significant planets or points in the chart of the annual return of the Sun to its birth position.

3. Find the position of the current ***Age along the Zodiac (Age Point)*** by counting the years along the zodiac at a rate of **1° for each year of life, starting at 0° Aries.** With all of the symbolic measures, their **conjunctions** to natal planets, midpoints, Placi-

dus house cusps, and other sensitive chart points are the preeminent indicators. Which chart factors does the current *Age Point* conjoin or aspect within a 1° orb, primarily in the birth chart, but also in the solar return or secondary progressed chart (if you are using the latter two as part of your predictive system)? I use the major aspects plus the semisquare, sesquisquare, semisextile, and quincunx.

4. Find the position of the current *4/7° per year Age along the Zodiac (4/7° Age Point)* by counting the years along the zodiac at a rate of **4/7° for each year of life, starting at 0° Aries.** Study the major and minor aspects made by the *4/7° Age Point*, as in the previous step. Because this is a slower measure, it will have a smaller orb of about 30 minutes of arc before and after.

5. Broadly speaking, the ***Point of Life,*** found by counting **7 years per zodiac sign, starting a 0° Aries,** can be used to highlight the **specific 7-year period** belonging to the sign in which it falls. (See step 2c above.) This approach is akin to the use of whole-sign aspects in Hellenistic astrology. For example, if the *Point of Life* were traversing Virgo, it would be aspecting the zodiac signs in square to it, namely, Gemini and Sagittarius, by hard aspect, which implies that the 7-year periods covered by Gemini and Sagittarius would be characterized by stressful and challenging events.

6. Counting 7 years per zodiac sign, starting a 0° Aries, is equivalent to **advancing in the zodiac by 4 2/7° (4.286°) from 0° Aries for every year of life.** Thus, at any given age, the ***Point of Life*** will traverse a span of 4.286° until the native reaches the next birthday. If you are working with the specific age on a given date, you can calculate a more precise *Point of Life*. In this case, Frankland uses an orb of about 4° before and after, which corresponds to roughly a year before and after, in which the specific *Point of Life* is most active. Conjunctions of the *Point of Life* with natal planets, midpoints, house cusps, and other sensitive chart points will highlight important years and their related themes in the life of the native.

7. Study the **slower-moving planets,** which, by secondary progression, will remain close to their natal positions in the birth chart for many years. In this way, the ponderous planets (Jupiter, Saturn, Uranus, Neptune, Pluto) and their aspects form a secondary progressed background that can influence areas of life for long periods of time. Are any such areas being highlighted by Frankland's symbolic measures at the time of the consultation?

8. In addition to studying the slower-moving planets, also determine whether the current year's Solar and **Lunar Eclipses** and **planetary stations** make "hits" with any of Frankland's symbolic measures. Eclipses are especially powerful in this regard when they aspect a natal or directed planet or point in the chart.

9. **Symbolically direct** all the planets and points in the birth chart for the current age at the rate of…

10. (a) **1° per year,** as Charles Carter recommended; and

11. (b) **4/7° per year (0° 34' 17.14" per year),** Frankland's new operative influence; and

12. (c) **4 2/7° per year (4° 17' 8.57" per year),** Alan Leo's equating each sign of the zodiac with seven years of life.

13. Look for any significant aspects between the directed points and the natal planets or points in the chart. What do these symbolic directions highlight, and how are they likely to manifest?

14. The more often the above procedures emphasize a particular theme or region of the chart, the more likely and notably such an issue will manifest at the age under consideration.

A Final Example: Author's Birth Chart and the Writing of This Book

My father, who was present at my birth, made a note in his journal that I was born at 9:05 a.m. on 3 September 1945 (chart 63). My birth certificate indicates that my birth took place at 9:09 a.m. EWT, which is four minutes later than my father's record. In favor of the 9:05 a.m. time is the fact that the secondary progressed Sun, which is exalted in Aries on the 7th house cusp of marriage, exactly conjoined the Ascendant of the 9:05 a.m. chart on the day of my wedding in 1977.

As a final example, let's see how Frankland's measures relate to the writing of this book during the year 2022, which corresponds roughly to the span from 76.3 to 77.3 years of age. The planet Saturn is the timelord of this period in Ptolemy's *seven ages of man*. Saturn occupies the 10th house of professional activity and rules the signs on the cusps of the 4th (home, tradition) and 5th (creative projects) houses. Because of the pandemic, I had more time than usual at home to work on writing this book about the astrology of the early part of the previous century.

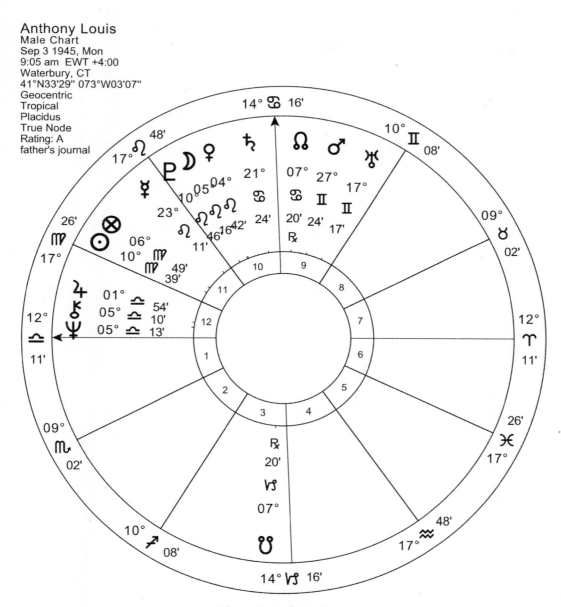

Anthony Louis
Male Chart
Sep 3 1945, Mon
9:05 am EWT +4:00
Waterbury, CT
41°N33'29" 073°W03'07"
Geocentric
Tropical
Placidus
True Node
Rating: A
father's journal

Chart 63: Anthony Louis
3 September 1945, 9:05 a.m. EWT, Waterbury, Connecticut, 41N33 73W03

In Alan Leo's scheme of *seven years of life per sign of the zodiac*, I was passing through the Aquarius period from ages 70 through 76, again ruled by Saturn as timelord and associated with the 5th house.

With regard to Frankland's symbolic measures:

- The *Age along the Zodiac* for ages 76.3 to 77.3 ranges from 16.3° to 17.3° of Gemini, conjoining and emphasizing natal Uranus at 17° 17' Gemini in the 9th house of publishing and astrology. This symbolic direction corresponds to transiting Uranus stationing direct on 18 January 2022 at 10°49' Taurus in the 8th house in close trine to my natal Sun. In addition, the position at which transiting Uranus stationed direct in January was "hit" by a Solar Eclipse at 10° 28' Taurus in the 8th house on 20 April 2022. Furthermore, the Lunar Eclipse of 8 November 2022 at 16°00' Taurus conjoined transiting Uranus at 16°56' Taurus Rx. Thus, Uranus was highly activated in my chart during 2022.

- The 4/7 Age along the Zodiac measure for ages 76.3 to 77.3 ranges from 43.6° to 44.2°, which is equivalent to 13.6° to 14.2° of Taurus in the 8th house of in-depth investigation and occult studies and in close sextile to the natal MC of professional endeavors. During the year 2022, the 4/7 Age along the Zodiac activated the following fixed midpoints in Solar Fire's midpoint modal sort: Mercury/Venus, Saturn/Fortuna, Moon/Mercury, Mars/Jupiter, and Uranus/Ascendant—all of which are symbolically related to a creative writing project involving astrology.

- The *Point of Life* for ages 76.3 to 77.3 ranges from 27° 00' Aquarius to 01° 17' Pisces, and entered 0° Pisces on my birthday in September of 2022. Thus, the *Point of Life* began the year in exact trine to natal Mars in Gemini in the 9th house, a perfect moment to put energy into writing a manuscript intended for publication.

We have spent little time in this book trying to understand *why* Frankland's symbolic measures should be so effective, that is, whether they have a plausible rationale. Sepharial would probably say that Frankland managed to reclaim some of the ground that the Cosmic Symbolism of astrology had ceded to the exact methods of modern science. Robert Hand would likely be in agreement, for he wrote in the foreword to Nancy Hastings's 1984 book *Secondary Progressions*: "Only a symbolic world-view in which symbolism has the same level of reality that science gives to energy and matter can serve to explain secondaries and other kinds of direction" (Hastings 1984, xii).

Let me close this volume by quoting the ending paragraph of Frankland's second and last book on symbolic directions, *New Measures in Astrology* (1928):

> The object in this book is to direct closer attention to the birth chart and its wonderful construction, to establish a system whereby periods of benefit or detriment may be approximately measured from the birth chart. My meagre knowledge of this vast subject leads me to a respect for astrology and all astrologers who labour for its welfare, and to humbly submit these theories in the hope they will prove of some value in directing. (Frankland 1928, 123)

Appendix A
THE *POINT OF LIFE*

This table was prepared with Excel to make it easy to calculate the *Point of Life*. This symbolic measure is calculated by assigning 7 years to each sign of the zodiac, commencing from 0° Aries to the current age of the client at a rate of 4 2/7° per year. For example, 21 years old would symbolically equate to 0° Cancer. The *Point of Life* highlights areas of life that may be significant at a given age, depending on which astrological factors, if any, are active at the time. Note that the cycle begins at age 0 and repeats at age 84, which is the orbital period of Uranus.

POINT OF LIFE		
Age	**Ecliptic Longitude**	**Sign**
0 / 84	0	0° ARIES
1 / 85	4.286	4° Ar 17'
2 / 86	8.571	8° Ar 34'
3 / 87	12.857	12° Ar 51'
4 / 88	17.143	17° Ar 9'
5 / 89	21.429	21° Ar 26'
6 / 90	25.714	24° Ar 43'
7 / 91	30	0° TAURUS
8 / 92	34.286	4° Ta 17'
9 / 93	38.571	8° Ta 34'
10 / 94	42.857	12° Ta 51'

POINT OF LIFE		
Age	**Ecliptic Longitude**	**Sign**
11 / 95	47.143	17° Ta 9'
12 / 96	51.429	21° Ta 26'
13 / 97	55.714	25° Ta 43'
14 / 98	60	0° GEMINI
15 / 99	64.286	4° Ge 17'
16 / 100	68.571	8° Ge 34'
17 / 101	72.857	12° Ge 51'
18 / 102	77.143	17° Ge 9'
19 / 103	81.429	21° Ge 26'
20 / 104	85.714	25° Ge 43'
21 / 105	90	0° CANCER
22	94.286	4° Cn 17'
23	98.571	8° Cn 34'
24	102.857	12° Cn 51'
25	107.143	17° Cn 9'
26	111.429	21° Cn 26'
27	115.714	25° Cn 43'
28	120	0° LEO
29	124.286	4° Le 17'
30	128.571	8° Le 34'
31	132.857	12° Le 51'
32	137.143	17° Le 9'
33	141.429	21° Le 26'
34	145.714	25° Le 43'
35	150	0° VIRGO
36	154.286	4° Vi 17'
37	158.571	8° Vi 34'

POINT OF LIFE		
Age	**Ecliptic Longitude**	**Sign**
38	162.857	12° Vi 51'
39	167.143	17° Vi 9'
40	171.429	21° Vi 26'
41	175.714	25° Vi 43'
42	180	0° LIBRA
43	184.286	4° Li 17'
44	188.571	8° Li 34'
45	192.857	12° Li 51'
46	197.143	17° Li 9'
47	201.429	21° Li 26'
48	205.714	25° Li 43'
49	210	0° SCORPIO
50	214.286	4° Sc 17'
51	218.571	8° Sc 34'
52	222.857	12° Sc 51'
53	227.143	17° Sc 9'
54	231.429	21° Sc 26'
55	235.714	25° Sc 43'
56	240	0° SAGITTARIUS
57	244.286	4° Sg 17'
58	248.571	8° Sg 34'
59	252.857	12° Sg 51'
60	257.143	17° Sg 9'
61	261.429	21° Sg 26'
62	265.714	25° Sg 43'
63	270	0° CAPRICORN
64	274.286	4° Cp 17'

POINT OF LIFE		
Age	**Ecliptic Longitude**	**Sign**
65	278.571	8° Cp 34'
66	282.857	12° Cp 51'
67	287.143	17° Cp 9'
68	291.429	21° Cp 26'
69	295.714	25° Cp 43'
70	300	0° AQUARIUS
71	304.286	4° Aq 17'
72	308.571	8° Aq 34'
73	312.857	12° Aq 51'
74	317.143	17° Aq 9'
75	321.429	21° Aq 26'
76	325.714	25° Aq 43'
77	330	0° PISCES
78	334.286	4° Pi 17'
79	338.571	8° Pi 35'
80	342.857	12° Pi 51'
81	347.143	17° Pi 9'
82	351.429	21° Pi 26'
83	355.714	25° Pi 43'
84	360	0° Aries

How to Calculate the *Point of Life* at a Given Age

The following method is useful if you are studying a specific age and want to calculate its *Point of Life*. The *Point of Life* is calculated by assigning 7 years to each sign of the zodiac, commencing from 0° Aries to the current age of the client at a rate of 4 2/7° per year (or, in decimal form, 4.285714° per year).

Divide the age in question by Alan Leo's *seven years per zodiac sign*. For example, Queen Elizabeth II died at age 96.3886. Thus, 96.3886 / 7 = 13.7696, which consists of a whole number part (13) and a decimal part (0.7696).

The whole number part represents the number of zodiac signs that the *Point of Life* has completely traversed. In this example, the Queen's *Point of Life* has passed through 13 zodiac signs, commencing in Aries, and must therefore now be in Taurus.

The decimal part indicates how far into the final zodiac sign the *Point of Life* has reached. In this case, it has gotten to 0.7696 of Taurus.

Multiplying the 30° of Taurus by 0.7696 gives the result 23.097°, or 23° Taurus, and .097' of Taurus × 60 minutes = 5.82, or 06 minutes of Taurus, for a final result of 23° 06' Taurus.

How to Calculate the Exact Age When an Event Takes Place

Queen Elizabeth II was born on 21 April 1926 and died on 8 September 2022.

Using the "Days Calculator: Days Between Two Dates" at the Time and Date website (https://www.timeanddate.com/date/duration.html), we find that the queen lived a total of 35,204 days. A google search will indicate several sites that offer calculators to determine how many days, months, and years there are between two dates. Some calculators allow you to indicate the time of day.

Dividing 35,204 days by the length of a tropical year (365.242 days), I determined that Queen Elizabeth II was 35,204 / 365.242 = 96.39 years old (rounded to the nearest hundredth) when she passed on.

Another Example of Calculating the *Point of Life* at a Given Age: Yevgeny Prigozhin

Mercenary Yevgeny Prigozhin rebelled against Russian President Vladimir Putin on 23 June 2023, and exactly two months later, on 23 August 2023, Prigozhin's plane mysteriously fell from the sky, killing all aboard. Some pundits suspect that Putin ordered the plane to be shot down. Prigozhin was born on 1 June 1961, time unknown, in Saint Petersburg, Russia (chart 64).

Using the "Days Calculator: Days Between Two Dates" at the Time and Date website (https://www.timeanddate.com/date/duration.html), we find that Prigozhin was 22,667 days old when he rebelled against Putin on 23 June 2023.

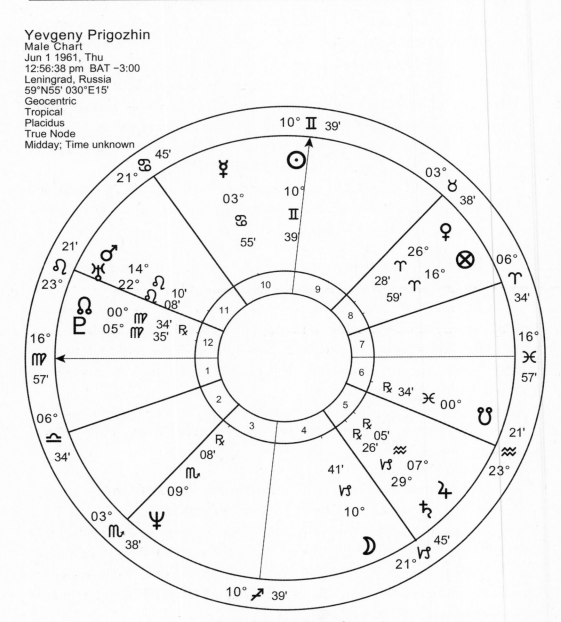

Yevgeny Prigozhin
Male Chart
Jun 1 1961, Thu
12:56:38 pm BAT −3:00
Leningrad, Russia
59°N55' 030°E15'
Geocentric
Tropical
Placidus
True Node
Midday; Time unknown

Chart 64: Yevgeny Prigozhin
1 June 1961, 12:56:38 p.m. BAT, Leningrad, Russia, 59N55 30E15

Dividing 22,667 days by 365.242 days in a year, we determine that Prigozhin was 62.06 years old when he rebelled.

The *Point of Life* assigns 7 years to each sign of the zodiac, so we divide 62.06 years by 7 to determine how many signs, starting at 0° Aries, it has traversed since birth:

62.06 / 7 = 8.866 signs. Eight signs take us to the end of Scorpio, and 0.866 signs takes us into Sagittarius: 0.866 × 30° = 25.98°, or 25° 59' Sagittarius as his *Point of Life* at the time of the rebellion.

In Prigozhin's birth chart, this *Point of Life* is closely quincunx the midday natal Sun at 10° 39' Gemini and semisquare natal Neptune at 09° 08' Scorpio, thus activating the natal Sun-Neptune quincunx. At the same time, this *Point of Life* is in trine to natal Venus at 26° 28' Aries, a favorable influence that perhaps protected him from being killed immediately by Putin's forces. On the other hand, natal Venus was afflicted by an applying square from retrograde Saturn in Capricorn, so Venus's ability to protect him was impaired.

Appendix B
THE *4/7° PER YEAR MEASURE (4/7° AGE POINT)*

For quick reference, here is a table of Frankland's *4/7° per year of life Age along the Zodiac Point (4/7° Age Point)*. This symbolic measure is calculated by taking 4/7 of the current age and adding that value to 0° Aries. To avoid having to write out "4/7 of a degree equals one year of life," I often abbreviate this symbolic measure as the *4/7° Age Point*. Frankland also used the *4/7° measure* to symbolically direct any point or stellar body in the chart.

4/7° PER YEAR OF LIFE (4/7° AGE POINT)			
Age	**4/7 of Age**	**Sign**	**Ecliptic Longitude (Rounded)**
0	0	**ARIES**	0°
1	0.571	Aries	0.57°
2	1.143	Aries	1.14°
3	1.714	Aries	1.71°
4	2.286	Aries	2.29°
5	2.857	Aries	2.86°
6	3.429	Aries	3.43°
7	4	Aries	4°
8	4.571	Aries	4.57°
9	5.143	Aries	5.14°
10	5.714	Aries	5.71°

4/7° PER YEAR OF LIFE (4/7° AGE POINT)			
Age	**4/7 of Age**	**Sign**	**Ecliptic Longitude (Rounded)**
11	6.286	Aries	6.29°
12	6.857	Aries	6.86°
13	7.429	Aries	7.43°
14	8	Aries	8°
15	8.571	Aries	8.57°
16	9.143	Aries	9.14°
17	9.714	Aries	9.71°
18	10.286	Aries	10.29°
19	10.857	Aries	10.86°
20	11.429	Aries	11.43°
21	12	Aries	12°
22	12.571	Aries	12.57°
23	13.143	Aries	13.14°
24	13.714	Aries	13.71°
25	14.286	Aries	14.29°
26	14.857	Aries	14.86°
27	15.429	Aries	15.43°
28	16	Aries	16°
29	16.571	Aries	16.57°
30	17.143	Aries	17.14°
31	17.714	Aries	17.71°
32	18.286	Aries	18.29°
33	18.857	Aries	18.86°
34	19.429	Aries	19.43°
35	20	Aries	20°

4/7° PER YEAR OF LIFE (4/7° AGE POINT)			
Age	4/7 of Age	Sign	Ecliptic Longitude (Rounded)
36	20.571	Aries	20.57°
37	21.143	Aries	21.14°
38	21.714	Aries	21.71°
39	22.286	Aries	22.29°
40	22.857	Aries	22.86°
41	23.429	Aries	23.43°
42	24	Aries	24°
43	24.571	Aries	24.57°
44	25.143	Aries	25.14°
45	25.714	Aries	25.71°
46	26.286	Aries	26.29°
47	26.857	Aries	26.86°
48	27.429	Aries	27.43°
49	28	Aries	28°
50	28.571	Aries	28.57°
51	29.143	Aries	29.14°
52	29.714	Aries	29.71°
53	0.286	**TAURUS**	30.29°
54	0.857	Taurus	30.86°
55	1.429	Taurus	31.43°
56	2	Taurus	32°
57	2.571	Taurus	32.57°
58	3.143	Taurus	33.14°
59	3.714	Taurus	33.71°
60	4.286	Taurus	34.29°

4/7° PER YEAR OF LIFE (4/7° AGE POINT)			
Age	4/7 of Age	Sign	Ecliptic Longitude (Rounded)
61	4.857	Taurus	34.86°
62	5.429	Taurus	35.43°
63	6	Taurus	36°
64	6.571	Taurus	36.57°
65	7.143	Taurus	37.14°
66	7.714	Taurus	37.71°
67	8.286	Taurus	38.29°
68	8.857	Taurus	38.86°
69	9.429	Taurus	39.43°
70	10	Taurus	40°
71	10.571	Taurus	40.57°
72	11.143	Taurus	41.14°
73	11.714	Taurus	41.71°
74	12.286	Taurus	42.29°
75	12.857	Taurus	42.86°
76	13.429	Taurus	43.43°
77	14	Taurus	44°
78	14.571	Taurus	44.57°
79	15.143	Taurus	45.14°
80	15.714	Taurus	45.71°
81	16.286	Taurus	46.29°
82	16.857	Taurus	46.86°
83	17.429	Taurus	47.43°
84	18	Taurus	48°
85	18.571	Taurus	48.57°

4/7° PER YEAR OF LIFE (4/7° AGE POINT)			
Age	**4/7 of Age**	**Sign**	**Ecliptic Longitude (Rounded)**
86	19.143	Taurus	49.14°
87	19.714	Taurus	49.71°
88	20.286	Taurus	50.29°
89	20.857	Taurus	50.86°
90	21.429	Taurus	51.43°
91	22	Taurus	52°
92	22.571	Taurus	52.57°
93	23.143	Taurus	53.14°
94	23.714	Taurus	53.71°
95	24.286	Taurus	54.29°
96	24.857	Taurus	54.86°
97	25.429	Taurus	55.43°
98	26	Taurus	56°
99	26.571	Taurus	56.57°
100	27.143	Taurus	57.14°

How to Calculate the *4/7° per Year of Life Age along the Zodiac (4/7° Age Point)*

Using the chart of Yevgeny Prigozhin from appendix A (chart 64), let's calculate his *4/7° per year of life Age along the Zodiac (4/7° Age Point)* at the time of his death.

Prigozhin was born on 1 June 1961 and died on 23 August 2023. Using the "Days Calculator: Days Between Two Dates" at the Time and Date website (https://www.timeanddate .com/date/duration.html), we find that he was 22,728 days old at the time of his demise.

Dividing 22,728 days by 365.24 days per year, we determine that he was 22,728 / 365.24 = 62.23 years old.

Thus, Prigozhin's *Age along the Zodiac* would be 62.23° from 0° Aries, which is 2.23° Taurus, or 2° 14' Taurus.

Next, we must calculate 4/7 of his *Age along the Zodiac*: 4/7 × 62.23° = 35.56°, or 35° 34', which corresponds to 5° 34' Taurus as his *4/7° Age along the Zodiac (4/7° Age Point)* at the time of his death.

Directing natal Saturn, which lies at 29° 26' Rx, by the arc 35° 34' (Prigozhin's *4/7° Age along the Zodiac* when the plane crashed), we arrive at 5° 00' Pisces, which is directly opposite natal Pluto at 5° 35' Virgo, so that symbolically directed Saturn was closely opposing natal Pluto when he perished.

Appendix C
PTOLEMY'S *SEVEN AGES OF MAN*

This table summarizes the second-century scheme of Claudius Ptolemy regarding the *seven ages of man*. Each period of life is ruled by a planetary timelord whose symbolism pervades the period. The ninth-century astrologer Abu Ma'shar began his delineation of annual revolutions with this technique.

PTOLEMY'S *SEVEN AGES OF MAN*			
Planet (Chaldean Order, Fastest to Slowest)	**Nature of Period**	**Begins at Age**	**Duration in Years**
Moon	Infancy	0	4
Mercury	Childhood	4	10
Venus	Adolescence	14	8
Sun	Early adulthood	22	19
Mars	Middle adulthood	41	15
Jupiter	Mature adulthood	56	12
Saturn	Old age	68	30

ALAN LEO'S ZODIAC SIGNS COMBINED WITH PTOLEMY'S *SEVEN AGES OF MAN*

This table presents Alan Leo's division of the 84-year life span among the twelve zodiac signs combined with Ptolemy's *seven ages of man* in a kind of Jyotish dasha timelord system, for easy reference.

ALAN LEO'S ZODIAC SIGNS COMBINED WITH PTOLEMY'S *SEVEN AGES OF MAN*			
Zodiac Sign and Ruler (Alan Leo)	**Age in Years**	**Ptolemy's *Seven Ages* Timelord**	**Age in Years**
Aries (Mars)	0–3.999	Moon	0–3.999
Aries (Mars)	4–6.999	Mercury	4–13.999
Taurus (Venus)	7–13.999	Mercury	4–13.999
Gemini (Mercury)	14–20.999	Venus	14–21.999
Cancer (Moon)	21–21.999	Venus	21–21.999
Cancer (Moon)	22–27.999	Sun	22–40.999
Leo (Sun)	28–34.999	Sun	22–40.999
Virgo (Mercury)	35–40.999	Sun	22–40.999
Virgo (Mercury)	41–41.999	Mars	41–55.999
Libra (Venus)	42–48.999	Mars	41–55.999
Scorpio (Mars)	49–55.999	Mars	41–55.999
Sagittarius (Jupiter)	56–62.999	Jupiter	56–67.999
Capricorn (Saturn)	63–67.999	Jupiter	56–67.999

ALAN LEO'S ZODIAC SIGNS COMBINED WITH PTOLEMY'S *SEVEN AGES OF MAN*			
Zodiac Sign and Ruler (Alan Leo)	**Age in Years**	**Ptolemy's *Seven Ages* Timelord**	**Age in Years**
Capricorn (Saturn)	68–69.999	Saturn	68–98
Aquarius (Saturn)	70–76.999	Saturn	68–98
Pisces (Jupiter)	77–83.999	Saturn	68–98
Aries (Mars)	84–90.999	Saturn	68–98
Taurus (Venus)	91–97.999	Saturn	68–98
Gemini (Mercury)	98–104.999	Moon	98–102

Appendix E
KEYWORDS FOR THE PLANETS, ASCENDANT, AND MIDHEAVEN

The significance of planets in predictive work depends on which house they occupy in the birth chart and the house cusps that they rule. In addition, the planets and other celestial bodies have general or universal significations, which often give clues to the type of event they may indicate. This section lists celestial objects *in alphabetical order* with some of their common universal meanings. I have included comments by Sepharial, whose writings influenced Frankland in the early decades of the 1900s. The quotations here are from Sepharial's 1921 book *Directional Astrology*. No doubt as you experiment with Frankland's symbolic measures, you will modify this list based on your own experience with charts.

Ascendant: Sepharial writes: "This point of the horoscope [the Ascendant] indicates things personal to the subject, as health, general welfare, comfort, environment, changes, and the common relationships of life, that which affects him through collective influence, the public state of affairs, etc. Good aspects (as above numerated) tend to benefit the subject by a variety of means differing as the nature of the planet which is in aspect by direction. Evil aspects signal bad health, obstacles, hindrances, incommodities, troubles and annoyances of various kinds, according to the nature and position of the planet directed" (Sepharial 1921, 46).

Chiron: Chiron is an icy centaur-object discovered in 1977, which has come to symbolize the "wounded healer" and our ability to heal from the pain of being hurt. It is often active astrologically when we undergo some type of emotional hurt or painful injury to the body. Chiron has an erratic 50.45-year orbit that crosses the path of Saturn and passes inside the trajectory of Uranus.

Jupiter: Jupiter is the supreme god in Roman mythology, equivalent to the Greek god Zeus, the Greater Benefic. Zeus rose to power by defeating his father, Cronos/Saturn, who in turn had wrested power from his father, Uranus, by castrating him. A bisexual philanderer, Zeus routinely cheated on his wife Hera (the goddess of marriage) with whoever tickled his fancy. In the process, he got countless females pregnant and fathered large numbers of children. Jupiter has become a signifier of progeny, abundance, the production of children, sowing wild oats, plenty, optimism, benevolence, enthusiasm, warmth, adventure, joviality, increase, expansion, good fortune, success, inflation, justice, ethics, philosophy, religion, prosperity, luck, lust for life, health, feeling good, overindulgence, and generosity. Jupiter loved to travel, meet new people, learn new things, expand his horizons, and, in general, do things on a large scale.

Sepharial writes: "*Jupiter* in good aspect denotes increase of fortune, opening up of new and lucrative opportunities, expansion of interests, advancement, progress, honours, confidence, good judgment, a general feeling of expansion and well-being, both physical and mental. In evil aspect Jupiter denotes losses, errors of judgment, vanity or excessive confidence, disfavour of legal men and clericals, physical disabilities arising from congestion and surfeit, excess or over-indulgence, 'too much of a good thing,' too much *confiance en soi*, and consequent loss of esteem with others. It indicates a period of low finance, due to lavish expenditure, severe losses, or heavy investments. Jupiter is anciently known as the Greater Benefic, but it is certain that its evil aspects denote anything but a beneficial state of affairs" (Sepharial 1921, 51).

Mars: Mars is the Roman god of war, the Lesser Malefic. He likes to give orders and be in charge. He is competitive, enjoys challenges, and loves a good fight. Mars has come to signify courage, action, initiative, energy, directed activity, the muscular system, kinetic energy, self-will, impulse, provocation, zeal, passion, anger, boldness, courage, willpower, assertion, challenge, a fighting spirit, wrath, aggression, struggle, accidents, strife, quarrels, contention, danger, drive, prowess, executive ability, and the determination to win. As the war god, Mars is symbolically linked to virility, young men, brothers, knives, guns, swords, blood-letting, the use of force, weapons, scalpels, inflammation, acute infection, surgical instruments, fevers, fires, hurts, injuries, piercing, cutting, penetrating, provoking, heating, burning, scorching, killing, butchering, bleeding, crashing, or anything that can be used to overpower his adversaries and achieve his goals. His action is to strive, pierce, cut, wound, injure, provoke, fight, challenge, penetrate, sever, and separate.

Sepharial writes: "*Mars* in good aspect denotes activity, new enterprises, great output of energy with commensurate good results, travelling, the executive powers are stimulated, and much profitable work is done. Benefits accrue from military men, business connected with iron, steel, and fire. The muscular system is strengthened and there is a disposition to increased activity. Honours due to deeds of daring and chivalry. Women frequently marry under this aspect. In evil aspect Mars denotes hurts by burns, scalds, fire, and steel, with loss of blood, abrasions and cuts, and also fevers and inflammatory conditions of the body or that part of it indicated by the position of Mars by direction. Loss by fire or theft, sometimes attended by violence. Sudden alarms and disasters of various sorts. Mars was anciently known as the Lesser Infortune" (Sepharial 1921, 51–52).

Mercury: Mercury is the messenger of the gods. Youthful, winged, and able to fly, androgynous Mercury rapidly carried news and messages back and forth among the deities. In astrology, Mercury signifies prepubescent children, young people, androgyny, transition, students, editors, writers, language, capacity for thought and observation, mental attitude, speakers, the media, news, communications, writings, documents, travel, journeys, mobility, transport, trade, bartering, commerce, sales, negotiations, markets, mercantilism, mental activities, intellect, wit, cleverness, quick thinking, and those who sell goods or advise others.

Sepharial writes: "*Mercury* acts in terms of the planet to which at birth it is in closest aspect; but if not within orbs of an aspect with any planet, then in terms of the ruler of the sign it occupies. In good aspect it usually signifies activity, much occupation of a profitable nature, connected with writings, science, and business of a general nature. Travelling, profitable journeys, good news, gain in connection with the avocation or trade. An active time generally. In evil aspect Mercury produces annoyances and disturbances, evil news, worry and anxiety, many short journeys to and fro to no purpose or profit, sleeplessness, irregular feeding, unrest" (Sepharial 1921, 53).

Midheaven: Sepharial writes: "This point of the horoscope [the Midheaven] stands for dignity, influence, authority, and position, the worldly honour and credit of the subject, and for all that is associated with his social and communal status. Good directions, such as the sextile and trine of all planets, and the conjunction and parallel of Jupiter, Venus (and Mercury when well aspected at birth), are indications of an enhanced position, higher honours, social distinctions, increase of prestige, etc. Evil directions, such as the semisquare, square, and opposition of all planets (including the Sun and Moon in this category), and the conjunctions and parallels of Uranus, Neptune, Saturn, and Mars, indicate assaults upon the good name and credit of the subject, hurt to the business affairs, loss of position, rivalries, and unprofitable associations" (Sepharial 1921, 45–46).

Moon: The Moon is a goddess who reflects the light of the Sun and illuminates the world at night. Most notable for its rapidly changing phases and its connection to the tides of the ocean and the female menstrual cycle, the Moon has become a symbol of changes, travel, cycles, periodicity, the flow of events, moods, feelings, emotions, one's inner life, women and women's issues, mothers, the womb, the body, mothering, nurturing, domestic life, the care of children and of those in need, milk and those who work with liquids of any kind, commodities, the public, popularity and public opinion, females in general, sailors, imagination, receptivity, and the mind.

Sepharial writes: "The *Moon* denotes the health, changes of fortune, the mother and female representatives of the family, the functional powers of the body, and, in its association with the Ascendant, public bodies, the populace, and public concerns generally. If in a hylegiacal position, it indicates the vital organs and life of the subject" (Sepharial 1921, 47). Also: "The *Moon* in good aspect denotes pleasant and profitable changes, a change for the better in the general state of affairs, gain by public associations and concerns, favours from women of mature age, popularity. In evil aspect it denotes loss by any of the above means, and a state of unrest both physical and mental which leads to neglect of duties and consequent loss. Hurts from women. Some public affronts may be suffered. Changes are unfortunate, and best avoided" (Sepharial 1921, 53–54).

Moon's North Node (Rahu): The Head of the Dragon is a "shadow planet" that causes eclipses to extract vengeance on the Sun and the Moon for informing Vishnu of his theft of some of the elixir of life to become immortal. Vishnu severed the dragon in two parts, the head becoming Rahu (the North Node, the point where the Moon begins to ascend in its precessional orbit around the Earth) and the tail becoming Ketu (the South Node, the point where the Moon begins to descend in its precessional orbit around the Earth). Rahu has become a symbol of materialistic ambition and an insatiable desire for the goods of this world at the expense of one's spiritual development. In Western astrology, Rahu is viewed as expanding, energizing, or increasing whatever it contacts. In Jyotish, Rahu is a symbol of strong attachments, gains, obsessions, addictions, sudden unexpected happenings, accidents, diseases (including epidemics), and foreign travel or residence. Cosmobiologists view the Moon's nodes as signifying associations, contacts, alliances, and personal connections with other people.

Moon's South Node (Ketu): Like Rahu, the Tail of the Dragon is a "shadow planet" and an immortal enemy of the Sun and the Moon. Ketu is the headless body of the dragon (see *Rahu* above). Cut off from the materialistic ambitions of Rahu, Ketu is a symbol of detachment, renunciation, decrease, and deprivation in the material realm but with the benefit of spiritual growth. In Western astrology, Ketu is viewed as reducing or diminishing whatever it contacts. In Jyotish, Ketu has become a signifier of spirituality, detachment, loss, letting go, leaving the material world behind, self-knowledge, otherworldly interests, pain and injury, and outcasts and those who are cut off from mainstream society. Evolutionary astrologers associate the Moon's South Node and its dispositor with karma from past lives.

Neptune: Neptune is the Roman god of the seas, similar to Poseidon, the Greek god of the seas, earthquakes, floods, droughts, and horses. As ruler of the world's oceans, with their waves and sea mists, Neptune was thought to signify boundlessness, mysticism, the unknown, spiritual awakening, fog, mist, illusion, chaos, confusion, unseen influences, misinformation, impermanence, fantasy, intrigue, fiction, escapism, lack of direction, dreams, imagination, daydreams, unreality, scandal, unsubstantiated beliefs, over-idealization, dreamlike states, intoxication, anesthesia, unconsciousness, paralysis, seances, the spirit world, occultism, connections to distant shores, ocean journeys, deception, fraud, misrepresentation, disillusionment, unreliability, dissolution, undermining, weakening, subversion, dissipation, diffusion, poisoning, letting go, fading away, mystery, vagueness, ambiguity, uncertainty, mirage (Fata Morgana), a lack of clear boundaries, otherworldliness, floods, tsunamis, ocean currents, emotions dominating rational thinking, matters related to liquids and gases, and the ability to loosen or dissolve structured forms. Modern astrologers associate Neptune with Hollywood and viewing the world through rose-colored glasses.

Sepharial writes: *Neptune* in good aspect indicates events of a beneficial nature connected with the use of the faculties or some special faculty, and frequently in connection with a form of art; benefits from unexpected sources coming mysteriously to the subject; unseen and intangible influences at work for the benefit of the subject; brilliant flashes and inspirations of the mind; spiritual aid; intuitive activity. In evil aspect by direction it denotes chaotic and mysterious events adverse to the interests; scandal, secret enmity; undermining of the credit by misrepresentation and fraud; treachery, ambush; an involved state of affairs; nervous leakage and depletion of energy; wasting of tissue; physical ennui and decline of the vital powers from inscrutable causes; apprehension, fear, and dread of consequence; danger of espionage; loss by fraudulent concerns and false investments; mental unrest and loss of faculty" (Sepharial 1921, 49–50).

Pluto: Infamous for his abduction and rape of Persephone, Pluto (aka Plutus, Ploutos, or Hades) came to symbolize immense power and also the manipulation and control of others. The name Pluto has its origin in the Greek word *ploutos*, meaning "wealth." The philosopher Plato regarded Pluto as governing the riches within the Earth, bestowing spiritual wealth, and acting as an agent of the cycle of death and rebirth. Zeus apparently blinded Ploutos so that he would distribute his wealth impartially. Pluto also possessed a Helmet of Invisibility to aid him in his fight against the Titans. As god of the underworld, Pluto can signify forces buried deep beneath the surface that eventually can be brought to light. It is a symbol of the afterlife, confronting human mortality, matters of life and death, *force majeure*, powerful influences, radical changes, turning points, complications, metamorphosis, intensity, profundity, buried secrets, obsessions, compulsions, transformation, regeneration (like the phoenix rising from its ashes), renewal, rebirth, evolution, reorganization, reformation, remodeling, reconstruction, renovation, purging, cleansing, elimination of waste, transition from one stage of life to another, inflection points, and reversals. Activation of Pluto in a birth chart often correlates with life-altering events of some urgency, which serve to eliminate that which is no longer useful or needed and to divide one's life into "before and after." As a god of great wealth, Pluto sometimes signifies large gains or expenditures of money.

Saturn: Saturn is the Roman god of time and agriculture (the sowing of seeds so that crops will grow), equivalent to the Greek god Cronus, the Greater Malefic. With the aid of a sickle fashioned by Gaia, Saturn ambushed and castrated his father, Uranus, thereby assuming command of the cosmos. No wonder Uranus is associated with sudden disruptions! As the outermost visible planet of our solar system, Saturn has come to symbolize remoteness, separateness, isolation, being apart, solitude, barriers, obstacles, hindrances, endings, boundaries, restrictions, estrangement, structures, stability, discipline, permanence, old age, ponderousness, burdens, gravity, lessons to be learned, contraction, concentration, heaviness, sorrow, loss, deprivation, fear, mistrust, affliction, mourning, falls, solidity, hardening, density, responsibility, inhibition, duty, deliberativeness, slowing down, perseverance, objectivity, maturity, restraint, limits, alienation, depression, disappointment, confinement, and distancing and separation from others. As the visible planet farthest from the Sun, Saturn travels slowly and cautiously, like an old man with a limp, through a cold, dark, inhospitable region of space and signifies places of a similar nature on Earth. Its action is to cool, congeal, condense, harden, weigh down, slow, delay, age, pause, limit, bound, restrict, confine, discipline, structure, face reality, act responsibly, and move slowly and deliberately.

Sepharial writes: "*Saturn* in good aspect indicates favours from aged persons and benefits from old associations, long investments, time contracts, and a general state of stability and steadiness in the fortunes, congenial retirement and sequestration. In evil aspect Saturn depletes the vital powers, causes physical hurts by falls and contusions, morbid diseases, colds and chills, inhibition of bodily functions; loss of money and property; mental and nervous depression; privations, obstructions, hindrances, and general misfortunes. Saturn is anciently known as the Greater Infortune" (Sepharial 1921, 50–51).

Sun: Sun god and giver of life. The Sun at the center of the solar system is its source of light and heat, which are necessary for creating and sustaining life. The Sun signifies those in power and command, such as leaders, kings, presidents, bosses, authorities, and father figures. The Sun illuminates the day and brings matters to light, thus revealing the truth. In good condition, it symbolizes advancement, benefits from superiors, honors, prominence, vitality, life force, power, warmth, brilliance, and those who stand out prominently or gloriously in public view. The Sun also signifies the goals in life and the spiritual life force that animates the soul of the native.

Sepharial writes: "The *Sun*, when in a hylegliacal place (as defined by Ptolemy), has significance of the vital constitution and life of the subject. Generally it stands for the father and male representatives of a family, and for the honour, credit, and position of the subject himself. It is thus associated more particularly with the Midheaven" (Sepharial 1921, 46). Also: "The Sun in good aspect indicates increase of prestige, honours and emoluments, new friends and associations of a creditable character, general advancement and good fortune. In evil aspect the Sun denotes losses, disfavour of superiors, troubles through male members of the family, the chief, overseer, or manager of a business; loss by governing bodies; ill-health due to fevers. Reverses of various sorts according to the house in which the direction is completed" (Sepharial 1921, 52).

Uranus: Uranus is the primordial god of the sky, who himself was fatherless and conceived by Gaia (Earth) alone. Ambushed and castrated by Saturn/Cronos, Uranus is a symbol of sudden and unanticipated breaks, disruptions, accidents, bolts from the blue, and freedom of thought and action. The strange orientation of the planet's axis of rotation, so that it points almost directly at the Sun, links Uranus to things that are sudden, abrupt, odd, unusual, unexpected, surprising, rebellious, explosive, unpredictable, impulsive, unsettled, impatient, tense, eccentric, original, and novel, and that go against the norm or upset the status quo. The discovery of the planet in 1781 associated Uranus historically with social uprisings, sudden changes, separations, estrangements, severing of ties, tension, excitement, explosiveness, dislocation, breaks, disruptions, discontinuities, reforms, progressive ideas, the desire for personal and political independence, democratic reforms, the Industrial Revolution, the development of modern science and technology, the harnessing of electricity, and the revival of interest in astrology after its decline during the Scientific Revolution of the 16th and 17th centuries.

Sepharial writes: "*Uranus* in good aspect denotes civic and governmental honours, preference, advancement; unexpected benefits arising out of public concerns and affairs; ingenuity, inventiveness; originality; success in mechanical and engineering business; strokes of good fortune coming from unexpected sources; new associations and alliances. In evil aspect this planet denotes the breaking down of existing relationships, lesions and fractures, partings and separations, loss of a sudden and unlooked-for nature; hurt by strikes and public demonstrations; nervous lesion, paralysis; breaks and dislocations" (Sepharial 1921, 50).

Venus: Venus is the Roman goddess of love and beauty, the Lesser Benefic. Legend has it that Venus gave birth to Cupid, a cherubic little god whose arrows made people fall in love. In astrology, Venus is a general signifier of affection, sentiments, erotic love, femininity, young women, sisters, intimate relationships, sex symbols, attractiveness, attachments, social benefits, love affairs, coitus, sperm, sexual pleasure, fun, enjoyment, hedonism, comforts, gifts, luxuries, fashion, charm, peace, happiness, harmony, balance, beauty, aesthetics, social graces, the arts, creative endeavors, artistic pursuits, indulgences, satisfaction, and a fondness for the finer things in life. Interestingly, in Mesopotamia Venus was identified with the goddess Inanna and later worshiped as Ishtar, a deity of sexual love, female sexuality, warfare, conflict, justice, beauty, and political power and ambition. In one myth, a young gardener rapes Inanna/Ishtar as she is sleeping under a tree. In another myth, she travels to the underworld, where she is turned into a corpse, only to later be brought back to life and able to return to the world of the living. These ancient associations of the planet Venus may be the source of some of the meanings found in Abu Ma'shar's work and in Jyotish texts linking Venus to the 12th house.

Sepharial writes: "*Venus* in good aspect signifies social and domestic success, pleasures and enjoyments, gifts and presents, decorations; the young court or marry, and the mature have children born or daughters engaged or given in marriage, and such events happen as cause pleasure and satisfaction. The affectional nature is stimulated and the health is good. In evil aspect Venus denotes sorrows, disappointments, bereavements, grief, and losses, domestic and social troubles, and hurts associated with young women or children. Venus was anciently known as the Lesser Benefic, and the less one has of it when in evil aspect the better for all concerned" (Sepharial 1921, 52–53).

BIBLIOGRAPHY

Abenragel, Haly (Abū l-Ḥasan 'Alī ibn Abī l-Rijāl al-Shaybani). *El libro conplido en los iudizios de las estrellas: Libro IV, traducción* [The complete book on the judgment of the stars: Book IV, translation]. Traducción a Castellaño de la Angigua Corona de Aragón. Zaragoza, Navarro & Navarro, 1988–1997. This book was first translated into Old Castilian by Yehudā ben Moshe at the court of Alfonso X, in Toledo, Spain, in 1254. The Castilian translation of 1254 was translated into Latin in 1485 in Venice and published by Erhard Ratdolt as *Praeclarissimus liber completus in judiciis astrorum* [The very famous complete book on the judgment of the stars], aka *De judiciis astrorum*. Augsburg, Germany: Erhard Ratdolt, 1485. A digital copy can be found at the Library of Congress website: https://www.loc.gov/item/2021666773. Accessed August 2023.

Adams, Evangeline. *The Bowl of Heaven*. New York: Dodd, Mead, 1926.

———. *Your Place in the Sun*. New York: Dodd, Mead, 1927.

Addey, John. *Harmonics in Astrology*. London: Urania Trust, 1996.

Al-Biruni. *Book of Instruction in the Elements of the Art of Astrology*. Written in Ghaznah, 1029 CE. Reproduced from British Museum ms. Or. 8349. Translation by R. Ramsay Wright. Reprint, London: Luzac, 1934.

Astro-Databank. "Shaw, George Bernard." Accessed August 2023. https://www.astro.com /astro-databank/Shaw,_George_Bernard.

Behari, Bepin. *Planets in the Signs and Houses*. Salt Lake City, UT: Passage Press, 1992.

Blaquier, Maria. *Astrología tradicional: Técnicas predictivas de los Señores del tiempo* [Traditional astrology: Predictive techniques of the time lords]. Madrid: Kier, 2020.

Blaschke, Robert. *Astrology: A Language of Life, Volume I: Progressions.* Lake Oswego, OR: Earthwalk School of Astrology, 1998.

Blavatsky, H. P. "Neros." In *The Theosophical Glossary.* London: Theosophical Publishing Society, 1892. https://universaltheosophy.com/hpb/theosophicalglossary.html.

Burk, Kevin. *The Complete Node Book.* St. Paul, MN: Llewellyn, 2003.

Cafe Astrology. "Astrology Topics: the Meaning of Midpoints." https://cafeastrology.com /astrologytopics/meaningsofmidpoints.html. Accessed August 2023. The site is run by astrologer Annie Heese.

Carmody, Francis J. *Arabic Astronomical and Astrological Sciences in Latin Translation: A Critical Bibliography.* Oakland, CA: University of California Press, 1955.

Carter, Charles E. O. *An Encyclopedia of Psychological Astrology.* London: Theosophical Publishing House, 1924.

———. *The Principles of Astrology.* 3rd ed. London: Theosophical Publishing House, 1939.

———. *Symbolic Directions in Modern Astrology.* London: Theosophical Publishing House, 1929.

Charak, Dr. K. S. *Elements of Vedic Astrology.* Delhi, India: UMA Publications, 1995.

Christino, Karen. *What Evangeline Adams Knew.* Brooklyn Heights, NY: Stella Mira Books, 2004.

Cochrane, David. "Venus Star Points: The Yin-Yang Polarity, Part 2." Evidence-Based Astrology channel. October 10, 2022. YouTube video, https://www.youtube.com /watch?v=zKeMqvqwGZ8.

Cornelius, Geoffrey. *The Moment of Astrology: Origins in Divination.* New York: Arkana, 1994.

Crawford, Elizabeth. "A Poster Speaks: The Mystery of the Disappearing Doctor." Woman and Her Sphere. October 1, 2013. https://womanandhersphere.com/2013 /10/01/a-poster-speaks-the-mystery-of-the-disappearing-doctor/.

Cristoff, Boris. *La predicción astrológica por el sistema de la Proluna y sus derivados* [Astrological prediction by the Proluna system and its derivatives]. Buenos Aires: Kier, 1994.

Davison, R. C. *The Technique of Prediction.* 1955. Reprint, London: L. N. Fowler, 1971.

DeLuce, Robert. *Complete Method of Prediction.* New York: ASI, 1978.

Dio, Lucius Cassius (c. 165–c. 235). *Roman History.* Volume 8, books 61–70. English translation by Earnest Cary. Loeb Classical Library edition. Cambridge, MA: Harvard University Press, 1925. https://www.loebclassics.com/view/LCL176/1925/volume.xml.

Ebertin, Reinhold. *The Combination of Stellar Influences.* Tempe, AZ: American Federation of Astrologers, 1972.

Esoteric Technologies. *Solar Fire 9 User Guide.* Seaford, Victoria, Australia: Esoteric Technologies, 2019.

Evans, Colin. *The Valentino Affair: The Jazz Age Murder Scandal That Shocked New York Society and Gripped the World.* Guilford, CT: Lyons Press, 2020.

Fagan, Cyril. *Astrological Origins.* St. Paul, MN: Llewellyn, 1971.

———, and Brigadier R. C. Firebrace. *Primer of Sidereal Astrology.* 3rd ed. Tempe, AZ: American Federation of Astrologers, 1971.

Frankland, William. *Astrological Investigations: How to Estimate the Important Areas of Life.* London: L. N. Fowler, 1926. https://archive.org/details/in.ernet.dli.2015.128190.

———. *Keys to Symbolic Directing: Measuring Our Years.* London: Fowler & Co., 1930.

———. *New Measures in Astrology: A Symbolic Basis in Directions.* London: L. N. Fowler, 1928. https://archive.org/details/in.ernet.dli.2015.128188.

Freeman, Martin. *Forecasting by Astrology.* Wellingborough, Northamptonshire: Aquarian Press, 1982.

Garcia, Mari, and Joy Usher. "An Introduction to Charles Carter." Skyscript. February 2013. https://www.skyscript.co.uk/carter_intro.html#BS.

Guttmann, Arielle. *Venus Star Rising: A New Cosmology for the 21st Century.* Santa Fe, NM: Sophia Venus Productions, 2010.

Hand, Robert. "Planetary Periods in Western Astrology." Arhat Media. Accessed August 2023. https://www.arhatmedia.com/periods.htm.

Harding, Michael, and Charles Harvey. *Working with Astrology: The Psychology of Harmonics, Midpoints and Astro*Carto*Graphy.* London: Arkana, 1990.

Hastings, Nancy Anne. *Secondary Progressions: Time to Remember.* York Beach, ME: Samuel Weiser, 1984.

Hephaistio of Thebes. *Apotelesmatics, Book II.* Translated by Robert Schmidt. Edited by Robert Hand. Cumberland, MD: Project Hindsight, 1998.

HistoryNet Staff. "Old Glory's Final Ill-fated Flight: New York to Rome in 1927." HistoryNet.com. June 12, 2006. https://www.historynet.com/old-glorys-final-ill -fated-flight-new-york-to-rome-in-1927.

Houlding, Deborah. "Astrology and Real Life: A Review of an Illness." *The Traditional Astrologer* 18 (March 1999).

———. *The Houses: Temples of the Sky.* Bournemouth, England: Wessex Astrologer, 2006.

———. "Ptolemy's Terms & Conditions." Skyscript. November 2010. https://www .skyscript.co.uk/terms.html.

Jones, Marc Edmund. *The Guide to Horoscope Interpretation.* Wheaton, IL: Theosophical Publishing House, 1981. Originally published in 1941 by Sabian Publishing Society.

Khullar, S. P. *Kalamsa & Cuspal Interlinks Theory.* New Delhi, India: Sagar, 2008.

Kurtik, G. E. "The Identification of Inanna with the Planet Venus: A Criterion for the Time Determination of the Recognition of Constellations in Ancient Mesopotamia." *Astronomical & Astrophysical Transactions* 17:6 (1999): 501–13. https://doi.org/10.1080 /10556799908244112.

Labouré, Denis. "Cours d'astrologie gratuit: la révolution solaire par Denis Labouré." Editions Spiritualité Occidentale channel. March 14, 2017. YouTube video, https:// www.youtube.com/watch?v=lvVwo_ZNYVE.

Leo, Alan. *Astrology for All, to Which Is Added a Complete System of Predictive Astrology for Advanced Students.* London: L. N. Fowler, 1899.

———. *Everybody's Astrology: A Book for Beginners.* Alan Leo's Astrological Manuals, No. 1. 10th ed. 1904. Reprint, London: L. N. Fowler, 1910.

———. *Horary Astrology.* Alan Leo's Astrological Manuals, No. 7. 1st ed. London: L. N. Fowler, 1907.

———. *The Progressed Horoscope.* Rochester, VT: Destiny Books, 1983. Originally pub- lished in 1906 by L. N. Fowler, London, UK.

———. *1001 Notable Nativities: An Astrological "Who's Who."* 4th ed. Edinburgh: Inter- national Publishing Co., 1917.

Lilly, William. *Christian Astrology.* 1647. Reprint, London: John Macock, 1659.

Louis, Anthony. *The Art of Forecasting Using Solar Returns.* Bournemouth, England: Wessex Astrologer, 2008.

———. *Horary Astrology: The History and Practice of Astro-Divination.* St. Paul, MN: Llewellyn, 1991.

———. "Will the Real Dr. J. Heber Smith Please Stand Up?" *The Astrological Journal* (September/October 2022): 13–16.

Lovretic, Cristina. "Atacires, una técnica predictiva milenaria." Centro Astrológico de Chile. May 17, 2014. https://www.centroastrologicodechile.cl/articulos-astrologicos /atacires-una-tecnica-predictiva-milenaria/.

Maciá, Tito. *Atacires: Los relojes del cielo.* New York: Little French's Media, 2019.

Ma'shar, Abu. *Persian Nativities IV: Abu Ma'shar: On the Revolutions of the Years of Nativities.* Translated and edited by Benjamin N. Dykes. Minneapolis, MN: Cazimi Press, 2019. Original text written in the 9th century.

Mason, Sophia. *Delineation of Progressions.* Tempe, AZ: American Federation of Astrologers, 1985.

Maternus, Julius Firmicus [Iulii Firmici Materni]. *Matheseos libri VIII.* In Latin and edited by W. Kroll and F. Skutsch. Germany: B. G. Teubneri, 1897. https:// www.hellenisticastrology.com/editions/Firmicus-Maternus-Mathesis-Vol-1.pdf.

Mercadé, Aleix. "Astrology as a Therapeutic Tool: A Study of a Complicated Grief Case." Presented at the 37th Iberian Congress of Astrology, Malaga, Spain, June 19, 2022. https://astrologiaexperimental.files.wordpress.com/2022/07/astrology-as-therapeutic -tool.-a-study-of-a-complicated-grief-case-aleix-mercadecc81.pdf.

Milburn, Leigh Hope. *The Progressed Horoscope Simplified.* Tempe, AZ: American Federation of Astrologers, 1936.

Mitchell, Glenn. *Discover the Aspect Pattern in Your Birth Chart: A Comprehensive Guide.* Woodbury, MN: Llewellyn, 2020.

Morin, Jean-Baptiste. *Astrologia Gallica.* Latin edition. The Hague: Adriani Vlacq, 1661.

———. *Astrologia Gallica, Book 22: Directions.* Translated from the Latin by James Herschel Holden. Tempe, AZ: American Federation of Astrologers, 1994.

Morrow, Glenn. *Plato's Cretan City.* Princeton, NJ: Princeton University Press, 1960.

Munkasey, Michael. "Comments on Progression, Direction and Return Techniques." NCGR San Diego. 1998. https://ncgrsandiego.org/articles.htm.

National Gallery of Ireland. "Five Things to Know about George Bernard Shaw." https://www.nationalgallery.ie/art-and-artists/exhibitions/shaw-and-gallery-priceless-education/five-things-about-GBS. Accessed August 2023.

Nobel Prize Outreach AB 2023. The Nobel Prize in Literature 1925: George Bernard Shaw. August 2, 2023. https://www.nobelprize.org/prizes/literature/1925/summary/.

Omarr, Sydney. *My World of Astrology.* New York: Fleet Pub. Corp., 1965.

Patry, Joni. *Neptune Secrets, Illusions and Scandals: A Neo-Vedic Approach.* Dallas, TX: Galactic Center, 2020.

Pessin, Dietrech. "The Lunar Gestation Cycle." *The Mountain Astrologer* (June/July 2012): 43–44.

Prabook. "Dorit Schmiel." Accessed August 2023. https://prabook.com/web/dorit.schmiel/2395149.

Ptolemy, Claudius. *Tetrabiblos.* Translated into English by F. E. Robbins. Loeb Classical Library. Cambridge, MA: Harvard University Press, 1980. The four books of the *Tetrabiblos* were written in the second century CE.

Ridley, Jane. "No Sympathy for Horrid Women: On the History of George V and the Demands of the Suffragettes." Literary Hub. January 7, 2022. https://lithub.com/no-sympathy-for-horrid-women-on-the-history-of-george-v-and-the-demands-of-the-suffragettes/.

Robson, Vivian. *Electional Astrology.* Philadelphia, PA: J. B. Lippincott, 1937.

———. *Fixed Stars and Constellations in Astrology.* Originally published in 1923 in London. Reprint, New York: Samuel Weiser, 1979.

Rout, Partha Sarathi. *Nakshatra Exploration: A Unique Exponent of KP Astrology Based on Research Study.* Chennai, India: Notion Press, 2021.

Sandbach, John. "Planets Activating the Node/Midheaven Midpoint." December 15, 2010. http://john-sandbach.blogspot.com/2010/12/planets-activating-nodemidheaven.html.

Santos, Demetrio. "El ciclo de 60 años." Temas de astrología. April 8, 2015. https://temasdeastrologia.blogspot.com/2015/04/el-ciclo-de-60-anos.html.

Savalan, Karen Ober. *Midpoint Interpretation Simplified.* Tempe, AZ: American Federation of Astrologers, 1978.

Scofield, Bruce. "Making Time Out of Space: An Introduction to Planetary Periods." *The Mountain Astrologer,* February/March 1998. Also available on the Astrolabe website: https://www.alabe.com/text/periods.html.

Sepharial [Walter Gorn Old]. *Astrology: How to Make and Read Your Own Horoscope.* Revised ed. 1904. Reprint, New York: Diehl, Landau & Pettit, 1920.

———. *Directional Astrology.* Philadelphia, PA: David McKay, 1921.

———. *Manual of Occultism.* London: William Rider & Son, 1914.

———. *Transits and Planetary Periods.* London: W. Foulsham, 1920. Text available at https://archive.org/details/transitsplanetar0000seph/mode/2up.

Smith, Dr. J. Heber [attributed to Dr. Smith, but the real author is unknown]. *Transits of the Planets.* XXX. Reprint, Washington, DC: American Federation of Astrologers, 1968. This booklet is reproduced in the appendix of Sydney Omarr's *My World of Astrology,* 1965, and also in part 3 of Celeste Teal's *Identifying Planetary Triggers,* 2000. Dr. Smith's name is sometimes listed incorrectly as Heber J. Smith.

Teal, Celeste. *Identifying Planetary Triggers: Astrological Techniques for Prediction.* St. Paul, MN: Llewellyn, 2000.

Time. "The Press: Under The Crabapple Tree." Vol. 8, no. 20 (November 15, 1926): 30.

Time and Date AS. "Days Calculator: Days Between Two Dates." https://www.timeanddate.com/date/duration.html. Accessed August 2023. This calculator can be used to determine how many days, months, and years there are between two dates.

Titus, Placidus de. *Astronomy and Elementary Philosophy.* Translated by Manoah Sibley. London: W. Justins, 1789.

———. *Primum Mobile.* Latin edition of 1675 translated into English by John Cooper. London: Davis and Dickson, 1814.

Unamuno, Miguel de. "¡Pistis y no gnosis!" *Obras completas, IV* [Complete works, IV]. Edited by Manuel García Blanco. 15 vols. Madrid: Afrodisio Aguado, 1958.

———. *Recuerdos de niñez y de mocedad* [Memories of childhood and youth]. 6a. ed. Madrid: Espasa-Calpe, 1968.

Valens, Vettius. *Anthologies, Book 1*. Translated by Mark T. Riley, Professor Emeritus, California State University, Sacramento. 1996. https://www.csus.edu/indiv/r/rileymt /Vettius%20Valens%20entire.pdf.

Valentine, Lesia. *Subject A: Tertiary Progressions*. Memphis Astrology. May 16, 2018. https://memphisastrology.blogspot.com/2018/05/subject-tertiary-progressions.html.

Volguine, Alexandre. *La technique des revolutions solaires* [The technique of solar returns]. Paris, Dervy, 1972.

Williams, Dr. David R. "Planetary Fact Sheet—Ratio to Earth Values." NASA. https:// nssdc.gsfc.nasa.gov/planetary/factsheet/planet_table_ratio.html. Last updated February 11, 2023.

Witte, Alfred. *Direktionen und planetenbilder* [Directions and planetary pictures]. *Astrologische Rundschau* [Astrological Review] 17, no. 2 (May 1925): 52–55. https://astrax.de/pdf/44_Direktionen%20und%20Planetenbilder.pdf.

———, Hermann Lefeldt, and Ludwig Rudolph. *Rules for Planetary-Pictures*. Boca Raton, FL: Penelope Publications, 1998. A summary of Witte's key midpoint delineations can be found in the article "Astrology Topics: the Meaning of Midpoints" at https://cafeastrology.com/astrologytopics/meaningsofmidpoints.html. Accessed August 2023.Cafe Astrology is a site run by astrologer Annie Heese.

Ward, Sue. *Sue Ward's Traditional Horary Course*. Lisbon: Prisma, 2021.

Wynn [Sidney K. Bennett]. *The Key Cycle*. Washington, DC: American Federation of Astrologers, 1970. This 55-page typed booklet reprints Wynn's original Key Cycle articles that he published in various editions of his *Astrology Magazine* in the 1930s and 1940s.

———. *Your Future: A Guide to Modern Astrology*. 1935. Reprint, Whitefish, MT: Kessinger, 2010.

INDEX

A

A to Z Horoscope Maker and Delineator (1910), 2

Abe, Shinzo, 46–50

Abenragel, Haly, 6, 15, 147–149, 350, 351, 399

Adams, Evangeline, 1, 30–32, 131, 333, 344–347, 399, 400

(Adams's) Gemini-rising chart for the USA, 347

Additional Double Digits Birth Number(s), 95, 98, 102, 103, 160, 217, 269, 288, 292, 307, 311

Additional Single Digits Birth Number(s), 94, 96, 101–103, 105, 160, 178, 216, 269, 288, 292, 307, 311

adverse charts, 131, 132

Age along the Zodiac (Age Point), 6, 9, 15, 16, 18, 31, 35, 69, 76, 78, 86, 88, 91, 98, 99, 105, 108, 111, 118, 121, 129, 134, 137, 145, 147, 151, 153, 154, 156, 159, 165–167, 173, 174, 176, 181, 183, 184, 188, 214, 216, 230–232, 238, 242, 259, 260, 262, 265, 270, 271, 273, 275, 280, 282, 285, 288–290, 293, 299, 300, 316, 318, 324, 325, 354, 355, 364, 365, 368, 379, 383, 384

Alan Leo on the significations of the twelve houses, 194–195

Al-Biruni's classical orbs, 273

Alcabitius house system, 148, 149

Alcyone (fixed star), 315

Almagest, 305

angular house(s), 105, 131, 210, 222

angular planet(s), 19, 151, 162, 164, 214, 270, 342

Aniston, Jennifer, 7–10

annual profections, 1, 2, 17, 18, 35, 250, 282, 296, 350–352, 356

Antinous, 304, 305, 307–310

Arabic part(s), 3, 16, 211, 248, 281

Aries Point (0° Aries), 3, 6, 9, 15, 16, 19, 24, 25, 31, 32, 43, 48, 69, 75, 76, 78, 84–86, 91, 111, 133, 134, 147, 151, 165, 170, 173, 174, 176, 177, 184, 188–190, 226, 242, 244, 270, 271, 280, 281, 308, 314,

324, 328, 362, 364, 365, 371, 374, 377, 379, 384

arrow of Heracles, 184

assassination, 46, 50

astrologer who died at age 46, 60, 254–257, 265

Astrological Investigations (1926), 5, 13, 14, 17, 19, 75, 79, 83, 85, 86, 101, 118, 127, 131, 134, 139, 141, 143, 167, 172, 188, 198, 233, 242, 253, 254, 271, 275, 321, 401

Astrological Lodge of London, 13, 76

Astrological Society, 13

astronaut, 181

(at the) bendings, 31, 129, 130, 162, 171, 185, 187, 262, 263, 286, 335

atacir, 147–149, 349–356

B

Bad Daemon, 203, 231

Barclay, Olivia, 283

Barrett, Wilson, 119, 123–127

Benjamine, Elbert, 347

Bennett, Sidney K. (a.k.a. Wynn), 139, 333–344, 347, 406

Bergoglio, Emanuel Horacio, 151

Bieber, Justin, 238–240

Birth Number, 15, 18–20, 79–82, 84–86, 88, 90, 94–96, 98–103, 105, 107, 109, 112, 113, 118, 159, 160, 162, 167, 178, 216, 217, 269, 286, 288, 292, 298, 305, 307, 309, 311, 313, 363

Blakely, David, 96

Blaquier, Maria, xvi, 11, 100, 267, 399

Blaschke, Robert, 18, 36, 400

Blavatsky, Helena, 7, 400

bombed, bombing, 267, 269, 271, 272

Bowl of Heaven, The (1926), 31, 344, 399

Brahe, Tycho, 305

British Journal of Astrology, 7, 355

Burk, Kevin, 185, 400

C

Campos, Olga, 278

Caput Algol, 314

Carter, Charles E. O., 1, 2, 6, 7, 13, 16, 17, 24, 25, 35, 36, 56, 70, 76–78, 81–84, 88, 103, 109, 214, 272, 280, 281, 354–356, 366, 400, 401

celestial equator, 32, 43, 349–351

celestial sphere, 22, 189, 349–351

Challenger disaster, 181, 183

Chiron, 9, 27, 29, 45, 69, 98, 99, 111–113, 127, 145, 151, 153, 156, 159, 160, 177, 180, 183–185, 187, 188, 203, 230, 231, 237, 238, 242, 244, 245, 256, 259, 265, 270, 272, 285, 290, 299, 313, 316, 389, 390

Christian Astrology (1647), 1, 21, 206, 212, 402

Christopher Ewart-Biggs literary award, 267, 269

chronocrator, 16, 51, 60

clusters of planets, 48, 154, 254, 256, 265, 308, 363

Cochrane, David, 59, 400

combining house cusps, 122–123, 219–248

Conder, Stanley (the "boy explorer"), 240–244, 330

Cornelius, Geoffrey, 2, 11, 249, 253, 283, 358, 360, 362, 400

Cosmic Symbolism, 13, 62, 63, 70, 356, 368

Cristoff, Boris, 326–329, 331, 352, 400

critical degree(s), 19, 133, 314

Cross, John, 164

D

Dance with a Stranger (1985), 96

dasha systems of Indian astrology, 4, 52, 60, 61, 387

Davison, Emily, 67, 69, 70, 73, 211, 400

De Saulles, Bianca, 180

De Saulles, John, 180

death by hanging, 96, 148–150

decumbiture, 342

DeLuce, Robert, 22, 401

dignities, 61, 131, 210, 214

Dio, Lucius Cassius, 309–310, 401

discovery of Uranus, 39

divisional charts, or Vargas, of Indian astrology, 351

divorce, 9, 10, 28, 29, 121, 180, 205

dominant note, 139

dominant planet, 139

Dorotheus, 351

Double Digits Birth Number, 80–82, 84, 95, 98, 101, 102, 103, 105, 109, 160, 217, 269, 286, 292, 307, 311

Dragon's Head, 140, 190

Dykes, Benjamin, 18, 51, 52, 403

E

Earth Point, 189, 190

eclipses, 9, 17, 37, 49, 56, 65, 70, 71, 90, 112, 113, 118, 145, 159, 173, 220, 273, 296, 300, 366, 393

ecliptic degree, 6, 24, 289

Edward VII of the UK, 71, 228

Eliot, George, 162–166

Ellis, Ruth, 85, 96–100

Emperor Trajan, 303, 304, 307

Encyclopedia of Psychological Astrology, An (1924), 83, 400

engineer who nearly died when his arm was torn off in an industrial accident, 109–113, 181, 321, 397

equatorial degree, 6, 189, 300, 356

Evans, Mary Ann (a.k.a. George Eliot), 162–166

excitants, 9, 35, 36, 90, 94, 99, 112, 116, 118, 154, 160, 216, 220, 221, 233

F

fateful chart, 134, 135

fateful horoscopes, 132

favorable charts, 131

Finger of Fate, 108

Finger of God, 108

Firdaria, 60

Firmicus Maternus and the twelve places, 202–203

fixed star(s), 19, 71, 309, 314, 315, 404

formula for naming an atacir, 351

found by the aid of the stars, 357–362

4.286° per year, 3, 59, 75, 325

4/7° per year of life Age along the Zodiac measure (4/7° Age Point), 4, 9, 16, 20, 24, 31, 35, 85, 86, 91, 99, 111, 119, 121, 122, 126, 127, 129, 130, 145, 151, 156, 173, 176, 183, 184, 188, 220, 230, 231, 232, 238, 259, 260, 262, 265, 271, 272, 273, 275–301, 316, 318, 320, 322, 323, 324, 326, 352, 355, 356, 364, 365, 366, 379–384

Frankland on the twelve houses, 198–202

Frankland, William, xv, xvi, 1–7, 9–11, 13–20, 24, 25, 29, 31, 32, 35–37, 39, 43–46, 48, 49, 52, 54–57, 59, 60, 63, 65, 66, 70, 75, 76, 78–86, 88, 90, 92, 94–96, 98–103, 105, 107, 109, 111–113, 115, 117–119, 121–123, 125–127, 130–134, 136–140, 142, 143, 145–147, 149, 151, 153, 154, 157, 159, 160, 162, 164, 165, 167, 168, 170–174, 176–178, 181, 183–185, 187–190, 193, 194, 198, 202, 209–211, 214, 216, 219–222, 224, 226–228, 231, 233, 234, 236, 238, 240, 242, 245, 247–254, 256, 257, 259, 260, 262, 263, 265, 267, 269–273, 275–278, 280–283, 285, 286, 289, 290, 292–294, 296, 298–300, 303, 305, 307–309, 313–318, 320–326, 328, 331, 333, 339, 344, 349, 352, 354–358, 360–366, 368, 369, 379, 389, 401

Freeman, Martin, 275, 401

Freud, Sigmund, 70

G

George V of the UK, 67–69, 73, 133, 157, 404

George, Llewellyn, 2

Georgiou, Steven Demetre (a.k.a. Yusuf/ Cat Stevens), 228–233

Gladstone, William Ewart, 44, 102, 103, 234–237

gradial transit, 72–74

Grand Cross, 4, 55, 56, 59, 83, 92, 94, 98, 100, 105, 127, 129, 130, 138, 149, 151, 153, 154, 188, 256, 257, 259, 260, 262, 263, 265, 270, 271, 285, 293

greater period of the Sun, 60–61

greater periods, 60, 61

Guttman, Arielle, 59, 401

H

Hamburg School, 5, 174, 253

Hand, Robert, 368, 402

hard aspects, 7, 83, 138, 146, 165, 250, 256, 257, 260

Harding, Michael, and Harvey, Charles, 2, 3, 137, 174, 189, 401

harmonic charts, 351

harmonics, 2, 399, 401

Harris, Pat, 283–285

Hastings, Nancy, 37, 368, 369, 401

hearing loss, 257, 259

Hearst, William Randolph, 346

heart failure, 286

Hickman, Sophia Frances, 91–96

hit by an electric trolley car, 278

hit-and-run accident, 334

honour and upliftment, 222, 224, 226, 227, 281

Houlding, Deborah, 11, 108, 257, 258, 260, 362, 402

house-related sensitive point, 17, 111, 112, 126, 236

houses in Jyotish, 204–206

Hoy, Garry, 263–265

hyleg/hylegiacal, 71, 130, 147, 148, 149, 259, 350, 392, 396

I

Ibn Ezra, Abraham ben Meir, 349

idealized human life span, 65

inconjuncts, 111, 280, 314, 316

Islam, Yusuf (*see* Yusuf/Cat Stevens)

J

joy(s), 213, 214

judging the overall tenor of the chart, 131–146, 270

K

Kahlo, Frida, 278, 279, 282

Ketu (a.k.a. South Lunar Node), 91, 134, 137, 140, 272, 282, 393

Kitchener, Horatio Herbert, 101, 102

Kite pattern, 164, 165

Knatchbull twins, 20, 267–273

Knatchbull, Nicholas, 267–272

Knatchbull, Timothy, 267, 269, 272

L

Labouré, Denis, 296, 298, 402

Law of Excitation, 35, 36

Leo, Alan, 3, 13, 16, 19, 25, 37, 39–43, 46, 48, 49, 52–56, 59, 70, 84–88, 92, 118, 119, 123, 125, 132, 139, 187, 193, 194, 236, 240, 244, 273, 324, 328, 329, 339, 349, 350, 358, 364, 366, 368, 375, 387, 402

Lewes, George Henry, 164–166

Lilly, William, 1, 2, 21–23, 67, 173, 194, 206, 208–210, 212, 213, 329, 402

Lindbergh, Charles, 88–91, 346

London, 2, 13, 53, 58, 67–69, 71, 76, 82, 87, 91–93, 123, 126, 142, 157–159, 161, 164, 170, 219, 228, 229, 239, 249, 253,

255, 267, 268, 287, 318–320, 333, 357, 359, 399–402, 404, 405

Lord of the Profected Ascendant, 364

lot(s), 16, 83, 211, 281

lottery, 214–217

Lunar Eclipse, 9, 49, 56, 70, 90, 99, 105, 112, 159, 160, 173, 342, 366, 368

lunar nodal axis, 32, 141, 282, 296, 314

lunar nodal cycle, 71

lunar nodes, 19, 94, 98, 129, 130, 134, 140, 162, 171, 172, 176, 177, 185, 189, 190, 244, 262, 263, 286, 293, 335, 339, 341, 346

lunation(s), 62, 70

M

MacDonald, Ramsay, 222–224

man from Nice, France, whose mother died in 1936, 290–296

man who drowned while on vacation, 339–341

man who had gone missing, 2, 11, 360–362

manifestation of the astrological symbolism, 14

marital separation, 29

Ma'shar, Abu, 6, 15, 17, 18, 51, 52, 147, 204, 213, 329, 351, 385, 397, 403

Mason, Sophia, 37, 217, 335

Maternus, Firmicus, 65, 194, 202, 203, 403

McAuliffe, Christa, 181–184, 210

mean daily motion of the Sun, 32

mean positions, 143, 256, 257, 259, 311

mean quotidian, 33

Metonic cycle, 51, 62, 64, 65

Michael, George, 286–290

midpoint modal sort, 4, 156, 159, 174, 176, 177, 183, 184, 214, 238, 256, 289, 368

midpoint of the Grand Cross, 130

midpoints, 2, 4, 5, 32, 43, 59, 83, 84, 127, 129, 130, 137, 138, 145, 153, 156, 157, 159, 167, 174, 176, 177, 181, 184, 188–190, 214, 228, 238, 249, 252–254, 256, 259, 263, 265, 278, 289, 299, 316, 364, 365, 368, 400, 401, 406

minor progressions, 36

missing lady doctor, 91–96

modality/modalities, 4, 15, 46, 156, 174, 330, 363

Moment of Astrology, The (1994), 2, 11, 249, 283, 362, 400

Moon's greater period, 60, 61

Moon's lesser or minor period, 60, 62

Morin, Jean-Baptiste, 23, 37, 139, 210, 403

Mountbatten, Lord, 267

mundane houses, 136

Munkasey, Michael, 34, 404

Muppets creator Jim Henson, 127–130

Mussolini, Benito, 224–226

mutable Grand Cross, 105, 127, 129, 260, 262, 271

mystical properties of whole numbers, 62

N

Naibod, 32, 33, 99, 107, 162, 188, 216, 262, 294

Naibod, Valentine, 32

(600-year) Naronic cycle, 7

Naros, 7

NASA, 146, 181, 406

natal potential(s), 9, 10, 24, 209, 245, 262, 313

natal promise, 4, 18, 20–24, 29, 35, 36, 55, 69, 117, 118, 153, 167, 210, 216, 270, 273, 276, 300, 337

near-death experience, 228, 230

new measures, 1, 3–7, 15–17, 20, 43, 44, 54, 56, 57, 76, 82, 83, 85, 86, 92, 95, 115, 117, 119, 136, 142, 174, 187, 219, 226, 240, 249, 250, 275, 300, 317, 318, 321, 326, 369, 401

New Measures in Astrology (1928), 3, 6, 7, 16, 17, 20, 43, 44, 54, 56, 57, 83, 85, 86, 95, 115, 117, 119, 136, 142, 187, 219, 226, 240, 249, 250, 275, 300, 317, 318, 326, 369, 401

90° midpoint sort, 4, 156, 159, 174, 176, 177, 183, 184, 214, 238, 256, 289, 290, 368

Nobel Prize, 5, 172, 173, 404

non-luminary planets, 19, 61, 62, 213

North Lunar Node, 9, 67, 100, 121, 140, 149, 164, 165, 172, 173, 176, 177, 181, 190, 214, 232, 236, 245, 270, 294, 298, 307, 309, 316, 341, 342, 393

Nova V1494 Aquilae, 309

number mysticism, 14

O

occult significance of the numbers 4 and 7, 3

Old Moore's Almanac, 70

Old, Walter Gorn (a.k.a. Sepharial), 7, 13, 70, 193, 195, 405

one degree along the ecliptic equals one year of life, 252

1° per year measure, 6, 17, 27, 29

1001 Notable Nativities (1917), 92, 119, 123, 240, 402

operative (astrological) influences, xvi, 4, 14, 18, 20, 79, 85, 99, 115, 117, 118, 121, 141, 167, 168, 170, 171, 173, 233, 270, 292, 294, 300, 301, 315, 364

O-ring gasket, 181

orb of influence, 20, 112, 356, 361

Osbourne, Fanny, 119, 121

overall pattern, 7, 10, 19, 149, 233, 363

P

pancreas, 342

paralysis, 130, 185, 188, 238, 263, 394, 397

Part of Fortune, 19, 23, 105, 137, 177, 211, 226, 242, 288, 299, 314

partial Solar Eclipse, 9, 49, 153, 154

Payne, Philip A., 346

Percy, Valerie, 245, 246

period of life, 16, 82, 167, 358, 385

personal planets, 18, 308

Philip Payne and the ill-fated flight of *Old Glory*, 346

Placidus, 19, 37, 39, 52, 82, 84, 88, 99, 100, 107, 122, 127, 140, 151, 154, 162, 173, 180, 181, 188, 193, 209–211, 214, 216, 219, 227, 244, 247, 249, 250, 254, 262, 267, 272, 273, 282, 294, 296, 318, 328, 330, 337, 344, 352, 405

planet within a house is its most immediate determining factor, 139

planetary period of human development, 51

planetary periods, 13, 16, 17, 51, 60, 63, 64, 66, 67, 69, 70, 72, 401, 405

Pluto, 10, 29, 45, 48–50, 69, 73, 85, 86, 90, 92, 94, 98–100, 105, 118, 125, 127, 129, 134, 138, 140, 141, 145, 151, 153, 154, 156, 159, 160, 170, 174, 176, 177, 181, 183, 185, 201, 214, 216, 232, 234, 238, 243, 244, 253, 259, 260, 263, 270, 271, 280, 285, 290, 293, 294, 296, 298–300, 307–309, 313, 315, 316, 324, 325, 330, 335, 339, 341, 342, 361, 362, 365, 384, 394, 395

Point of Danger to Life, 242, 243

Point of Dangerous Illness, 231, 232, 289

Point of Dangerous Injury or Illness, 232

Point of Death by a 12th House Secret Enemy, 248

Point of Friendship Leading to Marriage, 121, 125

Point of Honour and Upliftment, 222, 224, 226, 227, 281

Point of Illness at the End of Life, 123

Point of Illness in One's Final Days, 122

Point of Life, 6, 15–18, 20, 27, 29, 32, 35, 43, 44, 48, 49, 59, 69, 71, 75, 76, 78, 84–86, 90, 94, 98, 105, 108, 109, 118, 125, 134, 137, 138, 145, 151, 154, 159, 165–167, 170, 171, 173, 177, 180, 181, 183–185, 187, 188, 224, 226, 231, 234, 236, 238, 244, 247, 253, 254, 256, 259, 260, 262, 263, 271, 273, 275, 280–282, 285, 288, 293, 296, 299, 308, 309, 314, 315, 324, 328, 352, 354, 361, 362, 364, 365, 368, 371, 374, 375, 377

Point of Life-Threatening Illness, 111, 122, 231, 289

Point of Serious Illness, 122, 236

polio, 278, 281, 282, 310, 313, 314

ponderous planet, 45, 85, 86, 92, 118, 138, 141–143, 145, 256, 257, 260, 294, 301, 365

Pope Francis, 151–153

primary directed Ascendant, 32, 353

primary directions, 1, 5, 14, 17, 32–34, 36, 37, 70, 82, 85, 99, 107, 115–118, 125, 147, 180, 216, 221, 262, 276, 300, 320, 321, 333

priming a pump, 5

Princess Diana (a.k.a. Lady Diana Spencer), 46, 153–155

Principles of Astrology, The (1939), 35, 56, 214, 400

process of combination of two cusps, 220

profections, 1, 2, 17, 18, 35, 147, 250, 282, 296, 350–352, 356, 364

Progressed Horoscope, The (1906), 25, 37, 132, 273, 334, 349, 402, 403

progressing the solar return angles and cusps to the actual date of the event, 337

progression rates, 34–35, 352

progressions, 2, 4, 5, 14–18, 20, 21, 23, 24, 32–34, 36, 37, 50, 70, 72, 82, 85–87, 90, 112, 113, 115, 117, 118, 131, 132, 139, 141, 145, 177, 211, 214, 216, 217, 221, 233, 253, 260, 276, 286, 288, 300, 314–316, 320, 333–337, 357, 361, 364, 368, 400, 401, 403, 406

Progressions (1998), 18, 36

Proluna method of symbolic direction, 328–331

promissor, 22–24, 27, 29, 31

Promittor, 21, 22

Ptolemy, Claudius, 6, 15–17, 27, 32, 33, 48, 51, 52, 55–57, 59–61, 63–66, 69, 70, 76, 83–85, 92, 118, 125, 129, 149, 180, 181, 185, 193, 219, 254, 263, 285, 292, 294, 296, 305, 309, 328, 335, 349, 356, 363, 366, 385, 387, 396, 402, 404

Publius Aelius Hadrianus Afer, 303

Pythagoras, 62

Q

Queen Elizabeth II, 79, 157–162, 164, 375

quincunx, 10, 27, 29, 31, 48, 73, 99, 100, 108, 109, 111, 112, 122, 123, 126, 127, 134, 160, 165, 180, 181, 183, 217, 230, 237, 238, 243, 244, 248, 253, 259, 260, 262, 265, 270, 271, 285, 286, 289, 293, 294, 296, 298, 299, 301, 311, 335, 365, 377

R

racism, 310, 313

radix, 21, 22, 36, 316, 345

Rahu (a.k.a. North Lunar Node), 140, 164, 393

rate of 1° for every year of life, 9

rate of 1° per year, 6, 23, 31, 69, 70, 72–74, 147, 148, 151, 242, 288

rate of 7 years per zodiac sign, 17, 43, 49, 56, 85, 177

rate of one sign for every seven years, 6

rate of one zodiac sign (30° degrees) per 7 years of life, 3

real-time based, 6, 14, 15, 17, 69, 118, 153, 167, 177, 237, 294, 300

real-time measures, 18, 50

real-time movement, 3

rectification, 233, 356

rectifying the birth chart, 233, 272

Reeve, Christopher, 185–188

resonances, 57, 65, 69

ripe for effect, 219, 227

ripen/ripening, 4, 57, 65, 105, 216

ripple effect, 56, 57, 60, 63, 254, 325

ripples, 57, 59, 65, 67, 325

Robbins, Frank Egleston (translator of Ptolemy), 63, 404

Robson, Vivian, 116, 133, 315, 404

Roman Emperor Hadrian, 61, 303–311

rotation of the sky around the Earth, 14, 20

S

Sabina, Vibia, 304

Sahams, 281

Saturn, 4, 7, 10, 29, 31, 32, 45, 51, 54, 56–61, 63–67, 69, 70, 73–75, 85, 86, 91, 92, 94, 95, 98–100, 105, 107, 108, 112, 113, 117, 118, 122, 125, 127, 132–134, 137, 138, 140, 141, 145, 146, 151, 153, 154, 156, 157, 159, 160, 162, 165, 170, 172, 174, 177, 180, 181, 183, 184, 188, 194, 195, 201, 203–205, 210, 213, 221, 224, 228, 231, 232, 237, 238, 243, 245, 247–250, 252, 256, 257, 260, 263, 265, 270, 272, 273, 276, 280, 282, 285, 288–290, 293, 296, 298–301, 305, 307–309, 313–316, 318, 323–325, 329, 335, 339, 342, 345, 346, 350, 358, 360, 361, 365, 366, 368, 377, 384, 385, 387, 388, 390, 392, 395, 396

Savalan, Karen Ober, 46, 405

Schmiel, Dorit, 143, 144, 404

searching for major themes and patterns in the birth chart, 19

Second World War, 143

secondary progression, 5, 10, 35, 37, 57, 60, 75, 86, 94, 118, 134, 141, 142, 209, 211, 313, 315, 321, 355, 360, 365

semisextile, 31, 105, 111, 145, 177, 181, 237, 248, 265, 270, 280, 285, 286, 299, 311, 313, 315, 316, 365

sensitive point(s), 3, 5, 16, 17, 19, 24, 29, 43, 56, 57, 59, 108, 111, 112, 119, 122, 126, 151, 193, 211, 219, 220, 224, 227, 228, 231, 234, 236, 237, 240, 244, 245, 247, 248, 252, 281, 289, 314, 350

sensitive Point of Marriage, 119, 126

sensitive years, 220

Sepharial (a.k.a. Walter Gorn Old), 7, 13, 23, 61–63, 65, 66, 70–73, 116, 133, 145, 193, 195, 198, 355, 356, 368, 389–392, 394–398, 405

Sepharial on the twelve houses, 195–198

(Ptolemy's) *seven ages of man*, 16, 17, 27, 48, 51, 52, 56, 60, 63, 64, 70, 76, 85, 92, 118, 149, 157, 254, 285, 292, 328, 363, 366, 385, 387

seven years per sign, 3, 56, 59

severe illness, 318

sexual exploitation, 278

shadow planets, 140

Shaw, George Bernard, 5, 168–173, 399, 404

significator, 21–24, 27, 29, 31, 72, 74, 211–213

significators and con-significators of houses, 211–213

signing ceremony of the Declaration of Independence, 347

Single Digits Birth Number, 80–82, 84, 88, 94, 96, 99, 101–103, 105, 107, 109, 112, 159, 160, 178, 216, 217, 269, 286, 288, 292, 307, 311

Skinner, Christeen, 283

slow-moving planets, 45, 143, 221

Smith, Dr. J. Heber, 18, 31, 45, 46, 131, 132, 105

Smith, L. Protheroe, 7, 10, 275, 317–331

Society for Astrological Research, 13

solar arc, 3, 6, 15, 33, 171, 243, 281

Solar Eclipse, 9, 49, 71, 72, 84, 90, 100, 105, 112, 145, 153, 154, 173, 238, 296, 300, 315, 347, 368

Solar Fire astrology program, 33, 149, 174, 176, 184, 214, 222, 243, 249, 250, 256, 289, 339, 341, 360, 368, 401

solar returns, 1, 17, 18, 118, 148, 290, 296, 333, 337, 339, 364, 403, 406

solar type, 19

South Lunar Node (a.k.a. Ketu), 9, 91, 129, 134, 137, 140, 151, 153, 172, 185, 230, 245, 254, 272, 280, 282, 286, 290, 293, 318, 323–325, 393

Spencer, Lady Diana, 153, 155

Spirit of St. Louis, 90, 346

spiritual crisis, 25, 27

square to the Moon's true nodes, 185

stationary planets, 70

stationary position of a transiting planet, 74

stellium, 43, 44, 55, 105, 137, 143, 145, 153, 185, 187, 254, 256, 262, 271, 313, 314

Stevenson, Robert Louis, 119–123

Stewart, Martha, 106–108

Strauss, David Friedrich, 162

sudden windfall, 216

suffragette, 67, 69, 73

suicide, 2, 92, 296, 297, 300, 301, 353

summary of orbs, 272–273

summer solstice, 61, 187

Sun/Moon midpoint, 29, 137, 189, 214, 278

Sun's lesser or minor period, 60, 62

swimming accident, 230, 231

symbolic direction, 4, 20, 25, 31, 35, 37, 43, 56, 66, 86, 111, 119, 122, 145, 154, 237, 250, 272, 300, 323–325, 328, 349, 350, 352, 354, 355, 368

Symbolic Directions in Modern Astrology (1929), 1, 6, 16, 17, 88, 103, 109, 281, 354–356, 400

symbolic measures, xvi, 3–5, 9, 14, 15, 17, 18, 20, 31, 39, 48, 79, 109, 117, 118, 122, 123, 147, 153, 159, 167, 172, 173, 177, 181, 184, 211, 254, 262, 265, 270, 272, 273, 275, 280, 282, 283, 292, 294,

298–301, 303, 313, 316, 363–366, 368, 389

symbolic measures as intensifiers, 4

symbolic point related to the matter signified by the house in question, 125

symbolic rather than real time, 17

synodic month, 62

systems of directing, 17, 116

T

Teal, Celeste, 24, 37, 165, 405

tertiary progressions, 36, 214, 406

Tetrabiblos, 60, 63, 129, 130, 185, 263, 335, 404

Theosophy, 7, 70

Till, Emmett Louis, 310–316

timelord, 4, 16, 39, 51, 52, 60, 149, 157, 162, 352, 363, 364, 366, 368, 385, 387

Total Lunar Eclipse, 9, 49, 159, 342

Total Solar Eclipse, 71, 112, 145, 173, 315

transatlantic flight, 88, 346

transits, 1, 4, 5, 9, 13–18, 20, 23–25, 32, 33, 35–37, 45, 46, 57, 63, 66, 70–74, 82, 84, 85, 90, 99, 112, 113, 115, 116, 118, 131, 138, 140, 141, 143, 145, 154, 177, 220, 221, 233, 242, 243, 256, 257, 260, 273, 286, 288, 300, 307, 314, 320, 335, 337, 341, 342, 344, 347, 351, 352, 364, 405

Transits and Planetary Periods (1920), 13, 63, 66, 70, 72, 405

T-square, 29, 31, 48–50, 55, 69, 83, 84, 90, 112, 127, 138, 141, 154, 157, 159, 160,

162, 187, 245, 247, 257, 259, 270, 280, 290, 342, 362

tuberculosis, 228, 230–232

U

Unamuno, Miguel de, 25–27, 405

Uranus, 3, 7, 9, 18, 19, 27, 29, 31, 39–41, 43–46, 48, 50, 52, 56–60, 67, 69, 71, 73, 75, 76, 78, 85, 86, 88, 90, 92, 94, 99, 100, 105, 108, 111, 113, 118, 123, 129, 130, 132–134, 137, 138, 140, 141, 143, 145, 146, 151, 154, 156, 157, 160, 165, 170, 173, 176, 177, 180, 183, 185, 187, 188, 194, 201, 214, 216, 226, 227, 230, 231, 234, 236, 237, 242–245, 247, 249, 253, 254, 256, 257, 259, 260, 262, 263, 265, 270–272, 276, 278, 282, 285, 286, 289, 290, 293, 294, 299, 301, 307–309, 313, 315, 316, 318, 320–322, 324, 325, 328, 329, 335, 339, 341, 342, 345, 346, 352, 365, 368, 371, 390, 392, 395–397

Uranus as the "developer," 45

V

Valens, Vettius, 36, 37, 60, 65, 66, 217, 344, 406

Venus, 9, 13, 27, 29, 43, 44, 51, 54, 56, 57, 59–61, 63–67, 70, 76, 78, 84, 86, 94, 99, 107, 121, 122, 126, 127, 129, 130, 134, 136, 138, 140, 151, 154, 156, 157, 164, 165, 170–173, 180, 183, 185, 188, 194, 195, 201, 202, 205, 206, 213, 214, 216,

217, 224, 226, 227, 231, 236, 240, 244, 245, 249, 253, 254, 259, 262, 263, 270, 273, 276, 280, 282, 285, 286, 293, 294, 296, 299, 301, 308, 309, 313–316, 322, 324–326, 329, 330, 335, 341, 342, 345, 350, 352, 353, 368, 377, 385, 387, 388, 392, 397, 398, 400–402

"Venus Star" pattern, 59

Vimshottari dasha, 61

Virgo, 13, 14, 40, 41, 43, 44, 48, 54, 63–65, 75, 76, 82, 88, 111–113, 123, 125, 129, 133, 137, 138, 145, 148, 149, 151, 153, 154, 172, 177, 183, 184, 213, 216, 226, 233, 234, 237, 242, 249, 250, 253, 259, 262, 263, 265, 270, 271, 278, 286, 289, 290, 294, 308, 315, 318, 323, 325, 335, 350, 361, 365, 372, 384, 387

W

when the houses are more ripe for effect, 219–220

Whitehead, Edward, 11, 357, 359–362

Wilhelm II, Kaiser, 71

William Lilly and the twelve houses, 206–209

winter solstice, 187

Witte, Alfred, 5, 24, 29, 83, 174, 176, 183, 184, 188–191, 253, 254, 406

woman with abnormal liver function tests, 342–343

Working with Astrology (1990), 2, 137, 174, 401

Wryn, Rhiannon Leigh, 100, 101

Wynn (a.k.a. Sidney K. Bennett), 139, 333–344, 347, 406

Wynn's Astrology Magazine, 333, 339

Wynn's Key Cycle, 333–344, 347

Y

Yod, 55, 108

young man who was killed in a severe windstorm, 103–105

Yusuf/Cat Stevens, 228–233

Z

Zenil, Sara, 278

(Alan Leo's) zodiac signs and their associated ages, 40–42, 387–388

Zoller, Robert, on delineating the houses, 209–211

To Write to the Author

If you wish to contact the author or would like more information about this book, please write to the author in care of Llewellyn Worldwide Ltd. and we will forward your request. Both the author and the publisher appreciate hearing from you and learning of your enjoyment of this book and how it has helped you. Llewellyn Worldwide Ltd. cannot guarantee that every letter written to the author can be answered, but all will be forwarded. Please write to:

Anthony Louis
℅ Llewellyn Worldwide
2143 Wooddale Drive
Woodbury, MN 55125-2989
Please enclose a self-addressed stamped envelope for reply,
or $1.00 to cover costs. If outside the U.S.A., enclose
an international postal reply coupon.

Many of Llewellyn's authors have websites with additional information and resources. For more information, please visit our website at http://www.llewellyn.com.

Notes